AMONG THE RUINS

ALSO BY PAUL L. WILLIAMS

Operation Gladio

Crescent Moon Rising

The Day of Islam

The Al Qaeda Connection

Osama's Revenge

The Vatican Exposed

AMONG
THE
RUINS

THE DECLINE AND FALL OF THE
ROMAN CATHOLIC CHURCH

PAUL L. WILLIAMS

Prometheus Books

59 John Glenn Drive
Amherst, New York 14228

Inquiries should be addressed to
Prometheus Books
59 John Glenn Drive
Amherst, New York 14228
VOICE: 716–691–0133
FAX: 716–691–0137
WWW.PROMETHEUSBOOKS.COM

21 20 19 18 17   5 4 3 2 1

Library of Congress Cataloging-in-Publication Data Pending

Printed in the United States of America

For Peter H. Schmitt, the son I never had

By the waters of Babylon, we sat and wept when we remembered Zion.

—Psalm 137:1

CONTENTS

Apologia

THE LONG PROCESSION

I am not a Welsh Baptist. I come from a long line of Irish coalminers who eked a living within the anthracite regions of Northeastern Pennsylvania. They were boozers and brawlers and union organizers. But, above all, they were Roman Catholic with a fierce loyalty to the church.

My family parish was St. John the Baptist in West Scranton. At this parish, I received my first Holy Communion, underwent years of catechetical instruction, and submitted to the sacrament of confirmation. I sang "Panis Angelicus" with the church choir, inscribed JMJ on the upper-right-hand corner of my composition papers, wore a St. Christopher's medal, and made the sign of the cross before a foul shot. I fasted from meat on Friday, attended confession on Saturday, and went to Mass every Sunday morning and holy day of obligation.

The service was always the same, beginning and ending as it always had begun and ended. But, at our parish, the 10:15 Mass on Sunday morning (a Solemn High Mass and the last liturgy of the day) did not conclude when Father Joseph Oberholtzer, our parish priest, blessed the congregation, said "*Ite, Missa est*," and read the last gospel. Following this reading came the Benediction of the Blessed Sacrament.

By attending Mass, we had fulfilled our Sunday obligation and were not obliged to sit through this lengthy ritual. But no one left. Fr. Homer, the assistant pastor, stood vigil in the vestibule ready to accost any parishioner seeking to escape for a drag on a cigarette.

The benediction came replete with litanies to the saints. When the names of the hallowed members of the community of heaven were invoked, we were obliged to respond, "*Ora pro nobis*." The benediction concluded with a procession in which the members of the congregation walked behind Fr. Oberholtzer as he carried a monstrance bearing the sacred Host throughout the sanctuary. We never arrived home before noon.

The winter winds were still howling on Palm Sunday, March 28, 1958. On this day, we were obliged to wave palms about our heads during the procession. This would have been all well and good, if Fr. Oberholtzer had not been suffering from dementia. He led the congregation out of the church and into the street. We followed him, palms in air, past the convent house, where the religious sisters lived, the rectory, the church hall (where, to the outrage of Protestants, bingo was played and liquor was served), and the parochial school. Fr. Oberholtzer, monstrance still uplifted, proceeded to lead us down Luzerne Street past Betz's bar, the working-class row houses, the Handy Dandy store, the corner grocery stores, the West Scranton High School, and the Nehi bottling company. We were headed toward the end of the street and the Fiegleman junkyard.

Realizing that something was seriously amiss, a few men rushed back to the parish to fetch Fr. Homer, who came running down the street to prevent the sorry spectacle of the sacred sacrament ending up among mounds of scrap metal, castaway appliances, and the remains of rusty old automobiles. Fr. Homer recovered the monstrance and led the confused priest and the bewildered parishioners back to the sanctity of the church.

St. John the Baptist Church was closed in 1995. The hallowed ground where it once stood is now occupied by United Penn Bank. The convent house, the rectory, the church hall, and the school have been demolished to create a parking lot. Few remember the Te Deums that were raised to heaven at this site on Sunday morning, let alone Fr. Oberholtzer and the long procession to the junkyard. Perhaps in the priest's demented mind the mere sight of the sacred Host within the monstrance was supposed to cause Protestants who lived in the neighborhood to come to an awareness that the real presence of Jesus Christ abided in the Roman Catholic Church.

In 1958, Fr. Oberholtzer was not alone in his religious delusion. That same year, Pope John XXIII initiated his own long procession into the outside world that the faithful were summoned to follow. It was a procession that was supposed to make non-Catholics aware that the church had come of age, that it had shed its medieval trappings, that it sought to initiate a union with Protestants that would result in a new world religion. The pope brandished not a monstrance but a herald of enlightenment. In retrospect, he was no less quixotic than Fr. Oberholtzer. His procession led to an existential spiritual wasteland, with no way back to the hallowed ground from whence it had begun.

Among the ruins of my childhood faith, I have written this book. Striving for objectivity, I have included endnotes to document my every claim. But every story is told from the point of view of its author. And this story contains evidence of my outrage at Holy Mother Church and the abandonment of all that is sacred, as well as a good measure of my rue over what has been relinquished and forever lost.

Chapter One

THE GRAND ILLUSION

Introibo ad altare Dei,
Ad Deum qui laetificat juventutem meam.

(I will go to the altar of God,
To God, the joy of my youth)
—Introit of the Tridentine liturgy

The doctrines of Holy Mother Church were proclaimed as *semper eadem*—"always the same"—doctrines impervious to the winds of change and the demands of the zeitgeist. These teachings were upheld as "revealed truths" that the church had been divinely instituted to safeguard until the end of time. Some of the teachings were grounded in the scriptures (the Old and New Testaments), but others sprang from tradition—the revelations received by the vicarious representations of Christ on earth, that is, the bishops of Rome and the *egregi doctores ecclesia*, the "great doctors of the church" (Sts. Jerome, Augustine, Thomas Aquinas, et alia) throughout the centuries.

The divine nature of Roman Catholicism was grounded in the doctrine that the church had been established by Jesus Christ, who had singled out St. Peter for the "Great Commission," by saying, "Thou art Peter and upon this rock [*petrus*] I will build my church and the gates of hell shall not prevail against it" (Matt. 16:18). According to this same teaching, Christ also granted Peter exclusive sacerdotal authority—an authority which was not shared by the other eleven disciples: "I shall give to you [Peter] the keys of the kingdom of heaven. Whatsoever you bind on earth shall be bound in heaven; and whatsoever you loose on earth shall be loosed in heaven" (16:19).

St. Peter, according to Catholic doctrine, had established the church at Rome and passed on the authority of the episcopate to a fellow bishop named Linus, whose name appears in St. Paul's Second Epistle to Timothy (4:21). Linus, in turn, relinquished the office to Anacletus, and Anacletus to Clement. Linus and Anacletus left no mark in history save for their presumed martyrdoms. However, Clement, who was said to have been ordained by St. Peter, was the author of a sharp letter to the congregation of Corinth in Greece, demanding their obedience to their duly ordained presbyters.[1]

Regarding this chain of succession, St. Irenaeus, in 187 CE, wrote, "To this Clement there succeeded Evaristus . . . then, sixth from the apostles, Sixtus was appointed; after him, Telesphorus, who was gloriously martyred; then Hyginus; after him, Pius; then, after him, Anicetus. Soter succeeded Anicetus, Eleutherius does now, in the twelfth place from the apostles, hold the inheritance of the episcopate."[2] This chain leading to the prevailing bishop of Rome, the church steadfastly taught, remained unbroken, despite the fact that at one time there were three popes all claiming the right to St. Peter's throne.[3] Few Catholics were aware of this break in the chain, let alone historical evidence that the real leader of the primitive Christian community was not St. Peter but rather St. James, the brother of Jesus.[4]

THE ARK OF SALVATION

Since it was divinely established, the church claimed the right to pontificate on disputes, to settle religious controversies, to condemn heresies, and to establish universal doctrine. Despite the "False Decretals" (documents forged in the ninth century to establish the supreme authority of the pope) and the disturbing fact that several popes had been condemned as heretics, the church presented itself throughout the years as the sole source of truth for all of mankind. It was, as St. Cyprian said, "the Ark of Salvation, outside of which there is no hope of deliverance from sin and damnation."[5]

The moral and spiritual absolutism of Roman Catholicism was rooted in medieval realism and the medieval doctrine of the nature of God as espoused by Sts. Augustine, Anselm of Canterbury, and Aquinas. God, such fathers of the church taught, was immutable, omniscient, omnipotent, eternal, and perfect. His perfection mandated his existence, since nothing is perfect if it is lacking in life. God's nature also verified the existence of moral absolutes. Since such universals as goodness, truth, virtue, and beauty were concepts within the mind of God, as evidenced by his revealed word (sacred scripture), they possessed divine *reality* for all mankind.[6]

Not only was the Roman Church administered by the "Vicar of Christ" (a vicarious Jesus), but it also professed to be the sole dwelling place of the Holy Ghost. This indwelling, according to Catholic catechists, safeguarded the church from error so that Catholic *tradition* remained on equal footing with the Old and the New Testaments.[7] For this reason, the writings of the church fathers were as spiritually efficacious as the gospels of Matthew, Mark, Luke, and John; and the pronouncements of popes just as binding as the Ten Commandments.

ECCLESIOLOGY 101

The *Baltimore Catechism*, the official primer on Catholic doctrine, taught that the church possessed three attributes: authority, infallibility, and indefectibility. Authority meant that the pope and his bishops, as the lawful successors of the apostles, possessed the power from Christ "to teach, to sanctify, and to govern the faithful."[8] Infallibility meant that the church, due to the Holy Ghost's indwelling, cannot err in matters of faith and morality. Indefectibility meant that the teachings of the church would remain intact "until the end of time."

The rulings of the pontiffs and the great church councils were canonized into a body of law (*corpus iuris canonici*) that bound all Catholics into one system of belief. The chief precepts of the law were as follows:

1. To attend Mass on all Sundays and all holy days of obligation.
2. To fast and abstain on the days appointed.
3. To confess all sins to an authorized priest at least once a year.
4. To receive Holy Communion during the Easter season.
5. To contribute to the support of the church.
6. To observe all restrictions regarding wedding contracts, including "mixed marriages" (the marriage of a Catholic to a non-Catholic), which required a special dispensation.[9]

THE PROCESS OF PENANCE

To violate a law or moral ruling of Holy Mother Church was to defy "natural law" and divine revelation. Such a violation emptied the soul of all sanctifying grace, thereby requiring absolution by a Catholic cleric and satisfaction in the form of penance. Failure to acknowledge the guilt (*culpa*) of such an offense and to undergo the prescribed punishment (*poena*) was to dwell in the state of mortal sin, a condition that resulted in eternal damnation. Even a minor transgression—a venial sin—unless expiated by a priest and met with the proper satisfaction, meant years of suffering in a place between heaven and hell called purgatory. The exact duration of a sentence for each violation of ecclesiastical law was set forth in penitential books that had been developed in the sixth century.[10]

Prior to Vatican II, the vast majority of Catholics in America entered the confessional box every Saturday afternoon.[11] Forgiveness came when the priest said, "*Ego te absolvo*" (I absolve you). These words infused grace *ex opere operato* ("worked from the work" of Christ) into the sinner's soul, cleansing it of the stain of sin.[12] After uttering the words of absolution, the priest prescribed a punishment, such as the recitation of the rosary or a set number of Our Fathers and Hail Marys. This procedure, known as penance, stood as one of the church's seven sacraments. It alone enabled Catholics to obtain infusions of sanctifying grace by partaking of Holy Communion at morning Mass.

HYGIENIC CANNIBALISM

Prior to 1965, the Mass was celebrated in Latin by clerics who wore the vestments of the ancient pagan priesthood and performed acts of sacrifice before their congregants.[13] The victim remained the same, and the sacrifice, according to Catholic doctrine, was real. By pronouncing a precise formula, the Host (a thin, tasteless wafer of wheat flour and water baked by cloistered nuns and inscribed with the sign of the cross) became, in accordance with the doctrine of transubstantiation, the crucified body of Jesus, which the faithful and properly purified were called upon to consume.[14]

Catholics could reason that they were not engaging in tribal cannibalism by upholding the scholastic distinction that the *accidents* of the Host remained intact (the flour and the water) while the *substance* was actually body and blood.[15] Although such words and distinctions served to downplay the implied cannibalism, they often could not completely quell the queasy stomachs of first-time communicants.

CANONICAL DIGITS

The Host could only be touched by the "canonical digits" (the thumb and index finger) of an ordained priest. These digits had been specially wrapped and consecrated for this purpose. Aspiring young men who were missing one or more of their canonicals were deemed to be unfit for the priesthood. Special care was taken with seminarians. They were not allowed by their lay brothers to slice bread or cut meat for fear of lopping off a finger that was meant to elevate the Lord's body.[16]

To touch the sacred, the priests themselves had to undergo an ontological transformation that would separate them from the rest of mankind. This transformation occurred at the time of ordination through the laying on of the hands of a presiding bishop. This "imposition" elevated priests from ordinary men to supernatural agents, a process that could never be reversed or redone.[17] Their souls, according to Catholic doctrine, were sealed by an indelible mark—a mark that could not be removed, no matter how grievous their sin or how heinous their heresy.[18]

MAGICAL ACTS

During the Tridentine liturgy, the priests faced the marble altar in which the relic of a saint had been embedded. Unlike Protestant services, the emphasis was upon the sacrifice not the sermon. Homilies were superfluous and often bypassed, since they were not part of the "Ordinary" (i.e., the unchangeable parts of the Mass).

The rite was all by rote—day after day, week after week, year after year. The highlight of the Mass came when the priests elevated the Host and said, "*Hoc est enim Corpus meum*" (For this is my Body). These words performed the miracle, causing the congregation to look at it and say, "My Lord and My God."[19]

With the kneeling and rising, the bowing and blessing with incense, the swirling of the priest with the monstrance, the tinkling of bells and the chanting of the choir, the Mass resembled an elaborate dance before an untouchable thing. The only permissible change in the liturgy was the substitution of certain Latin prayers with other Latin prayers on various feast and fast days. There were "Low" Masses that lasted about an hour and Solemn High Mass with benediction that could last two hours or more. Such rituals, Catholics believed, mirrored the worship services held by first-century Christians in the catacombs of Rome. Nothing throughout time had changed or ever would change. The constant refrain throughout the liturgy was "*per omnia saecula saeculorum*" (through all the ages).

The Latin rite seemed to smack of pure magic. This etymological root of the phrase "hocus pocus" is the Catholic formula of consecration.[20] And the magic was enhanced by the witchery of the Latin words "*Sanctus, Sanctus, Sanctus*" and the intonation of the Latin hymns "O Salutaris Hostia" and "Panis Angelicus," which stressed the premise that an immolation of a pure and spotless victim was taking place before the eyes of the beholders.[21]

In truth, the church was a treasure trove of spells and charms: the sprinkling of holy water to sanctify a car, a house, or a business; the wearing of a scapular to ward off disease and evil spirits; the touching of a relic to effect a miraculous cure; the invoking of saints for special needs—St. Anthony to find a lost object, St. Claire to improve eyesight, St. Blaise to sooth a sore throat, St. Apollonia to relieve a toothache, and, as a last resort, St. Joseph to help with a lost cause.

PRIESTLY PRECAUTIONS

The faithful partook of the Lord's body and blood by marching to the altar rail (which separated the laity from the holy of holies) with folded hands, by kneeling in straight-line formation, and by sticking out their tongues to receive the paper-thin wafers. These wafers were transported to the communicants in gold chalices. A paten, or "communion catcher," was placed under the chin of every communicant by attending acolytes for fear that the sacred Host might slip from a tongue to the floor.

Should such a catastrophe occur, the priest would cover the consecrated element with a cloth specially provided for that purpose; then, after dispensing the remaining wafers to the flock, he would retrieve the fallen Host, consume it, and commence a through crumb hunt of the area in which the catastrophe occurred.[22] Every crumb was a communion unto itself, every piece the whole. For this reason, priests, at the conclusion of the liturgy, rinsed the chalice with wine that they drank to the last drop so that a morsel of the sacred body would not be left behind for a mouse to consume.

DEMANDS, DRESS, AND DECORUM

In preparation for communion, Catholics were compelled to fast from all food and drink. The fast began at midnight. The mere thought of the Eucharist ending up in a stomach filled with morning coffee and undigested food was horrifying to every devout casuist, who fathomed with the full meaning of transubstantiation. This prohibition on ingestion extended to a mechanical sip of water after brushing one's teeth.[23]

By 1958, 74 percent of the Catholics in America attended Mass on a weekly basis; those who failed to attend, for the most part, were ill, handicapped, or disabled.[24] The churches were so packed that a crew of ushers was required to seat them. Because the liturgy exposed mortal beings to the actual presence of Jesus Christ, the dress code was rigid and the decorum demanding. Men and boys were attired in suits and ties; women and girls wore dresses and head coverings. No one would dream of entering a church in jeans or shorts, let alone tee shirts and gym shoes. Within the sanctuary, no idle chatter, including the exchange of social niceties, was permitted, and no one walked away from the liturgy, once it commenced, to go to the bathroom.

The children were separated from the adults in the front pews so that their behavior could be monitored by religious sisters. No child moved a muscle without the sound of a religious sister's clicker. One click meant to stand, two clicks to kneel, and three clicks to sit. Youngsters who fell out of step with this regimentation were dragged by the ear from the sanctuary and taken to the convent, where corporeal punishment was meted out by the sisters *in loco parentis*.

SISTERS AND NUNS

After Mass, the children who had not reached their twelfth birthday were marched off to catechism. These classes were taught by the sisters, who always appeared in full habit (*habitus* meaning "appearance" or "dress"). Such attire for most religious orders of women consisted of long black dresses (most made of wool), cinctures or belts to hold the dresses in place, wimples that rounded the face, and black veils.[25] Many wore hair shirts underneath their habits for the mortification of the flesh. The sisters lived in convents under monastic rules and were bound by the "simple vows" of poverty, chastity, and obedience. They were forbidden to enter the rectory (where the priest lived) or any place where they might be alone with a man. For this reason, they never travelled alone, not even in the company of their parents.[26]

Unlike religious sisters, nuns professed the solemn vows of poverty, chastity, and obedience and lived in cloistered environments, where they lived lives of prayer and contemplation. Few were permitted to engage in "active" activities, such as teaching, nursing, or working among the poor.

The nuns wore wedding rings and claimed to be the "brides of Christ." The concept of a bride of Christ came from the writings of Tertullian, a third-century theologian, who issued this exhortation to the virgins of his native Carthage: "You married Christ, to him you gave your flesh and to him you betrothed your maturity."[27] All nuns wore wedding rings, but few realized that the idea of their spiritual marriage came from the writings of a heretic.

Catechism remained the same week after week. The sisters asked questions from the *Baltimore Catechism* and called upon students to stand and to provide the answers that appeared in the text. The weekly grill was conducted to prepare the children for the sacrament of confirmation.

SACRAMENTAL SLAP

Confirmation was administered every year in a parish by a bishop, who would appear in medieval attire—miter, stole, cope, crosier, and the episcopal ring that all Catholic were obliged to kiss. For the ceremony, the bishop was accompanied by Knights of Columbus in full regalia, including swords and sheaths. After grilling the class with the catechetical questions, he would summon candidates to kneel before him at the altar. The bishop administered the sacrament by placing his hands upon the heads of the adolescents and saying, "Almighty, everlasting God, who hast deigned to bring these Thy servants to a new life by water and the Holy Ghost, and hast granted them remission of all their sins, send forth upon them Thy sevenfold Spirit of Holiness, the Paraclete from heaven."[28] After making this intonation, he anointed them with chrism (holy oil) and gave them a slight slap on the cheek as a reminder that they must be ready to suffer for the sake of Holy Mother Church.[29]

At the conclusion of this rite, the confirmed sons and daughters of Holy Mother Church received new names in honor of their favorite saint. In this way, the sacramental *rite de passage* served not only to confirm adolescent faith in the claims of Roman doctrine, but also to reaffirm their Catholic identity in American society.

CATHOLIC IDENTITY

By 1960, the American people, by and large, identified themselves not by their ethnic heritage but by their religious affiliation. This phenomenon was a result of the fact that America, apart from the remnants of Native American tribes, possessed no autochthonous population. Its 160,000,000 people were either themselves immigrants or else descendants of more or less recent immigrants.[30] Such identification was essential for the process of socialization. Will Herberg, America's foremost authority on the sociology of religion, writes,

> Everyone finds himself in a social context which he shares with many others, but within this social context, how shall he locate himself? Unless he can so locate himself, he cannot tell himself, and others will not be able to know, who and what he is; he will remain "anonymous," a nobody— which is intolerable. To live, he must "belong"; to "belong," he must be able to locate himself within the social whole, to identify himself to himself and to others.[31]

The first generation of American immigrants identified themselves not by their place of origin but with all those who spoke the same language. Within the new land, they became Italians, Germans, Swedes, Russians, Greeks, and Hungarians, although very often the coverage of these names was not very clear in their own minds or in the minds of others. Eventually, the immigrants were expected to give up everything they brought with them—their language, their nationality, and their way of life—everything save their religion. For the third generation of American immigrants, religion alone remained to tell them who they were and where they came from. It represented their sociological roots. Indeed, by 1950, according to Herberg, not to be a Protestant, a Catholic, or a Jew in the American scheme of things was not to be anything; it was not to have a name.[32]

American Catholics naturally assumed their roots were firmly planted in a place that was *semper eadem*—a place that bound them to a sacred heritage that would always remain—a North Star from which they could always obtain their spiritual, moral, and sociological bearings.

Small wonder, therefore, that all aspects of Catholic life flourished in the years before Vatican II. By 1955, 87 percent of American Catholics claimed to be "active" members of the church,[33] and new parishes were being built at the rate of 150 to 200 a year, often averaging nearly four a week.[34] Five years later, the church in America could boast of its 54,682 priests, 8,887 seminarians, and 181,000 sisters and nuns.[35]

In those days, Catholics asserted their identity through a myriad of means: the "dog tags" around their necks (St. Christopher medals and scapulars); the aquamarine and white plastic statues of the saints on the dashboards of their cars, the meatless Fridays, the rosary beads in their pockets, the ashes on their foreheads, and the sign of the cross before diving into the swimming pool.

POWER AND PAROCHIALISM

Throughout the first fifty years of the twentieth century, the church wielded formidable political power that impacted all Americans. It prevented books on its *Index Librorum Prohibitorum*, including James Joyce's *Ulysses* and Henry Miller's *The Tropic of Cancer*, from being published, kept films condemned by the Legion of Decency, such as *The Moon Is Blue* and *Baby Doll*, from playing in movie theaters, and even shut down Broadway productions, including *Wine, Women and Song*, that were decried by the Catholic Theater Movement.[36] The church determined election results in major US cities and established public policy on such issues as pornography, homosexuality, abortion, and birth control.[37] It strengthened organized labor through Catholic Labor Schools and the Catholic Labor Movement and limited the boundary of free enterprise by its prohibition of "servile work" (work performed for gain) on Sunday.[38] The authority of the church was unquestionable, even though its demands on such matters as artificial contraception, premarital sex, child rearing, and "mixed marriages" were all but impossible to be met by most of its members.

The unbending posture of the church was most evident in the matter of parochial education. By order of the Third Plenary Council of Baltimore, a Catholic elementary and secondary education was required for all Catholic children. This placed an incredible onus on blue-collar families, since parochial education was costly, and married Catholics were obliged to breed like rabbits.[39]

Catholic school children attended daily Mass before the first morning class. Since most received communion, they had nothing to eat or drink for breakfast. All were dressed in parochial uniforms—girls in blouses and knee-length skirts, with Kleenex pinned to their hair, and boys in blazers, dress pants, white shirts, and ties. Every class began with the recitation of an Ave Maria, Pater Nostra, and Gloria. In high school, the students became steeped in Thomism and the distinctions between form and matter, substance and accident, nature and grace. Year after year, the instruction never wavered. Aquinas was more relevant than Einstein, Wittgenstein, or Sartre. The *Summa Theologiae* remained the summit of human knowledge for souls to scale. Nothing was out of date, superfluous or irrelevant about the thought of St. Thomas, the supreme doctor of Catholicism, not even his discussions of the means by which angels traveled through space. All truth was timeless. A standard text in parochial schools during the 1950s was *The Thirteenth, Greatest of Centuries* by James J. Walsh, first published in 1907.[40]

Prior to Vatican II, Catholics remained cocooned in a place where time stood still, where Latin was a living language, medieval caps and capes remained in style, and candles blazed before waxen figures. Catholics were assured that the church would always remain the same—the one home to which they could return always—a sanctuary against which "the gates of hell could not prevail."

Of course, it was all illusionary. Changes—significant changes—had crept into the church over the ages. The Tridentine Mass bore no semblance to primitive Christianity as outlined in such second-century texts as the *Didache* and the letters by St. Hippolytus.[41] The sacraments had lost their original significance. Baptism, for example, was the sole rite in the early church for the forgiveness of sins—a rite that could only be received once, by repentant adults. Clerical celibacy was not enforced until the Second Lateran Council in 1139.[42] And the notion of papal infallibility did not come into existence until the issuance of the Dogmatic Constitution *Pastor aeternus* by the First Vatican Council in 1869.[43]

Catholic were blissfully ill-informed of such developments, primarily because history had been periodically raided and ransacked by Catholic apologists to support the premise that nothing in the Roman Church really had changed, that the early Christians had submitted to auricular confession for sacerdotal absolution, that priests had never married, that virgins had always been consecrated as brides of Christ, that popes had never erred in judgments of faith and morals, that the veneration of holy relics had taken place in the catacombs, that the merits of Christ's work were kept in a heavenly treasure chest owned by the bishop of Rome, and that the doctrine of purgatory was grounded in the book of the Maccabees.

But, by 1965, the inconceivable had happened. The fixed star no longer appeared in the night sky. The timeless became temporal. The magical words were no longer spoken. The holy miracle became something tangible and mundane, and a state of grace was something that was neither expected nor required.

Chapter Two

THE SEISMIC SHIFT

The nature of the sin called usury has its proper place and origin in a loan contract. This financial contract between consenting parties demands, by its very nature, that one return to another only as much as he has received. The sin rests on the fact that sometimes the creditor desires more than he has given. Therefore he contends some gain is owed him beyond that which he loaned, but any gain which exceeds the amount he gave is illicit and usurious.

One cannot condone the sin of usury by arguing that the gain is not great or excessive, but rather moderate or small; neither can it be condoned by arguing that the borrower is rich; nor even by arguing that the money borrowed is not left idle, but is spent usefully, either to increase one's fortune, to purchase new estates, or to engage in business transactions. The law governing loans consists necessarily in the equality of what is given and returned; once the equality has been established, whoever demands more than that violates the terms of the loan. Therefore if one receives interest, he must make restitution according to the commutative bond of justice; its function in human contracts is to assure equality for each one. This law is to be observed in a holy manner. If not observed exactly, reparation must be made.
—Benedict XIV, *Vix Pervenit*, November 1, 1745

Few sins in traditional Catholicism were more grievous than usury—the practice of earning interest from loans and investments. Money, the church taught, was sterile.[1] Its sterility in accordance with natural law was evident: coins cannot grow more coinage and dollars cannot sprout more greenbacks. Producing money from money was making something out of nothing. For this reason, usury was condemned not only a manifestation of heinous greed, one of the seven deadly sins, but also a gross violation of natural law.[2]

This belief was rooted in scripture, including this injunction from Leviticus 25:36: "Do not take usurious interest from him, but revere your God that your countryman may live with you." In Luke 6:34–35, Jesus said, "And if you lend to those from whom you expect repayment, what credit is that to you? Even sinners lend to sinners, expecting to be repaid in full. But love your enemies, do good to them, and lend to them without expecting to get anything back. Then your reward will be great, and you will be children of the Most High, because he is kind to the ungrateful and wicked."

Every church father from the fifth to the fifteenth century who addressed the subject of usury condemned it, including St. Clement of Alexandria, Tertullian, St. Cyprian, Lactantius, St. Ambrose, St. Jerome, St. Augustine, St. Gregory the Great, St. Anselm of Canterbury, and John Duns Scotus.[3] According to St. Thomas Aquinas, usury represented a violation of commutative justice. "He who takes usury for a loan of money," he wrote, "acts unjustly for he sells what does not exist, and such an action evidently constitutes an inequality and consequently an injustice."[4] Dante, in his *Inferno*, placed usurers in the lowest level of the seventh circle of hell, a place reserved for those who commit acts of violence against the nature of God. By so doing, the poet expressed his belief that usurers deserved far greater punishment than violent murderers, violent suicides, blasphemers, and sodomites.[5]

Making money from interest had been decried by the church councils of Nicaea (325), Carthage (371), Orleans (538), Clichy (626), and Aix (769). The Third Lateran Council, in 1179, decreed that "usurers should not be admitted to communion of the altar or receive Christian burial if they die in this sin."[6] In 1274, the Second Council of Lyons affirmed that usurers should be stripped of their property, forced to give back their ill-gotten gains, and driven from Christian communities with all those who aid and abet them.[7] In 1311, the Council of Vienne declared, "If, indeed, someone has fallen into the error of presuming to affirm pertinaciously that the practice of usury is not sinful, we decree that he is to be punished as a heretic."[8]

VIX PERVENIT

Usury was such a noxious transgression of canon law that it became the sole subject of *Vix pervenit*, an encyclical issued by Pope Benedict XIV in 1745. This papal letter was circulated to every Catholic church and read to every Catholic congregant by parish priests and diocesan bishops. It let it be known that few moral transgressions were more loathsome in the eyes of God than exacting interest from financial loans. The fact that the use of money has changed since the Apostolic Age remained irrelevant. Usury, he said, can never be condoned, since it serves to rob the poor of their meager possessions. Benedict XIV concluded his diatribe as follows: "We exhort you not to listen to those who say that today the issue of usury is present in name only, since gain is almost always obtained from money given to another. How false is this opinion and how far removed from the truth!"[9]

RERUM NOVARUM

In 1891, Pope Leo XIII issued *Rerum novarum* (Of revolutionary things), which discussed the relationship between labor and capital, as well as the need for some amelioration of "the misery and wretchedness pressing so unjustly on the majority of the working class."[10] The encyclical supported the rights of labor to form unions, rejected socialism, and condemned unbridled capitalism. It also echoed *Vix pervenit* with these remarks against usury:

> We clearly see, and on this there is general agreement, that some opportune remedy must be found quickly for the misery and wretchedness pressing so unjustly on the majority of the working class: for the ancient working-men's guilds were abolished in the last century, and no other protective organization took their place. Public institutions and the laws set aside the ancient religion. Hence, by degrees it has come to pass that working men have been surrendered, isolated and helpless, to the hardheartedness of employers and the greed of unchecked competition. The mischief has been increased by rapacious usury, which, although more than once condemned by the Church, is nevertheless, under a different guise, but with like injustice, still practiced by covetous and grasping men.[11]

PERNICIOUS JEWS AND PROTESTANTS

This intransigent stance on a basic premise of monetary exchange produced dire consequences for the church. Since Catholics were forbidden to exact interest from loans, the business of moneylending was handed over to Jewish merchants. Such merchants advanced the capital to erect castles, cathedrals, and monasteries, and built for themselves some of the most lavish mansions in Western Europe.[12] The writings of Berthold of Regensburg, Walther von der Vogelweide, and Ulrich von Lichtenstein testify to the presumption that a *Wucherer* ("usurer") was a Jew during the medieval epoch.[13]

The problems produced by the church's position on moneylending worsened with the Reformation. Luther, Calvin, and other reformers sanctioned the practice of making money from money, a development that gave rise to the growth of capitalism in Northern Europe.[14] By the end of the seventeenth century, a wealthy and affluent middle class of Protestant merchants emerged, while their Catholic counterparts became increasingly impoverished.[15] The economic plight of the Catholic laity caused by the church's intransigent teaching would persist, as evidenced by the appearance of *Rerum novarum*, until the dawn of the twentieth century.

WORKS OF THE DEVIL

Even Protestant scoffers were obliged to acknowledge that the Roman Catholic Church remained true to its moral and spiritual teaching, although it was no longer "catholic" and its financial position was precarious. The revenue of the Holy Mother Church, in the form of taxes, tributes, legacies, and gifts from much of Northern Europe, thanks to the Reformation, was lost. Its only hope of retaining a portion of this revenue resided with the Holy See's willingness to venture into expanding economic markets, to invest in foreign colonies and foreign currencies, and to engage in international commerce by liquidating its vast real-estate holdings.[16] But the church failed to take advantage of emerging financial opportunities. It remained steadfast in the stance that money was sterile and that the exacting of interest violated natural law.

In addition to the ban on earning interest, the church became adverse to new technology. In the wake of the Industrial Revolution, it refused to take advantage of such innovations as the steam engine, the flying shuttle, and the water frame, which revolutionized means of production. The Holy See even condemned railroads as the work of the devil.[17]

THE LOSS OF TEMPORALITIES

Thanks to this position, the Papal States—the eighteen *patrimonia*, or estates, comprising sixteen thousand miles of Italian soil that were wholly owned by the Holy See—fell into a state of neglect and stagnation. At the time of the inauguration of Pope Clement XII in 1758, the population of the Papal States stood at 2,036,747. The provinces were plagued by famine, want, primitive sanitation, and widespread beggary. They suffered from lack of grain, shortage of coal and oil, inflationary prices, and onerous taxation. And there was scant hope of help from the Holy Father. The papal coffers were empty, and the church stood more than $80 million in debt.[18]

The situation continued to worsen until the Papal States broke out in open rebellion. One by one the provinces proclaimed their independence from the clutches of the Holy See. By 1860, the church had lost all of the provinces, save the patrimony of Rome.[19]

THE SYLLABUS OF ERRORS

On December 8, 1864, Pope Pius IX responded to the loss of his papal holdings by issuing his encyclical *Quanta cura* (Condemning current errors), with an attachment called *Syllabus errorum* (Syllabus of errors). Within the *Syllabus*, the following errors of the industrial age were set forth and condemned:

Error 15. Every man is free to embrace and profess that religion which, guided by the light of reason, he shall consider true.

Error 16. Man may, in the observance of any religion whatever, find the way of eternal salvation, and arrive at eternal salvation.

Error 17. Good hope at least is to be entertained of the eternal salvation of all those who are not at all in the true Church of Christ [i.e., the Roman Catholic Church].

Error 18. Protestantism is nothing more than another form of the same true Christian religion, in which form it is given to please God equally as in the Catholic Church.

Error 21. The Church has not the power of defining dogmatically that the religion of the Catholic Church is the only true religion.

Error 23. Roman pontiffs and ecumenical councils have wandered outside the limits of their powers, have usurped the rights of princes, and have even erred in defining matters of faith and morals.

Error 48. Catholics may approve of the system of educating youth unconnected with Catholic faith and the power of the Church, and which regards the knowledge of merely natural things, and only, or at least primarily, the ends of earthly social life.

Error 55. The Church ought to be separated from the State, and the State from the Church.

Error 77. In the present day it is no longer expedient that the Catholic religion should be held as the only religion of the State, to the exclusion of all other forms of worship.

Error 80. The Roman Pontiff can, and ought to, reconcile himself, and come to terms with progress, liberalism and modern civilization.[20]

THE DOGMA OF INFALLIBILITY

Four years after issuing the list of errors, Pius IX convened the First Vatican Council, which affirmed that the bishop of Rome possessed "full and supreme power of jurisdiction over the whole church, not only in matters of faith and morals, but also in those which concern the discipline and government of the church dispersed throughout the whole world." This power, the council declared, is "ordinary" (that is, not delegated) and "immediate" (that is, not exercised through some other party rather than "from this day forward").[21] The council went on to declare the dogma of papal infallibility:

> Faithfully adhering to the tradition received from the beginning of the Christian faith, to the glory of God our savior, for the exaltation of the Catholic religion and for the salvation of the Christian people, with the approval of the sacred council, we teach and define as a divinely revealed dogma that when the Roman Pontiff speaks EX CATHEDRA, that is, when, in the exercise of his office as shepherd and teacher of all Christians, in virtue of his supreme apostolic authority, he defines a doctrine concerning faith or morals to be held by the whole church, he possesses, by the divine assistance promised to him in blessed Peter, that infallibility which the divine Redeemer willed his church to enjoy in defining doctrine concerning faith or morals. Therefore, such definitions of the Roman Pontiff are of themselves, and not by the consent of the Church, irreformable.
>
> So then, should anyone, which God forbid, have the temerity to reject this definition of ours: let him be anathema.[22]

This dogma (a doctrine formally defined) made it clear to Catholic catechists that every time the pope as vicar of Christ issued a statement on faith and morals, including the Syllabus of Errors, he was making an infallible declaration. After all, all encyclicals were dispatched *ex cathedra* ("from the throne of St. Peter"), and hence represented teachings that were binding for all believers in every age.

This position eventually became embarrassing when the church of Vatican II commenced to cast aside many of its long-held claims, and councilor catechists began to argue that the dogma of infallibility applied only when the pope explicitly said that he was speaking *ex cathedra*. This catechetical assertion meant that only two infallible statements had been made by the vicars of Christ throughout the ages: the dogmas of the Immaculate Conception of Mary (as declared by Pius IX in 1854) and of Mary's bodily Assumption into heaven (as declared by Pius XII in 1950).[23] It also led contemporary Catholic thinkers to arrive at these conclusions: the dogmas of the divinity of Jesus, apostolic succession, and the Holy Trinity remained up for debate, along with such moral matters as same-sex marriage, contraception, and abortion; encyclicals, including *Humanae vitae*, could be viewed as conditional; and canon laws could be dismissed as temporal theories. Therefore, the dogma that was meant to bolster the power and prestige of the papacy eventually came to create a fissure within the Roman Catholic Church that would contribute to its collapse.

THE HERESY OF AMERICANISM

On August 18, 1870, one month after the issuance of the infallibility dogma, national troops of the unified Italy took possession of the patrimony of St. Peter, the Roman province itself. Pius IX, who held himself above reproach and correction, was left governor of a proverbial postage stamp—480,000 square meters on and around Vatican Hill. Stripped of his earthly possessions, the pope shut himself up in the apostolic palace and refused to appear in public, even to bless his people.[24]

As "prisoners of the Vatican," the supreme pontiffs became increasingly visceral in their denunciations of modernity, as evidenced by Pope Leo XIII's condemnation of "Americanism" in *Testem benevolentiae nostrae* (Witness to our goodwill), an encyclical that was promulgated on January 22, 1899. "Americanism," the pope declared, was a particularly vile heresy since it upheld the division of church and state and the right of individuals "to hold whatever opinion they please on any subject and to set such opinions forth in print."[25] Even more disturbing to Leo XIII was the demand by Americans for the church to surrender its cherished claims before the prevailing zeitgeist:

> The underlying principle of these new opinions is that, in order to more easily attract those who differ from her, the Church should shape her teachings more in accord with the spirit of the age and relax some of

her ancient severity and make some concessions to new opinions. Many think that these concessions should be made not only in regard to ways of living, but even in regard to doctrines which belong to the deposit of the faith. They contend that it would be opportune, in order to gain those who differ from us, to omit certain points of her teaching which are of lesser importance, and to tone down the meaning which the Church has always attached to them.[26]

It is small wonder that *Testem benevolentiae nostrae* remains an all-but-forgotten papal pronouncement, since the ramifications of its teaching would prohibit the vast majority of contemporary Catholics from receiving the sacraments.

THE LATERAN TREATY

The financial situation continued to worsen during the first three decades of the twentieth century. By 1929, the church was operating on an annual budget of $1 million and remained deeply in debt. Contributions from the "black nobility"[27] had declined to a trickle; legacies had all but disappeared; and creditors, including the Reichsbank in Germany, were demanding immediate payment on over $10 million in delinquent loans.[28]

When all seemed hopeless, a demonic figure appeared at the apostolic palace with a tantalizing temptation. Italian prime minister Benito Mussolini, seeking Catholic support for his fascist party in the 1929 national plebiscite, granted Pius XI an incredibly profligate reparation for the loss of the Papal States by signing the so-called "Lateran Treaty."

Within the annals of Roman Catholicism, few documents would prove to be of greater importance than this agreement with *Il Duce*. The first section of this document—called "the Conciliation Theory"—established Vatican City (*Stato della Città del Vaticano*) as a sovereign state, which consisted of the 108.7 acres on Vatican Hill that housed St. Peter's Cathedral, the Lateran and palace, and a cluster of other buildings. The new nation contained thirty squares and streets, four military barracks for the Swiss Guards, two churches (in addition to St. Peter's), and a population of 973 residents—most of whom were celibate priests. As a sovereign state, Vatican City also possessed several "extraterritorial holdings" in Italy: three basilicas in Rome (St. Mary Major, St. John Lateran, and St. Paul's), several office buildings, the papal summer palace at Castel Gandolfo (thirteen miles from Rome), and a score of estates from Milan in the north to

Reggio in the south. In exchange for sovereignty, the pope relinquished all claims to the lands that had been seized by the Italian government in 1870 and agreed to establish diplomatic relations with the Italian government.[29]

The second section of the treaty—called "the Financial Convention"—provided a payment of $90 million in cash to the Holy See and an undisclosed sum for the pope's "privy purse" as restitution for the former papal principalities. The Italian government further agreed to pay the salaries of all parish priests in the country.

The final section—known as "the Concordat"—provided the papacy with complete jurisdiction over all Catholic organizations in Italy. These organizations—called "ecclesiastical corporations" in the document—were declared exempt from taxation and state audit. Moreover, the Vatican was at liberty to create as many organizations as it pleased, all of which would be tax exempt in perpetuity. The Concordat further declared Catholicism "the official religion of Italy" and outlawed Protestant propaganda. Catechetical classes that prepared students for the sacraments of Holy Communion and confirmation were to be held in all public and private schools.[30]

And so, with one stroke of a pen, the Holy See went from rags to riches and gained a privileged position at the tables of international money markets where the future of the twentieth century would be charted. Ten years later, in 1939, when Hitler invaded Poland, the Roman Catholic Church would stand, once again, as the richest and, in many ways, the most powerful institution on earth.

NOGARA'S NEW AGENCY

On February 11, 1929, the day of the signing of the Lateran Treaty, Pius XI created a new financial agency called the Special Administration of the Holy See. The sole function of the agency was to safeguard the "donation of Mussolini" so that the church's newly found wealth would not be channeled into the pockets of friends and associates of Vatican officials or dissipated on social causes, such as feeding the poor or providing shelter to the dispossessed.[31] The pope appointed Bernardino Nogara, the financial wizard and manager who had reorganized the Reichsbank, as the agency's manager and director. Nogara accepted the position with the stipulation that no clerics were assigned to serve at the Special Administration for fear that parochial interest might interfere with financial gain. He further demanded and received total control over what to buy and what to sell with the $90 million, along with the right to operate the new agency in complete independence from all other Vatican bureaucracies.[32]

THE DOCTRINAL CHANGE

As the world fell into the grips of the Great Depression, Nogara's first move as the Vatican's chief financial officer was to take over principal interest in Banca di Roma, a firm that had many securities of no call value, that is, securities that were worth little or nothing if sold on the stock exchange.[33] He then managed to persuade Mussolini to include the bank in the creation of the Institute for Industrial Reconstruction (IIR). This was Italy's answer to the financial devastation that ravaged the country. The function of the IIR was to capitalize industrial companies to stimulate economic growth. The companies agreed to provide one lira for every two lira raised from the private sector. All investments were secured by the government. Under this arrangement the worthless securities of Banca di Roma were restored to their original value and the Vatican, as the major shareholder, boasted an overnight fortune of $632 million.[34]

The Banca di Roma deal draws scant attention from church historians. But it represented a crucial theological development within Roman Catholicism. The Holy See was now engaged in the practice of usury— abandoning a doctrine that it had professed throughout the ages. John T. Noonan writes,

> The doctrine [against usury] was enunciated by popes, expressed by three ecumenical councils, proclaimed by bishops, and taught unanimously by theologians. The doctrine was not some obscure, hole-in-the-wall affectation, but stood astride the European markets, at least as much as the parallel Islamic ban on usury governs Muslim countries today. . . . The great central moral fact was that usury, understood as profit on a loan, was forbidden as contrary to natural law, as contrary to the law of the Church, and as contrary to the law of the gospel.[35]

THE EMPTY EXPLANATION

Glossing over the issue of doctrinal abandonment, Catholic apologists argued that the church hadn't changed in its stance on moneylending.

What *had* changed, they said, was the nature of money. Money, they continued, was no longer sterile but fertile.[36] It was "not merely a medium of exchange, but as an instrument of production; and just as money may be charged for the use of land, or of a house, so money may be charged for the use of money."[37] Few, including Avro Manhattan and other rabid anti-Catholic writers, criticized this word play, despite the fact such argumentation could be employed to undermine the entire corpus of Catholic doctrine. By the same logic, one could maintain that other moral teachings must change; that teachings concerning fornication must be dismissed because of new findings regarding the nature of sexuality; that the notion of an all-male priesthood must be abandoned because of the contemporary understanding of gender; or that the concept of sexual perversity must be discarded because of breakthroughs in genetics.

With Banca di Roma, the ineffable had occurred, a change in basic doctrine that would result in the *aggiornamento* (updating) of Vatican II. A practice that had been condemned as worse than murder was now sanctioned by the Roman Catholic Church—not for the spiritual good of the faithful, but for the cause of its own material gain.

INFAMOUS INVESTMENTS

With the windfall from Banca di Roma, Nogara purchased IIR stock in the open market so that the Holy See, by 1935, emerged as the largest shareholder of state-secured businesses in Italy. One such company was Italgas, which became the sole supplier of natural gas to many Italian cities.[38] Another was Società Generale Immobiliare, one of Italy's oldest construction companies.[39] In time, Immobiliare would become an international conglomerate that would serve to topple governments, wreak financial havoc, and embroil the Vatican in a host of sensational scandals.

By the outbreak of World War II, the Holy See had acquired major interests in textiles, steel, mining, metallurgical products, fertilizer plants, farming products, timber, ceramics, railroads, timber mills, pasta products, and telephone and telecommunications companies. The list of these holdings filled over seventy pages of accounting ledgers. Several of these firms produced products that were antithetical to Catholic teaching, most notably Istituto Farmacologico Serono di Roma, Italy's largest producer of contraceptives.[40] But what was condemned by priests from the pulpit now served to enhance the pope's portfolio. In 1935, when Mussolini needed armaments for the invasion of Ethiopia, a substantial proportion of the weapons came from Breda, Reggiane, and Compagnia Nazionale Aeronautica, munitions plants that Nogara had purchased for the Holy Mother Church.[41]

In addition to Banca di Roma, Nogara acquired for the Vatican a host of medium-sized and small rural banks in southern Italy, along with controlling interest in such major banking establishments as Banca Commerciale Italiana, Credito Italiano, Banca Provinciale Lombarda, and Banco Ambrosiano.[42] He understood the most basic principle of capitalism, that the flow of revenue determines the success of economic enterprises. Through the Holy See's networks of banks, Nogara now could channel the flow of cash to Vatican-owned companies and away from the firms of all competitors. For this reason, the Roman Catholic Church was able to prosper and thrive during the lean years of the 1930s.

Money poured into the Holy See from all the corners of the country—so much cash that Nogara was faced with the problem of concealing the enormous holdings and vast earnings from public scrutiny. The money, under Nogara's direction, no longer flowed into the Special Administration for investment in private sector business or deposit in the Vatican-controlled banks. The excess revenue was rather diverted from the church's business interests, which were tax-exempt, into Swiss bank accounts, so that the money trail would lead to closed banks and concealed records.[43]

THE VATICAN BANK

But as hundreds of millions of dollars continued to pour into the coffers of the Holy See, these measures were insufficient. The church needed its own bank where the growing wealth could be concealed from public scrutiny. On June 27, 1942, Nogara and Pius XII created the Istituto per le Opere di Religione (IOR), which would become commonly known as the Vatican Bank, within the Bastion of Nicholas V, a round tower that had been constructed in 1452 to ward off the threat of a Saracen invasion. The bank was established as a sovereign financial agency within a sovereign state—an entity unto itself without corporate or ecclesiastical ties to any other agency of the Holy See. As such, it could not be compelled to redress wrongs—not even the most egregious violations of international law. Nor could it be forced to release the source of any deposit.[44]

Nogara initiated a process of destroying all records of the bank's transactions, including deposits and investments, on a regular basis. Anyone seeking information regarding the dealings of the Vatican Bank, even its corporate organization, would discover little more than empty file folders within the Vatican archives.[45]

The princes of the church would be poor no more. Thanks to the political ambition of a fascist dictator, they had transformed from intransigent moralists decrying the sin of greed and covetousness into modern businessmen and bankers. By embracing the sin of usury, the popes would become not only as wealthy as their medieval predecessors, but also as corrupt.

Chapter Three

THE CATHOLIC MASONS

*At this period, the partisans of evil seems to be combining
together, and to be struggling with united vehemence, led on or
assisted by that strongly organized and widespread association
called the Freemasons. No longer making any secret of their purposes, they are now boldly rising up against God Himself. They
are planning the destruction of holy Church publicly and openly,
and this with the set purpose of utterly despoiling the nations of
Christendom, if it were possible, of the blessings obtained for us
through Jesus Christ our Savior.*
　　　　　　　　—Leo XIII, *Humanum genus*, April 20, 1888

During his return flight from Rio to Rome on July 28, 2013, Pope
Francis spoke to reporters for eighty minutes and confirmed the
presence of a Masonic mafia within the Vatican. "Masonic lobbies," the
pope said, "this is the most serious problem for me."[1] Before Francis made
this disclosure, the mainstream press refused to grant credibility to reports
that the Roman Curia had become infested with a nest of Freemasons who
were intent upon undermining the traditional dogmas and doctrines of
the faith.

RED SCARE

The Masonic infiltration of Holy Mother Church began in 1945, when the
overriding concern of Pope Pius XII was the Italian Communist Party
(Partito Comunista Italiano, or PCI), which was poised to take control of
the Italian government in the national election of 1948. Between late 1943
and mid-1944, the PCI had doubled, and in the German occupied northern
half of the country an extremely radical Marxist movement was gathering
strength; in the winter of 1944, over 500,000 workers from Turin, waving
the red flag, shut down the factories for eight days despite brutal Gestapo

repression; and the Italian underground—consisting of Communist sympathizers—grew to 150,000 armed men.[2]

Post-war Italy stood ready to become the first Communist country in Western Europe. Hundreds of thousands of northerners had either actively supported or actively fought for the partisan movement that had finally forced the German army out of Italy. It was the partisans who had captured Mussolini and who had hung him upside down with his mistress; it was the partisans who continued to assassinate Fascists after the war ended; and it was the partisans who constituted the PCI. By 1946, the division in the country became acute, with the people in the north wanting a Communist republic, and the people in the south wanting a Catholic monarchy.[3]

In Sicily, the rise of the PCI was even more disconcerting. Girolamo Li Causi, the island's leading Communist, stirred up the masses with his demands for the redistribution of the land's feudal holdings. His words, "we plan no Soviet rule here," cut no ice with the mob and the propertied classes, but revitalized the longings of the landless poor for economic reform.[4] In 1947, the Left, never previously strong in Sicily, skyrocketed out of nowhere. All of Italy was stunned by the provincial elections, which produced resounding victories for the Communists.

If the Communists came to power, Pius realized, all would be lost for the church, including its tax-exempt status and its vast industrial wealth. Palmiro Togliatti, the PCI leader, called for the socialization of industrial firms that had been financed by Italy's Institute for Industrial Reconstruction (IIR) during the Great Depression. These firms included Italgas and Società Generale Immobiliare, the companies in which the Vatican had invested the lion's share of its newfound wealth.[5]

THE CIA CONNECTION

In desperation, the pope turned to the United States and the newly created Central Intelligence Agency. The Truman administration coughed up more than $380 million to reactivate the Christian Democratic Party (CDP); to establish twenty thousand CDP cells throughout Italy; and to create Catholic Action, an organization to generate propaganda against the Communists.[6] But more funds were needed for muscle—strong-arm tactics by made men who could ensure the church and its black nobility that the Catholic country would never become red.

In the months before the 1948 national election, the CIA dumped $65 million of its black money into the Vatican Bank. Much of the cash was hand delivered in large suitcases by clerics with affiliations to Calogero "Don Calò" Vizzini, Giuseppe Genco Russo, Lucky Luciano, and other members of the Sicilian Mafia, who were in the agency's employ.[7] In the closing months of 1947, hundreds of "made men" made their way to Italy from New York, Chicago, and Miami. Several arrived on US military transports.[8]

MUSCLE AND BLOOD

Murder, Inc. was now unleashed upon the Italian electorate. The Mafia army of thugs under the direction of the CIA burned down eleven Communist branch offices, made four assassination attempts on Communist leader Girolamo Li Causi, and opened fire on a crowd of workers celebrating May Day in Portella della Ginestra, killing eleven and wounding fifty-seven.[9] Throughout 1948, in Sicily alone, the CIA-backed terror attacks resulted in the killing on average of five people a week. The mob's tactics worked, and the Christian Democrats triumphantly returned to power.[10]

One year after the election, renewed fears of a Communist takeover of Italy arose from Stalin's creation of the Comecon to enforce the Soviet dominion of the lesser states of Central Europe. Faced with this development, the CIA opted to extend support for the CDP in Italy with annual infusions of $20 million in black funds. The money was deposited in Catholic banks throughout Italy, including Banco Ambrosiano. In exchange for this ongoing support, the pope allowed the CIA to establish a "Vatican desk," under the direction of James Jesus Angleton, a high-ranking CIA official.[11]

THE VATICAN DESK

The Vatican desk reviewed for pertinent data all of the intelligence reports that were sent to the Holy See from papal nuncios who were stationed behind the Iron Curtain. Strategies between the CIA and the church were drafted to undermine left-wing movements throughout Europe and South America. The affairs of politically suspect members of the Curia were monitored by moles, and the actions of progressive priests, particularly in Latin America, were thwarted by strong-arm techniques.

The Vatican now became a principal depository not only for black funds but also for top-secret documents, including CIA files relating to the development of nuclear weapons. One of these documents, never declassified, surfaced in 2006 during the process of discovery in *Alperin v. Vatican Bank*, a case that was tried in the federal district court of Northern California.[12]

The alliance between the Vatican and the CIA against the spread of Communism crystallized into a covert operation called Gladio, named after the short swords Roman gladiators used to kill their opponents in the arena. By 1955, ecclesiastical units of the operation—known as Catholic Gladio—popped up in Friuli-Venezia Giulia, a region of Italy that bordered the Communist bloc. Cardinal Giuseppe Siri and the Italian Episcopate Conference supervised its establishment.[13] Priests and bishops were now trained in guerilla warfare with Italian fascists to ward off a potential Soviet invasion of the Italian peninsula and to eradicate all left-wing dissidents who opposed the rule of the CDP.

CATHOLIC GLADIO

The Catholic units of Gladio were led by Fr. Augustin Bea, rector of the Pontifical Biblical Institute, Fr. Agostino Casaroli, his privy chamberlain, and Fr. Fiorenzo Angelini, master of pontifical ceremonies. These three clerics, who had been dispatched by the Holy Father, were soon joined by Fr. Michele Giordano, a diocesan assistant of Catholic Action, an organization that attempted to increase the influence of the church on society.[14] All four prelates eventually were elevated to the College of Cardinals for their work in the clandestine undertaking. Leading lay figures of the Catholic nobility also became prominent in Catholic Gladio, including Giulio Andreotti, a cofounder of the CDP, and Umberto Ortolani, the "secret chamberlain of the Papal Household" and member of the inner circle of the Knights of Malta.[15]

So many ethnic Slovenes who resided in Friuli-Venezia Giulia were terrorized by the activities of Catholic Gladio troops that two-thirds of them moved to more hospitable locations.[16] Throughout the 1950s, money for the activities of Catholic Gladio was provided by the CIA, which annually shelled out $30 to $50 million for covert operations in Italy. These funds were not only washed by the Vatican but also funneled by the pope to the groups and organizations that met with his approval.[17] Former CIA agent Victor Marchetti later testified:

In the 1950s and the 1960s the CIA gave economic support to many activities promoted by the Catholic Church, from orphanages to missions. Millions of dollars each year were given to a great number of bishops and monsignors. One of them was Cardinal Giovanni Battista Montini [who became Pope Paul VI].[18]

To protect the clandestine nature of Gladio, meetings of the anti-Communist forces were held in Masonic lodges amid all the trappings of Freemasonry. One such lodge became known as Propaganda 2, or "P-2."

PROPAGANDA DUE

The name of P-2 was derived from Propaganda Massonica, a lodge that was formed in 1877 by members of the Piedmont nobility in Turin. This lodge was distinctly different from other Masonic lodges since many of its members were Mafiosi and military officers, who were more concerned about political beliefs than other Masons. Initiates who entered Propaganda Massonica were threatened with "certain and violent death" if they revealed any of the society's secrets. The presence of the Mafia among the lodge members guaranteed that this demand for *omerta* was not an idle threat.[19] In 1924, Freemasonry in Italy was outlawed by Mussolini as politically subversive, and the Propaganda Massonica shut its doors and rolled up its ledgers.[20] At the close of World War II, the lodge was revitalized as Propaganda Due.

TACIT APPROVAL

Pius XII, by his silence, appeared to endorse the rise of Freemasonry in post-war Italy. This tacit approval was stunning since the Roman Catholic Church, in bulls and blasts, had condemned Freemasonry and banned its members, under threat of excommunication, from participating in Masonic rites.[21] The dangerous errors of this fraternal organization had been set forth as follows:

> God is described in Freemasonry as an impersonal "Great Architect of the Universe." He is neither the personal God of the Old and New Testaments nor the triune deity of Christian tradition.
> Masonic writings deny the dogmas of incarnation and the divine institution of the Roman Catholic Church.

In Freemasonry, Jesus Christ is portrayed as a mere mortal and an
  inspirational teacher like Socrates, Buddha, and Mohammad.

The Trinity is compared in Freemasonry to the "trinitiesî" of the
  ancient mystery religions.

Christianity is looked upon in Freemasonry as an offshoot of pagan
  religions and, therefore, laden with error. God is portrayed by
  Masonic writers as a deceiver who, like Satan, leads all those away
  from the truth who are not worthy to receive it.

Truth, according to Freemasonry, is relative to time and circumstance.
  It is not objective and binding as professed by the Roman Catholic
  Church.

Freemasonry presents itself as the foundation of all religion, since it is
  established on Naturalism, a system of belief that makes human
  reason supreme in all things.

Within the various degrees of Freemasonry, blood oaths are sworn,
  which bind initiates to the penalties of having their throats "cut
  from ear to ear," their tongues "torn out" by their roots, and their
  bodies "buried in the sands of the sea" for revealing any secrets of
  the secret society.[22]

But such teachings suddenly paled in importance before the rise of
Marxist doctrine in Italy and the threat to Holy Mother Church of the
socialization of Italian industry.

HIERARCHICAL HERETICS

By 1965, when Vatican II came to a close, the membership roll of P-2 contained the names of such ecclesiastical dignitaries as Alberto Ablondi,
bishop of Livorno; Msgr. Alessandro Gottardi, president of *Fratelli Maristi*;
Cardinal Augustin Bea, the Vatican secretary of state; Salvatore Baldassari,
bishop of Ravenna; Bishop Annibale Bugnini, secretary to the Commission
on Liturgical Reform; Msgr. Agostino Cacciavillan (later a cardinal), secretary of the nuncio to the Philippines and Spain; Msgr. Umberto Cameli,
director of the Office of Ecclesiastical Affairs in Italy; Agostino Casaroli
(later a cardinal), undersecretary of the Sacred Congregation for Extraordinary Ecclesiastical Affairs; Bishop Fiorenzo Angelini, vicar general of
Roman hospitals; Fr. Carlo Graziani, rector of the Vatican Minor Seminary;
Fr. Angelo Lanzoni, chief of the office of Vatican secretary of state; Virgilio

Levi, assistant director of the Vatican newspaper *L'Osservatore*; Cardinal Achille Liénart, bishop of Lille and grand master of Masonic lodges; Msgr. Francesco Marchisano (later a cardinal); Abbot Salvatore Marsili, head of the Order of St. Benedict of Finalpia; Bishop Marcello Morgante (later a cardinal), spiritual head of Ascoli Piceno in east Italy; Bishop Virgilio Noe (later a cardinal), head of the Sacred Congregation of Divine Worship; Vittore Palestra, legal counsel of the Sacred Rota of the Vatican State; Archbishop Michele Pellegrino (later a cardinal), spiritual head of Turin; Fr. Fiorenzo Romita, member of the Sacred Congregation of the Clergy; Fr. Pietro Santini, vice official of the Vicar of Rome; Msgr. Domenico Semproni, member of the Tribunal of the Vicarate of the Vatican; Cardinal Leo Suenens, protector of the Church of St. Peter in Chains (outside Rome); Bishop Dino Trabalzini, bishop of Rieti and auxiliary bishop of southern Rome; and Fr. Vittorio Trocchi, secretary for the Catholic Laity in the Consistory of the Vatican State Consultations.[23]

Within the next decade, scores of additional Vatican officials, including cardinals, Roman Catholic hierarchs, and prominent bishops and archbishops, would become members of Masonic lodges—many with ties to P-2.[24] It is difficult to believe that the supreme pontiffs (Pius XII, John XXIII, Paul VI, John Paul I, John Paul II, and Benedict XVI) were blissfully unaware that so many of the church's dignitaries were practicing Freemasons. And it remains equally mind-boggling that the pontiffs elevated these clerics to loftier dignitaries upon learning of their membership in P-2 and other Masonic lodges.[25]

KILLING AND THE CRAFT

As gladiators, the Catholic clerics helped to initiate the "years of lead" (*Anni di Piombo*)—a decade of false-flag attacks, including the Piazza Fontana and Bologna bombings, that were blamed on Communist agitators—condoned the wholesale killing of men, women, and children throughout Italy, and mounted a series coup d'états against left-wing regimes in Western Europe.[26]

As Masons, they became steeped in the tenets of a parallel religion—a religion with temples and altars, prayers, and a distinct moral code. The Catholic clerics adopted a deistic view of God as the impersonal Grand Architect of the universe before whom all manners of religious expression are equally efficacious. "The religion of Freemasonry," Albert G. Mackey explains in his *Encyclopedia*, "is not sectarian. It admits men of every creed within its hospitable bosom, rejecting none and approving none for his particular faith. It is not Judaism . . . it is not Christianity. It does not meddle with sectarian creeds or doctrines, but teaches fundamental truth. . . . At its altar, men of all religions may kneel; to its creed, disciples of every faith may subscribe."[27] The Catholic clerics involved in Gladio came to subscribe to the Masonic doctrine of "freedom of conscience," which is defined in an official publication of Freemasonry as "freedom from dogmatic principles," including the traditional teachings of Roman Catholicism.[28]

A NEW WORLD ORDER

The Catholic Mason clerics became bound to uphold the avowed purpose of the Masonic craft—the "creation of an international brotherhood of men bound in fellowship and pledged to mutual aid, religious toleration, and political reform"[29]—the very purpose for the convocation of the Second Vatican Council in 1962.

The Masonic infiltration of the church persisted after Operation Gladio was condemned by the European Parliament on November 22, 1990, and P-2 had been dismantled by the resolution of the Grand Orient of Italy, which regulated the activities of Italian lodges.[30] By 1993, according to Masonic officials, four Scottish Rite lodges had been set up within the eight city blocks that comprised the state of Vatican City.[31]

MASONIC POPES?

Testimony also surfaced that the list of Catholic Masons included Pope John XXIII and Pope Paul VI, the popes who had presided over the sessions of Vatican II. Carlos Vazquez Rangel, grand commander of the Supreme Council of the Masons of Mexico, offered this testimony: "On the same day in Paris, the profane [Masonic jargon for non-Mason] Angelo Roncalli (John XXIII) and the profane Giovanni Montini (Paul VI) were initiated into the august mysteries of the Brotherhood. Thus it was that much that was achieved at the Council was based on Masonic principles."[32]

Most Catholic apologists dismiss the allegation that John XXIII and Paul VI were members of Masonic lodges as a baseless conspiracy theory. But support for this contention was provided by Virgilio Guido, the former head of the Italian Grand Orient,[33] scattered newspaper accounts including feature articles in the *Portugal Daily News* and *30 Days*, an Italian monthly that is widely read by the Curia,[34] along with the findings of investigative reporters, such as Piers Compton, a former priest and the editor of the *Universe*, a Catholic weekly newsletter.[35]

But verification of Vazquez Rangel's revelation cannot be obtained from official Masonic records. Freemasonry is a secret society and membership lists remain shielded from public scrutiny. What's more, Masons who proceed through the various degrees of the craft are known by their codenames and membership numbers. Cardinal Agostino Casaroli, who served as John Paul II's secretary of state, was inducted into the secret society on September 28, 1957. Upon receiving his lodge number (41-076), he became known among his Masonic brothers as "CASA." Cardinal Sebastiano Baggio, the prefect of the Sacred Congregation of Bishops, became a Mason on August 14, 1967. He received the number 85-1640 and the Masonic moniker of "SEBA." Cardinal Pasquale Macchi, Paul VI's prelate of honor and private secretary, joined the lodge on April 24, 1953, gained the number 5463-2 and the codename "MAPA."[36] If, in fact, Roncalli and Montini submitted to the secret ceremony of Freemasonry on the same day in Paris, their Masonic names and numbers remain unknown.

CHAMPIONING FREEMASONRY

Although they may not have submitted to the initiation rite of Freemasonry, John XXIII and Paul VI certainly *acted* like members of the craft. Unlike their papal predecessors, they refused to condemn Freemasonry and to uphold the sentence of excommunication for all Catholics who joined Masonic lodges.[37] They championed the Masonic tenets of religious indifferentism and freedom of conscience. And they advanced the Masonic doctrine of universalism, "a worship in which all good men may unite, that each may share the faith of all."[38]

As soon as John XXIII convened the Second Vatican Council in 1959, Baron Yves Marsaudon, a thirty-third degree Mason and state minister of *Grande Loge Nationale Française*, the lodge that governs all Scottish rite members of the craft in France, exclaimed, "The sense of universalism that is rampant in Rome these days is very close to our purpose of existence."[39] One year later, John XXIII consecrated Marsaudon as a knight of the Sovereign Military Order of Malta (a Catholic lay religious order) and encouraged him to remain as the leading spokesman for French Freemasonry.[40] As a Knight of Malta, Marsaudon urged Catholics to support the reforms of Vatican II. "Catholics, especially conservatives," he said, "should not forget that all roads lead to God. They should abide by this brave idea of freedom of conscience which, and here one may speak of revolution, starting from our Masonic Lodges, has spread magnificently above the doctrine of Saint Peter."[41]

A "VIGOROUS ENDORSEMENT"

When John XXIII issued *Pacem in terris* in 1962, the *Masonic Bulletin* hailed the new encyclical as "a vigorous endorsement of Masonic doctrine."[42] Few could doubt this assessment, since *Pacem in terris* contains the following statement of support for the heretical positions of religious indifferentism and liberty of conscience:

> . . . among man's rights is that of being able to worship God in accordance with the dictates of his own conscience, and to profess his religion both in public and in private. According to the clear teaching of Lactantius, "This is the very condition of our birth, that we render to the God who made us that just homage which is His due; that we acknowledge Him alone as God, and follow Him. It is from this ligature of piety, which binds us and joins us to God, that religion derives its name."[43]

This passage from the encyclical is telling not only for its statement of support for heretical positions, but also for its reliance on Lactantius as the source of ecclesiastical authority. The fourth-century advisor of Emperor Constantine was not a Catholic saint, let alone a doctor of the church (*egregi doctores ecclesiae*), but rather a heterodoxical semi-Arian (i.e., one who believes that Christ is not eternal but rather created in time), whose theological claims, according to the authors of the *Catholic Encyclopedia*, displayed "a lack of grasp of Christian principles and almost complete ignorance of scripture."[44]

Within the same encyclical, the pope went on to reverse traditional doctrine banning Catholic membership in secret societies:

> Men are by nature social, and consequently they have the right to meet together and to form associations with their fellows. They have the right to confer on such associations the type of organization which they con-

sider best calculated to achieve their objectives. They have also the right to exercise their own initiative and act on their own responsibility within these associations for the attainment of the desired results.[45]

BROTHER MONTINI

Marsaudon and other Masonic officials were equally supportive of Paul VI, whose reign, they maintained, strengthened the ties between the church and the craft. "Born in our Masonic Lodges, freedom of expression has now spread over the dome of Saint Peter's," Marsaudon said. "This is the revolution of Paul VI. It is clear that Paul VI, not content to follow the policy of his predecessor [John XXIII] does in fact go much further."[46] Jacques Mitterrand, grand master of the *Grande Loge Nationale Française*, praised the church's new direction: "Something has changed in the Church. The replies set down by the Pope [Paul VI] to such burning questions as the celibacy of the clergy and birth control are fiercely contested within the Church. Some bishops, some priests, and members of the laity have questioned the word of the Sovereign Pontiff himself. In the eyes of the freemason, he who disputes dogma is already a freemason without his apron."[47]

Freemasonry's change of attitude toward the Roman Catholic Church was extraordinary. Prior to the pontificate of John XXIII, a state of war had existed between the craft and the church. The first volley in this war came from Pope Clement XII and his issuance of *In eminenti* in 1738. This bull forbade Catholics to join the Masonic movement under the pain of excommunication.

BARROOM BIRTH

The Masonic movement was created in 1716 at the Goose and Gridiron Ale House, where four secret societies with ties to the Jacobite movement decided to merge into the Grand Lodge of London. The members of these societies were British nobles, including Anthony Sayer, John Theophilus Desaguliers, and George Payne.[48] They were imbued with the thought of Sir Isaac Newton, who believed the doctrine of the Trinity was a "massive fraud" that had perverted the legacy of primitive Christianity and that the worship of Christ in place of God, the first cause and grand architect of the universe, was idolatrous.[49] Like Newton, they became fascinated with the geometry of Solomon's Temple, as described in the First Book of Kings, believing that the temple's harmonious components—the golden sections, the conic sections, and the spirals of orthographic projection, belied an ancient history that contained the secrets of the universe, secrets they were capable of discerning by proper use of mathematics.[50]

At the ale house, the so-called "freethinkers" decided to expand membership in their new society "to men of various professions," provided they were approved the ruling nobility and submitted to a secret ceremony of initiation.[51]

THE MASONIC CONSTITUTION

After the meeting, George Payne wrote *The General Regulations of a Freemason*, which was expanded by John Anderson, a Presbyterian minister, into *The Constitutions of the Freemasons Containing the History, Charges, Regulations, etc., of That Most Ancient and Right Worshipful Fraternity*, which became the standard text of the society. In the *Constitution*, Anderson expressed the brotherhood's belief that religion was a matter of opinion:

> A Mason is obliged by his tenure to observe the moral law as a true Noachide; and if he rightly understands the Craft, he will never be a stupid atheist nor an irreligious Libertine, nor act against conscience. In ancient Times, the Christian Masons were charged to comply with the Christian usages of each country where they traveled or worked; being found in all nations, even of diverse religions. They are generally charged to adhere to that religion in which all men agree (leaving each brother to his own particular opinions); that is, to be good men and true, men of honor and honesty, by whatever names, religions, or persuasions they may be distinguished; for they all agree in the three great articles of Noah, enough to preserve the cement of the lodge. Thus Masonry is the Center of Union, and the happy means of conciliating persons that otherwise must have remained at a perpetual distance.[52]

Anderson went on to insist that Freemasonry, since it espoused a "universal" religion, was the real "catholic" church:

> No private piques nor quarrels about nations, families, religions or politics must by any means or under any color or pretense whatsoever be brought within the doors of the lodge; for as Masons we are the most

ancient catholic religion and of all nations upon the square, level and plump.[53]

DECLARATION OF WAR

The movement soon spread to Ireland, France, Germany, the Netherlands, Russia, Spain, the United States, and Italy, where it captured the attention of Clement XII.[54] The pope, after sending agents to spy on the lodge meetings, proclaimed that the assemblies "have caused in the minds of the faithful the greatest suspicion, and all prudent and upright men have passed the same judgment on them as being depraved and perverted. For if they were not doing evil, they would not have so great a hatred of the light."[55] He condemned "the strict and unbreakable bond which obliges them, both by an oath upon the Holy Bible and by a host of grievous punishment, to an inviolable silence about all that they do in secret together." Noting that the Freemasons "do not hold by either civil or canonical sanctions," the pope called upon bishops and prelates to investigate them as "being most suspect of heresy."[56] Benedict XIV reiterated the condemnation in his Apostolic Constitution *Providas romanorum*, which was promulgated on March 18, 1751.[57]

The Masons, including Voltaire, responded to the condemnations by initiating a wave of Catholic anticlericalism, culminating in the French Revolution of 1789.[58] Louis Philippe II, the grand master of the *Grande Orient de France*, played a key role in the execution of Louis XVI, the Catholic king.[59] Other Masons who played leading roles in the revolution and the subsequent reign of terror were Mirabeau, Choderlos de Laclos, and Rouget de Lisle, who composed the national anthem "La Marseillaise."[60] In the course of the revolution, Catholic churches and monasteries were desecrated and destroyed throughout the country, 30,000 priests were send into exile, and hundreds more were sent to the guillotine.[61]

THE PERMANENT INSTRUCTION

In 1819, the Alta Vendita—the ruling body of Masonic lodges in Europe—issued "Permanent Instruction," an internal report outlining the means by which the craft would bring about "the final destruction of Catholicism." It called for Masons to infiltrate the church, pretend piety and orthodoxy, choose a pontiff from their ranks, and form "a council of the Sovereign." The report contained the following rallying call:

> You want to revolutionize . . . let the Clergy march under your standard, always believing that they are marching under the banner of the apostolic keys . . . lay your snares like Simon Bar-Jona; lay them in the sacristies, the seminaries, and the monasteries rather than at the bottom of the sea: and if you do not hurry, we promise you a catch more miraculous than his. The fisher of fish became the fisher of men; you will bring friends around the apostolic Chair. You will have preached a revolution in tiara and in cope, marching with the cross and the banner, a revolution that will need to be only a little bit urged on to set fire to the four corners of the world.[62]

SYNAGOGUE OF SATAN

Learning of this document, Pope Pius IX issued a new volley of six bulls and blasts against Freemasonry, culminating in *Etsi multa* (November 21, 1871), in which he spoke of the secret society as "the synagogue of Satan":

> Some of you may perchance wonder that the war against the Catholic Church extends so widely. Indeed each of you knows well the nature, zeal, and intention of sects, whether called Masonic or some other name. When he compares them with the nature, purpose, and amplitude of the conflict waged nearly everywhere against the Church, he cannot doubt but that the present calamity must be attributed to their deceits and machinations for the most part. For from these the synagogue of Satan is formed which draws up its forces, advances its standards, and joins battle against the Church of Christ.
>
> Our Predecessors, as watchers in Israel, denounced these forces from the very beginnings to rulers and nations. Against them they have struck out again and again with their condemnations. We Ourselves have not been deficient in Our duty. Would that the Pastors of the Church had more loyalty from those who could have averted such a pernicious plague! But, creeping through sinuous openings, never stinting in toil, deceiving many by clever fraud, it has reached such an outcome that it has burst forth from its hiding places and boasts itself lord and master. Grown immense by a multitude of followers, these nefarious bands think that they have been made masters of their desire and have all but achieved their goal. The have at last achieved what they have so long desired, that is, that in many places they obtained supreme power and won for themselves bul-

warks of men and authority. Now they boldly turn to this, to hand over the Church of God to a most harsh servitude, to tear up the supports on which it rests, and to attempt to distort the marks by which it stands out gloriously. What more? They would, if possible, completely wipe it out from the world after they had shaken it with frequent blows, ruined it, and overturned it.[63]

POPE VS. PIKE

And still, the war raged on. Alarmed that Freemasonry had gained "entrance into every rank of government" throughout the Christian world, Pope Leo XIII issued *Humanum genus* (April 20, 1884), an encyclical that condemned the craft's philosophy of naturalism, the belief that "human nature and human reason ought in all things to be mistress and guide," and its calculated attempt "to bring about the ruin of all forms of religion, and especially of the Catholic religion, which, as it is the only one that is true, cannot, without great injustice, be regarded as merely equal to other religions."[64]

Humanum genus prompted this response from Albert Pike, Southern grand commander of the Scottish Rites Southern Jurisdiction, at the assembly of the Grand Orient of Charleston, South Carolina, on October 19, 1884:

> . . . under the guise of a condemnation of Freemasonry, and a recital of the enormities and immoralities of the Order, in some respects so absurdly false as to be ludicrous, notwithstanding its malignity, it [*Humanum genus*] proved upon perusal to be a declaration of war, and the signal for a crusade, against the rights of men individually and of communities of men as organisms; against the separation of Church and State, and the confinement of the Church within the limits of its legitimate functions; against education free from sectarian religious influences; against the civil policy of non-Catholic countries in regard to marriage and divorce; against the great doctrine upon which, as upon a rock not to be shaken, the foundations of our Republic rest, that "men are superior to institutions, and not institutions to men;" against the right of the people to depose oppressive, cruel and worthless rulers; against the exercise of the rights of free thought and free speech, and against, not only republican, but all constitutional government. . . .[65]

THE ABYSS OF ALL ERROR

Throughout the first half of the twentieth century, Roman Catholic officials, including the presiding pontiffs, continued to rant and rave against Freemasonry as the "abyss of all errors."[66] Canon 2335 of the 1917 Code of Canon Law proscribed the following: "All those who enroll their names in the sect of Freemasons or similar associations which plot against the Church or legitimate civil authorities incur by this very fact the penalty of excommunication, absolution of which is reserved simply to the Holy See."[67]

MASONRY TRIUMPHANT

With Vatican II, the Masonic plan to topple the Roman Catholic Church, as outlined by the "Permanent Instruction" of the Alta Vendita in 1817, came to a successful conclusion. The Catholic cardinals and bishops, who had joined Masonic lodges, were placed in key positions of power to alter Catholic doctrine for the sake of *aggiornamento* ("updating"). Cardinal Augustin Bea became the driving force behind *Nostra aetate*, "Declaration on the Relation of the Church with Non-Christian Religions," and the president of the Secretariat for Promoting Christian Unity.[68] Cardinal Leo Joseph Suenens served as a moderator of the Vatican II Council and a major architect of *Lumen gentium* ("The Dogmatic Constitution of the Church") and *Gaudium et spes* ("The Pastoral Constitution of the Church in the Modern World").[69] Cardinal Achille Liénart assumed leadership of the progressive forces that managed to take control of the council.[70] Fr. Roberto Tucci was named the theological expert for preparing the official documents, including *Ad gentes* and *Gaudium et spes*. Archbishop Annibale Bugnini came to author *Novus Ordo*, the new liturgy, with this primary purpose: "We must strip from our Catholic prayers and from the Catholic liturgy everything which can be the shadow of a stumbling block for our separated brethren, that is, from the Protestants."[71]

Freemasonry had won the war.

Chapter Four

SPIRITUAL SUICIDE

There is a respect in which the Church can be compared to any great manufacturing company, and I hope that making this comparison will not appear too irreverent. The object of any manufacturer is to persuade the public to buy its product in preference to that of its competitors. Let us imagine that the chief executives of, say, the Ford Motor Company decided to give the company and its products a totally new image. In order to achieve this they made radical alterations in the appearance of Ford cars, threw out all their tried and tested marketing methods, and promoted their restyled vehicles in a completely new manner. Imagine then, that sales plummeted, and not only did they win practically no new customers, but lost a huge proportion of their established clients, in some countries as many as eighty percent. It would be an understatement to claim that these executive officers would have lacked credibility had they denied any connection between their new marketing policies and the collapse of their company. Imagine the reaction had the same executives not only tried to exculpate their new policies from any responsibility for the collapse, but denied that any collapse had taken place, despite the fact that in country after country Ford factories were closing down, and that sales were at the lowest level ever. Let us go one step further and imagine that they refused to abandon the disastrous policies they had adopted, and return to their traditional methods, but intended "to go forward on the same path" that had led to the self-destruction of Ford Motor Company. One can only conclude that under such circumstances their next shareholders' meeting would be somewhat stormy.[1]

—Michael Davies, *Pope John's Council*, 1977

Unlike any universal gathering of the Roman Catholic Church, including Nicaea (325) and Vatican I (1869), the Second Vatican Council was not convened to address a controversy or to settle a crisis. On

53

January 25, 1959, when John XXIII felt the urgent need to initiate change in the life and worship of the church, Roman Catholicism was flourishing in all aspects—attendance, membership, vocations, missions, and financial contributions—like never before since the time of Trent (1545).

In 1959 the Catholic Church in America counted 36,023 members in 111 dioceses and 27 archdioceses.[2] The US Catholic hierarchy consisted of four cardinals, 34 archbishops, and 183 bishops; the 17,000 parishes throughout the country were cared for by over 50,000 priests. Over 190,000 were in religious orders (164,000 sisters), most of whom taught in the parochial schools.[3] Roman Catholicism was far and away America's largest denomination. This achievement was remarkable. As late as 1908, the church in the United States was still part of the missionary field, under the jurisdiction of the Congregation of the Propagation of the Faith.[4]

In every American parish, there were social and recreational activities from bingos to baseball teams. In every American municipality, there were Catholic hospitals, homes for the elderly, and orphanages; Catholic Welfare Conferences and Altar and Rosary societies; Catholic fellowships of physicians, lawyers, teachers, students, and philosophers; Catholic Boy Scouts and Catholic War Veterans; Catholic leagues of policemen, firemen, and sanitation workers; Catholic newspapers and periodicals; and a Catholic Youth Organization with over six million members. In every city and suburb, there were Catholic elementary and secondary schools. Regarding the proliferation of Catholic education, Walter J. Ong wrote in 1953, "Never in the history of Christianity, including the height of the Middle Ages, has the Church as such been charged with an organized educational program which even remotely compares with that of the United States."[5] When the pope announced his plans for an ecumenical council, 4,000,000 elementary school pupils and over 780,000 high school students were enrolled in US Catholic parochial schools.[6]

Why, then, the need for the council? On July 5, 1961, Pope John XXIII provided the following answer:

> The ecumenical council will reach out and embrace under the widespread wings of the Catholic Church the entire heredity of Our Lord Jesus Christ. Its principal task will be concerned with the condition and modernization [in Italian: *aggiornamento*] of the Church after 20 centuries of life. May it be that side by side with this, God will add also, through whatever edification we may offer, but above all by merit of the omnipotence of the Most High who can draw new chosen sons from the very stones, one other result: a movement toward recomposition of the whole Mystical Flock of Our Lord.[7]

In short, Holy Mother Church was to be dressed in modern attire in order to attract "new chosen sons from the very stones" so that she could expand her household.

TEMPTING GOD

In his apostolic constitution *Humanae salutis*, promulgated on December 25, 1961, as an official proclamation of the Second Vatican Council, John XXIII acknowledged the church's robust health by saying, "The Church . . . has seen the rise and growth within herself of immense energies of the apostolate, of prayer, of action in all fields, first on the part of a clergy ever better equipped in learning and virtue for its mission and then of a laity which has become ever more conscious of its responsibilities within the Church and especially of its duty to collaborate with the Church's hierarchy."[8] Still and all, he decided, it was high time to administer a high colonic enema.

The results were supposed to be salubrious. Laymen would be stirred from their apathy and would join with priests and bishops in apostolic endeavors. The refined liturgy would become a new source of inspiration to the faithful. The religious orders, reformed in keeping with modern times, would find themselves overwhelmed with new candidates. The religious seminaries would be packed to overflowing. Catholic churches would sprout up on every street corner to accommodate the ever increasing number of new converts.[9] Apparently, no one reminded the Holy Father of the warning issued by Cardinal Henry Manning in 1909 that "to convoke a General Council except when absolutely demanded by necessity is to tempt God."[10]

PREPARING THE SCHEMAE

During the thirty-four months between the pope's summoning of the bishops and the opening session, the Roman Curia held the key positions on the planning committees that solicited suggestions for discussion at the council from bishops throughout the world. From thousands of these suggestions, the committee members selected seventy-five for development into detailed proposals or *schemae*.[11] The task was tedious and time consuming, forcing the committees to labor over their drafts from dawn to dusk. The topics ranged over a wide variety of subjects, including revelation, ecclesiastical benefices, political and social developments, threats to the welfare of Holy Mother Church, and the rise of new schools of thought, such as existentialism and phenomenology. Monsignor Vincenzo Carbone of the Vatican's General Secretariat was able to claim that no other council had had a preparation "so vast, so diligently carried out, and so profound."[12] Regarding the laborious task of developing the schemae, Monsignor Marcel Lefebvre wrote:

> Prior to the opening of the Council, I was a member of the Central Prepa-
> ratory Commission, and for two years, therefore, I attended all the meet-
> ings. The task of the Central Commission was to verify and examine all
> the preparatory schemae which were sent to us by the other commissions,
> consequently I was in a position to know what had been done, what had
> to be scrutinized, and what had to be presented to the Council. This work
> was done most conscientiously and with meticulous care. . . . A very fine
> work had been completed for presentation to the Council; these schemae
> conform to the doctrine of the Church, though adapted to the mentality of
> our generation, adapted after careful thought and with much prudence.[13]

If all went as planned, the bishops who gathered for Vatican II would simply put their stamp of approval on the proposals and return home.[14] The gathering would amount to little more than another glorious Roman pageant, replete with the standard pronouncements of excommunications and anathemas against the forces of modernity.

THE OPENING ADDRESS

On October 11, 1962, at the opening day of the council in St. Peter's Basilica, the pope announced the following to the 2,800 Catholic digni-taries in attendance:

> The Church, whose light illumines all, whose strength of supernatural
> unity redounds to the advantage of all humanity, is rightly described in
> these beautiful words of St. Cyprian:
> "The Church, surrounded by divine light, spreads her rays over the
> entire earth. This light, however, is one and unique and shines every-
> where without causing any separation in the unity of the body. She
> extends her branches over the whole world. By her fruitfulness she sends
> ever farther afield he [sic] rivulets. Nevertheless, the head is always one,
> the origin one for she is the one mother, abundantly fruitful. We are born

of her, are nourished by her milk, we live of her spirit" (*De Catholicae Eccles. Unitate*, 5).

Venerable brothers, such is the aim of the Second Vatican Ecumenical Council, which, while bringing together the Church's best energies and striving to have men welcome more favorably the good tidings of salvation, prepares, as it were and consolidates the path toward that unity of mankind which is required as a necessary foundation, in order that the earthly city may be brought to the resemblance of that heavenly city where truth reigns, charity is the law, and whose extent is eternity.[15]

And so, the Holy Father reiterated, the leaders of the church had been summoned neither to define a new article of faith nor to adopt a new stance against the spread of Communism. They had been called to devise a new means of proclaiming "the good tidings of salvation," so that all people might unite in one faith "where truth reigns, charity is the law, and whose extent in eternity." His words must have stupefied many of discerning cardinals, archbishops, and bishops, who now realized they had been beckoned to Rome for the sake of a papal pipedream.

PAPAL PELAGIANISM

Listening to the strange opening address, the same discerning clerics would have realized that serious trouble was in store. Although the pope cited St. Augustine, his statements smacked of Pelagianism, the fifth-century heresy which held that people are good by nature and can merit salvation without God's grace. Against the claims of Pelagius, St. Augustine had forged the doctrine of original sin and the theological contention that human nature had been "changed and vitiated" by the fall of Adam. By inheriting this nature, he wrote in *The City of God*, every person was born inherently evil—a slave to sin, utterly reliant on God's grace for salvation.[16] St. Augustine's views became formalized as dogma by the Council of Trent (1546–1563).[17]

Original sin was a keystone of Catholic theology. It provided the rationale for the doctrines of the Incarnation, the Atonement, and the Immaculate Conception of Mary. It explained the need for infant baptism and the spiritual realm of Limbo. It supported the view of the church as the sole source of spiritual redemption, Christ as the Second Adam, and the prohibitions regarding human sexuality.

THE NEW PERSPECTIVE

John XXIII, in his address, also abandoned the Catholic traditional world-view that came from the belief that all people are born sinners in need of redemption, by saying, "We feel we must disagree with those prophets of gloom, who are always forecasting disaster, as though the end of the world were at hand. In the present order of things, Divine Providence is leading us to a new order of human relations which, by men's own efforts and even beyond their very expectations, are directed toward the fulfillment of God's superior and inscrutable designs. And everything, even human differences, leads to the greater good of the Church."[18]

Those with ears to hear must have been aghast. The pope was negating the pronouncements of Trent in order to promote the humanistic and heretical teaching that people "by their own efforts" could fulfill the providential design for a new world order. This utopianism extended far beyond the pale of Pelagianism. It smacked of the writings of Albert Pike and the Masonic vision of a new world order. What the bishops were witnessing was not only the papal abnegation of *peccatum originale*, but also a radical change in the church's perspective of reality.

THE *PERITI* APPEAR

At the start of the council, members of the Curia and clerical traditionalists should have realized they had walked into a snare. They were informed that the *schemae* would be examined by a panel of *periti*, or "theological experts." The experts would ensure the conciliar documents would be fitting for presentation to the monumental gathering.

The *periti* included Fr. Karl Rahner, Fr. Hans Küng, Fr. Gregory Baum, Cardinal Henri de Lubac, Cardinal Yves Congar, John Courtney Murray, Fr. Edward Schillebeeckx, and Fr. Joseph Ratzinger (who would later ascend to the papal throne as Benedict XVI). All were affiliated with *Nouvelle Théologie*, a school of thought that rejected the teachings of St. Thomas Aquinas and his application of Aristotelian principles to Catholic thought as "out of touch with reality." All had been held under suspicion of heresy by Pius XII. A few, including Rahner, had been officially censured and proscribed from publishing works of theology.[19]

In place of the Scholasticism of St. Thomas, the *Nouvelle Théologie* proposed an existential methodology (subjectivism) in which the revealed truths no longer would be viewed as eternal but rather as teachings in constant flux to changing time and circumstance.[20] Fr. Karl Rahner expressed the need of abandoning the teachings of Aquinas as follows: "I want to emphasize again that I decidedly agree with (Hans) Küng when he makes a clear distinction between Roman theology (taught in the schools of Rome) and the Catholic Faith. To free itself from the constraining fetters of Roman Scholastic Theology represents a duty upon which, in my humble opinion, the possibility of the survival of Catholicism seems to depend."[21] Clinging to traditional doctrine, Cardinal de Lubac maintained, is "hugging a rotten corpse" and "going rotten with it."[22]

RESSOURCEMENT

These so-called "new theologians" sought to recover the original meaning of Christianity (*Ressourcement*) by stripping away the theological accretions of the early church by a rigorous application of historical-critical methodology to New Testament exegesis.[23] Setting aside the Gospel of John as unhistorical, they focused on the synoptic gospels—Matthew, Mark, and Luke—that shared the similar view of the historical Jesus. By separating the numerous contradictions between these three gospels, they believed they could uncover the *real* Jesus and his original Aramaic teachings.

The historical Jesus, they believed, was not the Son of God born of the Virgin Mary in a stable in Bethlehem to the song of a heavenly choir. A disciple of John the Baptist, he proclaimed an apocalyptic message of the coming of God's kingdom and end of human history. Jesus attracted a small band of followers, created a ruckus in Jerusalem by driving the moneylenders from the temple, and died on a cross as a common criminal. The accounts of the physical resurrection of Jesus were a product of the myth-making process. The meaning of this myth was that humans can achieve full acceptance by God and a sense of transcendence over temporal reality.[24] The proclamation that Jesus has risen from the dead, Rahner insisted, did not mean the occurrence was a "historical event" but rather a "spiritual reality."[25] Similarly, Hans Küng wrote,

> To maintain the identity God does not need the relics of Jesus' earthly existence. We are not tied to physiological ideas of the resurrection. There can be identity of the person even without continuity between the earthly and the "heavenly," "spiritual" body. Resurrection is not tied to the substratum—a priori constantly changing—or the elements of this particular

body. The corporality of the resurrection does not require the tomb to be empty. God raises the person in a new, different, unimaginable "spiritual corporality."[26]

ANONYMOUS CHRISTIANITY

Rahner, a Jesuit priest from Freiburg, Germany, would emerge from Vatican II as the leading *periti*. He championed "Anonymous Christianity," a faith that would embrace Buddhists, Hindus, Muslims, and all other religions, even atheists, as long as they were "conscientious and caring."[27] In an interview, Rahner explained:

Anonymous Christianity means that a person lives in the grace of God and attains salvation outside of explicitly constituted Christianity. . . . Let us say, a Buddhist monk . . . who, because he follows his conscience, attains salvation and lives in the grace of God; of him I must say that he is an anonymous Christian; if not, I would have to presuppose that there is a genuine path to salvation that really attains that goal, but that simply has nothing to do with Jesus Christ. But I cannot do that. And so, if I hold if everyone depends upon Jesus Christ for salvation, and if at the same time I hold that many live in the world who have not expressly recognized Jesus Christ, then there remains in my opinion nothing else but to take up this postulate of an anonymous Christianity.[28]

THE VIRGIN (?) MARY

Recognizing that Mariology was a stumbling stock to the expansion of "anonymous Christianity," Rahner interpreted the Catholic dogma of the Immaculate Conception of Mary as follows:

The dogma (of the immaculate conception) does not mean in any way that the birth of a being is accompanied by something contaminating, by a stain, and that in order to avoid it Mary must have had a privilege. The immaculate conception of the Blessed Virgin therefore consists simply in the possession, from the beginning of her existence, of the life of divine grace, which was given to her.—From the beginning of her existence Mary was enveloped in the redeeming and sanctifying love of God. Such is, in all its simplicity, the content of the doctrine that Pius IX solemnly defined as a truth of the Catholic faith, in the year 1854.[29]

Rahner may have been considered a *peritus* by John XXIII, but he wasn't very well versed in the dogma of the Immaculate Conception. In his apostolic constitution *Ineffabilis Deus* he stated repeatedly that Mary was preserved from all stain of original sin. He wrote:

> We declare, pronounce and define that the doctrine is revealed by God and therefore to be believed firmly and constantly by all the faithful, which holds that the Blessed Virgin Mary in the first instant of Her conception was, by a unique grace and privilege of Almighty God, in view of the merits of Jesus Christ the Savior of the human race, preserved from all stain of original sin.[30]

Regarding Mary's "perpetual virginity" (*virginitas in et post partum*), Rahner wrote that the teaching should not be interpreted to mean that she abstained from sexual congress but rather that she remained "wholly oriented to the will of God."[31] This interpretation negated the basis of the dogma of the Assumption set forth in 1950 by Pope Pius XII as the "glorification of the virginal body of the loving Mother of God—a truth that has been revealed by God and consequently something that must be firmly and faithfully believed by all children of the Church."[32]

TRANSIGNIFICATION

Another major impediment to Christian union, according to Rahner, was the dogma of transubstantiation, with its Aristotelian distinctions between accident and substance. No Protestant, Rahner realized, could stomach the teaching that the bread and wine was transformed into the body and blood of Jesus Christ by the priest's incantation. Yet the dogma was so deeply ingrained into the life of the church that it could not be discarded as an unfortunate accretion from the medieval epoch. Catholics continued to beat their breast and bow their heads before the elevation of the Host by priests with their canonical digits. They were mortified at the mere thought of touching it or chewing it. They confessed their sins, made penance, and refrained from food and drink after the stroke of midnight in order to become worthy recipients.

Transubstantiation represented the essence of Roman Catholicism, with all of its supernatural trappings and scholastic distinctions. To do away with this dogma, Rahner knew, would cause an outcry from every Catholic in every parish throughout the world. Although the dogma could not be obliterated, it could be imparted with a new signification that would be acceptable to the "separated brethren." To accomplish this objective, Rahner came up with the notion of *transignification*, which he explained as follows: "As regards transubstantiation, it may then be said that substance, essence, meaning and purpose of the bread are identical. But the meaning of a thing can be changed without detriment to its matter. . . . The meaning of the bread has been changed through the consecration. Something which formerly served profane use now becomes the dwelling-place and the symbol of Christ who is present and gives himself to his own."[33] This doctrine permitted Rahner and his fellow *periti* to insist that the words of consecration exacted a transformation by making the elements "symbols of Christ who . . . invites men to spiritual union."[34]

The appointment of Rahner, a scholar whose theological contentions had been condemned by the previous pope,[35] as a key *peritus* by John XXIII displayed the suicidal nature of Vatican II. The purpose of the council from the time of its inception was not to support the articles of the medieval faith but rather to subvert them before the inauguration of an innocuous new religion that would be acceptable to all Christians. The damage wreaked by Rahner on Holy Mother Church eventually came to supersede the devastation caused when a sixteenth-century Augustinian monk nailed ninety-five theses to the door of a cathedral in Wittenberg.

THE EPISCOPAL REBELLION

The agenda for October 13, the first work day of the council, included the election of members for the ten conciliar commissions. The task of these commissions (operating like US congressional committees) was to redraft the *schemata* in accordance with the demands of the *periti*. Each commission was to have sixteen elected and eight appointed members.[36]

In preparation for the vote, the Curia had developed lists of handpicked candidates for each commission, which they submitted to the gathering bishops for ratification. Control of the council, the Curia, which favored modernization, realized, depended on control of the commissions. If progressive bishops and priests associated with the modernist movement were appointed, then the most radical interpretation of Catholic doctrine would prevail and the teachings of tradition would be relegated to the trash heap of human history.

As soon as the lists of the handpicked candidates were distributed, Cardinal Achille Liénart took to the podium and addressed the assembly. He said that the bishops should not be expected to vote for the chosen candidates, since they were "total strangers" to most of the council members. Liénart moved that the bishops should draft their own lists in defiance of the Curia. His motion met with resounding approval.[37] A rebellion had been staged.

THE REBELLION LEADERS

Liénart and other leaders of the rebellion, including Cardinal Augustin Bea, Fr. Annibale Bugnini, and Cardinal Leo Joseph Suenens, were prominent Freemasons. Liénart had been initiated into the society in 1912 and attended lodges in Cambrai, Valenciennes, Paris, and Lille, where he ascended to the thirtieth order to become a grand master. After receiving his red hat as a member of the College of Cardinals, Liénart became instrumental in attracting other members of the Catholic hierarchy to the clandestine brotherhood.[38] Many of these recruits became active in Operation Gladio.[39]

By allowing the bishops to nominate their own candidates, Liénart and his cabal succeeded in gaining control of the council. The curialists in attendance (including Cardinals Ottaviani, Staffa, Vagnozzi, Browne, Spellman, and McIntyre) hailed, for the most part, from Italy, Spain, Ireland, and the United States. They were decisively in the minority. Many of the progressives (including Cardinals Doepfner, Alfrink, König, Suenens, and Frings) came from Germany and the Netherlands, where they had been steeped in the theology of *ressourcement*. The progressives were supported by bishops from Latin America and Third World countries, including Africa, who had quaffed the intoxicating brew of Marxism and Christianity known as "liberation theology."[40]

SCRAPPING THE SCHEMAE

As soon as the "modernists" gained control of the council, they opted to scrap all but one of the seventy-five schemae as "scholastic" and "outdated."[41] Monsignor Lefebvre noted, "Now you know what happened at the Council. A fortnight after its opening not one of the prepared *schemata* remained, not one! All had been turned down; all had been condemned to the wastepaper basket. Nothing remained, not a single sentence. All had been thrown out."[42]

The only acceptable schema had been penned by Fr. Annibale Bugnini, who remained intent upon transforming Catholicism in accordance with the precepts of Freemasonry.[43] This proposal, which Fr. Schillebeeckx hailed as an "admirable piece of work," called for a complete transformation of the Latin liturgy.[44]

In accordance with Rahner's notion of transignification, the Bugnini schema called for a mitigation of the conception of the Mass as a sacrifice in which a victim (Jesus Christ) was offered to God as atonement for sins of the world. For this reason, the term transubstantiation was completely eliminated from the schema. This was in violation of *Auctorem fidei*, a bull issued by Pope Pius VI in 1794, which ruled that any omission of the term transubstantiation from a discussion of the Eucharist must be condemned as "pernicious," "derogatory to the expounding of Catholic truth," and "favorable to heretics."[45]

THE PROTESTANTIZING PROCESS

Downplaying the doctrine of the real presence of Christ in the Eucharist, the schema maintained that Jesus was present *everywhere* throughout the liturgy, including the person of the priest, the readings of the words of scripture, and the prayers and songs of the congregation.[46] Since Christ was omnipresent, the unique holiness of the Eucharist was downplayed. It could be received standing instead of kneeling. It did not have to be placed on the tongues of communicants by a priest. It could be touched by ordinary lay people who lacked canonical digits. What's more, the wafer could be *chewed* like a mere morsel of bread or a potato chip. Such a distillation of doctrine could not arouse the ire of any Protestant, not even the most rabid Calvinist. This was Bugnini's intent. "We must strip from our Catholic prayers and from the Catholic liturgy everything which can be the shadow of a stumbling block for our separated brethren that is for the Protestants," he told a reporter from *L'Osservatore Romano*.[47]

Not only were the stumbling blocks removed, but Catholic congregants were obliged to act like Protestants by taking an active part in the worship service. They were to reply like acolytes to the ritual blessings and prayers of the priest; to serve as lay readers; and, even worse, to sing the new vernacular hymns. In preparation of participation by the laity, the marble altars, where prelates mumbled the Latin Mass with their backs to the congregation, were replaced by common tables, with priests facing the people, to whom they were obliged to speak in a clear and audible manner.[48]

END OF CATHOLICISM

The Bugnini schema also called for an end of the church's liturgical universalism. Prior to the convening of the council, Catholics could boast that the Mass was celebrated everywhere with the same unchangeable words, the same gestures and genuflections, the same plainsong chants and Latin hymns. But, in accordance with the Bugnini proposal, certain elements of the liturgy were to be subjected to continuous change with "allowance for legitimate variations and adaptations to different groups, regions, and peoples, especially mission lands."[49] The elements in question were not identified, so that the scope of interpreting them became virtually limitless. What's more, the schema stated, "In some places and circumstances an even more radical adaptation of the liturgy is needed and entails greater difficulties." Bishops in different provinces were granted the power "to direct, as the case requires the necessary preliminary experiments over a determined period of time among groups suited for the purpose."[50] And so the vast edifice of Catholicism was to be dismantled into thousands of parochial pieces for the sake of liturgical experimentation.

The liturgy was now to be an ever-evolving process—constant change from time to time and place to place. The new rites were to be "simplified." Elements of the Mass that had become "less harmonious" or "less functional" were to be discarded. When necessity arose, innovative elements were to be introduced.[51] Few of those in attendance at the opening session of the council would realize that ratification of the schema would result not only in marijuana Masses, Masses with crackers and whiskey as the elements of consecration, and teenage Masses with Coca-Cola and hot dog buns.[52]

THE ELIMINATION OF LATIN

This dismantling process was to be precipitated by the replacement of Latin, the universal language of the church, with the vernacular languages of the people. Article 36 of the schema declared, ". . . since the use of the mother tongue, whether in the Mass, the administration of the sacraments, or other parts of the liturgy, may frequently be of great advantage to the people, the limits of its employment may be extended."[53] In keeping with this stipulation, the church lost not only its universal language but also its distinctive character. In 1840, warning of the loss of the sacred language, Fr. Prosper Guéranger, the "father of the modern liturgical movement," wrote,

Hatred for the Latin language is inborn in the heart of all the enemies of Rome. They recognize it as the bond of Catholics throughout the universe, as the arsenal of orthodoxy against all the subtleties of the sectarian spirit. . . . We must admit it is a master blow to Protestantism to have declared war on the sacred language. If it should ever succeed in destroying it, it would be well on the way to victory.[54]

Introducing the *Novus Ordo Missae* (the implementation of the Bugnini schema) in 1969, Pope Paul VI said,

The introduction of the vernacular will certainly be a great sacrifice for those who know the beauty, the power and the expressive sacrality of Latin. We are parting with the speech of the Christian centuries; we are becoming like profane intruders in the literary preserve of sacred utterance. We will lose a great part of that stupendous and incomparable artistic and spiritual thing, the Gregorian chant. We have reason indeed for regret, reason almost for bewilderment. What can we put in the place of that language of the angels?[55]

The correct answer, as it turned out, was "nothing."

FALSE ASSURANCE

Despite the fact that it called for the reinterpretation of the dogma of transubstantiation, the transformation of the Mass into a Protestant rite, a mitigation of the sacrificial nature of the liturgy, the replacement of Latin with the secular language of the various Catholic nations, and the elimination of most sacramental blessings and signs of devotion (bowings, kneelings, and genuflections) that characterized the Roman rite, the Bugnini schema held that it honored sacred tradition and called for no substantial changes to existing dogma or doctrine. Article 4 of the proposal upheld the following: "In faithful obedience to tradition, this most sacred Council declares that holy Mother Church holds all lawfully acknowledged rites to be of equal authority and dignity; that she wishes to preserve them in the future and to foster them in every way."[56] Other assurances were added to placate the prelates into believing that any changes in the life and worship of the church would be superficial since "sound tradition" must be preserved. Article 23 of the schema stated, "There must be no innovations unless the good of the Church genuinely and certainly requires them, and care must be taken that any new forms should in some way grow organically from forms already existing."[57]

And so, the gathering was assured that they had nothing to worry about. The process of *aggiornamento* would leave all *sacra doctrina* intact. The changes would be made only to make the church more open and accessible. No cherished claim of tradition was really at risk. The entire process would amount to little more than ecclesiastical window dressing. Who could object? The end result would be more converts and an expansion of the one true religion throughout all of creation.

On December 2, 1962, the Bugnini schema was ratified by the council to become Vatican II's Constitution on the Sacred Liturgy. 1,922 bishops cast their *placet* ("Yes") votes in favor of the revolutionary plan.[58] Few realized they had engaged in an act of ecclesiasticide.

NOVUS ORDO MISSAE

The Constitution on the Sacred Liturgy stood as a blueprint for liturgical transformation. From this blueprint, Bugnini and the *periti* created the New Order of the Mass (*Novus Ordo Missae*), which was to be celebrated by Catholics throughout the world. The changes to the Roman rite, which were introduced from 1965 to 1969, cut to the very quick of Catholicism. The traditional Mass began with the priest reciting personal prayers of reparation to God called "The Prayers at the Foot of the Altar" ("*Judica Me*" and its antiphon). The New Mass commenced with a "Penitential Rite," which the priest and the laity recited together. This change promoted the idea that priests were no longer ontologically different than laymen.[59]

The offertory prayer ("*Suscipe, sancte Pater*"), which stressed the notion of the sacrificial offering to God of a "spotless Victim," was expunged from the new liturgy and replaced by a ceremony called "The Preparation of the Gifts." This ceremony included the prayer "Blessed are you, Lord God of all creation," based on a Jewish grace before meals.[60]

The traditional Mass contained only one "Eucharistic Prayer," the ancient Roman Canon ("*Te igitur*," with the commemoration of the saints). The New Mass possessed a number of "Eucharistic Prayers," including an "edited" version of the Roman Canon from which the lists of saints were expunged.[61] Further "editing" included the elimination of references to Christ as an oblation.

In the midst of the new celebration, the faithful, who had been instructed to retain a prayerful demeanor during the ritual, were now told to jump up and to greet their "brothers and sisters" (i.e., those in the same and nearby pews), with a "sign of Christ's peace."[62] This sign varied from handshakes to bear hugs. The disruption to the decorum was unsettling for many older congregants, who opted to ignore the intrusion by their newly created kinfolk by bowing their heads, closing their eyes, and fingering their rosary beads in spite.

To manifest the new spirit of ecumenism, the authors of the new Mass even changed the words of Christ, which were used in the Consecration. The words, as replicated in the traditional Mass, were as follows: *Hic est enim Calix Sanguinis mei, novi et aeterni testamenti, mysterium fidei, qui pro vobis et pro multis effundetur in remissionem peccatorum* ("For this is the Chalice of my Blood of the new and eternal covenant; the mystery of faith, which shall be shed for you and *for many* unto the forgiveness of sins"). These words were altered in the new Mass as follows: "This is the Chalice of my blood, the new and eternal covenant, the mystery of faith, which will be shed for you and *for all men* so that sins may be forgiven."[63]

Downplaying the notion of transubstantiation, various signs of respect toward the actual presence of Christ in the Host (genuflections, signs of the cross, bells, incense, etc.) were reduced or eliminated. Similarly, the communicants, like good Protestants, could now receive the Eucharist in their unholy hands. This was the final kiss off to St. Thomas Aquinas, who wrote, "The body of Christ must not be touched by anyone, other than a consecrated priest. No other person has the right to touch it, except in case of extreme necessity."[64]

Also cut from the Mass were the reading of the last gospel (*In principio erat Verbum . . .*) and the recitation of the prescribed prayers after Mass to the "glorious and Immaculate Virgin Mary," the Catholic saints (including the blessed Apostles Peter and Paul), and Holy Michael the Archangel, who could safeguard the faithful "against the wickedness and snares of the devil."[65] Gone were the trailing *Te Deums* and the Benediction of the Blessed Sacrament. Gone, too, were the litanies to the saints and the promises of indulgences.

The decline in attendance at weekly Mass, and all other phases of Catholic life and worship, can be traced to the institution of the liturgical changes at the close of Vatican II.

SESSION ONE CLOSES

After the ratification of the new Constitution on the Sacred Liturgy, Cardinal Suenens ascended to the podium to move that the focus of the council should be limited to the reform of the church—not the threat of godless ideologies such as Communism or the rise of new heresies, including religious indifferentism.[66] His motion was carried, and the tumultuous first session of Vatican II came to an inglorious close on December 8, 1962. The traditionalists hadn't been exposed to a revolution but rather a *blitzkrieg* from German and Dutch cardinals and theologians for which they had been totally unprepared. They watched their cherished claims of their faith being tossed to the winds of change by their fellow clerics with stunned disbelief. What had occurred was, for them, almost incomprehensible.

INCORRUPTIBILITY

Before the council was set to resume, John XXIII died of stomach cancer on June 3, 1963. No doubt several traditionalists uttered a sigh of relief. Sure, the Constitution on the Sacred Liturgy, the noxious Bugnini schema, had been ratified. But much of orthodox Catholicism could be salvaged. The constitutions of the church had yet to be drafted. With a new conservative pope on the throne, the ecumenical movement could be reversed. The injunctions against Catholics participating in non-Catholic worship services could be reaffirmed. The exclusivity of the Catholic claim to the keys to the kingdom of heaven could be restated. Old boogeymen—communism, socialism, modernism—could be rounded up and condemned. And the *periti* could be sent packing to the hinterlands of Northern Europe.

One proof of holiness in Roman Catholicism is the incorruptibility of a saint's body. For this reason, the bodies of dying popes had been infused with injections of oils and herbs. Their cadavers had been wrapped like mummies. But such efforts proved to be of no avail. Only days after his death, Pius XII's nose fell off.[67] On March 27, 2001, Catholic clerics were amazed when John XXIII's body was exhumed in preparation of his canonization. "None of the body had decomposed," Cardinal Virgilio Noe announced to the press. "It was as if he died yesterday." Noe went on to say the condition of the pope's remains could be "the result of a miracle."[68] What greater proof could anyone produce that the "good pope" had worked in cooperation with the Holy Spirit to effect changes in the church?

Cardinal Noe failed to say that the body of John XXIII had been embalmed by Gennaro Goglia in violation of canon law and the dictates of sacred tradition. For five hours, the mortician had infused the corpse with ethyl alcohol, formalin, sodium sulfate, and potassium nitrate. "Yes, it was just a body," Goglia said. "It didn't have to go to a beauty contest but it was the body of the pope."[69]

DRASTIC MEASURES

Shortly before the death of John XXIII, several members of the Curial party, including Cardinal Francis Spellman of New York and Cardinal James McIntyre of Los Angeles, were determined to change the course of the revolutionary council.[70] They realized that something was taking place within Roman Catholicism that ran significantly deeper than the proposed changes in the Mass. The church was changing politically as well. John XXIII had taken steps toward a rapprochement with the Soviet Union. He withdrew all ecclesiastical support from the Christian Democratic Party, thereby precipitating a sharp rise in the Italian Communist Party. And the pope had dissociated himself from strong-arm Catholic dictators in South America, including Nicaragua's Anastasio Somoza Debayle.[71] Drastic measures had to be taken to prevent the rabid ecumenists not only from totally dismantling nearly two thousand years of Catholic tradition but also from switching the allegiance of the Holy See in the midst of the Cold War.

Spellman met with CIA officials who shared his concern that the gathering of the bishops was abetting Communism. Liberal priests and bishops in Latin America, the officials confirmed, were speaking out against repressive strong-arm governments that had been set up by the US State Department.[72] The officials wanted to assure that the next pope would adhere to the goals and objectives of the US intelligence agency. Spellman was to serve as their mole at the next conclave, and the papal election was to be rigged.[73]

Chapter Five

THE THING WITH TWO HEADS

Urged by faith, we are obliged to believe and to maintain that the Church is one, holy, catholic, and also apostolic. We believe in her firmly and we confess with simplicity that outside of her there is neither salvation nor the remission of sins. There had been at the time of the deluge only one ark of Noah, prefiguring the one Church, which ark, having been finished to a single cubit, had only one pilot and guide, i.e., Noah, and we read that, outside of this ark, all that subsisted on the earth was destroyed.

We venerate this Church as one, the Lord having said by the mouth of the prophet: "Deliver, O God, my soul from the sword and my only one from the hand of the dog." [Ps 21:20] He has prayed for his soul, that is for himself, heart and body; and this body, that is to say, the Church, He has called one because of the unity of the Spouse, of the faith, of the sacraments, and of the charity of the Church. This is the tunic of the Lord, the seamless tunic, which was not rent but which was cast by lot [Jn 19:23- 24]. Therefore, of the one and only Church there is one body and one head, not two heads like a monster; that is, Christ and the Vicar of Christ, Peter and the successor of Peter, since the Lord speaking to Peter Himself said: "Feed my sheep" [Jn 21:17], meaning, my sheep in general, not these, nor those in particular, whence we understand that He entrusted all to him [Peter].
— Pope Boniface VIII, *Unam sanctam,*
November 18, 1302

Giovanni Battista Montini was the CIA's anointed candidate for the papacy. His father had been the director of Catholic Action, an anticommunist organization, and a member of the Italian Parliament.[1] During World War II, as the Vatican undersecretary of state, Montini had introduced officials from the Office of Strategic Services (OSS—the forerunner of the CIA) to Calogero "Don Calò" Vizzini, the *capo di tutti capi*— "boss of all bosses"—of the Vizzini/Agostino crime family, who played a significant role in the Allied invasion of Sicily.[2] After the war, he worked with the OSS in creating "ratlines" so that leading Nazi officials could escape to South America in order to escape prosecution as war criminals.[3]

As archbishop of Milan, Montini had arranged for the CIA's "black funds" to flow through the Merrill Lynch Brokerage House to a host of parochial banks in Italy and finally to the Vatican Bank for safe keeping.[4] In exchange for such service, the CIA regularly funneled millions to Montini for his charitable work.[5] The cash was delivered in satchels by Michele Sindona, the financial head of the Sicilian Mafia.[6]

MONTINI'S MASONS

Montini was elevated to the College of Cardinals by John XXIII on December 15, 1958. He worked behind the scenes at Vatican II to advance the pope's agenda, including the ratification of the Bugnini schema. In this way, he gained the favor of the *periti* and the reputation as a progressive.[7]

Continuing his work with the CIA, Montini remained active in Catholic Gladio and developed close ties to the members of the P-2 lodge, including Worshipful Master Licio Gelli. This affiliation gained him the support of the Catholic hierarchs who had become Freemasons, not only leading Vatican II figures Fr. Annibale Bugnini and Bishop Virgilio Noe, but also Cardinal Suenens, the leader of the progressive party at Vatican II and one of the council's four moderators; Cardinal Bea, the president of the Secretariat for Promoting Christian Unity (a pivotal position at the council); and Cardinal Liénart, a leading liberal at Vatican II and a member of the council's Board of the Presidency. The three Masonic cardinals, by gaining control of the council, wielded enormous influence over their fellow progressive hierarchs with red hats, including those from Germany, Belgium, France, the Netherlands, Latin America, and the Third World countries.[8]

When the conclave commenced on June 19, 1963, two candidates emerged from the progressive part: Montini and Cardinal Giacomo Lercaro of Bologna. Lercaro was an outspoken liberal and one of the architects of the Bugnini schema. The night before the conclave, Lercaro was summoned to the house of Count Umberto Ortolani, the "secret Chamberlain of the Papal Household" and a prominent member of P-2.[9] The meeting, attended by a host of other cardinals with ties to the famous Freemason, was held to arrange Montini ascendency to the papal throne. Lercaro's role as a *papabile* ("papal candidate") was to act as a spoiler.[10]

THE RIGGED PAPAL ELECTION

The Curial party's candidate was Cardinal Ildebrando Antoniutti, who supported Opus Dei, a right-wing clandestine religious movement.[11] Antoniutti was backed by Cardinal Giuseppe Siri of Genoa. Siri was a powerful force within the Curia and his support, coupled with the endorsement of the venerable old cardinal Alfredo Ottaviani (the Curial Head of the Holy See), transformed Antoniutti into a formidable *papabile*.

In compliance with the CIA's wishes, Spellman gained support for Montini from the other American cardinals—Ritter, Cushing, Wright, Meyer, and McIntyre—and from Cardinal Amleto Giovanni Cicognani, the influential Vatican secretary of state.[12] In first round of balloting, on June 20, Montini received thirty votes, Antoniutti twenty, Lercaro twenty, and the remaining ten votes scattered among minor candidates. At this point, Spellman managed to convince Ottaviani to join the Montini camp. On June 21, on the sixth ballot, Montini, at age sixty five, gained the two-thirds majority necessary for election.[13]

Proof of the rigging was later discovered by Roland Flamini. The *Time* correspondent uncovered tell-tale evidence that the CIA were able to confirm Montini's election before the puff of white smoke emanated from the Sistine Chapel and expressed their enormous pleasure that the conclave had proceeded in accordance with their plan.[14]

OPENING THE WINDOW

Assuming the name Paul VI, the new pope reconvened the ecumenical council on September 29, 1963. In his opening address, the new pope presented the four goals of the gathering: (1) to define the nature of the church and the role of the episcopacy; (2) to initiate a spiritual renewal of the church; (3) to restore unity among Christians (including seeking pardon for the church's contributions to the separation); and (4) to commence an ongoing dialogue with the contemporary world ". . . with the sincere intention not of conquering it but of serving it. . . ."[15] He concluded by saying that "the window of the council" should be "opened wide" to the winds of change.

In keeping with this address, Suenens and the *periti* commenced working on the schema on the church. Their central goal was not to support Paul VI as the duly appointed vicar of Christ but rather to put an end to the absolute rule of the bishop of Rome and to subvert, once and for all, the nineteenth-century dogma of papal infallibility. When they completed their proposal, their schema represented the longest and the most radical document of the council.

A MEDIEVAL FIEFDOM

Prior to the appearance of this schema, the Roman Catholic Church was structured as a medieval fiefdom. The pope served as the overlord to whom all the inhabitants of his fief pledge their absolute fealty. The cardinals served as his appointed henchmen. They were *hinged* to him and to his authority. The word "cardinal" comes from the Latin *cardo* meaning "hinge" or "support." By the end of the fourth century, cardinals were clerics who were *incardinated* to support the pope and to execute his commands.[16] The bishops were equivalent to nobles and knights in the feudal political system. Their duty was to enforce the dictates of the pope and to collect the feudal dues from his subjects. Priests were vassals to the bishops. The common laity represented the serfs, whose labor sustained the manor and its kingdom.

Cardinals, bishops, and prelates did not possess any authority in this system. Their authority came from the pope's position as the vicarious representative of Christ on earth. For this reason, they were *appointed* to their ecclesiastical positions; only the pope was elected. The pope alone could summon a general council, and its legislation had no force except when confirmed by his decree.[17] He was free to interpret, revise, or extend the canon law of the church (which had received its final formation by Gratian in 1148).[18] The pope was the final court of appeals for doctrinal disputes. He alone could absolve certain sins, issue indulgences, and canonize saints.

The advent of the Industrial Revolution and the nineteenth-century movements toward social equality only caused the church to fortify its medieval structure, with the bishop of Rome claiming more and more authority to preside over spiritual, moral, and political manners. Socialism and communism were condemned as godless ideologies. The American principles of individual liberty and the separation of church and state were decried as grievous errors.[19] The efforts toward solidification of Catholic feudal polity culminated in 1870 with the formation of the dogma of papal infallibility.

THE CONCEPT OF CONCILIARISM

The notion that the pope should be subjected to the will of an ecumenical council arose at the Council of Constance in 1414 to resolve the matter of three popes all claiming right to the Chair of St. Peter. The council, before selecting Martin V as the legitimate pontiff, issued this decree: "The Holy Synod of Constance ordains, declares, and decrees that this synod represents the Church Militant, and has authority directly from Christ; and everybody, of whatever rank and dignity, including also the pope, is bound to obey the Council in those things that pertain to the faith."[20] This victory by the so-called "Conciliarists" was short-lived since it was declared null and void on April 22, 1418, by Martin V, the very pope whom the gathering of bishops had elected.

In 1439, the Council of Florence, in an effort to make sure Conciliarism never rose again, restated the traditional Catholic system of church government as follows: "We define that the Holy Apostolic See of the Bishop of Rome possesses a primacy throughout the whole world; that the Roman pontiff is the successor of Blessed Peter, Prince of the Apostles; that he is the true Vicar of Christ, the Head of the Universal Church and of all Christians; that to him was given in Blessed Peter by our Lord Jesus Christ the fullness of power to feed, to rule, and to govern the Universal Church."[21]

A THEOLOGICAL WEED

But the theological weeds of heresy rarely die. Uprooted from one century, they inevitably sprout up in the next. Conciliarism was no exception. It rose again in the eighteenth century under the names of Gallicanism and Febronianism. These movements held that the bishop of Rome, although entitled to a certain primacy, should be subordinate to a universal church council. Gallicanism and Febronianism spread throughout Germany, France, and Italy, gaining footholds in such leading universities as Bonn, and prompting Pope Pius IX to convene the First Vatican Council in 1869. Like the Council at Florence, Vatican I also pronounced a sentence of excommunication on anyone who questioned the Roman pontiff's "full and supreme power of jurisdiction over the whole Church, not only in matters of faith and morals, but also in matters concerning the discipline and rule of the Church throughout the world."[22]

CONDEMNATION OF PAN-CHRISTIANITY

In the twentieth century, the heresy cropped up at Chevetogne Abbey in Belgium, a Benedictine monastery that had been established by Fr. Lambert Beauduin to promote Christian unity. In 1925, Beauduin and his monks held a series of talks with Anglican and Eastern Orthodox bishops and came to the conclusion that the major stumbling block to the reunion of Christendom was the dogma of papal primacy that granted the bishop of Rome complete jurisdictional authority over the church.[23] Pius XI intervened, ordered an end to the talks, and issued *Mortalium animos* (1928), an encyclical to draw the distinction between true and false ecumenism.[24] The encyclical stated:

> These pan-Christians who turn their minds to uniting the churches seem, indeed, to pursue the noblest of ideas in promoting charity among all Christians: nevertheless how does it happen that this charity tends to injure faith? Everyone knows that John himself, the Apostle of love, who seems to reveal in his Gospel the secrets of the Sacred Heart of Jesus, and who never ceased to impress on the memories of his followers the new commandment "Love one another," altogether forbade any intercourse with those who professed a mutilated and corrupt version of Christ's teaching: "If any man come to you and bring not this doctrine, receive him not into the house nor say to him: God speed you."[18] For which reason, since charity is based on a complete and sincere faith, the disciples of Christ must be united principally by the bond of one faith. Who then can conceive a Christian Federation, the members of which retain each his own opinions and private judgment, even in matters which concern the object of faith, even though they be repugnant to the opinions of the rest? And in what manner, We ask, can men who follow contrary opinions, belong to one and the same Federation of the faithful?
>
> How so great a variety of opinions can make the way clear to effect the unity of the Church We know not; that unity can only arise from one teaching authority, one law of belief and one faith of Christians. But We do know that from this it is an easy step to the neglect of religion or indifferentism and to modernism, as they call it. Those, who are unhappily infected with these errors, hold that dogmatic truth is not absolute but relative, that is, it agrees with the varying necessities of time and place and with the varying tendencies of the mind, since it is not contained in immutable revelation, but is capable of being accommodated to human life.[25]

CONGAR'S "COLLEGIALITY"

Fr. Yves Congar, a disciple of Beauduin, was a *peritus* for Vatican II. Drawing from his mentor's writings, he called for the creation of a permanent governing "college" of bishops to rule the church. Congar called his ecclesiological plan "collegiality" so that traditionalists would not dismiss it as the same heresy that had been condemned by the Council of Florence. Using the principles of *ressourcement*, Congar and his fellow *periti*, including Rahner and Ratzinger, argued that collegiality was the original structure of primitive Christianity as evidenced by Acts 15:19–20, which showed that the Christian mission was supervised by a church council in Jerusalem. This council, they pointed out, was led not by Peter but by James "the Just," the "brother of Jesus."[26]

THE NEW SYSTEM

Developing this notion, the *periti* postulated that the bishops, as the successors of the twelve apostles, received their authority directly from Christ by divine right (*iure divino*), not from delegation from the presiding bishop of Rome. The bishops, they maintained, shared supreme and plenary power over the church along with the pope. In accordance with this argumentation, they formulated a new system of ecclesiastical government analogous to American democracy. The congress of bishops represented the legislators, who required the pope (in place of the sitting president) to sign their juridical decisions into law. Thus the church was no longer to remain a monarchical institution with power flowing down from the pope to the bishops. The power now would flow from the bottom up—from the bishops to the pope.[27] Holy Mother Church was to be left standing on her head.

Within the old feudal system, the pope possessed complete authority over all Catholic clerics, both collectively and individually. He could demand the bishops to enforce his dictates within their dioceses. He could dispatch legates to supervise their activities. He could remove bishops from office and send them into ecclesiastical exile. But, with the new collegial system, the pope was bound to comply with the decisions of a permanent college of bishops. The Holy Father's authority was no longer to be singular and unique. It was to be shared, and the only infallible pronouncements were to be made in accordance with the majority vote of the episcopate.[28]

PROGRESSIVE SUPPORT

The notion of collegiality gained enormous support from the progressive members of the council, including Cardinals Suenens, Meyer, Leger, Alfrink, and De Smedt.[29] Cardinal Franz König of Vienna, who had chosen Rahner as his expert advisor, said,

> To cope with a rapidly changing world, the Catholic Church has to preserve its unity. But it also has to develop Catholic diversity. What style of leadership will enable it to do this? From the point of view of ecumenical endeavor, the very existence and exercise of Roman primacy are the real difficulty, but within the Catholic Church itself the question has long been: how can or should the present structure of command, which in the past century has become so centralized, be amended or improved.
>
> A gradual decentralization is needed, so as to strengthen the concern and responsibility of the college of bishops for the whole Church, under and with the Petrine office. . . . At the same time, the competence of individual bishops both locally and regionally needs to be strengthened too, for they are the shepherds of their local Churches, the vicars of Christ in their own dioceses. . . .
>
> Within the Catholic Church itself, no one has difficulties about the existence of the Petrine office, served by the necessary bureaucracy adjusted in line with the times. What is often felt to be defective is the present style of leadership practiced by the authorities in the Roman Curia in dealing with the diverse and multiple dioceses throughout the world.[30]

On October 30, 1963, the members of the council were asked to affirm or reject a ballot concerning collegiality. The ballot read:

Does it please the fathers that the Council should affirm:

1. That episcopal consecration is the highest degree of the sacrament of Holy Orders.
2. That each bishop who is legitimately consecrated in communion with the bishops and the pope, their head and principle of unity, becomes a member of the Episcopal College.
3. That this Body or College of Bishops succeeds the College of the Apostles in the mission of evangelizing, sanctifying and governing, and that this College of Bishops, united with its head, the Roman Pontiff and never without this head—it being understood that the primatial right of head remains whole and entire—possesses a supreme and plenary authority in the universal Church.

4. That this power belongs, by divine right, to the Episcopal College united with its head.
5. That the revival of the diaconate as a distinct and permanent grade of the sacred ministry is opportune.[31]

The result of the vote, which would determine the development on a schema on the volatile subject, was 1,610 votes in the affirmative, 477 in the negative, and 13 votes that were ruled invalid.[32]

The vote was momentous, causing Hans Küng to call it "the peaceful 'October Revolution' of the Catholic Church," in reference to the Bolshevik revolution of 1917.[33] Cardinal Suenens declared, "October 30 is a decisive date in the history of the Church. The battle of the Twelve (referring to the twelve disciples over the alleged Vicar of Christ) has been won."[34]

PAUL IN TEARS

Paul VI was completely unprepared for the fully developed schema on the church that was presented to him on August 14, 1964. After reading it, he broke into tears.[35] The plan called for a new-order church government in which the bishops, taken as a whole, would constitute the supreme authority, and the pope would be reduced to a symbolic figurehead. The pope called upon Archbishop Dino Staffa to meet with the Theological Commission of the Council to exact changes in the document.[36] The propositions in the new plan for church government, Staffa told the commission, were "opposed to the more common teaching of the saintly Fathers, of the Roman Pontiffs, of provincial synods, of the holy Doctors of the Universal Church, of theologians and of canonists, and to century-old norms of ecclesiastical discipline."[37]

But the commission members refused to define the term "collegiality" and to withdraw their demand for bishops to create the Episcopal College, a new entity, which was to be granted, along with the pope, "full power over the universal Church." In times past, a supreme pontiff would have disbanded the commission, branded the schema an anathema, and pronounced a sentence of excommunication upon all those who prepared it. But Paul was a milquetoast and a far cry from such militant popes as Pius XI and Pius XII. He acquiesced to the demands of the Theological Commission.

On November 10, 1964, Paul VI expressed his concerns that the schema, which was to be submitted for ratification, sought to unite the office of the papacy and the college of the bishops into one ecclesiastical entity. The offices, he told the council fathers, must be kept separate, with the collective episcopate subject to his sovereign rule. By ecclesiastical law, the pope pointed out, the jurisdictional power of the bishops, unlike their sacerdotal power, was conferred by him and revocable by him.[38] The pope was unaware that matters were no longer under his control.

THE NEW CONSTITUTION

The final version of the schema was ratified on November 20, 1964, by a vote of 2,134 to 10 in favor of the new plan for the church. Regarding collegiality, the official document read:

> For the discharging of such great duties, the apostles were enriched by Christ with a special outpouring of the Holy Spirit coming upon them, and they passed on this spiritual gift to their helpers by the imposition of hands, and it has been transmitted down to us in Episcopal consecration. And the Sacred Council teaches that by Episcopal consecration the fullness of the sacrament of Orders is conferred, that fullness of power, namely, which both in the Church's liturgical practice and in the language of the Fathers of the Church is called the high priesthood, the supreme power of the sacred ministry. But Episcopal consecration, together with the office of sanctifying, also confers the office of teaching and of governing, which, however, of its very nature, can be exercised only in hierarchical communion with the head and the members of the college. For from the tradition, which is expressed especially in liturgical rites and in the practice of both the Church of the East and of the West, it is clear that, by means of the imposition of hands and the words of consecration, the grace of the Holy Spirit is so conferred, and the sacred character so impressed that bishops in an eminent and visible way sustain the roles of Christ Himself as Teacher, Shepherd and High Priest, and that they act in His person.[39]

This remarkable paragraph (now article 21 of the Dogmatic Constitution on the Church, aka *Lumen gentium*) stated that the bishops receive their sacerdotal and juridical authority not from the pope, as the church formerly taught, but from Christ at the time of their ordination. Their power, therefore, was sacramental and could not be dissolved by any pontiff. This was a totally new doctrine in the annals of Catholicism. The bishops, along with the pope, were vicars of Christ. The paragraph further proclaimed that this teaching was based not on Catholic tradition but rather the established polity of Eastern Orthodoxy, a religion that had severed ties with the Roman Church in 1054.[40]

PAPAL DEMOTION

The new constitution on the church further stated:

> The order of bishops, which succeeds to the college of apostles and gives this apostolic body continued existence, is also the subject of supreme and full power over the universal Church, provided we understand this body together with its head the Roman Pontiff and never without this head. This power can be exercised only with the consent of the Roman Pontiff.[41]

In contradiction to traditional Catholic doctrine, this paragraph held that the bishops, along with the pope, possessed "supreme and full power" over the governance of the church. Moreover, it removed the pope from the papal throne and placed him as a bishop among fellow bishops, albeit it accorded him a place of prominence as head of the *collegium*. Granting the pope this position among his peers represents the new constitution's concession to the traditional claims of papal primacy. But this concession clearly implied that the college of bishops represented the one subject of supreme authority and that the pope merely served as its official spokesman.[42]

EXTRAORDINARY BECOMES ORDINARY

Finally, while never offering a definition of collegiality, the document went on to say:

> This college, insofar as it is composed of many, expresses the variety and universality of the People of God, but insofar as it is assembled under one head, it expresses the unity of the flock of Christ. In it, the bishops, faithfully recognizing the primacy and pre-eminence of their head, exercise their own authority for the good of their own faithful, and indeed of the whole Church, the Holy Spirit supporting its organic structure and harmony with moderation. The supreme power in the universal Church, which this college enjoys, is exercised in a solemn way in an ecumenical council. A council is never ecumenical unless it is confirmed or at least accepted as such by the successor of Peter; and it is prerogative of the Roman Pontiff to convoke these councils, to preside over them and to confirm them. This same collegiate power can be exercised together with the pope by the bishops living in all parts of the world, provided that the head of the college calls them to collegiate action, or at least approves of or freely accepts the united action of the scattered bishops, so that it is thereby made a collegiate act.[43]

This revolutionary statement, after noting an ecumenical council as a "solemn" exercise of collegial authority, sets the stage for the "non-solemn" or "ordinary" use of this power, by proclaiming, "This same collegiate power can be exercised together by the bishops living in all parts of the world." The meaning of this tortured phasing is that there is a mediate form of collegiate jurisdiction, beyond ecumenical councils, that can be exercised by bishops "living in all parts of the world." Thus regional or national gatherings of bishops have the same weight of authority as papal proclamations. The implications of this assertion are astonishing. It is not necessary, according to this statement, for the pope, as the Head of the College, to call such regional or national conferences into being. It is sufficient for him to simply *accept* their united actions by not stopping or opposing them.[44]

The following chart displays the shift in Catholic polity brought about by collegiality and the new Dogmatic Constitution of the Church:[45]

TRADITION	COLLEGIALITY
Pope derives authority from being the successor of St. Peter in the See of Rome.	Pope derives authority from his headship over the Apostolic college.
Pope has authority over every bishop individually *and collectively* (Vatican I, *Pastor aeternus*, 3).	Bishops collectively have "supreme and plenary authority in the Universal Church."
Bishops derive their jurisdiction from the pope, who can give it or take it away.	Because the bishops succeed the apostles, they collectively exercise a jurisdiction by divine law.
Bishops have an ordinary individual jurisdiction (in their diocese) and an extraordinary collective jurisdiction (in an ecumenical council).	Bishop have an ordinary individual jurisdiction, an extraordinary collective jurisdiction, *but also an ordinary collective jurisdiction*—the Episcopal College.

COLLEGIALITY'S DEVOLUTION

The breakdown of central authority precipitated by the new constitution spread below the episcopal level to local parishes, proliferating councils, commissions, and committees of every kind, on issues ranging from the role of women in the New Mass to the sanctity of same-sex marriages, all of which served to undermine the authority of parish priests. Lamenting the institutional chaos caused by collegiality, Fr. Basil Wrighton, of the Society of Saint Pius X, wrote:

> The sanctuary, the pulpit, and even the tabernacle have been invaded by the progressive laity, male and female. The net result of this collegial-democratic devolution is the destruction of Catholic unity, with a different religion in every parish. If the Pope is no longer to be monarch in the Church, neither will the bishop be monarch in his diocese. Everything will be put into commission, the talking will never cease, and the hungry sheep will not be fed. Can any sane Catholic pretend that this is the kind of charge that Christ laid on His apostles?[46]

TOO LITTLE, TOO LATE

After the ratification of the new Dogmatic Constitution on the Church, Paul VI decided to attach some notes to the document in an attempt to regain some measure of his supreme authority. He penned an explanatory note—*Nota praevia*—to the document, in which he maintained that, despite its issuance, no one should believe that the pope's supreme authority was confined to the college of bishops and that, apart from the college, the pope merely served as the figurehead of Roman Catholicism. In the *Nota*, he argued:

> As Supreme Pastor of the Church, the Supreme Pontiff can always exercise his power at will, as his very office demands. Though it is always in existence, the College is not as a result permanently engaged in strictly collegial activity; the Church's Tradition makes this clear. In other words, the College is not always "fully active [*in actu pleno*]"; rather, it acts as a college in the strict sense only from time to time and only with the consent of its head. The phrase "with the consent of its head" is used to avoid the idea of dependence on some kind of outsider; the term "consent" suggests rather communion between the head and the members, and implies the need for an act which belongs properly to the competence of the head.[47]

Never before in ecclesiastical history was a pope compelled to attach an explanatory note to a dogmatic constitution. It was an act of desperation—a final futile attempt to act as the sole "supreme and plenary" authority of the church. But it was too little, too late. He already had signed the constitution transforming it into an official decree. The Church of St. Peter, whether Paul VI liked it or not, had become a thing with two heads. Proof of this claim came with the council's treatment of the *Nota praevia*. The pope ordered that it be attached as an introductory note to *Lumen gentium*. The council fathers, also claiming "supreme and plenary" authority, relegated it to the appendix.[48]

THE MATTER OF INFALLIBILITY

Collegiality gave rise to profound uncertainty over the matter of papal infallibility. This uncertainty was addressed by the Sacred Congregation for the Doctrine of the Faith (SCDF), the oldest of the nine congregations of the Roman Curia. In 1973, the SCDF issued *Mysterium Ecclesiae*, a strange declaration, which held that the "chrism of infallibility" was not bestowed upon the pope alone as the successor of St. Peter, but rather is shared by all members of the church, including the common laity. The document declares, "The body of the faithful as a whole, anointed as they are by the Holy One, cannot err in matters of belief."[49] And so, the truth regarding divine matters resided not merely with the supreme pontiff and his college of bishops but also with the poor blokes in the pews.

Chapter Six

THE KISS OF JUDAS

*Moreover, some and even very many of the significant elements
and endowments which together go to build up and give life to
the Church itself, can exist outside the visible boundaries of the
Catholic Church: the written word of God; the life of grace; faith,
hope and charity, with the other interior gifts of the Holy Spirit,
and visible elements too. . . .*

*It follows that the separated Churches and Communities as
such, though we believe them to be deficient in some respects, have
been by no means deprived of significance and importance in the
mystery of salvation. For the Spirit of Christ has not refrained
from using them as means of salvation which derive their efficacy
from the very fullness of grace and truth entrusted to the Church.*
—Unitatis Redintegratio, Vatican II Decree
on Ecumenism, November 21, 1964

The dogmatic integrity of the Roman Catholic Church resided in its
claim of spiritual exclusivity—an adamant insistence that it alone
possessed the absolute, universal, and univocal truth. Any religious body
that deviated from the doctrines of the church was in error. The first expression of this teaching came from the following passage in St. Cyprian's "On
the Unity of the Catholic Faith" (240 CE):

The Spouse of Christ cannot become wanton. She is a virgin and chaste.
She knows one house, and guards the sanctity of one bridal chamber
with chaste reserve. She keeps us for God. She appoints to the Kingdom
the sons to whom she has given life. Whoever has been separated from
the Church is yoked with an adulteress, is separated from the promises
made to the Church. Nor shall he who leaves Christ's Church arrive at
Christ's rewards. He is a stranger; he is sacrilegious; he is an enemy. Who
has not the Church for mother cannot have God for his father. If anyone
outside the ark of Noah could escape, then may he also escape who shall
be outside the Church.[1]

SOLE SOURCE OF TRUTH

Extra Ecclesiam nulla salus ("Outside the church, there is no salvation") was affirmed by the great canonical doctors, including St. Ambrose, St. Jerome, St. Augustine, and St. Thomas Aquinas, and upheld by the fourth Lateran Council. The Council of Florence, in 1439, proclaimed:

> The most Holy Roman Church firmly believes, professes, and proclaims that those not living within the Catholic Church, not only pagans, but also Jews and heretics and schismatics, cannot become participants in eternal life, but will depart "into everlasting fire which was prepared for the devil and his angels" (Matt. 25:41), unless before the end of life the same have been added to the flock; and that the unity of the ecclesiastical body is so strong that only to those remaining in it are the sacraments of the Church of benefit for salvation, and do fastings, almsgiving, and other functions of piety and exercises of Christian service produce eternal reward, and that no one, whatever almsgiving he has practiced, even if he has shed blood for the name of Christ, can be saved, unless he has remained in the bosom and unity of the Catholic Church.[2]

In his encyclical *Singulari quidem*, issued on March 17, 1856, Pius IX maintained, "There is only one true, holy, Catholic Church, which is the Apostolic Roman Church. There is only one See founded in Peter by the word of the Lord (St. Cyprian, epistle 43), outside of which we cannot find either true faith or eternal salvation. He who does not have the Church for a mother cannot have God for a father."[3]

Five years before the convocation of Vatican II, Pius XII, in his allocution to the Gregorian University (October 17, 1953), said, "By divine mandate the interpreter and guardian of the Scriptures, and the depository of Sacred Tradition living within her, the Church alone is the entrance to salvation: She alone, by herself, and under the protection and guidance of the Holy Spirit, is the source of truth."[4]

PAGANS IN PARADISE

There were exceptions to this harsh declaration, including some pagan philosophers (Pythagoras and Plato) and the ancient Hebrew patriarchs and prophets, who were not united to the church in fact but in *desire*. Proof of this union, St. Justin Martyr and St. Thomas Aquinas agreed, came from their exemplary lives and their foreknowledge of the saving work of Jesus Christ.[5] The Pythagoreans, as the twelfth-century Catholic philosopher Peter Abelard pointed out, shunned all worldly contact and sought the solitude of desert places. Plato set up his academy on a site far removed from the city, a place that was unhealthy as well as deserted "so that fear and the presence of disease would break the assault of lust."[6] Not only the Greeks but many of the ancient Jews also testified to their prescient love of Christ by living a monastic life. The Nazarites, Abelard argues, lived as monks and dedicated themselves completely to the law of the Lord, and the "sons of the prophets" abandoned city crowds to live on barley meal and wild herbs by the river Jordan.

The chaste and holy lives of many of the pagan philosophers and ancient Jews posited the possibility that a few individuals who lived in ignorance of the true faith might make their way to heaven. This possibility, according to St. Thomas Aquinas, came with the proviso that they not only lived in accordance with the moral teachings of Roman Catholicism but also experienced a baptism of desire because of their prescient faith in Christ.[7]

A GRACIOUS CONCESSION

Upholding the tenet of baptism by desire, the church taught that the true faith was capable of germinating within the souls of primitive peoples— even those who had never been exposed to Catholic missionaries—because God had implanted a *conscience* within every man and woman. Conscience, according to traditional Catholicism, is the voice of God making known to every human being his eternal law and bestowing upon them a sense of duty. By conscience, men and women know they are required to submit to properly constituted authority, especially the authority of the church, whose dictates are final and should remain "unquestioned."[8] In addition, God granted mankind the gift of intelligence (*ratio*), by which even primitive people are capable of coming to a basic understanding of God and his divine attributes. The only reason that the majority of non-Catholics, especially those living in Christian nations, do not embrace the tenets of the Roman Church, according to the preconciliar church, was because they approached the study of Catholic doctrine "with minds full of prejudice and hearts full of sin."[9]

The gracious concession to non-Catholics of a possibility for salvation was affirmed by Pius IX in his encyclical *Quanto conficiamur moerore*, as issued on August 10, 1863:

We all know that those who are invincibly ignorant of our religion and who nevertheless lead an honest and upright life, can, under the influence of divine light and divine grace, attain to eternal life; for God who knows and sees the mind, the heart, the thoughts, and the dispositions of every man, cannot in His infinite bounty and clemency permit any one to suffer eternal punishment who is not guilty through his own fault.[10]

THE DIVINE ATTRIBUTES

Despite the East-West Schism and the Protestant Reformation, the church, in its glory days before Vatican II, insisted that it maintained perfect unity. This quality was manifested by the total agreement of parishes and dioceses throughout the world on matters of faith and morality.[11] It possessed perpetuity since its teachings "could not fail or become corrupt, since its Divine Founder Jesus Christ and the Holy Spirit" will abide with it until the end of the world."[12] The church claimed true catholicity, since it was "universal in time, doctrine, and extent."[13] It professed authority, since it was governed by the lawful successors of St. Peter.[14] And it was infallible, since its truths had been revealed by Jesus Christ.[15]

SACRED SERFDOM

Since there was no salvation outside the church, the concept of religious liberty was condemned. Such liberty, according to traditional Catholic catechistics, represented the liberty to err, since the Roman Church as an institution was "based on divine, infallible teaching."[16] Describing freedom of thought in matters of religion as a "disastrous heresy," Pope Pius VII wrote, "For when the liberty of all 'religions' is indiscriminately asserted, by this very fact truth is confounded with error and the holy and immaculate Spouse of Christ, the Church, outside of which there can be no salvation, is set on a par with the sects of heretics and with Judaic perfidy itself."[17] Pope Gregory XVI, condemned it as "an absurd and erroneous proposition" that propels men, who are to be "kept on the narrow path of truth" into "the bottomless pit."[18] Pope Pius IX termed religious freedom "the liberty of perdition,"[19] something that will "corrupt the morals and minds of the people, and . . . propagate the pest of indifferentism."[20]

Because Catholics alone possessed the absolute truth, they were forbidden to attend lectures in Protestant churches and to participate in Protestant worship services. In *Graves ac diuturnae* (1875), Pope Paul IX wrote:

They [the faithful] should totally shun their [Protestant] religious celebrations, their buildings, and their chairs of pestilence which they have
with impunity established to transmit the sacred teachings. They should
shun their writings and all contact with them. They should not have any
dealings or meetings with usurping priests and apostates from the faith
who dare to exercise the duties of an ecclesiastical minister without pos-
sessing a legitimate mission or any jurisdiction. They should avoid them
as strangers and thieves who come only to steal, slay, and destroy.[21]

Before Vatican II, any Catholic who took part in a non-Catholic worship
service (even by joining the congregation in singing a hymn) committed a
mortal sin. As Fr. Bertrand Conway pointed out in *The Question Box*, which
was first published by the Paulist Fathers in 1903 and sold over 2,300,000
copies, "Catholicism is essentially a religion based on a divine, infallible
teaching; a Catholic is logically a possessor of truth. Why, therefore, should
he seek for that which he already possesses? His faith precludes all possibility of doubt; it rests on the authority of God. He can never admit that
other churches, liberal or orthodox, may possibly be right."[22]

ECUMENICAL GUIDELINES

On December 20, 1949, the Holy Office issued its teachings on ecumenism
in the *Instructio de Motione Oecumenica*, which was based on Pius XI's
encyclical *Mortalium animos* (1928). This publication laid down the following canonically sanctioned principles for union with any Protestant
denomination:

1. Nothing can be added or subtracted from the fullness of Catholic
   doctrine. Protestantism has nothing to add to the revealed truth of
   the Roman Catholic religion.
2. Christian unity must not be pursued for the sake of assimilation
   (i.e., the incorporation of Protestant beliefs and practices into the
   life of the Church, and Catholic doctrine must never be adjusted to
   comply with Protestant sensibilities).
3. True unity between Christians can only come about by the return of
   Protestants to the Catholic fold.[23]

In keeping with these guidelines, converts to Catholicism were
required to manifest "supernatural sorrow for their past sins," to pro-

claim a "firm belief in all the teachings of Christ as handed down by the one divine Church," to study an approved catechism "under the guidance of a priest," and to swear the following oath: "With a sincere heart and with unfeigned faith, I detest and adjure every error, heresy, and sect, opposed to the said Holy, Catholic and Apostolic Roman Church. So help me God."[24]

THE BALTIMORE CATECHISM

Before Vatican II, almost every practicing Catholic knew the marks and divine attributes of the church; they believed that the church was the ark of salvation; they were aware of the ban on attending Protestant worship services; and they realized the dangers of religious liberty. Most could even intelligently discuss the concept of "baptism by desire" and the meaning of *ex opera operato*. All Tridentine Catholics had been subjected to years of exacting instruction in sacred doctrine. The instruction began as soon as Catholic children entered catechetical class at the age of six in preparation of their first Holy Communion. The lessons were the same in every parish within every diocese throughout the United States. The children were required to memorize the answers to the questions within the *Baltimore Catechism*, volume I, the basic text for religious instruction. Any deviation from the precise wording of the answers was unacceptable. And the children who failed to provide the properly prescribed responses were required to receive special instruction.

Following first Holy Communion, the children received the *Baltimore Catechism*, volume II, which was considerably thicker and riddled with such terms as "indefectibility," "indifferentism," "apostasy," "laicization," "plenary indulgence," and "transubstantiation." The answers to the questions within this volume also had to be put to memory and recited in weekly catechetical classes before stern and exacting religious sisters. This exercise was conducted in preparation for the Sacrament of Confirmation, which duly trained Catholic children would receive at the age of twelve. Confirmation was administered not by the parish priest but by a presiding bishop, who would grill the sacramental candidates on questions from the official catechetical text. Most of the questions inevitably concerned matters of ecclesiology.

HERESY #1: CHURCH NOT CATHOLIC

These years of indoctrination served to make Catholics aware that many of the pronouncements of Vatican II were not only in sharp contradiction to the teachings of the *Baltimore Catechism* but that they also smacked of unadulterated heresy. False teachings were lodged in *Unitatis redintegratio*, the decree on ecumenism, and *Lumen gentium*, the Dogmatic Constitution on the Church. Both of these decrees were promulgated on November 21, 1964. Additional heresies were contained in *Nostra aetate*, the Declaration on the Relation of the Church with Non-Christian Religions, which was issued on October 28, 1965, *Gaudium et spes*, the Pastoral Constitution of the Church in the Modern World, and *Dignitatis humanae*, the Declaration on Religious Freedom. The latter two decrees came into being on December 7, 1965.

Heresy was evident in the very opening paragraphs of *Unitatis redintegratio*, which held that the Catholic Church was not really Catholic. The decree read, "For almost everyone regards the body in which he has heard the Gospel as his Church and indeed, God's Church. All however, though in different ways, long for the one visible Church of God, a Church truly universal and set forth into the world that the world may be converted to the Gospel and so be saved, to the glory of God."[25] True universality, therefore, was not a divine attribute of the church, and Catholics had been wrong to affirm the following from Apostles' Creed as the basic formula of their faith: "I believe in the Holy Catholic Church . . ."

What's more, Catholics had been wrong in believing, as Pope Leo XIII pronounced in *Satis cognitum*, that the church stood in a "state of absolute perfection."[26] But since the church according to *Unitatis redintegratio* was lacking in true catholicity, a divine attribute, it was less than perfect. Like other worldly institutions, it was inherently flawed, and, therefore, *human*. This assertion was restated throughout the decree on ecumenism, including this passage from chapter 1: "Nevertheless, the divisions among Christians prevent the Church from attaining the fullness of catholicity proper to her, in those of her sons who, though attached to her by Baptism, are yet separated from full communion with her. Furthermore, the Church herself finds it more difficult to express in actual life her full catholicity in all her bearings"[27] The strange passage implied that Holy Mother Church for centuries had been delusional, since she had lived in a fantasy life in which she fancied herself as truly universal. Thanks to the council, the church regained her sense of reality and "longed" "in actual life" to experience "full catholicity in all her bearings" so that the "world may be converted to the gospel."

How were the faithful to respond to such statements? Since childhood, they had been taught that anyone who declared that Holy Mother Church is not fully and truly Catholic should be viewed as heretics and schismatics. Catholicity was one of the chief marks of the church.[28] But these statements were not coming from the Missouri Synod of the Lutheran Church or the Southern Baptist Convention. They were being issued by an ecumenical gathering of Catholic bishops in a decree that had been signed by the supreme pontiff. *Roma locuta est!* Rome had spoken, and they were bound to obey, even though these pronouncements represented a repudiation of the teachings they sworn to uphold.[29]

HERESY #2: PROTESTANTS ARE CATHOLICS

The decree on ecumenism declared men and women born into religious communities that had separated from Rome no longer should be viewed as heretics or schismatics but rather embraced "with respect and affection" as brothers and sisters.[30] It went on to say:

> Even in the beginnings of this one and only Church of God there arose certain rifts, which the Apostle strongly condemned. But in subsequent centuries much more serious dissensions made their appearance and quite large communities came to be separated from full communion with the Catholic Church—for which, often enough, men of both sides were to blame. The children who are born into these Communities and who grow up believing in Christ cannot be accused of the sin involved in the separation, and the Catholic Church embraces upon them as brothers, with respect and affection. For men who believe in Christ and have been truly baptized are in communion with the Catholic Church even though this communion is imperfect.[31]

And so, the church had been wrong in administering an oath to new members, demanding them "to detest and abjure every error, heresy and sect, opposed to the Holy, Catholic, and Apostolic Roman Church."[32] Pope Leo XIII had been wrong in issuing *Satis cognitum* (1896), an encyclical that stated, "The practice of the Church has always been the same, as is shown by the unanimous teaching of the Fathers, who were wont to hold as outside Catholic communion and alien to the Church, whoever would recede *in the least degree* from any point of doctrine proposed by Her authoritative Magisterium."[33] Now Catholics were told that Protestants, even those who rejected almost every pronouncement from the Holy See, were not "aliens" to the church but "separated brethren." And Pope Pius XII had been wrong in promulgating *Mystici corporis Christi* (1943), which spoke of the members of the Roman Catholic Church as follows: "Actually only those are to be included as members of the Church who have been baptized and profess the true faith, and who have not been so unfortunate as to separate themselves from the unity of the Body, or been excluded by legitimate authority for grave faults committed."[34] By the new meaning of Catholic, even rabid Pentecostals, who railed against the Church of Rome as the Whore of Babylon, were, in fact, genuine believers.

HERESY #3: THERE IS NO HERESY

Before the issuance of *Unitatis redintegratio*, Catholics were obliged by the constitution of the Fourth Lateran Council (1215) to "condemn all heretics, whatever names they may go under."[35] St. Thomas Aquinas had made the distinction between *formal* and *material* heresy that became incorporated into the canon law.[36] Formal heretics were individuals who *pertinaciously* (i.e., willfully) doubted or denied any "revealed truth" of the Church.[37] By this definition, Methodists who understood the teaching of apostolic succession but denied that the pope was the legitimate bishop of Rome were formal heretics. Presbyterians who could comprehend the dogmas of the Immaculate Conception and Assumption of the Virgin Mary but refused to accept them since they lacked any grounding in scripture were formal heretics. Baptists who came to grips with the doctrine of transubstantiation but rejected it as a theological aberration of medieval Scholasticism were formal heretics.

Material heretics, according to traditional Catholic teaching, did not merit condemnation and could be accepted upon strict conditions into the church's fold. Such heretics were simple folk who assented to the condemned doctrines of the Reformers without fully understanding their content. Granted the opportunity, these victims of the herd mentality could be enticed to graze in any religious pasture, including the sacred fields of Rome. Their willingness to accept Catholic doctrine made them meritorious of acceptance in the one true church (*votum ecclesiae*), although they remained "deprived of many gifts and heavenly aids."[38] For this reason, Pope Pius XII in his encyclical *Mystici corporis* invited them "to favor interior movements of grace and to remove themselves from their present state, in which they cannot be sure of their salvation."[39]

But, in accordance with the decree on ecumenism, no heresy—formal or material—was to be condemned. Heretical doctrines were to be treated "with respect." Heretics were to be embraced as spiritual kin.

HERESY #4: SPIRITUAL PARITY
EXISTS BETWEEN CHRISTIANS

In keeping with this ruling, Catholics were now not only allowed but encouraged to step foot within these places once decried as "seedbeds of heresy"[40] and to join Protestants in prayer services "for unity." *Unitatis redintegratio* said, "In certain special circumstances, such as the prescribed prayers 'for unity,' and during ecumenical gatherings, it is allowable, indeed desirable that Catholics should join in prayer with their separated brethren. Such prayers in common are certainly an effective means of obtaining the grace of unity, and they are a true expression of the ties which still bind Catholics to their separated brethren."[41]

This teaching was in violation of canon law 1258 which stated, "It is unlawful for the faithful to assist in any active manner, or to take part, in the sacred services of non-Catholics."[42] Those who violated this prohibition were subject to a sentence of excommunication. The only concession was saying grace, a practice allowable only "to avoid serious danger."[43]

But now, by decree, Catholics and Protestants should unite not only in prayer but also in theological meetings and discussions:

> We must get to know the outlook of our separated brethren. To achieve this purpose, study is of necessity required, and this must be pursued with a sense of realism and good will. Catholics, who already have a proper grounding, need to acquire a more adequate understanding of the respective doctrines of our separated brethren, their history, their spiritual and liturgical life, their religious psychology and general background. Most valuable for this purpose are meetings of the two sides—especially for discussion of theological problems—where each can deal with the other on an equal footing—provided that those who take part in them are truly competent and have the approval of the bishops.[44]

Granting Protestants "equal footing" with Catholics in matters of theology was an affirmation that both positions shared the same spiritual status and that neither sect possessed sole claim to the truth. In 1928, Pope Pius XI, decrying false ecumenism in his encyclical *Mortalium animos*, expressed outrage at the offer of non-Catholic assemblies to come to "the Church of Rome . . . on equal terms, that is as equals with an equal."[45] Even if such meetings were arranged, the pope argued, the Protestant assemblies that "loudly preach fraternal communion in Christ Jesus" would still remain unwilling "to submit to and obey the Vicar of Jesus Christ either in His capacity as a teacher or as a governor." Based on this realization, Pius XI declared, "It is clear that the Apostolic See cannot on any terms take part in their [Protestant] assemblies, nor is it anyway lawful for Catholics either to support or to work for such enterprises; for if they do so they will be giving countenance to a false Christianity, quite alien to the one Church of Christ."

HERESY # 5: THERE ARE PROTESTANT MARTYRS

Before Vatican II, the church recognized that a formal heretic could be converted and could die for the one true faith before becoming an official member of the church. Such an individual belonged to the Catholic fold through *votum ecclesiae* and died a Catholic, even though this may remain "God's secret."[46] But *Unitatis redintegratio* maintained that even militant Protestants, who never gave witness to the truth of Catholic doctrine, deserve the title of martyrs if they died for the sake of their sect: "Catholics must gladly acknowledge and esteem the truly Christian endowments from our common heritage which are to be found among our separated brethren. It is right and salutary to recognize the riches of Christ and virtuous works in the lives of others who are bearing witness to Christ, sometimes even to the shedding of their blood."[47]

A Protestant martyr, in Catholic theology, was an oxymoron. The church taught that those who burn, are tossed to wild beats, or put to the sword in the name of Christ cannot merit a martyr's crown unless they remain within "the bosom and the unity of the Catholic Church."[48] But Vatican II's new pronouncement took root and granted enormous impetus toward religious indifferentism, the teaching that all religions are equally efficacious in the eyes of God.

As saints and martyrs, the champions of Protestantism were now worthy of veneration by the Catholic faithful. This belief became crystallized in pronouncements made by John Paul II throughout his long pontificate, including this statement in *Ut unum sint* (May 25, 1995):

The courageous witness of so many martyrs of our century, including members of Churches and Ecclesial Communities not in full communion with the Catholic Church, gives new vigor to the Council's call and reminds us of our duty to listen to and put into practice its exhortation. These brothers and sisters of ours, united in the selfless offering of their lives for the Kingdom of God, are the most powerful proof that every factor of division can be transcended and overcome in the total gift of self for the sake of the Gospel.[49]

HERESY #6: ATHEISM IS ACCEPTABLE

Turning from *Unitatis redintegratio* to *Lumen gentium*, Catholics discovered a host of additional heresies, including the assertion that some people, through no fault of their own, fail to recognize the existence of God. The Decree on the Church stated, "Nor does Divine Providence deny the helps necessary for salvation to those who, without blame on their part, have not yet arrived at an explicit knowledge of God and with His grace strive to live a good life."[50]

This assertion undermined the doctrine that God can be known by the natural light of reason—a teaching that had been set forth as follows by St. Paul in his Letter to the Romans:

The wrath of God is being revealed from heaven against all the godlessness and wickedness of people, who suppress the truth by their wickedness, since what may be known about God is plain to them, because God has made it plain to them. For since the creation of the world God's invisible qualities—his eternal power and divine nature—have been clearly seen, being understood from what has been made, so that people are without excuse. (Romans 1:18–21)

In the *Summa Theologiae*, the central text of Catholic theology, St. Thomas Aquinas set forth five proofs of God's existence that can be established by anyone with a brain.[51] These proofs were known by every Catholic student in every Catholic high school. Moreover, the premise that atheism is excusable had been condemned as follows by the First Vatican Council: "If anyone says that the one, true God, our creator and lord, cannot be known with certainty from the things that have been made, by the natural light of human reason: let him be anathema."[52] Once again, by a former proclamation of the infallible church, the fathers of Vatican II, including Pope Paul VI, stood condemned as spokesmen of evil.

HERESY #7: CATHOLICS WORSHIP ALLAH

After confirming that atheists are without blame, *Lumen gentium* made the amazing proclamation that Muslims have a part in God's plan of salvation. It decreed, "The plan of salvation also includes those who acknowledge the Creator. In the first place amongst these there are the Mohamedans [*sic*], who, professing to hold the faith of Abraham, along with us adore the one and merciful God, who on the last day will judge mankind."[53]

This curious assertion that Catholics and Muslims "adore the one and merciful God" represented a denial of the dogma of the Holy Trinity, a dogma that Muslims condemned throughout their history as polytheism. It implied that Allah, not Jesus Christ, will serve as mankind's supreme judge at the last day. And it turned a blind eye to the following teachings from the Koran:

1. "Fight those who believe not in Allah nor the Last Day, nor hold that forbidden which hath been forbidden by Allah and his Messenger, nor acknowledge the religion of truth, [even if they are] the People of the Book [Christians and Jews], until the pay the *jizya* with willing submission and feel themselves subdued." (9:29)
2. "Slay the idolaters wherever you find them." (9:5)
3. "Take not Jews or Christians as friends." (5:51)
4. "Remember your Lord inspired the angels with the message: 'I am with you, give firmness to Believers: I will inspire terror in the hearts of the Unbelievers: you smite them above their necks and smite all their fingertips off them.'" (8:12)
5. "Good women are the obedient, guarding in secret that which Allah hath guarded. As for those from whom ye fear rebellion, admonish them and banish them to beds apart, and scourge them." (4:34)

What's more, this teaching stood in sharp contradiction to the teachings of former popes who condemned Islam as an "abominable sect."[54] Pope Clement V, at the Council of Vienne in 1312, prohibited the Muslim call to prayer, which involved "the public invocation of the sacrilegious name of Mahomet [Mohammad]."[55] And Pope Benedict XIV forbade Catholics from giving their children Muslim names under pain of eternal damnation.[56]

The Vatican II teaching that Catholics and Muslims professed the faith of Abraham and worshipped the same God was dramatized by Pope John

Paul II's raising and kissing of the Koran before an audience of startled onlookers on May 14, 1999.[57]

HERESY #8: RELIGIOUS LIBERTY MUST BE UPHELD

After encountering landmine after landmine of heresy implanted within the teachings of Vatican II, Catholics came upon the endorsement of a teaching that had once been described as "insane." The decree *Dignitatis humanae* (A Declaration of Religious Freedom) proclaimed, "This Vatican Council declares that the human person has a right to religious freedom. This freedom means that all men are to be immune from coercion on the part of individuals or of social groups and of any human power, in such wise that no one is to be forced to act in a manner contrary to his own beliefs, whether privately or publicly, whether alone or in association with others, within due limits."[58] And so, the "disastrous heresy" that would "corrupt the morals and minds of the people and propagate the pest of indifferentism" became the official church doctrine.

In Tridentine theology, the dogma condemning religious liberty went hand in hand with the teaching that the church should be united with the state. This union was necessary to prevent false religions and heretical beliefs from spreading. The ultimate ruler and authority on all matters temporal and spiritual in accordance with Christ's teaching—or, so the church taught—was the bishop of Rome. In *Unam sanctam* (1302), which appears to be the first infallible pronouncement of a Roman pontiff, Boniface VIII maintained,

> We are informed by the texts of the gospels that in this Church and in its power are two swords; namely, the spiritual and the temporal. For when the Apostles say: "Behold, here are two swords" [Lk 22:38] that is to say, in the Church, since the Apostles were speaking, the Lord did not reply that there were too many, but sufficient. Certainly the one who denies that the temporal sword is in the power of Peter has not listened well to the word of the Lord commanding: "Put up thy sword into thy scabbard" [Mt 26:52]. Both, therefore, are in the power of the Church, that is to say, the spiritual and the material sword, but the former is to be administered *for* the Church but the latter *by* the Church; the former in the hands of the priest; the latter by the hands of kings and soldiers, but at the will and sufferance of the priest.[59]

The pope added a final authoritative touch so there would be no mis-understanding of his meaning: "We declare, state and define that it is altogether necessary for salvation that every creature to be subject to the Roman Pontiff."[60]

This insistence on a union of church and state earmarked Catholic doctrine throughout the ages. In his Syllabus of Errors (1864), Pope Pius IX pointed out that a principal error is to uphold the notion that "the Church ought to be separated from the State, and the State from the Church."[61]

But *Dignitatis humanae* endorsed this separation and the heresy of Americanism, by proclaiming, "Government therefore ought indeed to take account of the religious life of the citizenry and show it favor, since the function of government is to make provision for the common welfare. However, it would clearly transgress the limits set to its power, were it to presume to command or inhibit acts that are religious."[62] Since the state exceeds its authority by seeking "to command or inhibit" religious acts of any kind, national governments must assume the posture of secular humanism. Small wonder that this teaching resulted in a host of Catholic nations, including Spain, Portugal, Italy, Ireland, and Argentina, aban-doning their Catholic constitutions.

HERESY #9—THERE ARE OTHER ARKS OF SALVATION

At last, Catholics came upon the final heresy, which was a betrayal of all they had believed: the Roman Catholic Church was not the only ark of sal-vation. The Holy Spirit was not a dove confined to a cage within Vatican City. According to *Unitatis redintegratio*, the third person of the sacred Trinity had winged its way into non-Catholic churches, filling their sanc-tuaries with grace and granting Protestants the means of salvation, even though they opposed sacred dogmas regarding the papacy, the Virgin Mary, the communion of saints, the forgiveness of sins, and the seven sac-raments. The decree said,

> Moreover, some and even very many of the significant elements and endowments which together go to build up and give life to the Church itself, can exist outside the visible boundaries of the Catholic Church: the written word of God; the life of grace; faith, hope and charity, with the other interior gifts of the Holy Spirit, and visible elements too. All of these, which come from Christ and lead back to Christ, belong by right to the one Church of Christ.[63]

Since non-Catholic churches possess such spiritual gifts, the decree continued, "the Spirit of Christ has not refrained from using them as a means of salvation."[64] And so, the catechetical lessons had been in error: the proclamations that the Roman Church alone possessed the truth, that the Roman Church alone remained the dispenser sanctifying grace, that the Roman Church alone possessed the means of salvation. Since Protestant churches contained the spiritual elements necessary for humanity's salvation, while denying cardinal tenets of the Roman Church, why should Catholics abide by the special precepts of their faith? Why weren't they allowed the religious liberty of Protestants—the right to eat meat on Friday, to skip Mass on Sunday and other holy days of obligation, to practice birth control, to divorce their spouses? Why were they obliged, unlike the separated brethren, to confess their sins to their parish priest and obtain pronouncements of absolution? Why were they compelled to make satisfaction in the form of penance for all of their transgressions? Why were their marriages only recognized as valid when performed before Catholic clerics? What was the need for Protestants wishing to marry Catholics to sign pre-Cana agreements? And, finally, why the need to obey the dictates of the Holy Father that Protestants could opt blissfully to ignore?

After standing Holy Mother Church on her head, stripping her of her traditional attire, and surrendering her cherished claims to the prevailing spirit of the age, the council fathers maintained that the decrees of Vatican II were merely "pastoral."[65] This was the ultimate statement of deception—the final kiss from Judas. Catholics, subjected to the effects of Vatican II, knew that the changes cut to the quick of their faith. The great exodus from the church was about to begin.

Chapter Seven

HOLY MOTHER CHURCH'S SEX CHANGE

Catholicism taught an especially strict sexual ethic. This is not to say that Protestantism taught a lax sexual ethic, for it did not. Yet, in general, Protestants were not so thoroughly convinced as were Catholics of the extreme wickedness of sexual impropriety. Here again, the Catholic doctrine of mortal sin played a major role in raising the stakes. Fornication could land you in Hell for eternity; so indeed could touching your girlfriend's breast; in fact, even thinking about this illicit touch, if you dwelled on it and took carnal pleasure in the thought, could land you in Hell.
      —David Carlin, *The Decline and Fall of the Catholic Church in America*, 2003

U nlike other religions, including Judaism, Roman Catholicism upheld an intransigent position on sexuality that included the ideal of male virginity. The primary source of this ideal was Christ himself. Jesus never married, and Jewish bachelors in their thirties were a rarity in Palestine, since they lived in opposition to the Biblical injunction "be fruitful and multiply" (Genesis 1:22).[1]

In the synoptic gospels, Jesus commanded his apostles to relinquish their wives and children (Matt. 19:29; Mark 10:29; Luke 18:29), and, in the Gospel of Luke, added, "The children of this age marry and are given in marriage but those judged worthy of a place in the world to come do not" (20:34–35). He spoke of a sexless existence as a statement of complete dedication to the Kingdom of God:

> Jesus said to them, "Moses permitted you to divorce your wives because your hearts were hard. But it was not this way from the beginning. I tell you that anyone who divorces his wife, except for sexual immorality, and marries another woman commits adultery."
> The disciples said to him, "If this is the situation between a husband and wife, it is better not to marry."

Jesus replied, "Not everyone can accept this word, but only those to whom it has been given. For there are eunuchs who were born that way, and there are eunuchs who have been made eunuchs by others— and there are those who choose to live like eunuchs for the sake of the kingdom of heaven. The one who can accept this should accept it." (Matt. 19:8–12)

This teaching gave rise to the doctrine of clerical celibacy and also caused several early church fathers to encourage castration. St. Justin Martyr, for example, wrote of a young Christian who asked a physician in Alexandria to castrate him. Since castration was banned by Roman law, the physician instructed him to apply for permission to undergo such surgery from the provincial governor. The youth complied and was filled with chagrin when the governor denied his request. The incident is significant primarily because St. Justin spoke of the young man's efforts to sever the source of his libidinal urgings as something admirable.[2]

THE IDEAL STATE

The exhortations of Christ concerning the virtue of a sexless existence were echoed by St. Paul in his first Epistle to the Corinthians:

Now for the matters you wrote about: "It is good for a man not to have sexual relations with a woman." But since sexual immorality is occurring, each man should have sexual relations with his own wife, and each woman with her own husband. The husband should fulfill his marital duty to his wife, and likewise the wife to her husband. The wife does not have authority over her own body but yields it to her husband. In the same way, the husband does not have authority over his own body but yields it to his wife. Do not deprive each other except perhaps by mutual consent and for a time, so that you may devote yourselves to prayer. Then come together again so that Satan will not tempt you because of your lack of self-control. I say this as a concession, not as a command. I wish that all of you were as I am. But each of you has your own gift from God; one has this gift, another has that. Now to the unmarried and the widows I say: It is good for them to stay unmarried, as I do. But if they cannot control themselves, they should marry, for it is better to marry than to burn. (7:1–9).

From such scriptural teachings, the church fathers, almost to the point of monotony, spoke of celibacy as a higher state.

Celibacy was viewed not as a negative virtue that denied the goodness of creation but rather as a positive virtue, a means by which the faithful could aspire to the state of angels and reverse the tragic effects of Adam and Eve.[3] St. Cyprian argued that, whereas sex takes a man's mind from God, sexual abstinence permits him to concentrate on God alone and thereby obtain increased freedom from the fetters of the material world.[4]

Primitive Christianity's emphasis on the virtue of chastity was stressed by the accounts of Mary and the Virgin Birth of Jesus. By the second century, these accounts were greatly embellished by apocalyptic words such as "The Gospel of the Nativity" and "The Protoevangelium of James." In the latter work, Salome (the stepdaughter of Herod the Great), after learning of the miraculous birth of Jesus from a midwife, set out to verify Mary's alleged "intactness" for herself. As Mary was sleeping, Salome stole into the cave and "put forth her finger to test her condition," only to have her finger severely singed for her sinful curiosity.[5]

THE LESSER STATE

Wedlock was a state for spiritual weaklings. St. Gregory of Nyssa mourned over the marriage of one of his students as a "sad tragedy,"[6] and St. Ambrose labeled it a "galling burden" and urged those of his disciples who were contemplating marriage to think of the state of domestic servitude to which wedded bliss soon deteriorated.[7] The most sincere praise of marriage during the Patristic age came from St. Jerome, who said, "I praise wedlock. I praise marriage, but it is because they produce virgins for me. I gather the rose from the thorn, the gold from the earth, and the pearl from the oyster."[8] This teaching of the superiority of virginity became defined as a solemn dogma by the Council of Trent in 1563, which decreed, "If anyone says that the married state excels the state of virginity or celibacy, and that it is better or happier to be united in matrimony than to remain in virginity or celibacy, let him be anathema."[9]

But even within the confines of holy matrimony, the church maintained that sexual congress can be mortal sin. St. Augustine argued that married couples turn intercourse into a sinful act when they use it exclusively for the gratification of lust (concupiscence) to the exclusion of the desire for offspring.[10] Such an act is sinful, he wrote, even if no attempt is made to prevent propagation "either by wrong desire or evil appliance."[11]

CONJUGAL CONCUPISCENCE

Throughout the Middle Ages, the church instructed couples to restrain the likelihood of marital concupiscence through periods of sexual abstinence. Priests sometimes advised couples to abstain from intercourse on Thursdays in memory of Christ's arrest, on Fridays in memory of his death, on Saturdays in honor of the Virgin Mary, on Sundays in honor of his Resurrection, and on Mondays in honor of the faithful departed.[12]

The question concerning the sinfulness of sexual congress within the confines of matrimony were still debated by scholastic theologians in the twelfth and thirteenth centuries. St. Thomas Aquinas believed that marital sex on occasion could be either venial or mortal sin, depending on the degree of lust. He wrote, "If pleasure be sought in such a way as the exclude the honesty of marriage, so that, to wit, it is not as a wife but as a woman that a man treats his wife, and that he is ready to use her in the same way if she were not his wife, it is mortal sin; wherefore if such a man is said to be too ardent a lover of his wife, because his ardor carries him away from the goods of marriage, so that it would not be sought in another than his wife, it is venial sin."[13]

MARITAL HEDONISM

The virtue of chastity in marriage was upheld in the church in the twentieth century until the time of Vatican II. In 1951, Pope Pius XII, in an address to midwives, condemned the unbridled pursuit of sexual pleasure in marriage as "hedonism," by saying,

> As with the pleasure of food and drink so with the sexual they must not abandon themselves without restraint to the impulses of the senses. The right rule is this: the use of the natural procreative disposition is morally lawful in matrimony only, in the service of and in accordance with the ends of marriage itself. Hence it follows that only in marriage with the observing of this rule is the desire and fruition of this pleasure and of this satisfaction lawful. For the pleasure is subordinate to the law of the action whence it derives, and not vice versa—the action to the law of pleasure. And this law, so very reasonable, concerns not only the substance but also the circumstances of the action, so that, even when the substance of the act remains morally safe, it is possible to sin in the way it is performed.[14]

He added,

> If nature had aimed exclusively, or at least in the first place, at a recip-
> rocal gift and possession of the married couple in joy and delight, and if
> it had ordered that act only to make happy in the highest possible degree
> their personal experience, and not to stimulate them to the service of life,
> then the Creator would have adopted another plan in forming and con-
> stituting the natural act.[15]

SELF-MORTIFICATION

By the fourth century, spiritual counselors encouraged the virgins in their
care to enhance the holiness of their lives through acts of mortification of
the flesh, including self-flagellation and prolonged periods of fasting from
food and wine. Such measures often resulted in amenorrhea, the cessation
of menstruation. Amenorrhea, in the eyes of St. Jerome, came to represent
tangible proof of the virgin's being able to reverse the effects of the Fall of
Adam and Eve and to achieve a pristine wholeness of being.[16]

The teaching that mature women—sexual women—could be transformed by rigid discipline into innocent children of God was passed
down the centuries in Catholic convents, where nuns and religious sisters
attempted to attain sanctity by the hair shirt, the scourge, and the stone,
which they used to beat against their breast in the manner exemplified
by St. Jerome in painting after painting, including Leonardo's unfinished
masterpiece in the Vatican. Prior to Vatican II, ascetic practices were still
in play. In the 1950s, the novices at Woodstock, the former Jesuit seminary
in Maryland, were given a spiked band to wear on their thigh as an act of
penance.[17]

NATURAL LAW

The Stoic philosophers from Chrysippus to Cicero upheld nature as a
guide for conduct and believed that a person should be rationally self-
sufficient and not a slave to the demands of his or her body. Such freedom
could only be achieved by a spirit of disinterestedness to base passions
and instincts. Moreover, according to the Stoics, reason decreed that sexual
activity must be guided by the finality inscribed within it by nature. The
finality of sexual congress, of course, was the production of children. By

nature, the male sex organ was external and the female internal. The two anatomical parts were designed by nature to fit together. Any other use of the sex organs was perverse, since it was against their biological purpose.[18] Imbued with such ideals, St. Paul in his Letter to the Romans wrote of women changing the "natural use" of sex into that which is "against nature," and of men giving up "natural relations" with women by being "consumed with passion for other men" (1:26–27).

Upholding the Stoic principle that anything that thwarts conception is unnatural, St. Justin Martyr wrote that Christians live in the manner of true philosophers since they marry only to have children. Otherwise, he said, they remain completely continent.[19] Similarly, St. Clement of Alexandria held that Christians who intend to beget children should approach their wives with a chaste and controlled will, for to engage in sexual congress for purposes other than procreation was to transgress the laws of nature.[20]

CRIMINAL CONDUCT

Of particular repugnance to the church fathers was any attempt at birth control. St. John Chrysostom held that the use of contraceptives was worse than homicide.[21] And St. Augustine spoke of married couples who practice birth control as fornicators engaged in "criminal conduct."[22]

St. Thomas Aquinas divided sins against nature into the following four categories: (1) procuring ejaculation without coitus (i.e., masturbation), (2) copulation with nonhuman creatures (i.e., bestiality), (3) venereal acts between members of the same sex, and (4) deviation between married partners from the proper manner of sexual intercourse—*naturalis modus concumbandi* (i.e., face-to-face contact with the woman on her back). Of these, he concluded, the most grievous sins were bestiality and homosexuality.[23]

PRESCRIBED PUNISHMENTS

How strict was the Catholic sexual code? The answer was lodged not only in the teachings of the church fathers (as cited above) but also in the *Cummean Penitential*, a seventh-century guide for priests to prescribe the correct acts of penance. For "unintentional pollution" (i.e., wet dreams), the recitation of fifteen psalms; if the nocturnal emission came from deliberately entertained thoughts of lust, a sentence of a seven-day fast on bread and water. For the first offense of masturbation, a penance of one hundred days on bread and water; for a repeated act, the punishment was extended for a year. For an act of fornication, a penance of one year on bread and water; if a child was begotten from the union, the punishment was increased to three years.[24] For an act of sodomy, the penitential mandated four to seven years of fasting and prayer. While the gravity (*culpa*) of these sins remained fixed through the ages, many of these penalties became mollified—but not for homosexuality. By the fourteenth century, homosexual sins were viewed with such gravity that they could only be absolved by the pronouncement of a bishop.[25]

FIXED TEACHINGS

In *Casti connubii*, an encyclical promulgated on December 31, 1930, Pope Pius XI addressed premarital and extramarital sexual activity and the evil of sexual incontinence by quoting St. Augustine:

> By conjugal faith it is provided that there should be no carnal intercourse outside the marriage bond with another man or woman; with regard to offspring, that children should be begotten of love, tenderly cared for and educated in a religious atmosphere; finally, in its sacramental aspect that the marriage bond should not be broken and that a husband or wife, if separated, should not be joined to another even for the sake of offspring. This we regard as the law of marriage by which the fruitfulness of nature is adorned and the evil of incontinence is restrained.[26]

Regarding chastity within marriage, Pius XI again quoted St. Augustine: "Intercourse even with one's legitimate wife is unlawful and wicked where the conception of the offspring is prevented."[27] Upholding the doctrine of natural law, the pope maintained, "The conjugal act is destined primarily by nature for the begetting of children, those who in exercising it deliberately frustrate its natural power and purpose sin against nature and commit a deed which is shameful and intrinsically vicious."

For the common laity, these teachings did not constitute mysteries, such as the dogmas of the Trinity, the Immaculate Conception, and the Assumption of Mary that must be accepted *sola fides*, "by faith alone." They were principles that could be verified by anatomy and the process of procreation. The teachings made sense and they governed the intimate lives of the faithful. Although there existed an obvious discrepancy between standard and practice, the standard by the vast majority of Catholics was upheld. In 1960, over 74 percent of the Catholics in America maintained that premarital sex was absolutely immoral even for couples engaged to be married.[28]

WARNINGS TO YOUTH

Anyone interested in the rigidity of Catholic doctrine regarding sexual behavior in the years before Vatican II should turn to *Modesty, Chastity, and Morals*, a quaint booklet by Monsignor J. D. Conway, published in 1955 and placed in the vestibules of parishes throughout the United States. Regarding impure thoughts, Conway wrote, "The sin connected with impure thoughts comes from the carnal (sexual, venereal) pleasure which they arouse and to which we consent. It is a mortal sin to entertain such thoughts for the purpose of getting such carnal pleasure."[29] Regarding the wearing of sundresses and shorts, he held, "A woman would be guilty of mortal sin if she deliberately dressed in a manner intended to provoke men to sin—if she simply wanted to arouse and excite them"[30] Concerning books and magazines, Conway said, "Habitual reading of most of the books and magazines distributed at the corner drug store is a narcotic for the intellect and a palliative for the will . . . disruptive of moral standards and conducive to neurotic irregularity in youthful development."[31]

SEXUAL TRANSFORMATION

On October 29, 1964, Cardinal Suenens, while presenting a new schema on marriage before the Second Vatican Council, said that the church in the past had placed too much emphasis on the words of scripture, "Be fruitful and multiply" (Genesis 1:22) and not enough on the teachings of Christ, "The two shall become one flesh" (Mark 10:8). He argued that the church, at last, should affirm that conjugal love, not fecundity, should be recognized as a primary purpose of marriage. He further advanced the idea— shared by the *periti*—that married couples should be granted the right to control their number of offspring.[32]

Traditionalists were aghast. Cardinal Ottaviani stood and said, "I am not pleased with the statement that married couples may determine the number of children they have. Never has this been heard in the Church. Does this mean that the inerrancy of the Church will be called into question?"[33]

The answer, of course, was yes. The radical schema on marriage was approved on November 13, 1965, by 1,596 votes to 72, and 484 affirmative votes with qualifications.[34] The document failed to recognize procreation as the primary purpose of marriage; made no mention of natural law; spoke of sexual congress as a sacrament; and left it to married couples to decide whether or not to use artificial contraception. The cat was now out of the Catholic bag. The intransigent teachings of the church on sex that had stood for nearly two thousand years were being altered by the council to meet the demands of contemporary society and the findings of the Kinsey report (studies conducted in the 1940s and 1950s on human sexual behavior).

AMENDED AMENDMENTS

Paul VI, realizing the disastrous effect the new teachings would have on the laity, sent four amendments (*modi*) to be included in the ratified document. When copies of the amendments were handed out to members of the commission on marriage, several, including Cardinal Paul-Emile Leger of Montreal, sprang to their feet in protest. But the pope remained adamant and, to some degree, prevailed. One amendment demanded the inclusion of "artificial contraception" among the "deformations" detracting from the dignity of conjugal love, along with the deformations of "polygamy, divorce, and free love." The commission refused to insert "artificial contraception," only agreeing to insert the ambiguous phrase "illicit practices against human generation." The commission further refused to acquiesce to the papal demand for a reference to Pius XI's encyclical *Casti connubii*.[35]

A second amendment dictated that the procreation was the primary purpose of marriage, not conjugal love. The commission, after considerable debate and with profound reluctance, acquiesced to this demand. Another amendment demanded the inclusion of a statement regarding conjugal chastity in the document, since it appeared to sanction not only artificial birth control but also abortion. The pope's modus said that couples who are faced with such choices regarding unwanted pregnancies must practice "the virtue of conjugal chastity sincerely."[36]

The commission, in rewording the amendment, excluded any statement regarding conjugal chastity, opting instead to insert this ambiguous statement, which implied that divine law was not fixed but ever evolving: "Sons of the Church may not undertake methods which are found blameworthy by the teaching authority of the Church in its unfolding of divine law."[37] The revised and final text was adopted on December 7, 1965, by a vote of 2,309 to 75. Paul VI, at his wit's end, reluctantly promulgated the document into a new decree.[38]

HUMANAE VITAE

Despite the fact that the members of the commission on marriage and the *periti* took an oath of secrecy, news of the conflict between the pope and the council members regarding artificial contraception, natural law, and conjugal chastity spread like wildfire throughout Rome and captured headlines in such leading Italian newspapers as *L'Avvenire d'Italia*.[39] The pope realized that he would have to issue a ruling on birth control that, by the power of his position, would be binding on all believers. In *Humanae vitae*, an encyclical issued on July 25, 1965, Paul VI condemned all artificial means of birth control (including condoms, pills, withdrawals, and postcoital dousing procedures) as immoral and unnatural. He proclaimed,

> We are obliged once more to declare that the direct interruption of the generative process already begun and, above all, all direct abortion, even for therapeutic reasons, are to be absolutely excluded as lawful means of regulating the number of children. Equally to be condemned, as the magisterium of the Church has affirmed on many occasions, is direct sterilization, whether of the man or of the woman, whether permanent or temporary. Similarly excluded is any action which either before, at the moment of, or after sexual intercourse, is specifically intended to prevent procreation—whether as an end or as a means.[40]

In the encyclical, Paul VI also attempted to uphold the doctrine of marital celibacy, by maintaining,

> The right and lawful ordering of birth demands, first of all, that spouses fully recognize and value the true blessings of family life and that they acquire complete mastery over themselves and their emotions. For if with the aid of reason and of free will they are to control their natural drives, there can be no doubt at all of the need for self-denial. Only then will the expression of love, essential to married life, conform to right order. This is especially clear in the practice of periodic continence. Self-discipline

of this kind is a shining witness to the chastity of husband and wife and, far from being a hindrance to their love of one another, transforms it by giving it a more truly human character. And if this self-discipline does demand that they persevere in their purpose and efforts, it has at the same time the salutary effect of enabling husband and wife to develop to their personalities and to be enriched with spiritual blessings. For it brings to family life abundant fruits of tranquility and peace. It helps in solving difficulties of other kinds. It fosters in husband and wife thoughtfulness and loving consideration for one another. It helps them to repel inordinate self-love, which is the opposite of charity. It arouses in them a consciousness of their responsibilities.[41]

By issuing this encyclical, the Holy Father remained blithely unaware that the council had ushered in a new age of moral subjectivism that no papal pronouncement could banish from the sanctified realm of the church.

THE SOUND AND THE FURY

The furor created by *Humanae vitae*, as Thomas Bokenkotter points out in *Essential Catholicism*, was "unprecedented."[42] Outcries of anger and resentment, directed not so much against Paul VI as against the papal office itself, came from progressive priests and bishops. A petition signed by six hundred American Catholic theologians took issue with the implied ecclesiology and the employed methodology of the encyclical and concluded that married couples should come to their own decisions regarding artificial contraception.[43] The triumph of subjectivism in this issue came from statements of Catholic hierarchies throughout the world, including the United States, Canada, the Netherlands, Germany, Austria, Scandinavia, and Belgium, which stressed the right of Catholic couples to follow their own consciences regarding birth control.[44]

The results of the uproar were telling. In 1965, 57 percent of married couples in America practiced some form of birth control. Most adhered to the church-sanctioned rhythm method, which allowed married couples to avoid pregnancy by attempting to pinpoint the woman's fertility period from month to month. By 1975, 67 percent of Catholic couples employed birth control—almost all by artificial means.[45]

CATHOLIC SEX STUDY

In 1972, the midst of the sexual revolution, the Catholic Theological Society of America established a committee to conduct a study on human sexuality with the hope of "providing some helpful and illuminating guidelines in the present confusion."[46] The committee's pronouncements represented a sharp repudiation of every traditional teaching regarding sexual morality. The proper meaning of sexuality, the committee concluded, was not the satisfaction of an animal urge but the means by which people can break out of their isolation and "attain communion with one another." Sexual congress, whether premarital or extramarital, was thus elevated to the status of a sacrament.[47] Regarding sexual morality, the committee decided that sex was moral if it contributed toward "integration" (i.e., communion with the partner). "Destructive sexuality," in the committee's opinion, "resulted in personal frustration and interpersonal alienation."[48]

Thanks to the pronouncements of Vatican II, the reaction to *Humanae vitae*, and the proclamations of progressive clerics and theological studies, the Catholic laity was forced to face the conclusion that they had been deluded by Holy Mother Church and her proclamations of the divine law governing the most intimate aspect of their lives. Their years of self-denial, of sexual abstinence, of making satisfaction for every minor sexual transgression had been wasted to uphold spurious claims that had arisen from Stoic philosophers and sex-crazed ascetics. The notion of natural law and the virtue of chastity were tossed out along with the church's other medieval baggage regarding usury, the liturgy, and the papacy. Their lives had been misspent by living in accordance with a code of morality that was philosophically misconceived and theologically outmoded. Sex, they now were taught, could be enjoyed simply for self-gratification.

The door was now opened for Catholics to join the sexual revolution. Married couples were not bound to employ the missionary position; masturbation was not mortal sin; and homosexual acts were not unnatural. A 1981 Knights of Columbus study of eighteen to thirty-year-old Catholics in the United States showed that 90 percent disagreed with the pronouncements of *Humanae vitae* and 88 percent disagreed with the Catholic norms on divorce and premarital sex.[49] From 1973 to 1983, the rate of divorce among Catholics grew from one in seven to one out of four. A 1985 Gallup poll showed that the general Catholic population had become more tolerant of premarital sex than Protestants—only 33 percent disapproving, compared to the Protestants' 46 percent.[50] According to the same poll, 77 percent of US Catholics said they relied on their own conscience rather than the proclamations of the church in making sexual decisions.[51]

The moral teachings of the church had granted Catholics a distinct identity, a means by which Catholics identified themselves to others. But by 1970, the Catholic substructure, with its own blend of rituals and rules, mystery and manners, vanished from the American scene. The editors of *Newsweek* on October 4, 1971, concluded, "Largely because of Vatican Council II and the turmoil that has followed, there is now as much diversity in theology and life-style among Catholics as there is among US Protestants. A Catholic, in effect, is anyone who he says he is, and his attitude toward the Church is likely to be shaped essentially by his income, education, and where he floats in America's still bubbling melting pot."[52]

Stripped of their sociological identities, their spiritual moorings, and their system of morality, Catholics didn't know what to believe or where to turn. The council had created an abyss that threatened to suck them into existential nothingness.

Chapter Eight

DISSENT, DELUSION, AND DESERTION

To those unacquainted with the power and scope of secret societies, the personality of Pope Paul VI presents a veritable enigma. No other Pope, even in the most tempestuous times, has been the subject of such conflicting reports; no other Pope has been so apparently self-contradictory. Even a casual reading of his reign leaves an impression of doubt, equivocation, and a pathetically weak kind of hedging that is a far remove from the assertive Pontificates of the past. On 14 September, 1972, he came down heavily against the suggestion that women might play some part in the ministry of the priesthood. Such a departure from custom was unthinkable. Yet his was not a decisive voice, for only some three weeks later the Vatican issued a hand-out to journalists announcing that the Pope might change his mind. The final contradiction came on 29 March, 1973, when the Associated Press reported: "Pope Paul ruled today that women, regardless of whether they are nuns, may distribute Communion in Roman Catholic churches." The Pope had already, in May 1969, condemned a new departure that had crept in whereby Communion was received in the hand. Yet later he took that stricture back, with the meaningless proviso that Communion bread could be so received "after proper instruction." It was said that the Pope's correspondence, before it reached him, passed through the hands of Casaroli, Villot, and Benelli, the Cardinals in virtual control of the Vatican. Statesmen and churchmen who paid official visits found Pope Paul diffident, almost vague, and more ready with comments and opinions than with definite answers. He lacked clarity; and as wonder gave way to a feeling of disquiet, various theories emerged to account for the air of mystery around Peter's Chair.
— Piers Compton, *The Broken Cross*, 1983

The findings of surveys conducted from 1970 to 1974 on American Catholics remain more illuminating and eloquent than any statement by religious analysts and social commentators. Church attendance among Catholic communicants, according to the National Opinion Research Center, dropped from 74 percent in 1965 to 50 percent in 1973, the decline strongest not among Catholic youth, as many would assume, but among adults over thirty years of age.[1] A study published by the Archdiocese of New York showed that attendance at Sunday Mass in the archdiocese fell by 23 percent from 1959 to 1970. In 1965, 824,475 Catholics, living within the Archdiocese of New York, attended Mass on a typical Sunday. By 1970, that number had dropped to 627,235.[2] In 1970, the Roman Catholic Church experienced its first decline in membership since its establishment in the United States.[3] By 1975, weekly confession by US Catholics had dropped 50 percent from 71 percent in 1964, and 38 percent of the Catholics polled said they "never" or "practically never" went to confession, as opposed to 18 percent a decade earlier.[4] On October 4, 1971, *Newsweek* published the following findings from a Gallup poll:

- One-half of the US Catholics polled favored a relaxation of the church's stance on abortion.
- Less than 10 percent believed their children would "lose their souls" by leaving the church.
- Two-thirds of the American Catholics no longer believed that Catholics who divorced and remarried outside the church were "living in sin."
- Over one-third said they no longer attended Mass with any regularity.
- Two-thirds admitted they had not gone to confession in the two-month period before being polled.
- Forty-one percent said that it was no longer a sin to miss Mass on Sundays and holy days of obligation.
- Fifty-eight percent said they never recited the rosary.
- Only 4 percent said that the pope provided guidance on what to believe.
- Fifty-eight percent said that a good Catholic could ignore the pope's teaching on birth control.[5]

A Greeley, McCready, and McCourt study conducted by the National Opinion Research Center between 1963 and 1974 uncovered these findings:

- Thirty-five percent of American Catholics held that sex before marriage was wrong, compared to 74 percent in 1963.
- Fifty percent maintained that sex for pleasure alone was acceptable, compared to 29 percent in 1963.
- Sixteen percent said that artificial contraception was always wrong, compared to 56 percent in 1963.
- Fifty percent would support the decision of a son to become a priest, compared to 66 percent in 1963.
- Forty percent believed that Jesus had appointed St. Peter and the pope as heads of the church, compared to 70 percent in 1963.[6]

THE PASSING OF PRIESTS

From 1963 to 1968, a total of 7,137 priests asked to be dispensed from the obligation of the priesthood; 5,652 of these requests were granted.[7] In 1968, Bearings for Reestablishment, a nonprofit organization, was established in New York City to help former priests find their way in the secular world. The firm was soon handling 165 new priest-clients a month.[8] By 1970, the church in America was losing five priests through death, retirement, and resignation for every two seminarians. Twenty-five hundred Roman Catholic clergymen—4 percent of all priests in the United States were dropping out annually.[9] The peak year for US Catholic seminarians was 1965, when enrollment reached 48,992. By 1971, the number of men studying for the priesthood had fallen to 22,963, a decrease of 53 percent.[10] The situation continued to worsen. By 1974, one out of seven—10,000 in all—had left the priesthood, and the number of Catholic seminarians had plummeted to 4,039.[11]

Cardinal Gabriel Garrone, prefect of the Congregation for Catholic Education, blamed the drop out of priests and the decline in seminarians on a "crisis in faith." He said, "Our fundamental concern must spring from the fact that we live in a very complex and very new environment; and that we, therefore, run the risk of remaining passive, either through discouragement and cowardice, or else we lose sight of the most fundamental impulse of all in the matter of vocations—faith."[12]

Sociologist Eugene Schallert reported in 1970 that many priests thought they were leaving to marry, only to discover that their real reason ran much deeper. His survey of ex-priests showed that almost all of them had embraced the reforms of Vatican II. But the changes in the church only created in the priests a loss of self-worth and spiritual belief. According to

Schallert, they no longer could believe in the teachings of the church and began to question the very basis of their existence. They sought a sense of direction from "critical others"—fellow priests, confessors, ecclesiastical superiors—only to discover that no help was forthcoming. Some of the ex-priests said that they had left for a woman, but discovered, in Schallert's words, "it wasn't a woman at all."[13]

NUNS IN REBELLION

From 1965 to 1970, religious sisters in record numbers abandoned their habits and left their convents to appear in blouses and blue jeans in rallies, marches, and sit-ins for a host of social causes, including gay rights. A group of defectors from the Immaculate Heart of Mary Sisters in Los Angeles dropped out of their order to form Sisters for a Christian Community, free-form religious settlements in thirty-two states that included married couples and Protestants.[14] Essential to the understanding, according to founding sister Lillanna Kopp, was the elimination of bureaucratic ties to the Roman Church. "We must be a pilgrim people on the road, unencumbered by luggage," Sister Kopp told a *Time* reporter. "Marble houses are what destroyed the old orders."[15]

Other religious sisters became involved in the women's liberation movement and shunned any semblance of adherence to the rule of episcopal cloister. This position was upheld by Sr. Margaret Traxler, founder of the National Coalition of American Nuns, who said, "We hope to end domination by priests, no matter what their hierarchical status."[16] Similarly, Sisters Barbara Ferraro and Patricia Hussey of the Sisters of Notre Dame di Namur and twenty other members of the order signed an advertisement in support of abortion on demand. When the Vatican attempted to pressure the order into expelling the sisters, the order responded by threatening a strike against the church.[17]

RELIGIOUS LYCANTHROPY

The transformation of nuns and religious sisters into hippies, radical feminists, and social activists smacked of religious lycanthropy. Prior to Vatican II, religious sisters lived under monastic rules. They rose around dawn for prayers first, then Mass and Holy Communion. This was followed by breakfast in silence. Following breakfast, they performed their convent chores: cleaning, cooking, baking, gardening, sewing, etc. Upon completion of these chores, they were permitted to report to the site of their apostolic mission—for example, the classrooms of the Catholic schools or the wards of Catholic hospitals. After work, they returned to the convent for more work, prayers, a simple supper, and evening devotions. At all times, the sisters wore the habit of their order. Some, like the contemplative nuns, wore hair shirts underneath their habits for mortification. They never entered a rectory, or any place where they might be alone with a man. For this reason, they never traveled alone, not even in the company of their parents.[18]

By the 1950s, the first cracks began to appear in the organization of convent life. Under the demands of medical practices and the shortage of trained nurses, sisters in the nursing profession were permitted to adjust their horarium in order to fulfill their professional duties. The sisters who served beyond the convent bedtime were permitted to sleep beyond the five o'clock summons to prayer and were relieved of some of their daily chores. Other fissures occurred. In 1953, Sister Mary Emil Penet organized the Sisters Formation Conference of the National Catholic Education Association and by forceful argumentation obtained ecclesiastical permission for sisters engaged in the teaching profession (many with only high-school degrees) to depart from the convent routine to attend colleges and universities in order to improve the quality of Catholic education. By 1965, the religious sisters in America, by and large, were left to manage their own schedules.[19]

QUITTING THE HABIT

The rebellion by the religious sisters got underway in 1966, when the Sisters of Loretto abandoned their habits for modern dress.[20] In 1967, the Vatican's Congregation for the Religious issued a statement upholding the principle that American bishops and local ordinaries possess the authority to determine whether grave circumstances warranted the waiving of the wearing of religious garb. But when the bishops attempted to lay down the law, the sisters rebuked ecclesiastical authority by maintaining their obedience was not to the Holy See but rather (in the words of Sr. Mary Luke Tobin, the mother-general of the Sisters of Loretto) to "the needs of the people and to the community."[21]

Paul VI attempted to clamp down on the rebellious sisters by issuing *Evangelica Testificatio*, an apostolic exhortation, on June 29, 1971, in which he said, "While we recognize that certain situations can justify the abandonment of a religious type of dress, we cannot pass over in silence the fittingness that the dress of religious men and women should be, as the Council wishes, a sign of their consecration and that it should be in some way different from the forms that are clearly secular."[22] His words were wasted. The secessionist sisters refused to return to the convent, to abide by the canonical hours, or to don the distinctive dress of their order. Sister Anita Caspary, mother superior of the Immaculate Heart of Mary in Los Angeles, said that the church "stands to lose the whole community of religious sisters, if it stands in the way."[23]

But the community of religious sisters, by and large, was already lost. From 1965 to 1980, the number of religious sisters in America diminished from 179,954 to 126,517. By 2014, only 48,546 were left—of that number, the average age was 65.[24] Due, in part, to the loss of religious sisters and the rising cost of hiring replacement teachers, parochial school enrollments in the United States dropped from 6.6 million in 1966 to 2.9 million in 1986.[25] Empty parochial schools were becoming just as commonplace as empty churches.

A NEW SCHISM

Vatican II produced a cleft between traditional clerics, who believed that the changes cut into the heart of sacred doctrine, and progressives, who maintained that the process of *aggiornamento* fell short of meeting the demands of modernity. In France, Archbishop Marcel Lefebvre caused the first schism in the church since 1870 by forming the Society of Saint Pius X at Écône, Switzerland, and erecting a seminary to train priests in the Tridentine tradition. He refused to celebrate the new Mass as instituted by Paul VI, which he called a "bastard rite." He rejected the church's decision to conduct an ongoing dialogue with Protestants, Jews, and Muslims, stating that the decision lent "credibility" to other religions. And Lefebvre opposed Vatican II's endorsement of religious liberty, which he condemned as "misguided" since it exposed faithful Catholics to false religious teachings.[26]

Lefebvre soon attracted an enormous following. At a church that he established in Lille, France, Lefebvre celebrated the traditional Latin Mass before a flock that numbered six thousand. In 1975, Paul VI ordered the rebellious archbishop to disband his followers and to shut down the seminary he had established. Lefebvre refused, causing the pope to suspend the sacerdotal authority of the archbishop and three hundred priests he had ordained at his seminary.

In 1975, John Paul II tried to establish a truce with Lefebvre in 1978, by allowing him to resume his priestly functions and, eventually, even by offering to name a traditionalist bishop whom Lefebvre would nominate. The archbishop rejected the compromise, which would not have obliterated the changes that he so disdained, and opted, instead, to ordain his own bishops. On July 2, 1988, John Paul II issued *Ecclesia Dei adflicta*, an apostolic letter, in which he proclaimed that Lefebvre and his followers had incurred "the grave penalty of excommunication envisaged by canon law."[27]

THREE BETRAYALS

To his dying day, Lefebvre insisted that he had not betrayed the church but that the church had betrayed him. At a conference of the Society of Saint Pius X, which was held on Long Island, New York, on November 5, 1983, he listed the betrayals of Holy Mother Church as follows:

> Let me sum up the whole situation as it took place at the Council . . . by saying that there were, in fact, three betrayals of the Church. . . .
>
> The first betrayal was the betrayal with the Freemason, the second with the Protestants, and the. third was the betrayal with the Communists.
>
> There was an understanding before the Council and during the Council through men commissioned by the Church who were the instruments of these betrayals, namely, the Secretariat for the Unity of Christians, which was specially created for that, directed by Cardinal Bea with, as Vice President, Msgr. de Smedt, Bishop of Bruges, and with, as Secretary, Msgr. Willebrands, who became Cardinal of Holland. These were the personalities who were the instruments of betrayal. There were direct contacts precisely between Cardinal Bea and the Masonic Lodge here in New York and in Washington . . . and with the lodges of the whole world.
>
> Why did these contacts take place? Why did Cardinal Bea come in the name of the Vatican, in the name of Rome, to meet these Freemasons? In order that we would accept the "rights of man" at the Council. How could we accept them? By accepting Religious Liberty, which is one of the "rights of man." Hence, to accept Religious Liberty was in principle to accept the "rights of man" within the Church. . . .

The second betrayal was the betrayal with the Protestants. It is Msgr. Willebrands who was entrusted . . . with the fostering of relations with the Ecumenical Council of Churches in Geneva. He went to Geneva to make peace with the Protestants, and the Protestants said to him, we can make peace with you, we can all unite and work together, but you must remove everything in the liturgy of the Church and in the concept of the Church which does not agree with Protestant principles. Hence, the whole liturgy and the whole structure of the Church was to be modified and there was to be a new Canon Law to establish this new structure of the Church and to put it into practice, a democratic structure. . . .

The third betrayal was through Msgr. Willebrands also, and Cardinal Bea, through their meeting with delegates of Moscow at Constantinople and also in Greece, with representatives of the Orthodox Church, the Patriarch Pimen of the Orthodox Church delegated by Moscow. What had to be done in order to please the Communists? The Communists required that there should be no condemnation of Communism at the Council, firstly; secondly, that all the bishops opposed to the Communist regime should be dismissed and replaced by collaborating bishops.[28]

THE EMPTY CHAIR

The sedevacantist movement arose in conjunction with the Lefebvre schism. Deriving its name from the Latin phrase *sede vacante*, meaning "with the chair [of St. Peter] vacant," the movement held that neither John XXIII nor Paul VI were legitimate popes since they had sanctioned the changes of Vatican II, which contradicted the essential teachings of the church, including the traditional insistence that Roman Catholicism represented the one true religion, outside of which there was no salvation. By issuing the heretical decrees, they became antipopes in accordance with the fourth part of canon 188 of the 1917 Code of Canon Law, which held that any cleric who publicly defects from the tenets of the Catholic faith automatically forfeits his ecclesiastical position.[29]

This position was set forth by Father Joaquin Saenz y Arriaga, a Jesuit theologian from Mexico, in his work *The New Montinian Church* (1971).[30] His claims were echoed by Fr. Michel-Louis Guérard des Lauriers, a Dominican professor of philosophy at the Pontifical Lateran University in Rome.[31] Their arguments gave rise to a movement that spread throughout Europe, attracting the support of several students and priests from Lefebvre's Society of Saint Pius X, including Fr. Daniel Sanborn, Fr. Daniel Dolan, and Fr. Anthony Cekada.[32] In the United States, the movement crystallized into the Religious Congregation of Mary Immaculate Queen, the Mater Boni Consilii Institute, and other sedevacantist groups, which established churches in Alabama, Arizona, Arkansas, California, Colorado, Florida, Illinois, Louisiana, Michigan, Minnesota, New Mexico, New York, North Dakota, Ohio, Texas, Virginia, Washington, and Wisconsin. In addition, a sedevacantist seminary was set up on fifty acres of land in Brooksville, Florida. The total membership of the movement remains anyone's guess, ranging from tens of thousands to hundreds of thousands.[33] One of the most prominent supporters of the movement was Academy Award winning actor Mel Gibson, who built a sedevacantist church—Church of the Holy Family—in Agoura Hills, California.[34]

PAPAL PROLIFERATION

The movement produced bizarre developments. Maintaining that the presiding pontiff at the Vatican was a heretic, the sedevacantist groups elected not only their own bishops and archbishops but also their own popes, each prancing about in full papal regalia and each making solemn papal pronouncements. One "pretender" was a French priest, Michel-Auguste-Marie Collin, who claimed that he had been called by heaven to become "Pope Clemens XV" during Vatican II, in 1963. Collin established an alternative "Vatican" in Clémery, Lorraine, where he also founded the Church of the Magnificat. One of Collin's followers, Fr. Gaston Tremblay, a priest from Quebec, ceased to recognize the French claimant's authority in 1968 and proclaimed himself "Pope Gregory XVII." His movement was called the Apostles of Infinite Love.[35]

Fr. Clemente Domínguez y Gómez of Palmar de Troya, Spain, also laid claim to the empty chair of St. Peter. In 1976, according to Domínguez, Jesus Christ appeared to him in a vision and crowned him as the rightful supreme pontiff. Assuming the name "Pope Gregory XVII" (the same name as Tremblay, his rival antipope in Quebec), Domínguez established the "Catholic, Apostolic and Palmarian Church" (named after Palmar de Troya) and attracted more than a thousand followers in Spain, and several hundreds more internationally.

Sedevacantist popes also popped up in the United States, including Lucian Pulvermacher, an Oblate priest, who became mystically consecrated as Pope Emmanuel I in Springdale, Washington, and David Allen Bawden, a former seminarian at the Society of Saint Pius X, who became elected at a conclave consisting of six laypeople, including his parents, in Delia, Kansas.[36]

THE DUTCH REVOLT

In 1969, the threat of another schism erupted in Noordwijkerhout with a gathering of the Dutch Pastoral Council, an organization representing the Catholic bishops and priests in the Netherlands. By a nine–to-one majority, the council voted for the abolition of priestly celibacy, the ordination of women, the rights of bishops to determine the validity of any papal decision or decree.

Paul VI penned a letter in which he expressed his "well founded reservations about the criteria for representation of Dutch Catholics at the plenary council." He then expressed his dismay that the teachings of Vatican II were "very rarely cited" by the prelates at the gathering that that their proposals "do not seem to harmonize at all with conciliar and papal acts."[37] At a time when the Dutch clerics were openly denying the sacramental priesthood and the pope's authority as St. Peter's successor, Paul VI could only muster enough courage to conclude his letter by raising this inconsequential question: "But before the danger of deviations that could be seriously damaging to the faith of the Catholic people of the Netherlands, the awareness of our responsibility as Pastor of the Universal Church obliges us to ask you frankly: what do you think that We may do to help you to strengthen your authority to enable you to better overcome the present difficulties of the Church in Holland?"[38]

Paul VI's handling of the crisis produced disastrous consequences. In 1960, Dutch Catholics stood as the most devout members of the Roman Church in Western Europe. Seventy-five percent attended Mass every Sunday and on every holy day of obligation. The Dutch bishops ordained 318 new priests every year. But the bottom fell out after the close of Vatican II. By 1977, Mass attendance in the Netherlands dropped to 30 percent, 2,000 priests defected or were laicized, and 4,300 religious sisters and brothers abandoned their religious lives.[39]

A BEWILDERED AGNOSTIC

In the midst of the madness, Paul VI began to act like a bewildered agnostic. Before a General Audience on December 6, 1972, he asked, "Does God exist? Who is God? And what knowledge can man have of him? What relationship must each of us have with him?"[40] To answer each of these questions would lead us to endless and complex discussions. Any Catholic school child with a *Baltimore Catechism* knew that these questions did not lead to endless discussions and complex discussions. Does God exist? Yes: "We can know by our natural reason that there is a God, for it tells us that the world we see about us could have been made only by a self-existing Being, all-wise and almighty."[41] Who is God? "God is the Supreme Being, infinitely perfect, who made all things and keeps them in existence."[42] What knowledge can man have of him? "We learn to know God from Jesus Christ, the Son of God, who teaches us through the Catholic Church."[43] What relationship must each of us have with him? "We must know Him, love Him, and serve Him in accordance with the teachings of the holy Catholic Church."[44] Prior to Vatican II, a Catholic unable to provide answers to these questions would have been deemed unfit for confirmation.

THE WORSHIP OF MAN

Before a General Audience on June 27, 1973, Paul VI claimed that human liberation does not come from the teachings of Christ or the tenets of the church but rather from human evolution. He said, "Everything must change, everything must progress. Evolution seems to be the law that brings liberation. There must be a great deal that is true and good in this mentality."[45]

On several occasions, the Holy Father sounded more like a proponent of secular humanism than the protector of the Catholic faith. Addressing the last general meeting of Vatican II, he said, "The attention of our Council has been absorbed by the discovery of human needs. But we call upon those who term themselves modern humanists, and who have renounced the transcendent value of the highest realities, to give the Council credit at least for one quality and to recognize our own new type of humanism: We, too, in fact, We more than any others, honor mankind; we have the cult of man."[46] In 1971, he issued this press statement to commemorate the success of the Apollo mission: "Man is the king of the earth and the prince of heaven. Honor to man, honor to thought, to science, to technology, to labor, to the synthesis of scientific and organizational activity of man."[47]

BETWEEN BRAHMA AND BUDDHA

All the while, Paul VI, the real pope, persisted in promoting religious indifferentism. "In Hinduism," Paul VI proclaimed in his decree *Nostra aetate* (October 28, 1965), "men contemplate the divine mystery and express it through an inexhaustible abundance of myths and through searching philosophical inquiry. They seek freedom from the anguish of our human condition either through ascetical practices or profound meditation or a flight to God with love and trust."[48] On August 22, 1969, he continued his praise of the Hindus by stating that Mahatma Gandhi was "ever conscious of God's presence."[49] Brahma, Vishnu, and Shiva, it appeared, had come to replace the holy Trinity.

"Buddhism," Paul VI maintained in *Nostra aetate*, "teaches a way by which men, in a devout and confident spirit, may be able either to acquire the state of perfect liberation, or attain, by their own efforts or through higher help, supreme illumination."[50] On September 30, 1973, he greeted the Dalai Lama, by saying, "We are happy to welcome you today. You come from Asia, the cradle of ancient religions and human traditions which are rightly held in deep veneration."[51] But Asia was the cradle of neither Judaism nor Christianity, and the faith that the pontiff now held "in deep veneration" denied the "revealed truths" of the Old and New Testaments and Catholic tradition.

Such statements of religious indifferentism caused Catholics to question the purpose of the Society of the Propagation of the Faith and the need for non-Catholics to convert from their native religions, and the purpose of Catholic missionaries. It was little surprise that Paul VI's statements regarding other religions produced a sharp decline in US Catholic missionaries, their number dwindling from 9,655 in 1968 to 4,164 in 1996.[52]

THE SMOKE OF SATAN

While the Roman pontiff was headed on his merry way toward a one-world religion, a theory emerged that the real Paul VI had been kidnapped

or killed after his coronation and replaced by an evil double. Such theorists noted changes in the pope's appearance: a rounding of his face, a change in eye color, an extension of the upper half of his ears, and the disappearance of a prominent facial birthmark.[53]

Was the cleric sitting on the throne of St. Peter an imposter? Was a diabolical double intent upon the subversion of *sacra doctrina* to secular humanism? What accounted for the sudden transformation of the pope's appearance? No answers were forthcoming. But it appeared to some that the devil had made his appearance within the Holy See. On June 29, 1972, Paul VI gave credence to this belief, by saying, "From some fissure, the smoke of Satan has entered the temple of God."[54]

The smell of sulfur may have arisen from Paul VI's ongoing support of the clandestine agenda of the CIA. Proof of this support came with the pope's appointment of Licio Gelli as *Equitem Ordinis Sancti Silvestri Papae* (a Knight in the Order of St. Sylvester), one of Catholicism's highest awards.[55] The knighting was extraordinary since Gelli was an avowed atheist, a CIA operative, a thirty-third degree Mason, and the Grand Master of P-2, who had never performed an act of service to Holy Mother Church.[56] Nevertheless, the ceremony was of profound significance since it confirmed the close ties between the Vatican and P-2, as well as the Holy See's reliance on Gelli and the CIA to maintain its privileged place of power and independence within Italy.

Waves of terror were about to be unleashed throughout Latin America and Western Europe.

The church was set to become a criminal organization.

Chapter Nine

A CRIMINAL ORGANIZATION

At the Vatican Bank [IOR], [Luigi] Mennini was one of the few who knew about [Archbishop Paul] Marcinkus's decision to join Cisalpine's board. He did not think it wise for the IOR to become entwined in offshore deals. But Marcinkus dismissed him as well intentioned but old fashioned. The IOR had to adapt to new and more sophisticated times. "You can't run the Church on Hail Marys," he said.

—Gerald Posner, *God's Bankers*, 2015

According to Malachi Martin in *Rich Church, Poor Church*, the Vatican became a criminal organization in 1969, thanks to Paul VI's association with Michele Sindona, who became the Vatican's chief financial officer, and Licio Gelli, who initiated the "years of lead."[1] But the Holy See's criminality dates back to the post–World War II era, when Pius XII allowed the CIA to make use of the Vatican Bank as a laundry for its black funds. To aid in the process of washing the billions from the heroin trade, the US intelligence agency worked in tandem with Henry Manfredi, who established the Federal Bureau of Narcotics' (FBN's) first overseas operation in Rome in 1951. Manfredi had established close ties to Monsignor Giovanni Battista Montini, then the Vatican undersecretary of state and later Pope Paul VI.[2] Through Montini, the FBN arranged to divert the flow of cash, at first through the Merrill Lynch Brokerage House and, eventually, through a host of parochial banks in Italy, before it finally arrived at the IOR.[3]

The transactions were supervised by Massimo Spada, a senior official at the Vatican Bank. Spada, a Knight of Malta, chaired or served on the boards of the astonishing array of companies owned by the Holy See, including Società Italiana per il Gas (Italy's central source of natural gas), Riunione Adriatica di Sicurtà insurance company, Istituto Bancario Italiano, Credito Commerciale di Cremona, Banca Privata Finanziaria, Banca Cattolica del Veneto, and FINSIDER, a conglomerate that owned the Italia shipping line, Alitalia airlines, Alfa Romero, and Italy's telephone system, along with producing 90 percent of Italy's steel.[4] For assistance in this task of managing the billions, Spada turned to tax attorney Michele Sindona.[5]

ENTER SINDONA

Sindona was a respected member of the Luciano/Don Calò crime family and one of the Sicilian Mafia's leading financial advisors. Between 1952 and 1955, he spent a considerable amount of time in New York, acting as Luciano's emissary to Vito Genovese.[6] By 1955, he had also become a CIA operative, providing a steady flow of black funds to leading Catholic dignitaries, including Giovanni Montini, who had been appointed archbishop of Milan.[7] Montini, in turn, introduced the ambitious young lawyer to Massimo Spada. Sindona now formed an integral part of the nexus between the CIA, the mob, and the Vatican.

Sindona used mob money and CIA funds to create Fasco AG, a Liechtenstein holding company, which became the cornerstone of his financial empire.[8] Through Fasco, he purchased his first bank—the Banca Privata Finanziaria (BPF) in Milan. The BPF served as a principal means of transferring drug money from the IOR for the purpose of Gladio and other CIA covert operations. William Harvey, the new CIA station chief in Rome, arranged for the financial firms of Sir Jocelyn Hambro, the owner of the Hambros Bank, and David M. Kennedy, chairman of the Continental Illinois Bank in Chicago and later the US treasury secretary under Nixon, to become minority shareholders, with each firm purchasing 22 percent of the bank's stock.[9]

SINDONA'S BANKS

Sindona also acquired the Banca di Messina, which gave the Gambino, Inzerillo, and Spatola crime clan unlimited access to a financial firm in Sicily. The Sicilian financier went on to buy a third bank—the Banque de Financement (Finabank)—in Geneva, which was largely owned by the IOR and, like the BPF, used as a conduit for the flight of money from Italy.[10] After Sindona's purchase of majority interest, the Vatican retained a 29 percent share based on its awareness of the benefits of owning a Swiss bank for the transfer of laundered funds.[11] Hambro and Kennedy, on behalf of their financial firms, gobbled up the remaining shares.

A TERRIBLE PROBLEM

In the spring of that year, Sindona was summoned late at night to the pope's private study on the fourth floor of the Apostolic Palace. The short, slender, and well-spoken Mafia don wore a meticulously tailored "navy blue suit, a white shirt with gold cuff links, and a gray silk tie. He appeared fresh and confident."[12] The pope was seated in one of his satin-covered chairs. His body was bent forward, and he appeared tired and ill. The Holy Father "did not offer his ring for Michele to kiss; instead, they greeted each other with the handshake of old friends."

"There is a terrible problem," Paul VI told Sindona. He was referring to the collapse of the "first republic" and the long reign of the Christian Democratic Party. The new government had moved to discard the Lateran Treaty of 1929 and the tax-exempt status of Catholic holdings throughout the country. The measure spelled financial destitution for the church and an annual tax bill in excess of $250 million. Even worse, the measure could prompt other countries to follow suit, until the Holy Mother Church became stripped naked of her vast wealth. "No matter," the pope said, "is of greater importance."[13]

Sindona replied by proposing a strategy to move Vatican resources out of Italy into the United States and the tax-free Eurodollar market, through a network of offshore financial firms.[14] This move would not only cloak the Vatican's holdings in *omerta*—a quality the Holy See valued as much as the Mafia—but it would also demonstrate to other countries that the Roman Catholic Church was financially powerful and that any interference with the Vatican's finances could produce dire consequences for national economies.[15]

THE PAPAL COMMISSION

Upon hearing the proposal, Pope Paul handed Sindona an agreement he already had prepared. The agreement was even more than the Mafiosi could hope for or dare to suggest. It named Sindona *Mercator Senesis Romanam Curiam*, "the leading banker of the Roman Curia," and granted him complete control over the Vatican's foreign and domestic investment policy.[16] In accordance with the agreement, Sindona would work closely with Bishop Paul Marcinkus, who now became secretary of the IOR, and Cardinal Sergio Guerri, governor of Vatican City. However, both clerics remained merely his advisors. The agreement placed the Vatican's billions at Sindona's disposal.

When the Mafia chieftain turned to the last page, he looked up at the Holy Father and smiled. The pope already had signed and sealed the document. It was the highest display of trust anyone could hope to receive from the vicar of Christ.[17] Such trust, of course, was not blind. It was based on the pope's awareness that Sindona remained in almost sole control of the billions in black funds that were flowing into the Holy See.

THE VATICAN'S ASSETS

Before Sindona took control of its assets, the Vatican held major interests in the Rothschild Bank in France; the Chase Manhattan Bank, with its fifty-seven branches in forty-four countries; the Credit Suisse in Zurich and also in London; the Morgan Bank; the Banker Trust; General Motors; General Electric; Shell Oil; Gulf Oil; and Bethlehem Steel. Vatican officials sat on the board of FINSIDER, which, with its capital of 195 million lire spread through twenty-four companies, produced 90 percent of Italian steel. The Holy See controlled two shipping lines and the Alfa Romeo car manufacturing company. What's more, controlling shares of the Italian luxury hotels, including the Rome Hilton, were in the Vatican portfolio.[18]

But the Vatican's central holding was Società Generale Immobiliare, a construction company that had produced a future in earnings for the Holy See since it had been acquired in 1934. In 1969 Immobiliare shares were selling for 350 lire. Sindona purchased 143 million shares from the Vatican at double the market price—700 lire per share—with money that had been illegally converted to his account from deposits at Banca Privata Finanziaria.[19] Sindona was willing to pay double the market value since the money, after all, would be spent, in part, to bring about significant changes in the political order.

In the same way, Sindona purchased the Vatican's majority ownership of Condotte d'Acqua, Italy's water company, and Ceramica Pozzi, a chemical and porcelain company. To spare the pope any embarrassment, he also bought Serono, the Vatican's pharmaceutical company that produced contraceptive pills.[20]

SUB SILENTIO

These transactions were conducted with extreme secrecy to escape the attention of Italy's tax collectors. The shares of Immobiliare were transferred first to Paribas Transcontinental of Luxembourg, a subsidiary of the Banque de Paris et des Pay Bas, and next to Fasco AG in Liechtenstein. Despite Sindona's diversionary tactics, the press got word of the sales of the Vatican companies and pressured the Holy See for a response. Through a spokesman, Pope Paul said, "Our policy is to avoid maintaining control of our companies as in the past. We want to improve investment performance, balanced, of course, against what must be a fundamentally conservative investment philosophy. It wouldn't do for the Church to lose its principal in speculation."[21] When Sindona was asked about the sales, he refused to comment, saying that he was obliged to maintain the confidentiality of his client, Holy Mother Church.[22]

LIQUIDATION SALE

The pope's banker proceeded to liquidate the church's remaining holdings in Italian companies to buyers, including Hambros Bank, Continental Illinois, and the American conglomerate Gulf & Western.[23] He invested much of the Vatican's revenue from these sales in American companies, such as Chase Manhattan, Standard Oil, Westinghouse, Colgate, Proctor and Gamble, and Dan River.[24] Several of these firms remained under the control of David Rockefeller.[25]

The liquidation of the Vatican's holdings, as engineered by Sindona, produced a disastrous effect on the Italian economy. The lira dropped precipitously in value. Unemployment rose. The cost of living increased. The savings of millions of families were wiped out almost overnight.[26]

LODGE BROTHERS

Sindona became a member of Propaganda Due in 1964. Licio Gelli officiated at the initiation ceremony, which took place in a Tuscan villa.[27] At the lodge, Sindona developed a close associate with Roberto Calvi, a P-2 member who served as the assistant manager of Banco Ambrosiano, a wealthy, parochial bank in Milan. Few banks were more prestigious. Established in 1894, Banco Ambrosiano operated "to provide credit without offending the ethical principles of Christian teaching," an explicit rebuke to lay lending institutions.[28] To ward off the interests of outsiders, the statutes of the bank required shareholders to produce a voucher of their good character from their parish priest. In addition, no shareholder could own more than 5 percent of the bank's wealth.[29]

Sindona realized that the "priests' bank" would be an ideal complement to his growing financial empire. Nothing he controlled could match Ambrosiano for resources, or its standing in Milan. Best of all, it had no dominant shareholder, so that those who ran it had an unfettered hand. Sindona and his new friend quickly came up with a plan to gain control of Ambrosiano through the creation of a series of shell companies in Panama, the Bahamas, and Luxembourg. The scheme would require the participation of Archbishop Paul Marcinkus, since the Catholic nature of the companies would have to be verified. The archbishop, of course, was most pleased to cooperate and arranged for Calvi to be appointed as Ambrosiano's new *direttore generale*, or general manager.[30]

THE RAT LINES

During the Allied occupation of Italy, Licio Gelli volunteered to serve with the Counter Intelligence Corps of the Fifth Army.[31] In this capacity, he worked in close contact with the US Office of Strategic Services (the precursor of the CIA) in the establishment of the Office of Reserved Affairs. This shadowy agency, located on Rome's Via Sicilia, was manned by a secret force of the Carabinieri under the command of Federico Umberto D'Amato, Mussolini's former chief of police. Its sole purpose was to exercise control "over the most delicate activities of the state."[32]

Through the Office of Reserved Affairs, Gelli gained entry to the Vatican, where he united with Fr. Krunoslav Draganovic, a Franciscan monk and member of the Ustashi (a Croatian Revolutionary Movement) high command, to set up the "rat lines" by which war criminals, including members of the Nazi high command, could escape to South American and other havens of refuge.[33] Many of the escapees were issued Vatican passports and traveled to their new hiding places in clerical garb.[34] A memo from an intelligence official working at the US State Department in 1947 explained that "the Vatican justifies its participation by its desire to infiltrate not only European countries, but Latin American countries as well,

[with] people of all political beliefs as long as they are anti-Communists and pro-Catholic Church."[35]

The operation of the rat lines brought Gelli in close contact with the future Pope Paul VI. At the close of the war, Monsignor Montini had been placed in charge of Caritas Italiana, a Vatican charity that provided "protection" for German soldiers and Nazi sympathizers. The protection came to include the issuance of refugee travel documents (replete with new identities) to such illustrious figures as Hans Hefelman, one of the principal figure in the Third Reich's euthanasia program, and Martin Bormann, Hitler's personal secretary.[36]

VATICAN GOLD

In addition to the rat lines, Gelli played a key role in the smuggling of over $80 million in gold and silver bars from the Ustashi treasury in Croatia to the Vatican Bank. Holy Mother Church was very pleased to receive the deposit for "safe-keeping," even though Gelli squirreled away 150 gold bars for himself.[37]

Gelli, upon making the deposit, became a frequent guest at dinner parties hosted for Vatican dignitaries at palatial home of Count Umberto Ortolani, the former head of military intelligence in Italy and Rome's most powerful layman. At these affairs, he befriended Cardinal Giacomo Lercaro, who became one of the four "moderators" of the Second Vatican Council; Monsignor Agostino Casaroli, who would become the Vatican's secretary of state under John Paul II; Giulio Andreotti, the cofounder of the Catholic Democratic Party; Massimo Spada, the lay *delegato* of the IOR; and Michele Sindona.[38]

P-2'S EXPANSION

By 1969, Gelli emerged as P-2's new Worshipful Master and became known by the code name Filippo.[39] The lodge now received massive infusions of cash—estimated at $10 million per month—from the CIA's black funds. This money was used to purchase the weaponry and materiel necessary to mount terrorist attacks throughout Italy, Greece, Turkey, and South America.[40] The subversive Masonic lodge, at this time, could boast of such members as Italy's armed forces commander Giovanni Torrisi; secret service chiefs Giuseppe Santovito and Giulio Grassini; Orazio Giannini, the head of Italy's financial police; Italy's chief surgeon Dr. Joseph Micheli; General Vito Miceli of the Italian Intelligence Agency; General Raffaele Giudice of the Financial Guard; Supreme Council Magistrate Ugo Zilletti; and, of course, Sindona, who became Gelli's principal advisor. In addition, the membership list contained the names of leading cabinet ministers, thirty generals, eight admirals, newspaper editors, television executives, and top business executives.[41]

Gelli took special pride in the induction of Carmelo Spagnuolo to his secret society. Spagnuolo was the chief public defender in Milan, and later the president of the Italian Supreme Court. This ensured that P-2, despite its acts of terrorism, would have justice on its side.[42]

THE GORILLA

The number of Catholic dignitaries within the lodge (see chapter three) continued to swell and now included Cardinal Francesco Marchisano (prelate of honor of the pope), Cardinal Marcello Morgante, Cardinal Roberto Tucci (director general of Vatican Radio), and Cardinal Jean-Marie Villot (Paul VI's secretary of state).[43] Another new member of the secret fraternity was an up-and-coming cleric from Cicero, Illinois, the hometown of Al Capone. Known as "the Gorilla," Paul Marcinkus stood at six feet four inches in his stocking feet. He was a scratch golfer, a gifted street fighter, and the lover of good bourbon, fine cigars, and young women. Within the effete and rarified environment of the Vatican, Marcinkus became singled out to serve as Paul VI's protector. On one occasion, the Gorilla picked up the tiny pope and carried him through an overly enthusiastic crowd that threatened to trample him to death.[44] On another, he saved the Holy Father from an attack by a knife-wielding Bolivian artist by breaking the would-be assailant's arm.[45]

Michele Sindona became instrumental in gaining the Gorilla his position as head of the Vatican Bank. This position made Marcinkus a bishop, a *prelate d'onore*, and he became assigned as a special assistant to Cardinal Alberto di Jorio. The gruff cleric from Cicero was now responsible for more than ten thousand accounts belonging to religious orders and to private Catholic dignitaries, including the pope.[46] In defiance of Canon 2335, Marcinkus had submitted to initiation into the Masonic lodge on July 2, 1963. His Masonic code name was "Marpa."[47]

The unholy trinity of Sindona, Calvi, and Marcinkus caused the Roman Church to become a leading player in the emerging cocaine trade, by offering the Latin American drug cartels money laundering services in exchange for stiff processing fees. To initiate this process, they established a chain of shell companies in Panama and the Bahamas, which transferred deposits from the cartels to Banco Ambrosiano and the Italian banks under Sindona's control. From these private and parochial banks, the money flowed to the IOR and from the IOR to financial firms in Switzerland, Luxembourg, and Liechtenstein. The first shell company established by the Vatican for this purpose was the Cisalpine Overseas Bank in the Bahamas.

Cisalpine had been set up in 1970 through Banco Ambrosiano Holding, a Luxembourg company under the Holy See's control, and immediately began to receive regular deposits of millions in cash from Pablo Escobar and other Latin American drug chieftains. The firm functioned solely as a laundry for black money. On any given day, throughout the 1970s, the shell company held $75 million in cash deposits. Cisalpine's immediate success caused Bishop Marcinkus to proclaim that the shell company represented a "perfect crime."[48]

TIME FOR ACTION

Within ten years of Gelli's emergence as Worshipful Master, P-2 had branches in Argentina, Venezuela, Paraguay, Bolivia, France, Portugal, Nicaragua, West Germany, and England. Within the United States, its members and associates included not only leading figures from the Gambino, Genovese, and Lucchese crime families, but also such notable political figures as General Alexander Haig, President Nixon's chief of staff, and Henry Kissinger, President Nixon's secretary of state.[49]

With Gelli in place as P-2's Worshipful Master, the Vatican could take further action against the left-wing Italian government that threatened its financial holdings. It could sanction the CIA to unleash the full force of Operation Gladio throughout Italy and the Western World. Paul VI realized the need for such action. In the national election, Italy's Communist Party (PCI) gained 27 percent of the overall vote. To make matters worse, the country established regional elections that enabled the Communists to gain control of Bologna, Florence, Tuscany, Umbria, Liguria, the Marches, Piedmont, and Emilia-Romagna and to form a coalition government with the Christian Democrats and the Italian Socialists in Rome, Milan, and Turin.[50]

To protect its financial assets and political power, Holy Mother Church was now willing not only to embark in acts of fraud and grand theft with Sindona and the Sicilian Mafia but also to endorse the "years of lead" (*anni di piombo*) to devour her own children.

Chapter Ten

YEARS OF LEAD

The official figures say that alone in the period between January 1, 1969, and December 31, 1987, there have been in Italy 14,591 acts of violence with a political motivation. It is maybe worth remembering that these "acts" have left behind 491 dead and 1,181 injured and maimed—figures of a war without parallel in any other European country.
—Giovanni Pellegrino, president of Italy's parliamentary commission investigating Gladio, 1995

To create a "strategy of tension," Operation Gladio launched a series of false-flag attacks that could be blamed on left-wing and Communist agitators, so that the Italian people would come to view Communism as a threat to their lives and well-being. A primary purpose of the attacks was to fortify the Christian Democratic Party (CDP) so that it could remain a central bastion against the spread of Communism throughout Western Europe and Latin America.

The CDP was an outgrowth of the Italian People's Party (Partito Popolare Italiano, PPI), which had been created in 1919 by Fr. Luigi Sturzo, with the imprimatur of Pope Benedict XV, to oppose the rise of the Italian Socialist Party. The social teachings of the church as contained in *Rerum novarum* represented the platform of the party, and all Catholics were called upon by their parish priests to vote for PPI candidates in regional and national elections.[1] The party was disbanded in 1924 so that the Holy See could forge an alliance with Mussolini and the National Fascist Party—an alliance that resulted in the Lateran Treaty of 1929. In 1942, it was reactivated by Alcide De Gasperi, an ardent Catholic whom Pius XII shielded from Mussolini's fascist army during the war. The party received enormous funding from the CIA and the Truman administration in 1947 so that it could ward off the rise of the Italian Communist Party (Partito Comunista Italiano—PCI).[2]

Throughout the subsequent decades, the CDP continued to receive enormous infusions of cash from the CIA and remained the leading polit-

ical party in Italy. The leaders of the CDP (including Italian prime ministers De Gasperi, Amintore Fanfani, Giovanni Leone, Arnaldo Forlani,
Aldo Moro, and Giulio Andreotti) remained devout Catholics who sought
the Holy Father's approval before initiating governmental policy and who
governed the country in line with the social doctrine of the church.[3]

REDS RESURGENT

All was well and good until 1968, when a series of developments threatened the ruling status of the Christian Democrats. The first was the rise of
the Community Party in the 1968 election. The PCI garnered 26.9 percent
of the vote, thereby becoming the country's second-largest political party.
The CDP remained stable at 39 percent, while the newly created United
Socialist Party amassed less than 15 percent.[4]

A second development was the resurgence of the Italian Radical Party
(Partito Radicale), which, after proclaiming 1967 as an anticlerical year,
mounted a campaign for the dissolution of the Lateran Treaty and the
elimination of the church's special status in Italy.[5] In 1970, the strength of
the Radicals became apparent when Italy's legislators voted to repeal the
government's prohibition against divorce.[6]

Overshadowing these developments was the CIA's concern over the
NATO bases in Italy, including the Mediterranean Naval Command in
Naples. With a total of ten thousand military personnel in place throughout
the country, the US government remained paranoid that the emergence of
the PCI as Italy's dominant party would mark the end of the US presence
in a country of enormous strategic importance.[7]

The false-flag attacks began in 1969 at the initiative of Henry Kissinger,
President Nixon's national security advisor, who issued orders to Licio
Gelli through his deputy, General Alexander Haig. The financial spigots
were opened without concern of leakage. In addition to the millions being
channeled to P-2 by CIA officials, millions more were funneled to Sindona
for the implementation of the strategy through US ambassador Graham
Martin. In 1970 alone, Sindona received more than $10 million from the
ambassador.[8] P-2 instantly morphed into a deep state that was governed
not only by Italy's leading military and political figures but also by principal Catholic dignitaries, including the Vatican's secretary of state. These
dignitaries, like the political leaders of Christian Democracy, remained in
constant contact with Paul VI.

THE FIRST ATTACKS

The first attack occurred on December 12, 1969, when a bomb exploded in the crowded lobby of the Banca Nazionale dell'Agricoltura in Milan's Piazza Fontana. Seventeen people were killed and eighty-eight injured. The victims, for the most part, were farmers who had deposited their meager earnings in the bank. Within an hour, three bombs exploded in Rome: one in a pedestrian underpass, which injured fourteen people, and two on Victor Emmanuel's monument, which houses Italy's Unknown Soldier.[9] The attacks were attributed to left-wing agitators, including Giuseppe Pinelli, an anarchist railway worker.[10] There were 398 additional attacks throughout the year.[11]

On May 31, 1972, a car bomb exploded in a forest near the Italian village of Peteano. The explosion gravely wounded one and killed three members of the Carabinieri, Italy's paramilitary police force. Two days later, another anonymous call implicated the Red Brigades, the far-left Communist group that had engaged in assassinations and kidnappings. Two hundred Communists with an affiliation to the group were rounded up and held in custody.[12] Throughout 1972, 595 terror incidents were reported throughout the country. The increase in attacks reflected the fact that the PCI's electoral support had reached 27.2 percent.[13]

On May 28, 1974, a bomb was set off within a garbage container that had been placed in the midst of Piazza della Loggia in Brescia. The blast killed eight people and wounded one hundred more. Following the attack, a series of anonymous callers to the police and the press attempted to implicate Lotta Continua ("Continuous Struggle"), a militant Communist organization, for the incident. Members of the group were rounded up and placed in custody, only to be acquitted due to lack of evidence.[14] On August 4, 1974, another major terrorist incident occurred when a bomb was detonated on the Italicus Rome-Munich express, as the train pulled out of a tunnel near the village of San Benedetto Val di Sambro. Twelve people were killed and 105 injured. Both attacks represented reactions to the May 12 vote, which abolished Italy's arcane divorce laws. The outcome represented a sharp rebuke to the Vatican and the Christian Democratic Party.[15]

The incidents continued to escalate as the PCI continued to amass more and more political support. In 1976, the Communist managed to gain 34.4 percent of the vote, thereby giving rise to 1,353 attacks. The peak period for terrorist activity came in the following three years: 1,926 attacks in 1977, 2,379 in 1978, and 2,513 in 1979.[16]

THE MORO MURDER

On March 16, 1978, Aldo Moro, Italy's prime minister was kidnapped while on his way to parliament for the opening of debate on the newly formed government of national unity—a coalition of Communists, Socialists, and Christian Democrats. All five of his bodyguards were mowed down by machine-gun bullets.[17] Moro had initiated plans to form a political coalition with the PCI policy that had been decried by fellow Christian Democrats, including Giulio Andreotti. But no one had been more outraged at the Italian prime minister's attempt at rapprochement than US secretary of state Henry Kissinger. In 1974, when Moro paid a visit to the United States, Kissinger warned him, "You must abandon your policy of bringing all the political forces in your country into direct collaboration, or you will pay dearly for it."[18] As soon as the crime occurred, the military secret service placed the blame on the Red Brigades, a Communist terror organization, and launched an enormous crackdown on all left-wing organizations.[19] On May 9, 1978, Moro's body, riddled with bullets, was found in the trunk of a red Renault that was parked equidistant between the offices of the PCI and the CDP in the heart of Rome.[20]

THE CATHOLIC CONNECTION

The fact that the Red Brigades had been infiltrated by the CIA and the Italian secret services remains no longer contested. The purpose of the strategy of tension was to encourage violence from the radical left in order to convince the Italian people of the need to repress the rise of Communism. The Brigades were a perfect foil. With unflinching radicalism, they considered the Italian Communist Party (PCI) too moderate and Moro's opening too compromising. Thanks to the infiltration, which occurred in 1973, the Brigades began to work closely with the Hyperion Language School in Paris, with most brigadiers unaware that it had been founded by the CIA. Hyperion opened an office in Italy shortly before the kidnapping and closed it a few months later. An Italian police report singles out Hyperion as "the most important CIA office in Europe."[21]

Fr. Felix Morlion, a Belgian priest, was affiliated with the Hyperion Language School and served to establish a branch of the "school" in Rome.[22] During World War II, he had worked closely with "Wild Bill" Donovan and the Office of Strategic Services by creating Pro Deo, a Catholic intelligence agency.[23] In 1945, the priest relocated to Rome, where he became the private emissary of Pope Pius XII and four of the pope's successors, including Paul VI.

In 1966, Morlion established, with funding from the CIA, the Pro Deo University, which became Libera Università Internazionale degli Studi Sociali (the International University of Social Studies). As president of the new university, he became a force in the formation of the right-wing policies of the Italian government. He also reportedly became a recruiter of terrorists and assassins, including Mario Moretti, who was found guilty of murdering Moro, and Mehmet Ali Agca, who attempted the hit on John Paul II.[24]

NAGGING QUESTIONS

Questions about Morlion's involvement in the Moro matter first arose from the discovery of photos, taken by Carmine Pecorelli, an Italian journalist, of the prominent priest in the company of leading Italian military intelligence officials at the time of the kidnapping. Such questions became more pressing when the Rome office of the Hyperion School, which Morlion had helped to establish, opened shortly before the Moro kidnapping, only to close the following autumn.[25] Even more puzzling was the fact that the Pro Deo founder received prominent mention in the secret files of Licio Gelli (which were seized in 1982).[26]

Fr. Antonio Mennini, a Vatican official, served as the intermediary between Moro and his family during the time of the captivity. How Fr. Mennini came to serve in this capacity raises questions about the extent of the Vatican's involvement in the crime. Fr. Mennini, who claimed to have heard Moro's last confession, was the son of Luigi Mennini, who served under the direct supervision of Archbishop Paul Marcinkus. Why would the brigadiers—avowed atheists—employ the services of a priest? And why would they seek the service of the son of a high ranking IOR official? Were Luigi or Antonio somehow in league with the kidnappers? Fr. Mennini, following Moro's death, rose through the ranks of Holy Mother Church and presently serves as the papal nuncio to Great Britain. And the Vatican, to this day, continues to shield Moro's confessor from ever having to testify in state hearings concerning the prime minister's abduction and death.[27]

ECCLESIASTICAL TREASON

Why would the Vatican seek the murder of Moro? Since 1967, a series of investigative stories had run in *L'Espresso*, Italy's leading left-wing publication, which dubbed the Vatican as "the biggest tax evader in postwar Italy."[28] A published estimate of the yearly amount due to the Italian government from the Holy See on just the dividend tax was $720 million (the equivalent of $4.8 billion in 2016).[29] Moro, in seeking to create a establish a new coalition government with the PCI, made several requests for the Holy See to demonstrate "good will" by making token payments to the government and by providing a list of all its stock holdings. The requests were adamantly denied. Moro, by seeking such a settlement, was acting like a traitor to the church that had established his political party. Secretaries of State Amleto Cicognani and Jean Marie Villot insisted that Italy possessed no right to ask for financial disclosures from the church, nor should the Italian government expect to receive one lira in remuneration, since the Vatican remained a sovereign country.[30] While Moro persisted in seeking some financial gesture from the Holy See, Monsignor Fausto Vallainc said that the demands for payment should be reversed. The Holy See, he argued, should receive an annual stipend from the Italian government, since the Vatican was an international attraction that brought millions of tourists with their vacation money to Rome.[31]

The demand for money from the Italian government intensified until the Italian government under Prime Minister Giovanni Leone pressed the pope's nose to the grindstone: Pay tax on the demands from the Italian stockholders or lose the hundreds of millions given annually to the church in direct subsidies, a practice that had been initiated by Mussolini in 1929. Paul VI acquiesced and commenced the liquidation of the church's vast Italian holdings with the help of Michele Sindona. With the cash from the liquidation sale, the Holy See invested heavily with Sindona in Banca Privata Finanziaria and Banca Unione, Italy's national union bank. Sindona merged the two firms into a new financial institution called Banca Privata. Upon its creation in July 1974, Sindona's new institution displayed a loss of 200 billion lire.[32] Three months later, Banca Privata went into compulsory liquidation. The loss to Holy Mother Church, according to Swiss estimates, was in the range of $1 billion.[33]

THE PURPLE FUNK

When Italian investigators uncovered the Vatican's ties to Banca Privata, Pope Paul VI became an object of scorn and derision. Stories appeared in the press that the Holy Father had lost up to $1 billion because of his clandestine deals with Sindona. On the left of the theological spectrum, the Jesuits attacked the pope for his interference in Italian politics and "the placement of the Church's future in the hands of the devil."[34] On the right, Tridentine conservatives, including French archbishop Marcel Lefebvre, demanded Paul VI's abdication. *The Traditionalist*, a Catholic weekly newspaper, after publishing a detailed account of the Sindona affair in February 1975, called the pope "a traitor to the Church."[35]

Pope Paul VI fell into a purple funk. His behavior became erratic. He spoke with his confidants about the possibility of resigning. Before he would agree to set aside his tiara, the pope said that he would have to make amends for the financial loss he had caused Holy Mother Church. He wished to retain the right to name his successor, and he requested the abolition of the four-hundred-year-old decree that prohibited popes from selling their sanctified positions as vicars of Christ to the highest bidders among the College of Cardinals.[36] This return to the time-honored practice of simony would permit Paul VI to raise a fortune for the church—the fortune he had lost thanks to his dealings with Sindona and the Mafia.

FRIENDS ARE EXPENDABLE

The Holy Father complained of lack of sleep. He wandered through the corridors of the papal apartments in the Apostolic Palace in the wee small hours of the morning, often complaining to guards and attendants of an ominous presence within the Holy See.[37] The situation, he realized, had been caused by Moro's willingness to make concessions to the socialists and Communists at the expense of Holy Mother Church.

And now, in 1978, Moro stood ready to form a new coalition government with the PCI that could spell financial ruin for the church. The pope had known Moro since 1935, when the future prime minister established the Catholic University Students' Association (Federazione Universitaria Cattolica Italiana).[38] But the *compromesso storico*, the plan for a new coalition, must never become a reality.[39] Moro was a friend. But friends were expendable.

NO REST FOR THE WICKED

Moro's murder served its purpose. It solidified national support for Arnaldo Forlani, Italy's new CDP prime minister. And it halted the rise in public popularity of the PCI, whose share of the vote fell to 30.4 percent in 1978.[40] The Lateran Treaty would remain intact and the Vatican had secured a respite from any public scrutiny of its financial transactions. Yet the attacks continued. The country was still under the influence of the Left as evidenced by Law 194, enacted on June 6, 1978, which granted women the right to free abortion upon demand during the first ninety days of their pregnancy.[41] The legislation had been vehemently opposed by the pope and leading CDP officials, including Forlani and Andreotti. What's more, a "red-belt" of Communist administrations remained deeply entrenched within the central regions of Emilia-Romagna, Tuscany, and Umbria.[42] But, after 1980, which witnessed 1,502 attacks, the number fell to 634 in 1981 and 347 in 1982.[43]

THE BOLOGNA BOMBING

Gladio's role in the "strategy of tension" might have gone undetected save for the massacre in Bologna. At 10:25 a.m. on August 2, 1980, a time bomb in an unattended suitcase exploded within the crowded, air-conditioned waiting room of the Central Station in Bologna, destroying most of the main building. Eighty-four people were killed in the bombing and more than two hundred wounded, making it the most savage attack to take place on Italian soil since World War II.[44]

Blame, of course, was placed on the Red Brigades and the radical Left. But there was a problem that could not be resolved by the roundup of the usual suspects. The bomb that had been used in Bologna was not an ordinary explosive. It was a sophisticated device made of TNT and Composition B—a device that had been developed for use by the US military. What's more, the bomb was very similar to the explosives that the Italian police had found in the arms dump near Trieste, an arms dump that had been set aside for the Italian Gladio unit.[45]

THE POLICE RAID

On March 7, 1981, a raid on Licio Gelli's villa uncovered a list of 962 P-2 members that included top Italian intelligence, military, media, and political officials in SISMI (Italy's Military Information and Security Service), along with several prominent Argentines.[46] The publication of the names created a national furor that resulted in the collapse of the government of Arnaldo Forlani. The Italian people were aghast to learn that their most powerful political, military, and media leaders were members of the clandestine lodge.

But the discovery did not directly link the lodge with the Bologna bombing or the other attacks that had taken place during the years of lead. That link would be eventually found at the Fiumicino Airport in Rome on July 17, 1982. Within the false bottom of a suitcase belonging to Gelli's daughter were two documents outlining the master plan of the Masonic group, which, coupled with a top-secret US Army document, were enough to convince Judge Felice Casson and his team of investigators that P-2 had been involved in the attacks and that the secret society was acting as a proxy for the CIA.[47] What's more, the investigators realized that the secret society, acting under orders of US officials, had been initiating acts of terror throughout the Western World with the blessing of Holy Mother Church. The end result of the years of lead was the formation of a repugnance to Roman Catholicism that continues to permeate Western Europe.

RELIGIOUS HYPOCRISY

The years of lead displayed the hypocrisy of Holy Mother Church. Despite Vatican II's ruling in favor of the separation of church and state, the Holy See was involved in political machinations at the most nefarious level. Despite Vatican II's pronouncements concerning the sanctity of human life, the church was complicit in the wholesale slaughter of political dissidents, along with hundreds of innocent Catholic men, women, and children. Despite Vatican II's endorsement of religious liberty and ecumenism, the Vatican was engaged in securing its place of privilege and entitlement within Italy. The decrees of the council, in the final analysis, meant nothing at all.

But no example of the disparity between the Holy See's pronouncements and its participation in political oppression was as glaring and disconcerting than Operation Gladio. In *Populorum progressio*, Paul VI called upon wealthy countries, institutions, and individuals to take "concrete action" against the growing imbalance between the rich and the poor and to promote human rights within the social and political order of developing nations.[48] While issuing this teaching, the church was supporting military juntas and strong-arm dictators throughout Latin America, so that the oppressed masses would remain subservient to their leaders. This insistence permitted the church to crush the rise of liberation theology and to participate in the financial gain of the developing nations, including taking an active part in the rise of the drug cartels.

Chapter Eleven

CATHOLIC CONDOR

Catholicism plays a crucial role in this new military order, not only because of its influence among the masses, but also because the Church had provided the moral legitimacy for authority in Latin America ever since the Conquest. Hence the archbishop must be present at the dictator's inauguration, a High Mass marks the regime's first year in power, and other symbols of Church-state collaboration are scrupulously observed. Like the Spanish conquistadors, Latin America's generals feel that the Church should be an active agent in their regimes.
—Penny Lernoux, *Cry of the People*, 1980

L iberation theology first reared its head at a conference of Latin American bishops in Medellin, Colombia, in 1968, when the bishops, instead of upholding the latest encyclicals from Pope Paul VI, called upon the Vatican to "defend the rights of the oppressed" and to uphold a "preferential option for the poor" in the struggle for social justice. The bishops condemned the Holy See's alignment with the powerful elite and denounced the oppression of the Latin American people by strong-arm dictators and also by the United States and other first-world countries. The most pressing issue of the day, they declared, was not economic development but political oppression. What's more, in an official proclamation known as "the Medellin document," the clerics declared that violence is sometimes necessary when directed against the government and social institutions.[1]

New York governor Nelson Rockefeller foresaw the danger of the new theology. After his 1969 tour of Latin America on President Nixon's behalf, he warned the US business community of the antiimperialist nature of the Medellin documents. The Rockefeller Report, which became the basis of Nixon's Latin American policy, spoke of the need for the emergence of military regimes that would put an end to the movement and warned the Nixon Administration that it had better keep an eye on the Catholic

149

Church south of the border, since it suddenly had become "vulnerable to subversive penetration."[2]

PRIESTS IN REVOLT

The report proved prescient. Priests formed left-wing organizations in seven countries, some doing so in open support of coups against democratic governments, as in Chile and Bolivia. In several dioceses, ugly clashes erupted between priests and bishops. Thirty diocesan priests in Mexico demanded the resignation of Bishop Leonardo Viera Contreras, and in Maracaibo, Venezuela, twenty-two pastors called on Archbishop Domingo Roa Pérez to resign. Several hundred priests and laymen petitioned the Guatemalan Congress to expel Archbishop Mario Casariego, cardinal of Guatemala City; in Argentina a group of priests from Cordoba and Rosario demanded the dismissal of Bishop Victorio Bonamin, chief military chaplain. Similarly, activist priests in Rio de Janeiro and Peru insisted on their right to elect the local archbishop, while Chile's left-wing religious movement, Christians for Socialism, attacked Santiago's cardinal Raul Silva.[3]

Pope Paul VI was at his wit's end. After trying to appease the leftists with a series social-justice encyclicals and pronouncements, he realized that the only way he could reassert his papal authority was by force. Such force, of course, could not be overt. It could only be unleashed by Catholic organizations, including Opus Dei and Catholic Action, working in tandem with the Nixon administration and the CIA.

WORKS OF GOD

Operation Condor, a program intended to eradicate Communist groups and movements throughout South America, got underway in the early 1970s, when Opus Dei elicited support from Chilean bishops for the overthrow of the democratically elected government of president Salvador Allende. The Catholic group began to work closely with CIA-funded organizations such as Fatherland and Liberty, which subsequently became the dreaded Chilean secret police. In 1971, the CIA began shelling out millions to the Chilean Institute for General Studies (IGS), an Opus Dei think tank, for the planning of the revolution. IGS members included lawyers, free-market economists, and executives from influential publications, such as Hernán Cubillos, founder of *Que Pasa*, an Opus Dei magazine, and publisher of *El Mercurio*, the largest newspaper in Santiago (and one that was subsidized by the CIA). After the coup, a number of IGS technocrats became cabinet members and advisors to the ruling military junta, and Cubillos came to serve as Chile's new foreign minister.[4] Immediately upon seizing control of the presidency, General Augusto Pinochet rounded up thousands of alleged Communists in the national stadium for execution.[5]

"GOD WILL PARDON ME"

The full fathom of the Vatican's involvement in Condor has never been sounded. But every phase of the operation, including the purging of the left-wing clerics, received the tacit approval of the pope. Leaders of the military juntas, including General Pinochet, were devout Catholics. Indeed, when Pinochet was taken into custody in England for the murder of thousands of Chileans in 1998, he was mystified by the charges. His bafflement was justifiable. When Pinochet initiated his pogrom, Archbishop Alfonso Lopez Trujillo, general secretary of the Latin American Episcopal Conference, said, "The military juntas came into existence as a response to social and economic chaos. No society can admit a power vacuum. Faced with tensions and disorders, an appeal to power is inevitable."[6] Following his arrest, Vatican secretary of state Cardinal Angelo Sodano, on behalf of the Holy Father, sent a letter to the British government demanding the general's release.[7]

When General Pinochet finally went on trial in 2005, a Chilean judge asked him about his reign of terror, which had resulted in the murder of over four thousand Chileans, the torture of over fifty thousand, and the "disappearance" of hundreds of thousands. The general piously answered, "I suffer for these losses, but God does the deeds; He will pardon me if I exceeded in some, which I don't think I did."[8]

COCAINE AND THE CHURCH

In 1975, the Bolivian Interior Ministry—a publicly acknowledged subsidiary of the CIA—drew up a master plan with the help of Vatican officials for the elimination of liberation theology. Dubbed the "Banzer Plan"—after Hugo Banzer, Bolivia's right-wing dictator, who fancied himself the "defender of Christian civilization," the scheme was adopted by ten

Latin American governments.[9] Banzer had come to power in Bolivia as the result of a three-day coup in August 1971 that left 110 people dead and 600 wounded. The coup, as recently declassified US State Department documents show, was funded by the CIA as part of Operation Condor.[10]

In order to mount the master plan, Banzer relied on Klaus Barbie, who recruited a mercenary army of neofascist terrorists, including Stefano Delle Chiaie.[11] To fund the army, Banzer ordered coca trees to be planted throughout the country's ailing cotton fields. Between 1974 and 1980, the land used in coca production tripled.[12] The coca was exported to Columbian cartel laboratories, including Barbie's Transmaritania. A multibillion-dollar industry was born. The tremendous upsurge in coca supply from Bolivia sharply drove down the price of cocaine, fueling a huge new market and the rise of the Colombian cartels. The street price of cocaine in 1975 was $1,500 a gram. Within a decade, the price fell to $200 per gram.[13] The CIA became an active participant in this new drug network by creating a pipeline between the Colombian cartels and the black neighborhoods of Compton and Los Angeles. The pipeline was unearthed by Gary Webb, a reporter for *San Jose Mercury News*, in 1996. Webb's findings resulted in an investigation by the US Senate that served to confirm his claims.[14]

The money from the network was often deposited by priests and bishops in Cisalpine and six shell companies that were set up in Panama by Sindona, Calvi, and Marcinkus. These companies—Astolfine SA, United Trading Corporation, Erin SA, Bellatrix SA, Belrose SA, and Starfield SA—were owned by the Vatican. These firms generated no actual capital by investing in other banks and companies, fulfilled no international financial service by managing funds from legitimate investors, and served no legitimate business purpose by transferring foreign currency from earnings in overseas operations. The companies existed only as transfer stations of laundered cash for the Colombian drug cartels. From Panama the drug money was routed to Banco Ambrosiano in Milan and eventually to the Vatican Bank, which charged a processing fee of 15 to 20 percent. From Vatican City, the funds were transferred to numbered bank accounts at Banca del Gottardo or Union de Banques Suisses (UBS) in Switzerland.[15]

FIGHTING PROSTITUTION

The laundering service to the cartels was supervised by Archbishop Darío Castrillón Hoyos of Colombia. The archbishop was a close friend and confidant of Pablo Escobar, the leader of Colombia's most notorious cartels, who gave Castrillón a share of his profits from the drug trade for Catholic charities. The archbishop argued that such gifts were justified since some of the hundreds of millions of dollars that Escobar gained from the sale of cocaine would not be spent on prostitution.[16]

Eventually, the Vatican established two other shell companies—Manic SA in Luxembourg and Nordeurop Establishment in Liechtenstein. The additional companies were necessary to handle the enormous cash flow. By 1978, money coming into the Panamanian companies from the Medellin Cartel alone was enormous, since Escobar, at the height of his power, was smuggling fifteen tons of cocaine into the United States every day.[17] The Vatican was now playing with drug money in a game of very high risks.

THE DIRTY WAR

No Latin American country, not even Pinochet's Chile, could equal the levels of violence that followed the military coup of March 24, 1976, in Argentina. Indeed, the only regime to create a state of fear approximating that of Argentina was Hitler's Germany.[18] (There were other parallels to Nazism, including a government-sponsored hate campaign against the country's four hundred thousand Jews). As many as thirty thousand political prisoners (including students, union organizers, journalists, and even pregnant women) were killed or disappeared during the 1976–1983 "Dirty War," which was fully endorsed by the Ford, Carter, and Reagan administrations.[19] Political killings took place on the average of seven a day in 1977. Nor were Argentines the only victims. An estimated fourteen thousand refugees from other South American military regimes were told to leave the country or face the possibility of arrest. Torture was automatic for anyone arrested, according to a spokesman for the World Council of Churches.[20]

Archbishop Pio Laghi, the papal nuncio in Argentina, developed a close relationship with the leaders of the junta, playing tennis with them on a daily basis. In his sermons, Laghi quoted the Catholic just war theory, as developed by St. Augustine, and used it to sanction the military campaign against all dissent. Keeping in line with the nuncio, the Argentine bishops failed to denounce the daily atrocities that were taking place in the country. Their only acts of mercy came with their assignment of priests to accompany tortured prisoners on their last journey. The priests dutifully blessed the prisoners and granted them the last rites before their handcuffed bodies were tossed out of military helicopters into the South Atlantic.[21]

THE US ENDORSEMENT

Recently declassified National Security documents show that the CIA and the U-S State Department remained primary sponsors of the military junta, which was led by General Jorge Videla. On February 16, 1976, six weeks before the coup, Robert Hill, the US ambassador to Argentina, reported to Secretary of State Henry Kissinger that the plans for the coup were underway and that a public-relations campaign had been mounted that would cast the new military regime in a positive light. Hill added that even though "some executions would probably be necessary," the leaders of the junta remained determined "to minimize any resulting problems with the US."[22]

On March 25, 1979, two days after the coup, William Rogers, assistant secretary for Latin America, advised Kissinger that the military takeover of Argentina would result in "a fair amount of repression, probably a good deal of blood." To this warning, Kissinger responded, "Yes, but that is in our interest."[23]

On March 30, 1976, Ambassador Hill sent a seven-page assessment of the new regime to Kissinger. In the report, Hill wrote, "This is probably the best executed and most civilized coup in Argentine history."[24] One week later, the US Congress approved a request from the Ford administration, written by Kissinger, to provide $50 million in aid to the new military regime.

CATHOLIC COMPLICITY

On the eve of the coup, General Jorge Videla and other plotters received the blessing of the Archbishop of Paraná, Adolfo Tortolo. The day of the takeover itself, the military leaders had a lengthy meeting with the leaders of the bishop's conference. As he emerged from that meeting, Archbishop Tortolo said that, although "the Church has its own specific mission, there are circumstances in which it cannot refrain from participating even when it is a matter of problems related to the specific order of the state."[25] He went on to urge all Argentines to "cooperate in a positive way" with the new government. After thousands had disappeared, the bishop said, "I have no knowledge, I have no reliable proof, of human rights being violated in our country" and praised the military regime, saying that the armed forces were simply "carrying out their duty."

The vicar for the army, Bishop Victorio Bonamin, characterized the campaign as a defense of "morality, human dignity, and ultimately a struggle to defend God. . . . Therefore, I pray for divine protection over this 'dirty war' in which we are engaged." He told a university audience in December 1977 that the world was divided into "atheistic materialism and Christian humanism." Though he denied any knowledge of individual cases, he said: "If I could speak with the government, I would tell it that we must remain firm in the positions we're taking: foreign accusations about disappearances should be ignored."[26]

PAPAL SANCTION

General Videla, who is currently serving a life sentence for his part in the Dirty War, told reporters that he had conferred with Cardinal Raúl Francisco Primatesta, the leading Argentine cleric, about the regime's policy of eradicating left-wing activists. He further insisted that he maintained ongoing conversations with Archbishop Laghi and the leading bishops from Argentina's Episcopal Conference. These dignitaries, he insisted, advised him of the manner in which the junta should deal with all dissidents, including clerics who advocated liberation theology.[27]

The general's claim is supported by Bishop Tortolo, who in 1976 said that the clergy was advised of all actions made by the junta, particularly in regard to troublesome priests and nuns.[28] Tortolo made this statement when questioned about the disappearance of two Jesuit priests—Francisco Jalics and Orlando Yorio—and six members of their parish. The disappeared priests were under the charge of Fr. Jorge Mario Bergoglio, the provincial general of the Society of Jesus in Argentina. They were espousing liberation theology among the poor in the slums of Buenos Aires.[29]

THE TORTURE CHAMBER

Fr. Jalics and Fr. Yorio—the two Jesuit priests in Bergoglio's charge, were taken to the notorious Navy School of Mechanics (ESMA) in Buenos Aires.

ESMA was the most important of the military government's 340 detention and torture centers. A trip to ESMA typically began with an introduction to "Caroline," an electric prodding rod with two prolonged wires. The visitors were stripped and tied to a steel bed frame. Electricity was applied to the victims, who were periodically doused with water to increase the effects. If the subject was a woman, the interrogators went for the breasts, vagina, or anus. If a man, they applied the wires to the genitals, tongue, or neck. Sometimes victims twitched so uncontrollably that they not only lost control of their bowels but also shattered their own arms and legs. Fr. Patrick Rice, an Irish priest who had worked in the slums and was detained for several days at ESMA, recalled watching his flesh sizzle as the electricity flowed through his body. What Fr. Rice most remembered was the smell. "It was like bacon," he said.[30] Children were tortured in front of their parents, and parents in front of their children. One torturer estimates that about sixty babies passed through the facility and that all but two (whose heads had been smashed against the walls) were sold to suitable Argentine couples.[31]

At ESMA, which also served as a disposal site for other naval camps, corpses were initially buried under the sports field. After the field was filled, the bodies were burned daily, at 5:30 in the afternoon, usually after having been cut up with a circular saw. Eventually, the ESMA officials hit upon the idea of aerial disposal at sea. The dead were dumped from airplanes hundreds of miles off the coast of Buenos Aires, along with torture victims who had been drugged into a comatose state. One pilot testified that prisoners fell like ants from the planes.[32]

THE NAKED PRIESTS

Fr. Jalics and Fr. Yorio were released five months after captivity. They were found half naked in a field outside Buenos Aires. Fr. Bergoglio later insisted that he had secured their release but no documentation exists that he had intervened on behalf of the two priests in his charge. Fr. Yorio, at the 1985 trial of the leaders of the junta, said that Bergoglio had handed them over to the death squad: "I am sure that he himself [Fr. Bergoglio] gave over the list with our names to the navy." He further refuted the claim that Bergoglio had saved the lives of the priests, saying, "I do not have any reason to think he did anything for our release, but much to the contrary."[33]

In addition, Fr. Yorio said that Bergoglio had expelled him from a teaching position at a Jesuit school and had spread false rumors to the Argentine high command, stating that Yorio was "a communist" and "a subversive guerilla, who was after women."[34]

Fr. Jalics also refuted Bergoglio, saying, "From subsequent statements by an official and 30 documents that I was able to access later, we were able to prove, without any room for doubt, that this man [Bergoglio] did not keep his promise [to protect the priests], but, on the contrary, he presented a false denunciated to the military."[35] Fr. Jalics, who has retreated to a monastery in Germany, said that he is now reconciled with the past because "forgiveness is a central tenet of Christianity."

THE DAMNING EVIDENCE

Journalist Horacio Verbitsky recently uncovered a military document from 1976 in the archives of Argentina's Ministry of Foreign Affairs that appears to provide proof that Fr. Bergoglio provided damning testimony about the two priests in his charge to the junta. The document, bearing the signature of Anselmo Orcoyen, who served as the director of the Catholic Division on Ministry, appeared on the front page of *Pagina12*, the Argentinean daily newspaper, on March 17, 2013.[36] It reads:

> Father Francisco Jalics
>   Activity of Disseverment in the Congregation of Religious Sisters (Conflicts of Obedience)
>   Detained in the Navy School of Mechanics 24/5/76 XI/76 (6 months)—accused with Fr. Yorio of suspicious contact with guerillas.
>   They lived in a small community which the Jesuit Superior dissolved in February of 1976 but they refused to obey the order to leave the community on March 19. The two were let go. No bishop of Buenos Aires would receive them.
>   This notification was received by Mr. Orcoyen and given to him by Fr. Bergoglio, who signed the note with special recommendations not to approve of their requests.
>   (signed) Orcoyen.

The Vatican, at this writing, continues to affirm Bergoglio's innocence in this matter, insisting that there has never been a "concrete or credible accusation" against him.[37]

STEALING BABIES

But other criminal allegations were directed against Bergoglio. The Grand-mothers of the Plaza of Mayo, a human rights group established to locate children stolen during the Dirty War, state that the Jesuits' provincial general failed to assist a family of five, who were awaiting execution by the death squad. One member of the family, Elena de la Cuadra, was a pregnant young woman. The five had appealed to the superior general of the Society of Jesus at the Vatican. The superior general turned the matter over to Bergoglio, who remained the provincial general of the order in Argentina. Bergoglio, in turn, sat on the case for several months, only to pass it off to a local Catholic bishop. The bishop reportedly returned to Bergoglio with a letter from the junta stating the four members of the family had been killed but the young woman had been kept alive long enough to deliver her baby.[38] No one in the junta apparently wanted to be accused of abortion. The baby was given to a prominent family and could not be returned to its maternal grandmother or any other blood relative.[39]

Fr. Bergoglio later claimed that he had no knowledge of stolen babies, of which there were hundreds, if not thousands, until the collapse of the regime. He said that he did what he could but had little influence "to save people from the regime."

"BERGOGLIO KNEW EVERYTHING"

"Bergoglio has a very cowardly attitude when it comes to something so ter-rible as the theft of babies," Estela de la Cuadra, whose husband, brother, brother-in-law and pregnant sister had been executed, said. "He doesn't face this reality, and it doesn't bother him. The question is how to save his name, save himself. But he can't keep these allegations from reaching the public. The people know how he is."[40]

Ms. de la Cuadra also expressed her outrage that Bergoglio, when serving as the head of the Argentine Bishops' Conference, refused to defrock Fr. Christian von Wernich, even after he had been "jailed for life in 2007 for seven killings, 42 abductions, and 34 cases of torture, in which he told victims: 'God wants to know where your friends are.'"[41] Von Wernich had served the dictatorship as chaplain of the Buenos Aires Provincial Police.

"I've testified in court that Bergoglio knew everything, that he wasn't—despite what he says—uninvolved," Ms. de la Cuadra said.[42]

CRIMINAL CHARGES

In 2005, Argentine human rights attorney Myriam Bregman filed a criminal suit against Bergoglio, who had been elevated to the College of Cardinals, accusing him of complicity in the kidnapping and torture of Fr. Yorio and Fr. Jalics, along with six members of their parish. Bergoglio refused to respond to the subpoena to appear in court, invoking his immunity from prosecution as a Vatican official under Argentinean law.[43]

"He finally accepted to see us in an office alongside Buenos Aires cathedral sitting underneath a tapestry of the Virgin Mary," Ms. Bregman said. "It was an intimidating experience. We were very uncomfortable intruding in a religious building."[44] She added that "Bergoglio did not provide any significant information on the two priests. 'He seemed reticent, I left with a bitter taste,' she said."

Later, in an interview with Sergio Rubin, his official biographer, Bergoglio said that he regularly hid people on church property during the Dirty War, and once gave his identity papers to a fugitive with similar facial features so that the man could escape across the border. But, Bergoglio added, these acts were performed in secret since church leaders were called upon to support the junta.

Responding to these comments, Ms. Bregman said that Bergoglio's words condemn him and prove that he condoned the torture and the killing. "The dictatorship could not have operated without this key support," she said.[45]

"WASHINGTON'S POPE"

On March 13, 2013, Cardinal Jorge Mario Bergoglio ascended to the throne of St. Peter as Pope Francis I. The nagging questions about his background may never receive a satisfactory answer. Nor will concerns that the CIA manipulated the election as it had in the past. Argentinean journalists and scholars with insight into the agency's activities in their country already have labeled Bergoglio "Washington's Pope."[46] Certainly, the new pontiff upheld the interests of General Jorge Videla and Admiral Emilio Massera during the Dirty War, and served to suppress all manifestations of liberation theology. And, certainly, he can serve to influence policy (including the agenda of neo-conservatives) throughout South and Central America. His installation, it has been noted, took place one week following the death of Venezuelan president Hugo Chavez.[47] By the end of 2013, Bergoglio emerged as the most popular cleric on planet earth, earning an approval rating of 88 percent among American Catholics.[48] Few appear to take heed that Francis is the first pope to be charged in a criminal suit of conspiring with a military junta.[49]

Chapter Twelve

THE CONTAGION OF CORRUPTION

The plain truth is that this is an institution, as we all remembered before Benedict XVI resigned, retired, this is an institution that is corrupt and riddled with corruption, irredeemably corrupt from top to bottom and we are just deceiving ourselves.
—David Starkey, British historian, interview on
Broadcasting House, BBC Radio 4, March 17, 2013

The Vatican was engaged not only in bank theft but also in an assortment of other crimes, including the attempted sale of $1 billion in counterfeit securities. On June 29, 1971, Leopold Ledl, an Austrian con man, met with Vincent Rizzo, a leading *capo* of the Genovese crime family, at the Churchill Hotel in London to purchase $1 billion in counterfeit securities for the Vatican.[1] Ledl, who was involved in gunrunning, drug trafficking, and counterfeiting securities, had established friendships with a host of ecclesiastical dignitaries, including Cardinal Giovanni Benelli, Paul VI's assistant secretary of state; Cardinal Egidio Vagnozzi, head of the Vatican's Office of Economic Affairs; Cardinal Amleto Giovanni Cicognani, secretary of state emeritus; and Cardinal Eugène Tisserant, dean of the College of Cardinals. Such exalted figures were regular dinner guests at Ledl's lavish wooded estate outside Vienna.[2]

Early in 1971, Cardinal Tisserant summoned Ledl to his office in the Vatican. He spoke about the declining funds within the Vatican's treasury due to a series of "ill-considered" investments in Sindona's banks. The cardinal then asked Ledl to help in securing "first class counterfeit securities in large American companies" with a face value of $1 billion.[3] Tisserant wasn't concerned about the risk. The American government, he told his Austrian friend, would never accuse Holy Mother Church of dealing in bogus bonds and stocks. If it were discovered that the Vatican possessed such phony securities, US authorities would assume that the church had fallen victim to some unscrupulous swindlers and would step in to make restitution for any losses.[4]

THE COUNTERFEIT SECURITIES

A deal was struck. The Vatican would receive 65 percent of the cash when the bogus securities were sold. The remaining 35 percent would go to Ledl and his associates within the Genovese crime family of New York. The phony stock, which was printed by the mob at a print shop owned by Louis Milo on Avenue A and Twelfth Street in Little Italy. The trial run consisted of 498 bonds of American Telephone and Telegraph (AT&T), valued at $4,980,000; 259 bonds of General Electric, valued at $2,590,000; 412 bonds of Chrysler, valued at 2,060,000; and 479 bonds of Pan American World Airways, valued at $4,780,000. The total face value of the paper was $14,410,000.[5] These bonds were delivered to Bishop Paul Marcinkus, who now served as the head of the Vatican Bank. In July 1971, Marcinkus called upon "Count" Mario Foligni, a Ledl accomplice, to make a trial deposit of $1.5 million. When he opened the account, Foligni named Monsignor Mario Fornasari, a secretary at the Vatican, as the beneficiary. The securities passed inspection by the bank officials, a testimony to the forgery skills of the Genovese family.[6]

THE TRIAL RUN

In September, Marcinkus directed Foligni to make a second trial deposit—this time of $2.5 million at the Banco di Roma. Alfio Marchini, the owner of the Leonardo da Vinci Hotel and close friend of Bishop Marcinkus, was beneficiary. The securities were examined and certified as authentic.[7]

The problem arose when officials of both banks sent samples of the bonds to New York for physical examination. The Bankers Association in New York determined that the securities were counterfeit. Word was sent to Interpol. When Foligni was questioned he sang like a canary about his associations with Ledl and Marcinkus. When Ledl was taken into custody, he, too, broke into song and chirped about Vincent Rizzo, the Genovese family, the Vatican, and Cardinal Tisserant.[8]

By the time William Lynch, chief of Organized Crime and Racketeering of the US Department of Justice, and William Aronwald, assistant chief of the New York Strike Force, managed to cut through the red tape to arrange an interview with Tisserant, the cardinal was dead of natural causes and already buried. The investigators then sought to question Bishop Marcinkus. It took more than a year before their request to enter the inner sanctum of the Vatican Bank was granted.[9]

The interview, as taped by Lynch and Aronwald, began with the investigators questioning Marcinkus about Michele Sindona.

THE TAPED INTERVIEW

"Michele and I are good friends," Marcinkus said, as he puffed a large Cuban cigar. "We've known each other for several years. My financial dealings with him, however, have been very limited. He is, you know, one of the wealthiest industrialists in Italy. He is well ahead of his time as far as financial matters are concerned."[10]

When asked about his "limited" dealings with Sindona, Marcinkus replied, "I do not believe it necessary to break banking secrecy laws in order to defend myself."

"If it becomes necessary, are you prepared to testify in a United States court?" Lynch asked.

"Well, yes," Marcinkus said, "if it's absolutely necessary."

Lynch got down to business, and asked, "Do you have a private numbered account in the Bahamas?"

"No," Marcinkus responded.

"Do you have an ordinary account in the Bahamas?"

"No," Marcus said matter-of-factly, "I don't."

"Are you quite sure, Bishop?" Lynch pressed.

"The Vatican does have a financial interest in the Bahamas," Marcinkus replied, "but it's strictly a business transaction similar to many controlled by the Vatican. It's not for any person's private financial gain."

"No," Lynch continued, "we are interested in personal accounts you have."

"I don't have any private or personal accounts in the Bahamas or anywhere else," Marcinkus said.

The investigators knew that everything Marcinkus said was untrue. The bishop was a member of the board of directors of Cisalpine Overseas Bank in Nassau and had been since 1971; he made regular visits to the Bahamas and personally owned 8 percent of the bank's stock. They also knew of the bishop's private accounts at Sindona's banks throughout Italy and the small fortune Marcinkus had squirreled away, compliments of his dealings with Sindona and P-2, at the Banque de Financement in Geneva.[11]

HANDS OFF

Following the meeting, US officials pursued the prospect of ordering the indictment of Marcinkus. The bishop, after all, was an American bishop and subject to American justice. This meant that he could be extradited to stand trial. Such a measure seemed warranted. More than $10 million in phony securities were still held by the Vatican, and there existed a strong possibility that even more of the $1 billion order might have been signed, sealed, and delivered.[12]

But the Nixon administration put the skids to the investigation. The matter was too delicate and could result in a political backlash by American Catholics.[13] It was decided that it was best to forget about the $10 million, the mob, and Marcinkus. After all, the government couldn't send agents across the Tiber with semiautomatics, search warrants, and handcuffs. "We were not about to waste that amount of taxpayers' money," William Aronwald later said. And so, the case against Marcinkus was dropped because of "lack of evidence."[14]

MISSING MILLIONS AND A MISTRESS

The corruption was not confined to Vatican City. It was contagious and spread to other places throughout the Catholic world. In Chicago, Cardinal John Cody ran the nation's largest diocese into the ground. Labeled a "psychopathic paranoid" by Fr. Andrew Greeley, a leading American sociologist of religion, Cody regularly removed his clerical collar to check into hotels in southeast Chicago for weekends of binge drinking.[15] More troubling was the cardinal's refusal to provide an accounting for millions of dollars in diocesan funds that had gone missing.[16] No one knew the amount of the missing money. But, in 1971, the Catholic cemetery revenue for the Archdiocese of Chicago stood at $50 million. Six months after this figure was reported, the sum in the cemetery fund mysteriously dropped to $36 million.[17]

Later, information emerged about Cody's lavish lifestyle, including his relationship with Helen Dolan Wilson, who appears to have been his lifetime mistress. Cody shelled out more than $1 million in church funds to Wilson, a divorcee and the cardinal's step-cousin. He bought her a vacation home in Boca Rotan, Florida; placed her on the payroll of the archdiocese; padded her hours so that she would receive a generous pension; and steered the priests in his charge to the insurance agency of David Wilson, Helen's son, who amassed over $150,000 in commissions from policies with the archdiocese.[18]

TOSSED TO THE STREETS

Priests within the archdiocese were subjected to Cody's tyrannical rule. Those who failed to win his favor received Sunday afternoon visits from the cardinal, who summarily dismissed them, giving them two weeks to remove their possessions from their rectories. The dismissed priests were granted no pension funds or retirement stipends. They were tossed to the street without as much as a kiss on the cheek for good luck.[19]

The situation grew so severe that the priests formed the Association of Chicago Priests, a makeshift trade union to create a united front against Cody's actions. Cody ignored their requests. Phone calls found the cardinal constantly "unavailable." Letters went unanswered. Some priests stayed on to fight for job security and retirement benefits. Many left. By 1978, one third of Chicago's Catholic clergy had called it quits.[20]

VOLCANIC CONFRONTATION

While the plight of the priests failed to merit Paul VI's concern, he was compelled to take action over the missing millions. Not wanting to create a controversy, he opted for a plan that would remove Cody as the despotic ruler of the archdiocese in a face-saving manner. Cardinal Sebastiano Baggio, the prefect of the Sacred Congregation of Bishops, was dispatched to Chicago in early August of 1978. His mission was to inform Cody that the Holy Father wanted to appoint an episcopal coadjutor to oversee the day-to-day operations of the archdiocese. The press release would state that cardinal's declining health necessitated the need for an assistant bishop.

During his volcanic meeting with Baggio, Cody was not forthcoming about the missing funds and refused to comply with the papal order for a coadjutor. Baggio prepared a damning report, but the pope, true to his weak-kneed manner, failed to demand Cody's resignation in accordance with canon law.[21]

MISCHIEVOUS MONKS

The corruption spread to Doylestown, Pennsylvania, where a group of Pauline monks operated Our Lady of Czestochowa, a shrine to the "Black Madonna" who had spared a Polish monastery from Swedish invaders during the seventeenth century. Reports of financial malfeasance and criminal activity at the shrine began to arrive at the Holy See with mounting regularity. By 1975, the Vatican appointed two prelates—Bishop George Guilfoyle of the diocese of Camden, New Jersey, and Fr. Paul Boyle, the provincial chief of Chicago's Passionist Fathers—to unearth the basis of the complaints.[22]

What they discovered sent shockwaves through the Holy See. Many of the Pauline monks had violated their vows of poverty and chastity by pilfering nearly $20 million in contributions from pious pilgrims, buying expensive goods, driving luxurious cars, and keeping women of questionable character in their cells. They had raised $400,000 in contributions for bronze plaques in the memory of loved ones that were to be placed throughout the shrine. But no plaque was made or mounted. The pilgrims had shelled out over $250,000 to the greedy monks for Masses that were never celebrated and $64,000 for cemetery work that was never performed. The monks also defaulted on a multimillion-dollar bank loan. The security on the loan was a letter of guarantee from Father George Tomzinski, the supreme head of the Pauline Order.[23]

CADILLACS AND CONCUBINES

Although the monks also defaulted on $4.3 million in church bonds purchased by Polish-American Catholics, they continued to live with their 130-acre monastery that was, in the words of Guilfoyle and Boyle, "more like a resort hotel than a monastic institution."[24] Within his finely appointed apartment, Fr. Michael M. Zembrzuski, the vicar-general of the monks, lived like a married man with his longtime mistress on money that had been donated to the shrine. When even this amount proved to be insufficient to maintain his lifestyle, the vicar-general began to demand a kickback from all those who worked at the estate, including the managers of the cemetery. Zembrzuski avoided criminal charges by threatening to go to the press with what he knew about similar prelates in the church.[25]

When Guilfoyle and Boyle ordered the monks to turn over their credit cards, the keys to their Cadillacs, and the funds in their checking accounts, half of them cast off their cowls and called it quits.[26]

ENTER KAROL WOJTYLA

The report of the two investigators, which numbered several hundred pages, was sent to the Vatican. The recommendation that Zembrzuski should be forced into retirement and that the offending priests be "severely disciplined" was signed by Cardinal John Krol of Philadelphia.[27] But before such action could be taken, Zembrzuski called upon his good friend Cardinal Karol Wojtyla of Poland to intervene. Wojtyla, who would soon ascend to the papal throne as John Paul II, flew to Rome and managed to persuade Paul VI and his Vatican advisors to cast aside the investigation and to ignore the recommendation. His intervention was successful. The Holy See opted not only to leave Zembrzuski in charge of the shrine but also to remove from the Pauline order every monk who had cooperated with the investigation.[28]

THE DUPLESSIS ORPHANS

The climate of corruption that permeated Catholicism did not arise from the permissiveness of the 1970s. It emerged from the donation of Mussolini, the creation of the Vatican Bank, and the abandonment of the teachings governing usury. The bottom line for the church was the dollar sign. This became evident in the case of the Duplessis Orphans.

In post–World War II Montreal, thousands of children, who had been placed in Catholic orphanages, were suddenly proclaimed as mentally retarded and handed over to Catholic asylums for the insane. The motive for the reclassification was money. Subsidies for orphans, under the government of Quebec premier Maurice Duplessis, were $1.25 per day for orphans and $2.75 per day for mental patients. Moreover, the church could receive substantial financial assistance for building new psychiatric hospitals. Mr. Duplessis was much praised by the press for his commitment to the mental health of the people of Quebec.[29]

FORCED LABOR, SEXUAL ABUSE, AND PHYSICAL TORTURE

Over twenty thousand children, most from unwed mothers, ended up in the Catholic asylums.[30] The asylums were run by such religious orders as the Sisters of Providence, the Sisters of Mercy, the Gray Nuns of Montreal, the Sisters of Charity of Quebec, the Little Franciscans of Mary, the Brothers of Notre Dame-de-la-Misericorde, and the Brothers of Charity.[31] Children were subjected to forced labor and physical torture. "They would plunge our heads into ice-cold water if we did something wrong," Clarina Duguay, a surviving Duplessis orphan, said. Duguay also testified to being chained to a bed and forced to scrub the floors of the asylum from morning to night.[32]

Martin Lecuyer, another survivor, said that the children received no schooling but were sent to work on nearby farms. "The farmers would pay the religious community for the work we did," he said. "This was slavery, that's the word for it."[33] At night, Lecuyer claimed that he was regularly sexually assaulted by a religious brother from the time he was eleven. When he complained to a superior about the abuse, he was beaten with a leather strap.[34]

CHEMICAL EXPERIMENTATION

But the sexual abuse, forced labor, and torture paled in comparison with the drug experimentation. The children served as guinea pigs for chlorpromazine, a drug known as a "chemical bully club" because of its mental and physical consequences. A possible side effect of the drug is tardive dyskinesia, a central nervous system disorder that results in distorted facial expressions and involuntary body movements. The use of chlorpromazine on the orphans was part of the MKUltra mind-control program of the CIA.[35] Dr. Ewen Cameron, the psychiatrist who conducted appalling tests on human subjects at McGill University, spearheaded much on the experimentation.[36]

In addition to chlorpromazine, the children were also subjected to electric shock, lobotomies, and doses of additional drugs, many hallucino-genic. Clarina Duguay said that she began receiving chlorpromazine two weeks after she arrived at St. Julien Hospital. The nuns had told her the drug would help her sleep. It did more than that. "It made me a zombie," she maintained. "I had no energy. I was always feeling sleepy, had a hard time getting up. I was getting the drug every night."[37]

Paul St. Aubain, another Duplessis orphan, said he was lobotomized at St. Michel Archange, a Catholic asylum in Joliette, when he was eigh-teen. "I wasn't ill," Mr. St. Aubain said. "They did it without my consent, without my permission. They were experimenting on me. I was their pris-oner."[38] He said he was also subjected to electroshock therapy and daily doses of psychiatric drugs.

PIG STY

Many of the children, like Mr. St. Aubain, suffered permanent brain damage. Some died. Their bodies were buried on an eight-hundred-acre plot of ground on the outskirts of Montreal that was next to a pig sty. The land was owned by the Archdiocese of Montreal, which was governed by Cardinal Paul-Emile Leger, a leader of the progressive party at Vatican II. Albert Sylvio, a Duplessis orphan who had been placed at St. Jean de Dieu, recalled transporting more than sixty bodies of fellow orphans to a mass grave site during the 1950s. "We put them in cardboard boxes," he said. "There was never any ceremony. Some had died on the operating table. Some had been sick and some committed suicide."[39]

Death had its reward for the religious sisters and brothers in charge of the orphans. The bodies of many of the children were sold to local medical schools for dissection. A Quebec law passed in 1942 allowed the members of religious orders to sell unclaimed remains for $10.[40]

LOVING KINDNESS

The story of the orphans came to light during the waning days of Paul VI's pontificate. The cries for redress were ignored by the pope and his two immediate successors. Eventually, the surviving orphans organized to pressure the church and the Canadian government for justice. After nearly fifteen years of litigation, the Quebec government, in 2001, granted the survivors the meager sum of $10,000 per person, plus an additional $1,000 for each year of wrongful confinement to a mental institution.[41] But the church refused to apologize or to provide a dime.

Alain Arsenault, a Montreal-based attorney who represented the orphans, said, "The Catholic Church of Quebec is the main perpetrator in this case, while the government assisted it. The Church has never apologized for anything," What's more, according to Arsenault, the Vatican and the Archdiocese continue to insist that Holy Mother Church showed loving kindness to the orphans by providing them with food and shelter.[42]

Regarding the torture, the forced labor, the sexual abuse, and the horrific experimentation, Archbishop Christian Lépine of Montreal recently said, "If it's someone in an institution, even if it's someone who's there in the name of his own religion—being a Christian—if he does something unjust, well, it's still as a member of the church. It's not the church itself."[43]

Along with the corruption came a profound change in the sexual orientation of the Catholic clergy, including the Vatican hierarchy.

By 1978, reliable reports emerged that over 50 percent of the inhabitants of Vatican City were practicing homosexuals.

Chapter Thirteen

THE GAY CHURCH

For a village [Vatican City] where the overwhelming majority have sworn a vow of celibacy there is an unusual preoccupation with sexual matters. Homosexuality, if not rife within the Vatican, is constantly evident, and is a frequent factor in career advancement. Young attractive priests, invariably referred to as Madonni, *use their charm to accelerate their promotion. Certain bishops have found the need to work late in a locked room with only a* Madonno *to assist them. Satanic masses have happened regularly with hooded semi-naked participants and porn videos have been shown to a carefully selected audience.*
—David Yallop, *The Power and the Glory*, 2007

In 1999, shortly before he died of bone and liver cancer, Monsignor Luigi Marinelli, who had worked at the Vatican for forty-five years, testified that a gay lobby had emerged as a dominant force within the Roman Curia under the pontificate of Paul VI and had begun to use sex as a carrot for advancement to ambitious up-and-coming clerics. In his memoir *Via col Cento in Vaticano* (*Gone with the Wind in the Vatican*), Marinelli wrote that being a practicing gay prelate "can help a hopeful candidate advance more quickly and cause a rival to lose the desire to present himself for promotion. The one who gives himself from the waist down has a better chance than the one who gives his heart and soul to the service of God and his brothers. For many in the Curia, the beautiful boy attracts more goodwill and favor than the intelligence one."[1]

The list of alleged gay Catholic clerics, provided by Marinelli, included the names of Cardinal Tarcisio Bertone, who became the Vatican secretary of state, Bishop Mauro Parmeggiani, reigning cleric of Tivoli, Archbishop Józef Wesolowski, apostolic nuncio to the Dominican Republic, and Monsignor Francesco Camaldo, official of the Vicariate of Rome at the Vatican.[2] Under Bertone's direction, the Vatican purchased properties in Rome that served to house gay saunas and massage parlors where priests paid for sex. The most notorious of these places was Europa Multiclub, the largest gay bathhouse in Italy. Tales of Vatican dignitaries frequenting Multiclub captured headlines in Rome's tabloids, and the website for Multiclub promoted special "bear nights," where hairy young men stripped and changed into clerical outfits.[3]

THE PINK POPE

The most prominent name on Marinelli's list of gay clerics was that of Giovanni Montini, who reigned over the church as Paul VI. Testimony about the pope's sexual proclivity was from several reliable sources, including Franco Bellegrandi. A member of the honor guard of the sovereign pontiff (*camerieri di spada e cappa*), Bellegrandi served as a professor of modern history at Innsbruck University in Austria and as a correspondent for *L'Osservatore Romano*, the Vatican newspaper. In his book *Nichitaroncalli: Controvita di un Papa* (*Nikitaroncalli: Counterlife of a Pope*), Bellegrandi writes, "When he was Archbishop of Milan, he was caught by the police one night wearing civilian clothes and in not so laudable company. Actually, for many years he has been said to have a special friendship with a red-haired actor. This man did not make any secret of his relationship with the future Pope. The relationship continued and became closer in the years ahead."[4]

The red-haired actor and lifetime lover of Paul VI whom Bellegrandi describes reportedly was Paolo Carlini, who appeared in *Roman Holiday* (1953) with Audrey Hepburn and Gregory Peck and *It Started in Naples* (1960) with Clark Gable and Sophia Loren.[5] As long as Paul VI occupied the papal throne, Carlini was allowed to come and go as he wished within Vatican City. He often would take the elevator to the papal bedchamber in the dead of night.[6]

Under Paul VI, according to Bellegrandi, offices within the Vatican were suddenly staffed by effete young men in tight-fitting uniforms with makeup on their faces. These newcomers replaced venerable old employees who were suddenly fired or removed to a different post. Bellegrandi writes, "The *Gendarmeria Pontificia* [the Vatican police] had to steer carefully along those floating mines and keep one eye closed—and sometimes both eyes—hushing up reports, and discouraging a diligent editor or two. I underwent such an experience myself."[7]

The relationship of the pope to the movie actor might have remained concealed from the public, save for Paul VI's denunciation of homosexuality and other "perversions" on December 29, 1975. In his "Declaration on Certain Questions concerning Sexual Ethics," the pope condemned homosexuality as "a serious depravity" that represented "a sad consequence of rejecting God."[8] This statement struck several members of the European gay community as "galling hypocrisy." Roger Peyrefitte, a former French diplomat, published an article in *Tempo*, an Italian news journal, which exposed the Holy Father's long-standing affair with Carlini.[9] The article created a furor, causing Paul VI to appear on the balcony of St. Peter's to denounce the "horrible and slanderous accusations." But Peyrefitte remained steadfast and repeated his accusations on a host of television news programs that were broadcast throughout Italy.[10]

THE RATZINGER RUMOR

Another rumored member of the Vatican's gay subculture was Joseph Ratzinger, who ascended to the papal throne as Benedict VI. In an article for *The Atlantic*, Andrew Sullivan wrote, "[Ratzinger's] gayness is almost wince-inducing. The prissy fastidiousness, the effeminate voice, the fixation on liturgy and ritual, and the over-the-top clothing accessories are one thing."[11] Similarly, Richard Sipe, a former Benedictine monk and well-known sociologist, said, "I have asked a number of Roman clerics and members of the Roman press corps if they think the pope is gay. None, of course, wish to be named for obvious reasons, but every one was convinced that Pope Benedict XVI is gay."[12]

Those who alleged Ratzinger's homosexuality pointed to his longtime relationship with Fr. Georg Gänswein, his handsome and fawning private secretary. Angelo Quattrocchi, a longtime Vatican observer, wrote, "About ten years before he became pope, when age was beginning to take its toll and was maybe sharpening the secret internal rage, Ratzy [Ratzinger] met Don Giorgio [Gänswein]. And it was a spark of life amid the doctrinal darkness. . . . So we can at least imagine how a pure soul becomes inflamed when it meets its soul mate, when a nearly 70-year-old prefect of the Congregation for the Doctrine of the Faith meets a brilliant 40-year-old priest from his native Bavaria who shares the same outlook on the world, . . . When we see the photos, which we publish in this book, of Georg putting Ratzy's little hat on for him, handing him his stole, watching his back, looking after him, accompanying him and helping him as he walks, we cannot help being moved."[13]

THE MAUVE MASS

The gay culture in the Vatican, according to a research project by Sylvia MacEachern, played a significant role in the creation of the new liturgy. Due to its influence, the Mass became less rigid and legalistic and more open to participation by the laity, more expressive of pop culture and contemporary trends in music, and more expressive in signs of affection.[14] Fr. Richard Fragomeni, one of the leaders of the liturgical reformation said that he wanted the New Mass to be "as attractive as sex."[15]

HOMOSEXUAL HIERARCHS

American Catholic hierarchs who were "outed" as gay included Bishop Robert H. Brown (San Diego), Bishop Paul Dudley (Sioux Falls, South Dakota), Bishop Thomas Dupré (Springfield, Massachusetts), Cardinal Edward Egan (New York), Bishop Joseph Ferrario (Honolulu, Hawaii), Bishop Louis E. Gelineau (Providence, Rhode Island), Bishop Thomas Green (Tucson, Arizona), Bishop Joseph Green (Reno/Las Vegas), Archbishop Wilton Gregory (Atlanta, Georgia), Bishop George H. Guilfoyle (Camden, New Jersey), Bishop Joseph Hart (Cheyenne, Wyoming), Bishop Howard Hubbard (Albany, New York), Bishop Thomas Lyons (Washington, DC), Bishop Robert Lynch (St. Petersburg, Florida), Bishop Emerson More (New York), Bishop Francis Mugavero (Brooklyn), Bishop P. Francis Murphy (Baltimore), Archbishop John Myers (Newark, New Jersey), Bishop Anthony J. O'Connell (Palm Springs, Florida), Archbishop John R. Quinn (San Francisco), Bishop James Rausch (Phoenix, Arizona), Bishop Frank Rodimer (Paterson, New Jersey), Bishop George Rueger (Worcester, Massachusetts), Bishop Daniel Ryan (Springfield, Illinois), Bishop Lawrence Soens (Sioux City, Iowa), Cardinal J. Francis Stafford (Denver, Colorado), Bishop J. Keith Symons (Palm Beach, Florida), Archbishop Rembert Weakland (Milwaukee), Bishop Lawrence Welsh (Spokane, Washington), Bishop J. Kendrick Williams (Lexington, Kentucky), and Bishop G. Patrick Ziemann (Santa Rosa, California).[16] The list contained the names of several "princes of the church," including Cardinal Joseph Bernardin, Cardinal Theodore McCarrick, and Cardinal John Wright.[17]

QUEER CARDINALS

Cardinal Joseph Bernardin was one of the most influential religious figures in the history of the American church. He was the creator of the National Conference of Catholic Bishops and the United States Catholic Conference.[18] According to his biographer, Eugene Kennedy, Bernardin "was the senior active American prelate among the country's more than 350. But his influence far exceeded his seniority. His writing and speaking on national and even global issues caused him to eclipse megabishops of the past."[19] On November 13, 1993, the cardinal was accused of numerous coercive sexual acts against Steven Cook, a seminarian from the Archdiocese of Cincinnati, and of engaging in "sexual satanic rites" with seminarians in Winona, Minnesota.[20] The 10 million dollar lawsuit against Bernardin was settled and sealed out of court. Cook, however, never retracted his charges, nor did he say they were inaccurate.[21] In accordance with Bernardin's last request, the Windy City Gay Chorus performed at his funeral Mass at the Holy Name Cathedral in Chicago in 1996.[22]

Cardinal Theodore McCarrick, archbishop of Washington, DC, was charged with making sexual advances on two priests and one ex-priest during his well-known "sleepovers" at his shore home in New Jersey.[23] Cardinal John Wright, who presided over the Archdiocese of Pittsburgh, had been known to have a predilection for boys going back to his days as a priest in Boston. Fr. Raymond Page would take boys out to a holiday home in Massachusetts for Wright to sodomize. In the spirit of charity, the cardinal gave the boys $20 for their cooperation.[24] At Vatican II, Wright was a strong advocate for reform, especially in the areas of ecumenism and religious freedom.

Notable among the practicing homosexual American cardinals was Cardinal Francis Spellman, one of the most influential Catholic clerics of the twentieth century. After his death, members of the media discovered that Spellman was well-known in New York's gay community as "Nelly." One of Spellman's lovers was a Broadway dancer who appeared in the show "One Touch of Venus." Several nights a week, the cardinal would send his limousine to pick up the dancer for bouts of rough-and-tumble sex. When the dancer asked Spellman how he could get away with living such a debauched life, the cardinal answered, "Who would believe it?"[25]

SEMINARY SEXCAPADES

By the end of Paul VI's reign, 40 percent to 60 percent of the young men in Catholic seminaries studying for the priesthood were practicing homosexuals.[26] The gay environment was so pronounced at St. John's Provincial Seminary in Plymouth, Michigan, that the school came to resemble the set for *Fellini Satyricon* rather than a place for spiritual formation. Homosexual acts between the seminarians took place in open settings. During the night, aggressive gays would cruise the dormitory from room to room in search of new partners. By 1985, the seminary had become so notorious as a homosexual hothouse that it was shut down by the Vatican.[27]

At St. Mary's Seminary in Baltimore, which became known as "the Pink Palace," the students regularly dressed in leather or lavender silk for a night of frolicking on the "block," Baltimore's answer to Greenwich Village. School vans provided the transportation. The rector of the seminary said, "We don't ask our candidates about their sexual orientation. It would be a violation of a man's civil rights to deny him ordination on those grounds."[28]

"OUT, PROUD, AND OPEN"

At St. Mary's of the Lake in Mundelein, Illinois (commonly known as "Mundelein"), new students were often coerced into having sex with upper classmen and the priests who served on the faculty. Instructors managed to convince the aspirants to the priesthood that homosexual acts were not a violation of the virtue of chastity. Coming out parties for the closet seminarians became gala events that were celebrated by dining, drinking, and dancing. Few were able to retain their orthodox beliefs in such a bacchanalian setting. One student sent this complaint to Father John Canary, the rector at Mundelein:

> Upon my arrival at Mundelein, I assumed there would be some "gay" students. I also assumed that I could handle that. I am a straight man, not a homophobic monster, Still nothing prepared me for the "underculture" of homosexuality that has been supported by the formation staff . . .
>
> It's pretty offensive to a straight guy, because if I ever brought a woman in, played dance music rather than show tunes, and told jokes about which classmates were coupling with whom, I'd be booted out in a minute. . . . It's common knowledge there are "gay couples" [at Mundelein] and I mean "couples" not friends.

The other problem at Mundelein is that if a straight student complains about this, he gets blackballed as a "conservative." There are several of us who are trying to be chaste. It's difficult, but to have to live among this gay culture is too much. To be at events where guys seem to have their CAM [campus] priest's blessing to be "out, proud, and open" about their love life really bothers me. And I am not alone.[29]

Students such as Michael Shane, who penned the above complaint, were classified as morally rigid and sent to psychologists for vocational counseling. At the counseling sessions, they were encouraged to be tolerant of all manners of sexual expression. If they failed to take this counseling to heart, they were driven out of the seminary as spiritually unfit for ordination.[30]

OUR SEXUALITY

In order to mold the students into "open and affirming" clerics, *Our Sexuality* became a standard text at the Oblate School of Theology in San Antonio, Texas. This work by Robert Crooks and Karla Baur, two "good Catholic authors," taught that those studying for the priesthood must relinquish many of their "biases," including the belief that sex is only for reproduction. The authors said,

Many people have learned to view activities and other practices—such as masturbation, sexual fantasy, and anal intercourse—with suspicion. The same is true of sexual activity between members of the same sex, which certainly does not fit into the model of intercourse for reproduction. All these noncoital sexual behaviors have been defined at some time as immoral, sinful, perverted, or illegal. We will present them in this text as viable sexual options for those who choose them.[31]

They insisted that students must abandon the traditional teachings of the church concerning sexual morality as expressed by St. Thomas Aquinas. Aquinas, according to *Our Sexuality*, "maintained that human sexual organs were designed for procreation and that any other use—as in homosexual acts, oral-genital sex, anal sex, or sex with animals—was against God's will and therefore heretical. Aquinas's teachings were so influential that from then on homosexuals were to find neither refuge nor tolerance anywhere in the Western World."[32]

Once ordained, many of the priests who graduated from these "hotbeds of homosexuality" came under the jurisdiction of gay bishops. They had been trained to be open and accepting of homosexual coupling. They had been exposed to teachers who insisted that seminarians adopt a nonjudgmental stance toward sexual deviancy. They had been encouraged by clerical formation teams to emerge from their closets and to acknowledge their sexual orientation. Those who fancied that these methods of preparing men for Holy Orders were all well and good remained blithely unaware that 10 percent of the new prelates were pedophiles.[33]

Chapter Fourteen

YEAR OF THREE POPES

Was John Paul I murdered? Certainly, there were reasons to believe so. For a man of sixty-five he was in excellent health; there was no post-mortem or autopsy; the Curia obviously panicked and was caught out in any number of small lies as to the manner of his death and the finding of his body; and if, as was widely believed, he was on the point of exposing a major financial scandal in which the Vatican Bank and its director, Paul Marcinkus, were deeply implicated, there were at least three international criminals—one of whom, Roberto Calvi of the Banco Ambrosiano, was later found hanging under Blackfriars Bridge in London—who would have gone to any length to prevent him from doing so. The Vatican, moreover, is an easy place for murder. It is an independent state with no police force of its own; the Italian police can enter only if invited—which they were not.
—John Julius Norwich, *Absolute Monarchs*, 2011

As his health began to fail in 1978, Paul VI ruminated about his sense of selfhood: "What is my state of mind? Am I Hamlet? Or Don Quixote? On the left? On the right?"[1] His questions remained unanswered. On Friday, August 4, he was confined to his bed at Castel Gandolfo (the papal summer residence) due to a flare up of arthroses, a disease of the joints, and a severe bladder infection.[2] From his bed, the pope participated in Sunday Mass at 8:00 a.m. As the liturgy drew to a close, Paul VI suffered such a massive heart attack that he seemed to explode from within. Fr. John Magee, who was at the pope's side, believed that the Holy Father would have been thrown from his bed by the violence of the attack if he had not been held by attending prelates.[3] Twelve hours later, he was dead.

THE STENCH OF DECAY

Cardinal Jean Villot, the Vatican secretary of state, was summoned. Following church protocol, he called out the pope's baptismal name (Giovanni) three times while tapping the head of the pope with a small silver mallet. After the pope was dressed in a red chasuble with a gold-and-white miter on his head, his body was placed in a hearse and transported fifteen miles to St. Peter's Basilica. For a time the body was sealed in a casket. But as cardinals began to gather, demands were made that the casket be opened and the body placed in view of the ecclesiastical mourners.[4]

The pope had died in the middle of the *ferragosto*, Italy's traditional August vacation break, and in the midst of a scorching heat wave, with temperatures soaring to 98 degrees in Rome. When the casket was opened, audible gasps could be heard. Paul VI's body had taken on a green tinge and already had begun to putrefy. The stench was appalling. Makeup was applied to the cadaver and the body was injected with more formaldehyde. Throughout the Novendiales, the nine days in which the pope's remains are placed on display, the same procedure had to be repeated several times a day, while fans were installed to disperse the smell.[5]

NO TOILETS

Before his death on August 6, 1978, Pope Paul VI decided to put to task the College of Cardinals by making the process of electing his successor as grueling as possible. Knowing that previous conclaves had been bugged,[6] he left instructions that all cardinal-electors swear a solemn oath not to divulge the results of the balloting to any outside source or to discuss the results with other princes of the church. Swiss Guards were placed outside every entrance and beneath every window, just in case one of the septuagenarian cardinals attempted to escape from a high tower.

Within the Sistine Chapel, where the conclave was held, the cardinals, who were accustomed to living in regal splendor within luxurious apartments, were confined to single cells without any amenities. Before entering the cells, the cardinals were searched by guards for "bugging" devices or other means of communication, including pencils and notepads. "The cells have no toilets and no running water," Cardinal Giuseppe Siri complained to an attendant. "It is impossible to live any longer under these conditions."[7]

"THEY'VE MADE PETER SELLERS A POPE!"

At the start of the conclave, on August 25, 1978, the 111 cardinals were marched in silence to the chapel. The presiding cardinal—the *camerlengo*—took roll call and ordered the purpled prelates to kneel while beating their breasts and chanting the Latin hymn, "Veni, Creator Spiritus." Many within the sacred assembly were disgruntled to find that they were not treated like princes of Holy Mother Church but prisoners in San Quentin.[8]

To make matters worse, the heat wave continued. The situation within the chapel soon became unbearable, with every door locked and barred and every window boarded and sealed. Small wonder that the traditionalists and progressives came to an immediate compromise by electing Albino Luciani, a "strange, little fellow," who became Pope John Paul.[9] The appearance of the smiling new pontiff on the central loggia of St. Peter's Basilica caused noted journalist and Vatican insider John Cornwell to gasp, "My God! That's Peter Sellers! They've made Peter Sellers a pope."[10]

THE OPEN LETTER

As soon as the election results were made known by the appearance of white smoke from the Sistine Chapel, the Italian press asked the new pope to restore "order and morality" to the Holy See. *Il Mondo*, Italy's leading economic journal, published an open letter to ask John Paul a series of sharply pointed questions. "Is it right for the Vatican to operate in markets like a speculator?" the journal inquired.[11] "Is it right for the Vatican to have a bank whose operations help the illegal transfer of capital from Italy to other countries? Is it right for that bank to assist Italians in evading taxes?"

Il Mondo went on to question the Vatican's association with "the most cynical financial dealers," such as Michele Sindona. The letter asked, "Why does the Church tolerate investments in companies, national and international, whose only aim is profit—companies which, when necessary, are willing to trample on the human rights of millions of the poor, especially in that Third World which is so close to your heart?"[12]

The letter, which was signed by the journal's financial editor, also offered the following observations about Bishop Paul Marcinkus, president of the Vatican Bank:

He is the only bishop who is on the board of a lay bank, which incidentally has a branch in one of the great tax havens of the capitalistic world. We mean the Cisalpine Oversees Bank in the Bahamas. Using tax havens is permitted by earthly law, and no lay banker can be hauled into court for taking advantage of that situation; but perhaps it is not licit under God's law, which should mark every act of the Church. The Church preaches equality but it does not seem to us that the best way to ensure equality is by evading taxes, which constitute the means by which the lay state tries to promote the same equality.[13]

THE PRELIMINARY REPORT

One week after the open letter appeared in *Il Mondo*, John Paul received a preliminary report on the internal workings of the Vatican Bank from Cardinal Villot, who remained the Holy See's secretary of state. The bank, which had been formed to further "religious works," was now serving a distinctly secular purpose. Of the 11,000 accounts within its registry, fewer than 1,650 served an ecclesiastical cause. The remaining 9,350 accounts served as "slush funds" for special friends of the Vatican, including Sindona, Calvi, Gelli, Marcinkus, and leading Sicilian Mafiosi, including the made men of the Corleone, Spatola, and Inzerillo families and members of the Camorra of Naples and Milan. The Banda della Magliana gang serviced the accounts of Giuseppe "Pippo" Calò, the Mafia's head cashier, who served as the boss of the Porta Nuova clan.[14] Other accounts were held by leading Italian politicians and businessmen; and still others for the foreign embassies of Iran, Iraq, Indonesia, Argentina, Chile, Colombia, and other countries.[15] The Santa Anna Gate within Vatican City opened to a busy thoroughfare as thugs with suitcases filled with drug money marched past the Swiss Guards, up the stairs to the IOR. Members of the Italian underworld, for the most part, remained traditionalists, who shied away from electronic bank transfers.[16]

WORSE NEWS

On September 7, Cardinal Giovanni Benelli, the archbishop of Florence, conveyed to the Holy Father even worse news: The Bank of Italy was investigating the links between Roberto Calvi of Banco Ambrosiano and the Vatican Bank, including Calvi's purchase of Banca Cattolica del

Veneto from the IOR in 1972. This purchase had occurred when John Paul was archbishop of Venice. The sale had been made without his consultation, let alone that of any other patriarch or prelate. Everything about this transaction was mysterious. Banca Cattolica del Veneto was one of Italy's wealthiest banks, with vast real-estate holdings in Northern Italy. Calvi, on behalf of Banco Ambrosiano, purchased 50 percent of the shares for $46.5 million (around $2 billion in today's money). But the shares never left the Vatican. Instead the stock was reassigned to Zitropo, a company owned by Michele Sindona. Zitropo was then sold to Calvi, and by 1978 the company was acquired by the Vatican. All this time the shares of Banca Cattolica del Veneto never left the Vatican safe.[17] The investigators sent a preliminary report concerning these irregularities to Judge Emilio Alessandrini. The final report, Cardinal Benelli told the pope, could result in criminal charges not only against Calvi but also against leading Vatican officials, including Archbishop Marcinkus and his two close IOR associates Luigi Mennini and Pellegrino de Strobel.

Neither Cardinal Benelli nor the pope were aware that the troublesome matter of Judge Alessandrini was under control and that criminal charges would not be filed against Calvi and his IOR cohorts. On January 29, 1979, five gunmen murdered the Italian magistrate, when his orange Renault 5 stopped for a red light on Via Muratori in Milan. The action accomplished its purpose. The investigation of Calvi and the Vatican officials came to an abrupt halt.[18]

MASONIC CABAL

The most appalling revelation came on Tuesday, September 12, when John Paul sat down at his desk to discover the latest copy of *L'Osservatore Politico*. This newsletter contained a list of 121 leading Catholic clerics and laymen who were members of Masonic lodges with alleged ties to Licio Gelli and P-2.[19] If the list proved accurate, the pope would have no recourse save to strip the cardinals, archbishops, bishops, and monsignors of their titles and offices and to subject them to the rite of excommunication in accordance with canon law. This action would constitute a pogrom of the *papabili*—the individuals closest to the Chair of St. Peter.[20] At the top of the list was the name of Cardinal Jean Villot, the Vatican secretary of state. Villot's Masonic name was "Jeanni" and he had enrolled in a Zurich lodge (#041/3) on August 6, 1966.[21]

The pope sought to see if the information was accurate by making contact with Italian officials through his close friends Cardinal Pericle Felici and Monsignor Giovanni Benelli, whose names did not appear in the newsletter. Since all secret societies in Italy were required to register the names of their members with the state, officials were able to locate Italian Masons of the Zurich lodge who confirmed that Cardinal Villot, indeed, had been inducted into the Order of Freemasonry.[22]

Another name on the list was that of Villot's assistant, Cardinal Sebastiano Baggio, Masonic name "SEBA," Lodge #85-1640, date of initiation August 14, 1967. Again, the pope and his associates made contact with the authorities and received confirmation that Cardinal Baggio, indeed, was a Mason in good standing. By the end of the day, John Paul received verification of the membership of other leading Catholic dignitaries in Masonic lodges, including Monsignor Agostino Casaroli, his foreign minister; Cardinal Ugo Poletti, the vicar of Rome; Monsignor Pasquale Macchi, who had been Paul VI's trusted secretary; and, last but not least, Archbishop Paul Marcinkus, who controlled the vast wealth of Holy Mother Church.[23]

A MILQUETOAST AT HEART

John Paul, however, was neither a spiritual warrior nor determined reformer. Of all the popes of the twentieth century, he was, perhaps, the most timorous. On one occasion, when a gust of wind blew a score of documents from his hands to the roof of the Apostolic Palace, John Paul became so distraught that his attendants had to place him in bed, where he remained with a rosary between his fingers until the papers were found.[24] Nevertheless, reliable sources contend that the new pope was moved to action as he learned more and more about the inner workings of Vatican, Inc. According to David Yallop, John Paul announced on September 28 his decision to remove Archbishop Marcinkus from the IOR, to transfer Cardinal Baggio to the diocese of Florence, and to force Cardinal Villot into retirement. This contention is supported by declassified documents from the US Department of State and the CIA.[25]

THE MACABRE GRIMACE

The morning after John Paul made these alleged announcements, he was found dead under conditions that continue to baffle investigators. At 4:30 a.m., Sister Vincenza, the papal housekeeper, following her morning routine, knocked at the door of the papal bedchambers and left a pot of coffee on a table in the hallway. When she returned a half hour later, she found the tray untouched. After knocking at the door and receiving no reply, she called out: "*Buon giorno, Papa.*" The room was still. Entering the room, she found the pope sitting up in bed with his eyeglasses half off his nose. His fingers were clutched around a file, and papers were strewn among the bed covers. As soon as she approached him, Sister Vincenza reeled back in horror. The pope's lips were pulled back in a macabre grimace; his gums were exposed; and his eyes appeared to have popped from their sockets.[26]

The nun shrieked with alarm and pulled a bell to summon Fr. John Magee, John Paul's secretary. As soon as Magee saw the pope's condition, he telephoned Cardinal Villot, who occupied an apartment within the Lateran Palace. Villot, according to Vatican sources, uttered in French the following cry of surprise: "*Mon Dieu, c'est vrais tous ca?*" ("My God, is all that true?"). Then he asked Magee an extraordinary question: "Does anybody else know the Holy Father is dead?" Magee replied on the phone that no one knew except the Vatican nun. Villot then told Magee that no one—not even Sister Vincenza—must be allowed to enter the pope's bedroom and that he, as the Vatican *camerlengo* ("presiding cardinal") would handle matters as soon as he arrived.[27]

VILLOT'S SATCHEL

Villot appeared in a matter of moments. To Magee's amazement, the cardinal was shaved, well groomed, and in full ecclesiastical attire. It seemed as though Villot was set to make a public appearance. The time was 5:00 a.m.[28]

Before proceeding with the rite of extreme unction, Villot began placing items from the pope's bedroom in a satchel, including the vial of low blood pressure medicine that John Paul kept on a bedside table, the papers that were scattered on the bedcovers, the pope's appointment book, and his last will. Finally, he removed John Paul's glasses and slippers. None of these things were ever seen again.[29]

A PHYSICIAN'S PRONOUNCEMENT

Villot telephoned Dr. Renato Buzzonetti, the Vatican physician, and instructed Magee to make arrangements for the immediate transfer of Sister Vincenza to her cloistered environment at her motherhouse in Venice. At this point in the story, the nun disappeared. No investigator—not even John Cornwell who became the official Vatican snoop in this case—was permitted to interview her. Cornwell was merely told that she had died shortly after arriving at the motherhouse.[30] The British journalist accepted this explanation without question. Neither he nor any other reporter who probed into John Paul's death has been able to uncover the proper name of Sister Vincenza, let alone reason for her abrupt dismissal from the Vatican.

Dr. Buzzonetti arrived at 5:45, examined the body, and announced to Magee and Villot that the pope had suffered "a coronary occlusion;" that he had died "between 10:30 and 11:00 the previous evening;" and that he had "suffered nothing."[31] But the Holy Father's bulging eyes and horrific grimace seemed to tell a different story.

BIZARRE POSTMORTEM

Shortly after the physician left, two morticians—Ernesto and Arnaldo Signoracci—appeared out of nowhere. It was 6:00 a.m. Villot must have summoned them as soon as he received the call from Father Magee (i.e., before 5:00 a.m.), before he called Dr. Buzzonetti, and before he had even seen the body.[32] What's more, the morticians had been transported to the Vatican by an official call that presumably had to be dispatched before Villot entered the papal bedchamber.[33] When Cornwell interviewed the Signoracci brothers, they were unable to confirm the time of their arrival. They only affirmed that it was early in the morning.[34]

Even though the bodies of the popes are traditionally not embalmed, the two morticians, under instructions from Villot, began to inject embalming fluid into John Paul's body as soon as they arrived. This unorthodox means of embalming without draining the corpse of blood would serve to prevent any possibility of a complete autopsy and any accurate determination of the cause of death.[35] The morticians also manipulated the distorted jaw of the pope, corrected his horrible grimace, and closed his eyes.[36] When interviewed by Cornwell, the brothers admitted that they had opened the dead pope's femoral arteries and injected an "anti-putrid" fluid before removing the body from the Vatican. They could not remember either the room or the place where they had performed this procedure.[37]

A FABRICATED STORY

While the pope's body was being infused with the fluid, Villot instructed Magee to relate to the world a fabricated story about the morning's events. Magee was to say that he, not Sister Vincenza, had found the pope's body. He was to make no mention of the papers that were strewn across the bed or the items that Villot had tucked away in his satchel. What's more, in order to provide a proper ecclesiastical spin to the tale, Magee was to say that John Paul had died with a copy of *The Imitation of Christ*, the great devotional work by St. Thomas à Kempis, clutched in his hand.[38]

At 6:30 a.m., Villot conveyed the news of the pope's death to Cardinal Carlo Confalonieri, the eighty-six-year-old dean of the Sacred College; Cardinal Agostino Casaroli, head of the Varian Diplomatic Corps; and Sergeant Hans Roggen of the Swiss Guards.[39] The news was beginning to spread throughout the Vatican village. At 6:45 a.m., Sergeant Roggen came upon Archbishop Marcinkus in a courtyard near the Vatican Bank. This was most unusual. Marcinkus, who lived twenty minutes from the Vatican in the Villa Stritch, was a late riser, who never appeared at his office before 9:00 a.m. When the sergeant blurted out the news, Marcinkus stared at Roggen, displayed no emotion, and made no comment. Later, when questioned by Cornwell about his lack of reaction, Marcinkus offered this explanation: "I thought he [Roggen] said, 'Hey, I dreamed the Pope was dead.'"[40]

At 7:27 a.m., nearly three hours after Sister Vincenza discovered the pope's body, Vatican Radio made the following announcement: "This morning, September 29, 1978, about five-thirty, the private secretary of the pope, contrary to custom not having found the Holy Father in the chapel of his private apartment, looked for him in his room and found him dead in bed with a light on, like one who was intent on reading. The physician, Dr. Renato Buzzonetti, who hastened to the pope's room, verified the death, which took place presumably toward eleven o'clock yesterday evening, as 'sudden death' that could be related to acute myocardial infarction."[41]

THE STORY UNRAVELS

Despite Cardinal Villot's care in fabricating the fiction, the story quickly began to unravel upon inspection. The first problem came with *The Imitation of Christ*. John Paul's copy could not be found within the papal apartment. It remained among his belongings in Venice, where he had served as patriarch. On October 2, the Vatican was forced to admit that the Holy Father was not reading *The Imitation of Christ* at the time of his demise, but rather was holding in his hands "certain sheets of paper containing his personal writings such as homilies, speeches, reflections, and various notes."[42] On October 5, after continual badgering from the press, the Vatican came clean and admitted that the papers the Holy Father was clutching concerned his decision to make critical changes within the Roman Curia, including the Vatican Bank.

The second problem came with the work of the morticians. Italian law dictated that no embalming should be undertaken until twenty-four hours after death without dispensation from a magistrate. For this reason, the immediate injection of "anti-putrid" fluid into the body of the pope without drainage of blood smacked of foul play.[43] On October 1, *Corriere della Sera*, Milan's daily newspaper, published a front-page story entitled, "Why Say No to an Autopsy?" The story called for a complete disclosure of all facts relating to the pope's death and concluded by saying,

> The Church has nothing to fear, therefore, nothing to lose. On the contrary, it would have much to gain. Now, to know what the pope died of is of a legitimate historical fact, it is part of our visible history and does not in any way affect the spiritual mystery of his death. The body that we leave behind when we die can be understood with our poor instruments, it is a leftover; the soul is already, or rather it has always been, dependent on other laws which are not human and so remain inscrutable. Let us not make out of a mystery a secret to guard for earthly reasons and let us recognize the smallness of our secrets. Let us not declare sacred what is not.[44]

"NON STA BENE, MA BENONE!"

These demands intensified when John Paul's personal physicians said that the pope was in good health. "He had absolutely no cardiopathic characteristics," Dr. Carlo Frizzerio said. "Besides, his low blood pressure should, in theory, have made him safe from acute cardiovascular attacks. The only time I needed to give him treatment was for the influenza attack."[45] This diagnosis was verified by Dr. Giuseppe Da Ros, who examined the pope on Saturday, September 23, and told the press: *"Non sta bene, ma benone"* ("He is not well, but very well").[46] The pope's good physical condition was attributed to his lifestyle. He exercised regularly, never smoked, drank alcohol only rarely, and kept a healthy diet. At the time of his death, John Paul was sixty-five.

Numerous heart specialists throughout the world, including Dr. Christiaan Barnard of South Africa and Dr. Seamus Banim of London, took to task Dr. Buzzonetti's diagnosis of myocardial infarction without conducting an autopsy as "incredible" and "preposterous."[47] Such critiques caused Villot to concoct another story. He told his fellow cardinals, who pressed for an autopsy, that the real cause of John Paul's death was not a heart attack. The Holy Father, he assured them, had unwittingly taken a fatal overdose of Effortil, his blood pressure medicine. If an autopsy was conducted, Villot said, it would give rise to the belief that the pope had committed suicide.[48]

CANON LIES

When this explanation failed to quiet the clamor for an autopsy, Villot proclaimed that canon law expressly prohibited the body of a pope to be subjected to postmortem surgery. This statement gave rise to yet another problem. Canon law neither banned nor condoned papal autopsies. It failed to address the subject. What's more, scholars quickly pointed out that an autopsy had been performed on the body of Pius VII in 1830.[49]

Rumor quickly became rampant that John Paul had died of poisoning. Some speculated that a lethal dosage of digitalis had been added to the Effortil, which was in liquid form. Such a mixture would induce vomiting—vomiting that would account for the necessity of Villot's removal of the pope's glasses and slippers. Brother Fabian, the Vatican pharmacist, used this theory to provide a final explanation to the pope's demise. John Paul, he said, was taking digoxin for a heart problem and could have swallowed a few pills before taking a slug of Effortil, with tragic results. But this explanation also proved to be bogus. John Paul had never received a prescription for digoxin. That drug had been used by Paul VI.[50]

"*EGLI E POLACCO*"

On Monday, October 16, 1978, Karol Wojtyla ascended to the papal throne as John Paul II. The news of the selection of Wojtyla caught the teeming crowd that had gathered in St. Peter's Square by surprise. The people expected the election of some established member of the Vatican bureaucracy, such as the progressive Cardinal Benelli or the conservative Cardinal Siri. They were stunned to hear the name of Wojtyla. Even members of the press turned to one another to ask: "Who is Wojtyla?" His strange-sounding name led many to believe that the new pope might be an African or Asian. Eventually, Fr. Andrew Greeley of Chicago told them: "*Egli e Polacco*" ("He is a Pole").[51]

It was one thing to elect a Pole—such as the famous anti-Communist Cardinal Stefan Wyszynski—but quite another to elect one about whom so little was known. Who was Wojtyla? How had a junior cardinal come to the throne in less than two days of balloting? Not only was the election unexpected, but the new pope also looked unusual as a Holy Father. He lacked the delicate—almost effete—features of Paul VI and Pius XII. His hulking physical frame and his nonintellectual mannerisms seemed to some observers antithetical to the Roman grace and refinement of many of his predecessors. This "lack of refinement" came to the fore during his first public appearance. Wojtyla, as John Paul II, approached a group of American reporters and beseeched them with the folded hands of a penitent to be "good" to him. A few minutes later, in a further effort to ingratiate himself with the press, the new pope cupped his hands like a megaphone and shouted his blessing to the milling crowd like a cheerleader at a football game.[52]

THE UNKNOWN WOJTYLA

Gradually, the public came to learn that Wojtyla, as a young man, had sought not to become a priest but an actor.[53] They further learned that he had worked in a chemical factory under Nazi control during World War II—although no one knew for certain if he had been the leader of "an underground movement which assisted Jews" or a Nazi collaborator.[54] Rumors persisted that he had developed romantic attachments to many women and may have been married. The alleged marriage helped to explain the so-called "great gap" in John Paul's career—the five-year span of time between 1939 and 1944.[55]

But certain things about the new pope eventually came to light. Cardinal Villot and the "Masonic Cardinals" had engineered his campaign with the help of US Cardinals Cody and Krol and celebrated his election not with traditional *Te Deums* and official prayers but rather a gala champagne party in which the new Holy Father filled the empty glasses of the nearest cardinals and nuns while warbling his favorite song, a Polish number called "The Mountaineer."[56]

The stage was set for moral and financial disaster.

Chapter Fifteen

THE AMBROSIANO AFFAIR

> *On the eve of his death, Calvi wrote to Pope John Paul II, seemingly pleading for his life. That he should involve the Supreme Vicar of the Catholic Church in this way is inexplicable, unless it was understood as a form of implied blackmail. The full story of Roberto Calvi has yet to be told. We shall better come to understand it by first regarding John Paul II's papacy as institutionally corrupted, and Calvi's role and influence within it as far larger than hitherto appreciated.*
>
> —Richard Cottrell, *Gladio:*
> *NATO's Dagger at the Heart of Europe*, 2012

By 1978, when John Paul II ascended to the papal throne, the money coming into the six Vatican shell companies in Panama—Astolfine SA, United Trading Corporation, Erin SA, Bellatrix SA, Belrose SA, and Starfield SA—from the Medellin Cartel alone was enormous, since Pablo Escobar, at the height of his power, was smuggling fifteen tons of cocaine into the United States every day.[1] The drug business was booming to such an extent that the Holy See set up two additional dummy firms—Manic SA in Luxembourg and Nordeurop Establishment in Liechtenstein—to aid in the washing the black money.[2]

The eight laundries were simply storefronts, manned by secretaries and street thugs. The money they received was wired or transported by courier, often a cleric, to the central headquarters of Banco Ambrosiano in Milan. From Milan, the money was rerouted to the Vatican Bank.[3] With the money flowing between tax-sheltered banks, the Guardia di Finanza (Italy's financial police) and other bank-auditing agencies were hardpressed to obtain the names of the depositors, let alone evidence of criminal malfeasance.

In addition to the cash from the cartels, money poured into the eight shell companies in the form of loans from Banco Ambrosiano in Milan. The loans were easy to obtain. Roberto Calvi, who remained Ambrosiano's *direttore generale*, convinced the bank's directors that the offshore firms were concerns of the Vatican for the exportation of "parochial goods."[4]

Of all the directors of all the banks in all the world, the directors of Banco Ambrosiano were the least likely to question the integrity of the undertakings of Holy Mother Church. The bank had been established in 1896 by Monsignor Giuseppe Tovini to provide financial service to Roman Catholic institutions and families. Named after St. Ambrose, the firm's expressly Catholic character was protected by a statute that required shareholders and directors to submit a baptismal certificate and statement of good conduct from their parish priest before they could vote.[5] Ambrosiano's independence from secular interest was protected by a statute that barred any individual from obtaining more than 5 percent of its shares. The bank's purpose was to serve "moral organizations, pious works, and religious bodies set up for charitable aims."[6] Any objection that the directors might have to the strange, new offshore companies were offset by the fact that the loans were sent not to Liechtenstein or Luxembourg but directly to the Vatican Bank.[7]

INSIDE THE SCAM

Almost overnight, the eight phony firms became multimillion dollar businesses that had been established without capital expenditure. It was a mindboggling accomplishment. The Ponzi scam served several purposes. The first was to provide a new source of arms revenue for "gladiators" involved in the "strategy of tension" (mounting attacks that could be blamed on Communist agitators) and right-wing regimes, even the regimes at war with America's closest allies. Bellatrix, for example, used $200 million of its assets to purchase French-made Exocet AM39 missiles for Argentina's military junta in its struggle with England over the Falkland Islands.[8] Other offshore companies engaged in obtaining Libyan arms supplies for the Argentine troops and for Nicaragua's Anastasio Somoza Debayle, whose regime was threatened by left-wing Sandinistas.[9] Since the Vatican owned the companies, Holy Mother Church was becoming a principal source of murder and violence throughout Italy and Latin America.

HOW TO STEAL A BANK

A primary purpose of the scam was for the Vatican Bank to obtain financial control of Ambrosiano. The shell companies used a portion of the loans to purchase Ambrosiano stock. Since the bank's charter prohibited any institution or person gaining from more than 5 percent of the shares, the stock was purchased by a multitude of phony corporations that were spinoffs of the eight phony firms. The United Trading Corporation, for example, spawned a host of nominal subsidiaries, including Ulricor, La Fidele, Finproggram, Ordeo, Lantana, Casadilla, Marbella, Imparfin, and Teclefin. By 1982, Ulricor ranked as the eighth-largest shareholder of Ambrosiano stock with 1.2 percent.[10]

To conceal the fraud, Calvi opened Ambrosiano Group Banco Comercial in Managua. Its official function was "conducting international commercial transactions." But its real function was to serve as a repository beyond the purview of the Guardia di Finanza, where all evidence concerning the fraudulent and criminal devices used to acquire majority interest in the Milan parent bank could be concealed.[11] For this convenience, of course, there was a price to be paid. Calvi traveled to Nicaragua and dropped several million into Somoza's pocket. The dictator was so pleased that he not only pronounced his blessing upon the new branch but also granted Calvi a Nicaraguan diplomatic passport, which he retained for the rest of his life.[12]

To increase the value of the shares, Calvi announced huge stock dividends and rights offerings, along with optimistic pronouncements about the future of Banco Ambrosiano and its new Latin branches. The shares began to split and split again. The shells used their increased stock holdings to borrow more money with which they purchased more stock in the name of more and more new spinoff firms. They never paid interest on their borrowings. They simply added the accrued interest to their loan balances and backed their obligation for collateral with more of their bank stock.[13] It worked like a charm. By the start of 1981, the Vatican had succeeded in gaining ownership of 16 percent of Ambrosiano's shares.[14]

SOLIDARITY'S SHARE

Another purpose of the scam was to provide funding for Solidarity, the largest trade union in Poland. As soon as he was crowned with the tiara,

John Paul II met in private with Calvi to express his demand that an ample share of the money from the Ponzi scheme be channeled to Lech Walesa, who had been "sent by God, by Providence."[15] Such payments met with the approval of Zbigniew Brzezinski, President Carter's national security advisor, and General Vernon Walters, the US ambassador-at-large.[16] By 1981, over $100 million in funds from the drug cartels and the illegal bank loans had flowed into the coffers of the struggling Polish labor movement, making the new pope a great hero in his native country.[17] Few, including Walesa, opted to look the gift horse in the mouth to discern that the true source of the manna from heaven was the drug trade.

PERSONA NON GRATA

In 1978, Michelle Sindona no longer could play a part in the shell game. He had been indicted in Italy for issuing false balance sheets and for filing a fraudulent statement of bankruptcy concerning Banca Privata, which had collapsed in 1974 after suffering a financial hemorrhage in excess of $300 million. Sindona fled to New York City, where he took up residence in the discreetly elegant Hotel Pierre on Fifth Avenue.[18] In New York, he was charged with bank fraud and his involvement in the collapse of the Franklin National, the largest bank failure in American history.[19]

The Sicilian don had become a persona non grata among his former criminal accomplices. Calvi and Marcinkus removed Sindona's name as a director of Cisalpine, the Nassau financial front, which now became known as Banco Ambrosiano Overseas.[20]

But, thanks to Sindona, the ties between the Vatican and the Mafia had been tightened into a Gordian knot. The money from the drug trade flowed into the Vatican Bank through parochial banks, including Banco Ambrosiano, while P-2 used the dummy companies to sell arms to Latin American dictators.[21] The last thing the mob wanted was exposure of the shell game.

AN UNTIMELY AUDIT

So much money pouring out of the country into mysterious offshore companies with weird-sounding names didn't go unnoticed. In June 1978, a twelve-man team from the Bank of Italy launched a probe of Banco

Ambrosiano, only to discover that they had wandered into a bewildering labyrinth of shady financial transactions. Calvi refused to provide the team with requested information concerning the eight companies that had received hundreds of millions in loans and the branches of the bank in Luxembourg, Nassau, and Managua. He claimed that such disclosures would breach the banking regulations of other countries. Eventually, the team asked for more investigators to unravel the puzzle. But even twenty auditors pouring over the books day after day for six months could not discern the true nature of the subsidiaries and shell companies, let alone the ground plan of the financial scheme.[22]

On November 17, 1978, the examiners produced a five-hundred-page report that was painfully abstruse. But the overall verdict that the bank was "not at all satisfactory" in its operations sent shivers throughout Italy's financial community. The auditors added this recommendation: "There is a clear need to cut back the network of subsidiaries which Ambrosiano has created abroad. They [the bank officials] must also be forced to provide more information and figures about their real assets, to avoid the risk that a possible liquidity crisis on their part might also affect the Italian banks, with all the unfavorable consequences that might entail."[23]

The report devoted more than twenty-five pages to the torturous relationship between Banco Ambrosiano and the Vatican Bank. It stated, "Independently of its position as stockholder, the IOR is bound by strong interest connections to the Ambrosiano group, as is demonstrated by its [the Vatican's] constant presence in some of Ambrosiano's most meaningful and delicate operations."[24]

A WARNING TO THE POPE

When the news of the report was leaked to the public, shares of Ambrosiano fell 30 percent on the Milan exchange and a horde of panicked depositors descended on the once staid bank to withdraw their savings.[25] The findings garnered the attention of the financial police, who opted to take a closer look at the books of Banco Ambrosiano and the dealings of Roberti Calvi. The new investigation, headed by Judge Luca Mucci, prompted Calvi to move the base of his international operations even deeper within the heart of Latin America. In 1980, he opened Banco Ambrosiano de America del Sud in Buenos Aires.[26]

As soon as the new investigation got underway, Beniamino Andreatta,

Italy's treasury minister, met with Cardinal Agostino Casaroli, the Vatican's secretary of state, to urge the severance of all ties between the Holy See and Calvi. Casaroli presented these concerns to the Holy Father. But so much money was pouring into the IOR and Solidarity that John Paul II opted to ignore the warning.[27]

SETBACKS

Matters beyond the control of Calvi, the CIA, and the Vatican also served to undermine the shell game. Throughout 1979, interest rates throughout the world soared to astronomical heights, making it more expensive for Banco Ambrosiano to obtain money for the loans. The Ambrosiano officials, prompted by the nagging concerns of board member Roberto Orson and deputy chairman Roberto Rosone, began to demand from Calvi definite proof that the Vatican maintained control over the eight ghost companies. The situation worsened as the dollar rose sharply against the lira, diminishing the worth of the lira-denominated bank shares.[28]

In July 1980, after the Guardia di Finanza uncovered evidence of "illegal capital exportation, bank documentation forgery, and fraud," Judge Mucci ordered Calvi to surrender his passport and warned that criminal charges would be on the way.[29] The banker was not amused. He needed his passport. He intended to meet with the oil-rich Arabs to secure a bailout.[30]

Thanks to the intervention of Gelli and leading members of P-2 who provided bribes to Ugo Zelletti and other members of the Superior Court of the Magistrature,[31] Calvi managed to recover his passport, just in time to travel to Nassau, where he forged a link between Ambrosiano Overseas and Artoc, a leading financial institution of the Arab world. A temporary agreement between the two firms was signed in London. Calvi now believed that his hope for salvation would come from the Muslim world. His faith was misplaced. The millions never materialized.[32]

THE UNANSWERED LETTER

On January 21, 1981, a group of Milanese shareholders in Banco Ambrosiano, fearing that the balloon would burst and that their shares would be worthless, wrote a long letter to John Paul II, urging him to investigate the unholy ties between Marcinkus, Calvi, Umberto Ortolani, and Gelli and the huge flow of cash into the corporations under the "patronage" of the Vatican. The letter, which was written in Polish so that the pope could easily understand it, stated the following:

> The IOR is not only a shareholder in Banco Ambrosiano, but also an associate and partner of Roberto Calvi. It is revealed by a growing number of court cases that Calvi stands today astride one of the main crossroads of the most degenerate Freemasonry (P-2) and of Mafia circles, as a result of inheriting Sindona's mantle. This has been done once again with the involvement of people generously nurtured and cared for by the Vatican, such as Ortolani, who move between the Vatican and powerful groups in the international underworld.[33]

"APPALLING EFFRONTERY"

John Paul II neglected to give the shareholders the dignity of a response. Instead, in a gesture of cold indifference to their pleas, the pope elevated Marcinkus to the position of president of the Pontifical Commission for the State of Vatican City. This position made "the Gorilla" the governor of Vatican City, in addition to head of the IOR. The promotion was made on September 28, 1981, the third anniversary of the death of John Paul I. Regarding this "appalling effrontery," David Yallop wrote,

> Through his Lithuanian origins, his continual espousal, in fiscal terms, of Poland's needs, and his close proximity to the pope because of his role as personal bodyguard and overseer of all security on foreign trips, Marcinkus had discovered in the person of Karol Wojtyla the most powerful protector a Vatican employee could have. Sindona, Calvi, and others like them are, according to the Vatican, wicked men who have deceived naïve, trusting priests. Either Marcinkus has misled, lied to, and suppressed the truth from Pope John Paul II since October 1978, or the present pope also stands indicted.[34]

The elevation of Marcinkus was made despite the warnings from Italy's treasury minister, the Bank of Italy audit, the worsening financial condition of the shell companies, and the circulation of the P-2 list, which showed that "the Gorilla" remained a Freemason in violation of canon law. Why John Paul would make such a promotion at this stage in his pontificate defies all rules of logic, let alone moral rectitude. One must realize that the pope—not less than common laymen—was aware that Marcinkus was a principal player in the $1 billion counterfeit securities scam, the collapse of Banca Privata, P-2 and the strategy of tension, and the mysterious death of his predecessor. The real postmortem miracle of John Paul II remains the continual concealment of his complicity in high crimes from the legion of men and women of good faith who have proclaimed him a saint.

A LETTER OF PATRONAGE

Calvi was becoming increasingly desperate. The shareholders kept insisting on some proof that the eight shell companies that had been established in Luxembourg, Liechtenstein, and Panama were properties of the Holy See. By August 1, Calvi had no choice save to appear before Archbishop Marcinkus with hat in hand. The affair was about to explode unless he could present some assurance to the Guardia di Finanza that the eight companies, which had drained Banco Ambrosiano of all its cash reserves, were, in fact, legitimate Vatican concerns. Marcinkus realized that some action had to be taken to ward off financial disaster and came up with a course of action that represented one of the greatest acts of fraud in ecclesiastical history. He issued a "letter of patronage" stating that the dummy firms were legitimate financial organizations, whose purposes and financial obligations were known, secured, and approved by Holy Mother Church. The letter, dated September 1, 1981, was written on Vatican letterhead. It reads as follows:

> Gentlemen:
> This is to confirm that we directly or indirectly control the following entries:
>
> Manic SA, Luxembourg
> Astolfine SA, Panama
> Nordeurop Establishment, Liechtenstein
> United Trading Corporation, Panama
> Erin SA, Panama
> Bellatrix SA, Panama
> Belrose SA, Panama
> Starfield SA Panama
>
> We also confirm our awareness of their indebtedness toward yourselves as of June 10, 1981, as per the attached statement of accounts.[35]

The attached accounts showed "indebtedness" to the Lima branch of Banco Ambrosiano alone for $907 million. The letter was signed by Archbishop Marcinkus, along with his administrative assistants Luigi Mennini and Pellegrino de Strobel.[36] To compound the fraud, Calvi presented Marcinkus with a letter of his own—this one stating that the Vatican Bank "would entail no liabilities" or "suffer no future damage or loss" from its involvement with the eight companies.[37]

A PLEA TO THE POPE

But the letter failed to shore up the losses, which amounted to $1.5 billion. On May 31, 1982, the Bank of Italy wrote to Calvi and his board of directors in Milan requesting a full accounting of the lending to the Vatican's eight shell companies. The board, under increased pressure, voted eleven to three to comply, despite Calvi's protests.[38]

Knowing the shell game had been lost, Calvi turned to the Holy Father with a last request for deliverance. In a letter dated June 5, 1982, he wrote,

I have thought a lot, Holiness, and have concluded that you are my last hope. . . . I have been offered help by many people on condition that I talk about my activities for the Church. Many would like to know from me whether I supplied arms and other equipment to certain South American regimes to help them fight our common enemies, and whether I supplied funds to Solidarity or arms and funds to other organizations of Eastern countries. I will not reveal it. I will not submit to nor do I want to blackmail; I have always chosen the path of coherence and loyalty.[39]

He added: "The Vatican has betrayed and abandoned me."[40]

After documenting in writing the Holy See's involvement in arming guerillas, engaging in bloody war, and misappropriating funds, Calvi continued, "Summing up, I ask that all the money that I gave to the projects of serving the political and economic expansion of the Church, that the thousands of millions of dollars that I gave to Solidarity with the express will of the Vatican, and that the sums which I provided to organize the financial centers and political power in five South American countries will be returned to me. These sums would amount to $1.75 billion."[41] He concluded the letter by saying that he was "seeking serenity" and "to live in peace."

FINANCIAL DOOMSDAY

On Thursday, June 17, came the coup de grace. *Il Sole 24 Ore*, Italy's cautious and conservative financial newspaper, published the complete text of the Bank of Italy's letter to Calvi and the Ambrosiano directors. Ambrosiano stock went into a freefall that resulted in complete collapse. Rosone and two other directors appeared before Luigi Mennini, deputy director of the IOR, and Pellegrino De Strobel, the IOR's chief accountant, and demanded payment on the loans that the Holy See had received for its offshore holdings.[42] They presented the two IOR officials with the letter of patronage which they along with Archbishop Marcinkus had signed and sealed. By any banking standard, they insisted, the letter represented a statement of financial obligation. Marcinkus was contacted by telephone. He was accompanying the pope on a trip to Switzerland. He responded to the demands of the Ambrosiano directors by saying, "We just don't have that kind of money."[43] When warned that his response would be reported to the Bank of Italy, the Archbishop said, "I know. I did all this to help a friend and look where we are."[44] Rosone later recalled his reaction: "I became as angry as a buffalo. I told them [Mennini and De Strobel] this was a criminal conspiracy. They had committed fraud. The letter [of patronage] was from the IOR and it was a guarantee. All that was missing was the signature of Jesus Christ."[45]

An emergency meeting was held on the fourth floor of Ambrosiano's headquarters. Panic reigned. Accusations were exchanged. Threats were made. Lawyers were summoned. When a degree of order was restored, Calvi, by unanimous vote, was removed from his position at the bank. The board was dissolved, and the bank was placed in the hands of a commissioner from the Bank of Italy.[46] A new warrant was issued for Calvi's arrest. But the cause of so much turmoil was nowhere to be found. The previous week, Calvi had made his escape from Milan. He was now one of the world's most wanted fugitives.

The day after Calvi vanished, Graziella Corrocher, the banker's fifty-five-year-old personal secretary, fell or was hurled from the fifth floor of Ambrosiano. The body landed with a thump on the ramp leading to the bank's underground garage. No arrests were made, and the cause of her death remains undetermined.[47]

TELL-TALE DOCUMENTS

On June 11, while packing his bags, Calvi told his son Nino, "I shall reveal things, which once known, will rock the Vatican. The pope will have to resign."[48] He stuffed several documents in his black briefcase, which came to light in 1987. One was a note concerning Gelli, which read, "He had convinced me that all political and financial power really depended on him and that no deal of any importance could go ahead without his consent." The note further stated that Calvi had never made a decision regarding the transfer of funds to the shell companies or weapons for the Latin American dictators and guerilla armies without conferring with Licio Gelli, his Masonic Worshipful Master.[49]

In a letter, Calvi said that the Vatican needed him to launch "an effective politico-religious penetration into secular society by securing control over banking institutions. The enormous importance of what I have just said induced me to incur debts in foreign currency in order to buy Banco Ambrosiano shares in sufficient quantity to guarantee IOR control over the institution."[50] Working for the Vatican, he added, meant providing financial assistance to guerilla units and strong-arm regimes. He wrote, "On more than one occasion, I believed that my life was at risk as I rushed from one Latin American country to another, seeking to oppose the ferment of anticlerical ideologies. I did my utmost in every sense even to the point of concerning myself with the supply of warships and other war materiel to support those capable of contrasting the advance of well-organized communist forces." These efforts, he maintained, ensured that the Vatican would have an authoritative presence in such countries as Argentina, Colombia, Peru, Paraguay, and Nicaragua.

Nearly four years after Calvi made his escape from Milan, Bishop Pavel Hnilica of Czechoslovakia paid Flavio Carboni $6 million on behalf of the Vatican for the contents of the black briefcase. On April 1, 1986, an Italian television news program, with the permission of Bishop Hnilica, opened the briefcase before its viewing public with great flourish. The contents had been depleted, but the remaining documents showed that Calvi had been pushed beyond the breaking point and was ready to employ blackmail in order to obtain reparation for the Ambrosiano's losses. Seven years after the program was aired, a Roman court convicted Carboni and Bishop Hnilica of being in receipt of stolen property.[51]

ESCAPE TO LONDON

Leaving Milan, Calvi made his way to the seaport city of Trieste, where he boarded the *Outrango*, a launch that had been used by Stibam, the Milan shipping firm, for drug smuggling, and sailed to the small fishing village of Muggia in Yugoslavia.[52] He was met by Carboni, who drove him to a safe house in Austria, where he received a passport that was genuine in all respects except the name of its bearer. "Roberto Calvi" had been crudely but simply adjusted to "*Gian* Roberto Calvi*ni*."[53]

On June 14, he was flown to London on a plane that had been chartered by Hans Kunz, who had been a player in Stibam's guns for drugs operation.[54] The Austrian businessman had been involved in providing Exocet missiles for use by the Argentine military junta in the Falklands War. The order had been placed by Gelli. The funding had been provided by Ambrosiano through a Vatican dummy corporation in Panama.[55]

THE BROTHEL AND THE BRIDGE

In London, Calvi was placed in an eighth-floor flat of a seedy apartment building off King's Row that served as a brothel for a louche clientele.[56] The hiding place had been secured for him by Carboni, who had booked lodgings for himself at a luxurious London Hilton. Calvi, growing increasingly morose and frightened, spent the next two days in a squalid bedroom stretched out on a cot, staring at the television, and making telephone calls. He spoke several times with his daughter Anna in Zurich, telling her of the danger she faced and imploring her to leave Europe for the United States. "Something really important is happening," he said, "and today or tomorrow all hell is going to break loose."[57]

On June 17, the body of Roberto Calvi was found hanging from an orange noose under Blackfriars Bridge in London, his feet dangling in the muddy waters of the Thames. He was wearing a lightweight gray suit; an expensive Patek Philippe watch remained on his wrist; and $20,000 was stuffed in his wallet. In his pockets were four pairs of eyeglasses and his doctored Italian passport; five bricks had been stuffed in his trousers.[58]

MASONIC SYMBOLISM

The site of Calvi's demise immediately aroused suspicion. Members of various Masonic lodges in Italy wear black robes and address each other as "friar." "Black friars"—*fratelli neri*—is an Italian nickname for Freemasons. There is even a "Blackfriars" lodge, number 3,722, in the "List of Lodges Masonic," the official register of European masonry.[59] The fact that masonry in the form of bricks was found on the body was deemed significant, as well as the Masonic oath stipulates that traitors should be "roped down" in the proximity of the rising tide.

Chapter Sixteen

THE BOX OF BONES

"This was a crime with a sexual motive. Parties were organized, with a Vatican gendarme acting as the 'recruiter' of the girls. The network involved diplomatic personnel from a foreign embassy to the Holy See. I believe Emanuela ended up a victim of this circle," Father Amorth, the honorary president of the International Association of Exorcists, told La Stampa *newspaper. The debate over who kidnapped Emanuela and what became of her has raged in Italy for three decades.*
—Nick Squires, *The Telegraph* (UK), May 20, 2012

Archbishop Marcinkus had a beautiful apartment in Rome, very comfortable. And then he had lots of young female housekeepers, very young, who needed to make frequent confessions.
—Licio Gelli, interview with Philip Willan, 2012

One month after Calvi's death, commissioners from the Bank of Italy appeared at the Vatican Bank to confront Archbishop Marcinkus about his part in the collapse of Banco Ambrosiano. Most of the $1.75 billion remained missing, and Marcinkus had issued the letter of patronage, acknowledging the Holy See's ownership of the eight dummy corporations that consumed the cash. Marcinkus, in reply, produced the counter-letter, signed by Calvi, which stated that whatever happened to Banco Ambrosiano and the eight corporations mentioned in the patronage letter, the Vatican "would suffer no future damage or loss." The Archbishop then showed the commissioners to the door, informing them that neither the Bank of Italy nor the Guardia di Finanza possessed any jurisdiction within the sanctified walls of Vatican City.[1]

But the Italian government maintained pressure on the Holy See for full disclosure of its involvement in the Ambrosiano affair. "The government," said Italy's treasury minister Beniamino Andreatta after meeting with Marcinkus, "is waiting for a clear assumption of responsibility by

the IOR."[2] While the waiting continued, the Italian press ran daily articles about the Vatican and its relationship with the Sicilian Mafia and P-2.
Rome's daily newspaper *La Repubblica* began to publish a cartoon strip
entitled "The Adventures of Paul Marcinkus."

To quiet matters, Cardinal Agostino Casaroli, the Vatican's secretary of
state, proposed the creation of a six-man commission to make an investigation into the Vatican's involvement in the collapse of Banco Ambrosiano:
three were to be named by the Vatican and three by the Italian Ministry
of the Treasury. The Italian government complied with the proposal. The
results, as expected, were inconclusive. At the end of October 1982, the
Vatican officials ruled that Holy Mother Church had no interest in the
dummy corporations and had assumed no involvement in the plot to drain
the bank of its wealth, while the three treasury officials ruled otherwise.[3]

PROOF OF GUILT

Dissatisfied with the findings, Ambrosiano's creditors continued to mount
pressure for a settlement, since most of the $1.75 billion had vanished
within a black hole created by the Vatican's shell companies. The Italian
government was left with no option save to mount a criminal investigation
to determine if the Holy See was the culprit in a shell game that caused the
financial ruin of thousands of families throughout Italy. Documents were
unearthed in the records of the Banca del Gottardo in Switzerland that
the Vatican, indeed, had set up and controlled the dummy corporations
to plunder the assets of the Milan bank. One, dated November 21, 1974,
and signed by Vatican officials, was a request for the Swiss bank to open
accounts on behalf of its newly created company: United Trading Corporation of Panama.[4]

Other documents found within other banks revealed more acts of
fraud by the Holy See. One document showed that the IOR had received
two deposits from Banco Andino of Peru on October 16, 1979. The first
deposit was for $69 million, the second also for $69 million. When the
deposits matured in 1982, Banco Andino asked for its money back. But
the Vatican Bank refused, saying that the United Trading Corporation of
Panama now owed the money and the IOR had no control over it.[5]

Still and all, the pope refused to acknowledge the Vatican's ownership for fear that such an admission would reveal that the Bride of Christ
was no longer pure and without blemish but had engaged in wanton acts

of covetousness and greed. The impasse had to be addressed by another decisive act.

GONE GIRL

On June 22, 1983, Emanuela Orlandi, the fifteen-year-old daughter of a Vatican employee, disappeared without a trace while on her way to her home in Vatican City from a music lesson at the Pontifical Institute of Sacred Music, a building attached to the Basilica of Sant'Apollinare in the heart of Rome.[6] She was last seen entering a dark gray BMW with a well-dressed man, whom witnesses said bore a striking resemblance to Enrico "Renatino" De Pedis, the acting head of Banda della Magliana, Rome's most notorious street gang.[7]

Two weeks later, the Orlandi family received a call from a man with a heavy American accent, who said, "We have taken the citizen Emanuela Orlandi only because she belongs to the Vatican State. We are not a revolutionary or terror organization; we have never described ourselves as such; we consider ourselves people interested only in liberating [would-be papal assassin] Agca. The deadline is July 20."[8] He identified his organization as "The Turkes Anti-Christian Turkish Liberation Front," a group unknown to Turkish intelligence. The caller said that he would leave an important message regarding the demands of his organization with the Vatican.

Several days later, Ercole Orlandi, Emanuela's father, paid a visit to Monsignor Dino Monduzzi, prefect of the Pontifical House, to see if the message had arrived. The prelate, at first, said no—no one within the Vatican had heard from the kidnappers. Thanks to the persistent questioning by Mario Meneguzzi, Emanuela's uncle, Monsignor Monduzzi finally admitted that there had been a call and a message. "But absolutely nothing they said or wanted could be understood," the prefect insisted.[9]

Between July 10 and July 19, the "American" made other calls, some directing the press to locations where they found notes and taped messages from Emanuela. On July 20, the mysterious caller contacted ANSA, Italy's national news wire service, to say, "Today is the last message before the deadline of the ultimatum expires."[10]

REQUESTS DENIED

Throughout the investigation, SISDE (Italy's domestic intelligence service) found the Vatican strangely uncooperative and unwilling to share their conversations with "the American." Vincenzo Parisi, the deputy head of SISDE, came to believe that the Holy See had shrouded the Orlandi case by a campaign of sophisticated disinformation. The messages and calls from the representative of the Turkish organization, Parisi said, were episodes of "play-acting" to distract attention from the real heart of the matter.[11] In his confidential report on the mysterious caller, Parisi wrote, "Foreigner, very possible of Anglo-Saxon culture; high intellectual and cultural level; familiar with the Latin tongue and, it follows, of Italian; member (or in close contact) with the ecclesiastical world; serious ironic, precise and orderly in composure, cold, calculating, full of himself, sure of his role and strength, sexually amorphous; has lived a long period of time in Rome, knows very well all the city zones that have something to do with his activity; well informed about Italian judicial rules and above all the logistical structure of the Vatican."[12]

The SISDE official went on to write that it was "highly plausible" that the kidnapping of Emanuela was committed by someone "inside the ecclesiastical hierarchy and order," who was tightly wired to organized crime figures.[13] Parisi managed to provide this profile because of an intercept that the Italian police had placed on a phone line within the Vatican after the caller demanded access to Secretary of State Casaroli. But Parisi was unable to listen to the conversations between the "American" caller and Cardinal Casaroli. The tapes, along with the intercept, mysteriously vanished from the Holy See.[14]

At Parisi's insistence, the *carabinieri* taped the telephone of Raul Bonarelli, the second-highest-ranking officer within the Vatican's Central Office of Vigilance. In one taped conversation with other Vatican officials, Bonarelli said that he had sent boxes of documents on the Orlandi case to the office of Cardinal Casaroli. Parisi and his fellow magistrates sent requests to the Holy See asking permission to interview Casaroli, members of his staff within the Secretariat, and members of the Office of Vigilance about the content of the internal documents. All the requests were denied.[15]

EXTORTION ATTEMPT

At the end of July, ANSA reported, "In the Vatican, the prevailing opinion is that the people responsible for the kidnapping belong to the world of common crime and that the proposal for an exchange with Agca is just an excuse to extort considerable sums of money [from the Vatican] in exchange for the girl to throw investigators off track."[16] The money, Judge Rosario Priori, a leading magistrate in the case, concluded, belonged to members of Banda della Magliana, who had deposited it with Marcinkus and Calvi only to be left with a kidnapped girl as means of obtaining repayment. The judge estimated that the amount owed to the gang was in excess of $200 million.[17]

ONE TRAMP'S TALE

Years later, Antonio Mancini ("Nick the Tramp"), a bagman for De Pedis, said that his boss had arranged the kidnap in order to recoup the millions it had lost in the collapse of Ambrosiano. "There was money that had gone missing," Mancini told a reporter from *La Stampa*, "and the choice was between dropping a cardinal by the roadside or striking someone close to the pope. We chose the second option."[18] Mancini added, "What Judge Priori says about the Orlandi kidnapping is the absolute truth, what puzzles me is the figure of $200 million. Knowing the amount of money that flowed into the gang's activity and especially the money made by the 'Testaccio' group [the division of the Banda under De Pedis], I think that $200 million is an insufficient sum."[19]

CALL GIRL'S STORY

Critical insight into the possible fate of Emanuela came from Sabrina Minardi, the former lover of De Pedis and high-class call girl. Emanuela, she testified, had been kidnapped by De Pedis, who held her at an apartment on the coastal town of Torvaianica, not far from Rome. Archbishop Marcinkus, Ms. Minardi said, visited Emanuela several times while the school girl remained in captivity. The victim, she continued, was eventually killed, chopped into pieces, and her remains were cast into a cement mixer.[20]

In a 2010 interview with Gianluca Di Feo of *L'Espresso*, Ms. Minardi said that she had ongoing sexual relations with Roberto Calvi and Archbishop Marcinkus. She claimed that she had received a villa in Monte Carlo from Calvi, while Marcinkus provided a Vatican position for one of her relatives. Ms. Minardi added that she had provided Marcinkus with a steady stream of prostitutes and had delivered to him large sums of cash from De Pedis in a Louis Vuitton bag. "I left him the money," she said, "but I kept the bag."[21]

As a result of Ms. Minardi's testimony, Rome prosecutors arrested three underworld associates of De Pedis for kidnapping and murder: Sergio Virtù, Angelo Cassani, and Gianfranco Cerboni.[22] She had identified these men as individuals who had assisted De Pedis in arranging the kidnapping and contacting the Vatican with the terms for Emanuela's release.[23]

THE PAYOFF

Eventually, the investigating magistrates obtained evidence that the Vatican made the payoff to the Banda in a circuitous manner. In the fall of 1983, L'Opera Francesco Saverio Oddasso, a Roman Catholic society dedicated to the works of St. Francis Xavier, sold a luxurious villa surrounded by 24,000 square meters of gardens on the outskirts of Rome to Enrico Nicoletti, the "treasurer" of the Banda, at the rock bottom price of 1.2 billion lire ($860,000). Seven years later, the property was appraised at 27 billion lire. The sale had been engineered by Cardinal Ugo Poletti, the Vicar of the Diocese of Rome and a member of P-2.[24] Nicoletti transformed the villa into a nightclub called the House of Jazz, which received substantial loans from the IOR.[25]

Thanks to the sale of the villa, Cardinal Poletti emerged as a leading figure in the case of the missing girl. Poletti, at the time of the kidnapping, had received a great deal of adverse publicity because of his membership in P-2 and his alliance with Licio Gelli. He also received criticism for his advancement of the cause of Opus Dei, a secretive Catholic sect that had served to establish Gladio units throughout Europe.[26] As the vicar of Rome, he presided over the Basilica of Sant'Apollinare, where De Pedis remained a member in good standing.[27] He stood in a unique position to resolve the matter of Emanuela Orlandi and the Banda's demand for repayment of its drug money.

A SORDID SCENARIO

By 1983, when the villa was sold, most investigators, including Judge Parisi, had come to the conclusion that the kidnapping case revolved around sex and the problem of pedophilia that was mounting within the Holy See. If the matter was simply financial, Archbishop Marcinkus would have provided the restitution. If the matter was political, the resolution would have been made by Cardinal Casaroli, the secretary of state. But the extortion appeared to revolve around an episode considerably more sinister. Rumors had been rampant about Archbishop Marcinkus's taste for young girls and for sex parties within his private apartments.[28]

A scenario was gradually compiled that served to explain the kidnapping, the Vatican's attempts at obstruction, and Cardinal Poletti's participation in the payoff. Emanuela, by this account, had been sexually molested by Marcinkus. When the Banda received news of the incident, they kidnapped the girl in order to blackmail the IOR head for the money they had lost through Ambrosiano. Exposure of the statutory rape would have been devastating in the wake of the Sindona episode, the P-2 headlines, the collapse of the Vatican's shell companies, and the strange death of Roberto Calvi. Emanuela represented a $200 million baby. Marcinkus, after personally verifying that the girl was in the Banda's custody, worked through P-2 and Cardinal Poletti—not to secure Emanuela's immediate release but to ensure her perpetual silence.

BOXES OF BONES

On February 2, 1990, Enrico De Pedis was gunned down and killed on Via del Pellegrino in Rome. He was buried in a diamond-studded tomb within the Basilica of Sant'Apollinare, a place reserved for popes and cardinals.[29] Perhaps the gangster merited such hallowed interment. He had participated in the killing of Calvi, made peace between the Vatican and the mob by accepting a real-estate deal as a cash settlement, and prevented a fifteen-year-old schoolgirl from creating a scandal that would have rocked the foundation of Holy Mother Church. His place among the saints and ecclesiastical dignitaries was sanctioned by Cardinal Poletti.[30]

In 2006, an anonymous caller to *Chi l'ha Visto* ("Who Has Seen Them?"), an Italian current-events program, said, "Do you want to solve the Emanuela Orlandi case? Then look inside the tomb of De Pedis." On

May 14, 2010, Italian forensic examiners opened the tomb in response to widespread public demand. They discovered that the body of De Pedis remained "well-preserved." He remained dressed in a dark blue suit with a black tie. Next to his coffin they also found nearly two hundred boxes of bones that appeared to date from pre-Napoleonic times. They remain under examination.

PROCLAMATION FROM POPE FRANCIS

In 2013, Pope Francis met the missing girl's mother, Maria, and her brother Pietro, and said, "Emanuela's in heaven." Shocked by the remark, Pietro replied, "Until there is proof to the contrary, I live in the hope she is alive. And I hope you will help me find the truth." But the pope merely shook his head and said, "She's in heaven."

Following the meeting, Pietro attempted to obtain an explanation of the pope's remark from the Vatican. But no explanation was forthcoming. "I want to understand if she is dead or alive. He says she's dead now? How does he know?" Pietro asked.

"The truth must come from the Vatican," he said. "She was a Vatican citizen. But they have never collaborated with investigators. They have always obstructed the investigation. They have behaved in a way that is not Christian."[31]

THE "GOOD WILL" PAYMENT

On May 24, 1984, a "good will payment" of $250 million was made by the Vatican, which was still reeling from the Orlandi incident, to Ambrosiano creditors at the headquarters of the European Trade Association in Geneva.[32] The money for the reparation came from a mysterious deposit made in the IOR by Secretary of State Casaroli in the amount of $406 million.[33] The source of the cash was Opus Dei ("Work of God"), a deeply conservative Catholic organization that had amassed an estimated $3 billion in assets.[34] In its efforts to prop up the papacy from the damage wrought by the IOR, the organization assumed the debt of parochial banks within the Ambrosiano group, including Banca Cattolica del Veneto, Credito Varesino, and Ambrosiano itself (which launched an ill-fated attempt to return from financial ashes as Nuovo Banco Ambrosiano).[35]

In exchange for these benefactions, John Paul II granted the sect recognition as a "personal prelature." This status ensured that the secret society would answer only to the pope and the pope alone. No local bishop could discipline or sanction it. Overnight, Opus Dei emerged as a global ecclesiastical movement without a specific diocese. No organization within the history of the Roman Catholic Church, save the Society of Jesus, had been granted such power.[36]

OPUS DEI

Founded in 1928 by Josemaría Escrivá, a Spanish priest and lawyer, Opus Dei is a movement in which members adhere to "the Way," a rigorous daily order prescribed by Escrivá that includes Mass, devotional readings, private prayer, and physical mortification (self-flagellation with whips and chains) to subdue the flesh. The "numeraries" within the order are single people who make a "commitment of celibacy" and live within centers. They maintain private sector employment and donate their income to the movement—opting to live on a modest stipend. The "supernumeraries" are married couples united who maintain the Way within their private domiciles. The movement also includes "associates"—single people who cannot live in centers because of other obligations, such as caring for their elderly parents—and "cooperators"—single or married individuals who contribute a lion's share of their income to Opus Dei but have not yet adopted the "divine vocation" of daily spiritual regimentation.[37]

Despite Opus Dei's espousal of an intransigent obedience to Catholic doctrine, the movement violates a cardinal tenet of canon law by remaining a "secret society," like Freemasonry. Opus Dei does not publish its membership list, and members, according to the movement's 1950 Constitution, are forbidden to reveal their adherence to the movement without the express permission of their superiors.[38]

FOUNT OF FASCISM

Much of what is known about Opus Dei comes from John Roche, a professor at Oxford University, who left the order and broke his pledge of secrecy. In an essay entitled "The Inner World of Opus Dei," Roche writes, "Internally, it is totalitarian and imbued with fascist ideas turned to religious purposes, ideas which were surely drawn from the Spain of its early years. It is virtually occult in spirit, a law unto itself, totally self-centered, grudgingly accepting Roman authority because it still considers Rome orthodox."[39]

By 1984, when the reparation was made, Opus Dei had become a $3 billion enterprise, controlling six hundred newspapers, fifty-two radio and TV stations, twelve film companies, and thirty-eight news agencies.[40] Prominent Americans who became affiliated with the movement included William Simon of Citicorp, Francis X. Stankard of Chase Manhattan, and Sargent Shriver, a former Democratic candidate for vice president. David Kennedy of Continental Illinois, albeit a Mormon, became a friend of the sect, since his bank became a leading shareholder of an Opus Dei bank in Barcelona.[41]

THE CIA FUNDING

Because Opus Dei was vehemently anti-Communist, the CIA in 1971 began to funnel millions into the coffers of the secret Catholic sect to thwart the growth of liberation theology in Latin America. Much of this money ended up in the Chilean Institute for General Studies (IGS), an Opus Dei think tank. The members of IGS included prominent lawyers, free-market economists, and executives from influential publications. The leader of IGS was Hernán Cubillos, founder of *Que Pasa*, an Opus Dei magazine, and publisher of *El Mercurio*, the largest newspaper in Santiago and one that received CIA subsidies. The coup against the democratically elected regime of Salvatore Allende was planned within the corridors of the Chilean think tank. After the coup, IGS technocrats became the new cabinet ministers, and Cubillos emerged as a foreign minister.[42]

Throughout the 1980s, the CIA made use of Opus Dei's *milites Christi* as a primary force in Poland. The numeraries and supernumeraries provided ongoing support for Solidarity, which, by some accounts, reached nearly $1 billion by the end of the decade. The Catholic society also organized courses, seminars, and conferences to indoctrinate Polish teachers, scholars, and economists in the tenets of Western democracy and the plans of a unified Europe (as envisioned by the Council on Foreign Relations and the Trilateral Commission) in the wake of the imminent collapse of the USSR.[43] How much money the CIA provided to Opus Dei remains a mystery. The CIA refuses to release any records regarding its relationship to the secret sect on the grounds that any disclosure would undermine "national security."[44]

THE CAGED DON

On March 27, 1980, Michele Sindona, who caused the involvement of Opus Dei in Vatican financial affairs, was convicted of sixty-eight counts of misappropriation of funds, perjury, and fraud involving the Franklin National Bank. He was fined $207,000 and sentenced to twenty-five years of confinement at the Federal Correction Institute in Otisville, New York.[45] The situation for the Sicilian don grew increasingly worse. On July 7, 1981, the Italian government charged Sindona with ordering the execution of Giorgio Ambrosoli, the chief bank investigator who uncovered the Vatican's connection to the Mafia. On January 25, 1982, he was indicted in Palermo, along with seventy-five members of the Gambino, Inzerillo, and Spatola crime families, for operating a $600 million-a-year heroin trade between Sicily and the United States.[46] Two years later, Sindona was extradited to Milan, where he was tried and convicted of bank fraud and murder. He was sentenced to life at Voghera, a maximum security prison on the outskirts of Milan.[47]

"MI HANNO AVVELENATO"

On March 20, Sindona rose from his prison cot to take breakfast. As always, his plastic plate and Styrofoam coffee cup were sealed. It was eight-thirty. He carried the coffee cup with him through the door that led to the toilet. Minutes later, the Mafia don emerged from the bathroom, his shirt covered with vomit, his face convulsed with horror. *"Mi hanno avvelenato,"* he screamed. "They have poisoned me!"[48]

These were his last words. Sindona was rushed to a nearby hospital, where he was declared to be in an irreversible coma. A lethal dosage of potassium cyanide was detected in his blood. That afternoon a priest administered extreme unction. Forty-eight hours later, Michele Sindona— the man known as "St. Peter's banker"—was dead.[49]

ARCHBISHOP'S ARREST WARRANT

There were more matters for damage control. The good-will payment to Ambrosiano creditors from the coffers of Opus Dei did not close the criminal probe of the massive bank collapse. On February 26, 1987, the investigating magistrates concluded that the Vatican Bank had acted as an umbrella for Roberto Calvi's illicit transactions, that it owned a substantial share of Banco Ambrosiano as well as the dummy corporations, and that it was responsible for the theft of $1.75 billion. Arrest warrants were issued for the three top IOR officials: Archbishop Paul Marcinkus, Luigi Mennini, and Pellegrino de Strobel.[50]

The arrests were not made. To protect its officials, the Vatican pointed to Article 11 of the Lateran Treaty of 1929 that served to regulate matters between the Holy See and Italy. The article stipulated that there should be no interference by the Italian government in "the central institutions of the Catholic Church." Italy's highest court upheld this stipulation and ruled that Marcinkus and his two associates could not be arrested and brought to trial in Italy. The three Vatican bankers remained safe from extradition within the sanctity of the Sovereign State of Vatican City.[51]

Marcinkus stayed under papal protection until 1991, when he took up residence in Sun City, Arizona. Italian authorities throughout the next decade attempted to persuade US officials to return the archbishop to Italy so that he could face a jury. But such efforts proved fruitless. The US Justice Department made the strange ruling that Marcinkus possessed a Vatican passport and could not be extradited to Italy even though his crimes took place on Italian soil. No one in the CIA wanted "the Gorilla" to testify in court about his ties to P-2, the Sicilian Mafia, and the transfer of funds to Solidarity, the opponents of liberation theology, and the right-wing regimes in Latin America. And so, he stayed sheltered from justice not within Vatican City but in Sun City, Arizona, where he joined a prestigious country club, played daily rounds of golf, and smoked expensive cigars.[52] He died of undisclosed causes on February 20, 2006.

THE GOLD BARS

In 1987, Licio Gelli turned himself over to Swiss authorities in South America, claiming that he was at "the end of his tether" and suffering from heart problems. He surrendered only after negotiating the terms of his return to Italy. He would be charged only with financial offenses. After serving less than two months behind bars, Gelli complained of deteriorating health and was released on parole. In 1992 he was sentenced to eighteen years in prison for his involvement in the Ambrosiano affair. The sentence was reduced to twelve years upon appeal.[53]

For the next six years Gelli remained under house arrest (*detenzione domiciliare*) at his luxurious villa in Tuscany. In 1998, when the police came to transport him to a public facility, Gelli disappeared again. In the villa, police discovered 363 pounds of gold bars buried in patio flowerpots among his geraniums and begonias. The grand master of P-2 had stolen the gold from the Yugoslavian government while operating the ratlines for the Nazis.[54] Gelli died in 2016 at his villa in Italy. He had reached the ripe old age of 96.

THE NEW ORDER

In the reorganization of the Vatican finances under Opus Dei that got underway in 1989, a new five-member supervisory board of "lay experts" was set up at the IOR. Its president was Angelo Caloia, head of the Mediocredito Lombardo bank. The vice president was Philippe de Weck. The other three were Dr. Jose Sanchez Asiain, former chairman of Banco Bilbao; Thomas Pietzcker, a director of the Deutsche Bank; and Thomas Macioce, an American businessman. The new managing director of the IOR was Giovanni Bodio, also from Mediocredito Lombardo.

Caloia and Bodio were associated with Giuseppe Garofano, the onetime chairman of Montedison and president of Ferruzzi Finanziaria SpA, Italy's second-largest industrial firm. Garofano, an Opus Dei supernumerary, served with Caloia on the Vatican's Ethics and Finance Committee until 1993, when he was arrested in connection with a $94 million political kickback scheme. Known as "clean hands," the scheme involved the kickback of millions flowing through the Saint Serafino Foundation, an account Garofano set up at the IOR. Jose Sanchez Asiain was a disciple of Bishop Alvaro del Portillo, who served as the general president of Opus Dei.

Although Thomas Macioce may not have been a member of Opus Dei, he shared its reactionary ideology. Macioce was a knight of the Sovereign Military Order of Malta, along with Secretary of State Haig, CIA director Casey, Treasury Secretary William Simon, Licio Gelli, former CIA director John McCone, Prescott Bush Jr. (brother of Vice President George Bush), President Reagan's national security advisor William P. Clark, deputy CIA director General Vernon A. Walters, and Count Alexandre de Marenches.[55] Having gained entry to such a charmed circle, Macioce, who served as the chief executive officer of the Allied Stores Corporation, must have been keenly aware of the tentacles of Gladio within the Vatican and the steady flow of mob money into the IOR.

Thomas Pietzcker was a last-minute replacement for Hermann Abs, the head of the Deutsche Bank and Pietzcker's boss. Abs had been forced to resign from the committee due to an outcry from the Simon Wiesenthal Center in Los Angeles about his role as "Hitler's banker" and as a director of IG Farben, which ran its own slave-labor camp at Auschwitz. After the war, Abs was placed in charge of allocating funds from the Marshall Plan to German industry. This position made him a pivotal figure in the establishment of Gladio. Abs, like Macioce, was a knight of the SMOM.[56]

The finances of Holy Mother Church were now in the hands of a secret Catholic society that remained in the service of a clandestine group of global economists.

Chapter Seventeen

VATICAN, INC.

The atmosphere was crackling last April 28 [1999] in a conference room at the Hilton hotel in Jackson, Miss. The assembled group, which included a well-known New York lawyer (and Reagan Administration adviser) named Thomas Bolan and two prominent Catholic priests who had flown in from Rome, was trying to sort out what to say to the state's insurance commissioner at an emergency hearing the following day. The commissioner wanted answers as to why $600 million had seemingly moved from a Vatican-linked foundation in Italy to a Catholic charity in the British Virgin Islands, and then into a trust that had long controlled a group of Mississippi insurance companies. "Tomorrow is a critical day for Monitor Ecclesiasticus and Saint Francis of Assisi throughout the whole country," announced attorney Nicholas Monaco, referring to the two overseas foundations. "The commissioner and his staff are very, very concerned."
> —Richard Behar, "Washing Money in the Holy See,"
> *Fortune*, August 16, 1999

Throughout his long pontificate, John Paul II allowed the relationship between the Sicilian Mafia and the Holy See to remain intact. His reign resulted neither in progressive reforms nor a return to traditional Catholic teachings. It rather resulted in the stabilization of Vatican, Inc., as a financial and political institution. The primary goal of this institution was not the quest and dissemination of spiritual truths in an age of uncertainty, but the perpetuation of its own corporate interests through intrigue, mendacity, theft, and, when the situation demanded, bloodshed.

CURSES AND BLESSINGS

During his visit to Sicily on November 6, 1994, John Paul II blessed the memory of Fr. Giuseppe Puglisi, an ardent opponent of the Mafia, who was gunned down and killed in front of his parish in Palermo. The pope also condemned the organized crime families, saying, "Those who are responsible for violence and arrogance stained by human blood will have to answer before the justice of God. Today, there is a strong yearning in Sicily to be redeemed and liberated, especially from the power of the Mafia."[1]

But the pope's words rang hollow in the midst of persistent illicit financial transactions between the Sicilian crime families and the Vatican. On October 3, 1999, three years after John Paul II pressed for the beatification of Father Puglisi, twenty-one members of the Sicilian Mafia were arrested in Palermo for conducting an elaborate online banking scam with the cooperation of the IOR. Antonio Orlando, the *capo* who masterminded the operation, succeeded in siphoning off 264 billion lire (about $115 million) from banks throughout Europe. The money was sent to the northern Emilia Romagna region of Italy. From this province, it was channeled into numbered accounts at the Vatican Bank.[2]

SPIRITUAL CLEANSING

Just before the arrests, Orlando and crew had set in motion a plan to net 2 trillion lire (around $1 billion) from the Bank of Sicily. Giuseppe Lumia, head of Italy's anti-Mafia commission, said that the scheme showed how dangerous the mob had become in using the Internet for illicit purposes.[3] Despite the arrests and subsequent convictions, Italian investigators were prevented from probing into the IOR's part in the criminal operation because of the sovereign status of Vatican City.

As further proof that business had returned to usual at the Vatican in the wake of the Ambrosiano scandal, London's *Daily Telegraph* ran an article on November 19, 2001, that identified the IOR—along with banks in countries such as Mauritius, Macao, Nauru, and Luxembourg—as being one of the leading places in the world for laundering underworld cash.[4]

KING DAVID'S DESCENDANT

During the final years of John Paul II's reign, other scandals came to light, including an elaborate scheme involving Martin Frankel, a high-school dropout from Ohio. Frankel, who modeled himself after Roberto Calvi, came up with the idea of creating a billion-dollar insurance empire with the help of the Vatican Bank. To accomplish this goal, he secured the services of Tom Bolan, founder of New York's Conservative Party, law partner of the late Communist hater Roy Cohn, and an advisor to President Ronald Reagan on judicial appointments.[5]

On August 18, 1998, Bolan arrived at the Vatican to meet with Monsignor Emilio Colagiovanni, an emeritus judge of the Roman Rota (a church tribunal); Monsignor Gianfranco Piovano, an official at the Vatican's Secretariat of State; and Bishop Francesco Salerno, the secretary of the Holy See's Supreme Court.[6] Bolan told the Vatican officials he represented a Jewish philanthropist named David Rosse (an alias for Martin Frankel), who wanted to establish a Vatican foundation in order to donate millions of dollars to the church. Rosse, Bolan told the clerics, was a middle-aged tycoon and a direct descendant from Israel's King David.[7] The officials were mesmerized. Why should the Holy See turn down millions from anyone—Jewish or not—who offered to open his checkbook?

A CATHOLIC FOUNDATION

In an August 22 letter to Bolan, which Bolan presented to the Vatican officials, Rosse (Frankel) wrote that he would establish a Catholic foundation, which would be governed by a "secret set of by-laws"; Rosse would be the original grantor of $55 million in funds; and the money would be wired to the foundation from a Swiss bank. Of the $55 million, $50 million would be sent to a US brokerage account (run by Frankel) in the name of the foundation for exclusive use by Rosse, who wanted to select the Catholic charities to which he wished to disperse the cash. The additional $5 million would be diverted to an account controlled by the Vatican.[8]

The $5 million payoff came with a catch. "Our agreement," Rosse outlined in the letter, "will include the Vatican's promise that the Vatican will aid me in my effort to acquire insurance companies by allowing a Vatican official to certify to authorities, if necessary, that the source of funds for the Foundation is the Vatican."[9]

Frankel was presenting the same deal to the Vatican officials that Sindona and Calvi had presented to Marcinkus. The Vatican would serve as a money launderer in exchange for a 10 percent cut of the millions Frankel would drain from the assets of his US insurance companies in the name of Holy Mother Church.

If the deal had only offered $5 million, the Vatican officials very likely would have turned up their noses and left the conference table with spiritual indignation. But Bolan, on behalf of Frankel, was offering much more. With his 90 percent, Frankel would buy progressively larger and larger insurance companies throughout the United States until he had established a multibillion-dollar empire. Frankel would control the trust (the new foundation with Vatican credentials) that owned the insurance companies, even as he (under an alias) managed their assets through a brokerage agency under his control. And the Vatican stood to make a fortune in excess of $100 million simply by granting its imprimatur to the scheme.[10]

THE SWISS ACCOMPLICE

Before the agreement was signed and sealed, Frankel was obliged to provide the Vatican Bank with documentation that he possessed the funds for the plan. Frankel responded by releasing the private number of Swiss banker Jean-Marie Wery, a managing director of Banque SCS Alliance. Wery, who turned out to be one of Frankel's criminal accomplices, assured the Holy See that Frankel (Rosse) was an extremely wealthy man who possessed ample funds to launch a $1 billion venture.[11]

On September 1, 1998, Monsignor Colagiovanni, Monsignor Piovano, and Bishop Salerno contacted Bolan to affirm the church's willingness to create a new Catholic foundation with David Rosse (Frankel) as president. They also were pleased to report that Rosse could open his own account at the Vatican Bank, a privilege that was offered only to an honored few.[12]

THE SPIRITUAL UMBRELLA

One month later, the three Vatican officials concocted a scheme of their own in order to safeguard the Holy See from charges of theft and criminal conspiracy, while still allowing the Vatican to rake in millions from the proposed insurance empire. Rosse should establish his own charity—the

St. Francis of Assisi Foundation to Serve and Help the Poor and Alleviate Suffering—that would not be conspicuously connected to the Vatican. The St. Francis Foundation would be united to Monitor Ecclesiasticus, a cultural and charitable organization thought to be under the direct control of the pope.[13] Monsignor Colagiovanni wrote a letter to Rosse in which he offered the church's assurance that "any fund or donation given to Monitor Ecclesiasticus" would fall under the protection of the "very strict confidentiality and secrecy laws" that apply to an entity linked to the Vatican Bank, meaning any money transferred in from the St. Francis Foundation would not be scrutinized. "Only the Pope personally," Monsignor Colagiovanni wrote, "can disclose details of any deposits or donations."[14]

With Monitor Ecclesiasticus as an umbrella, Holy Mother Church was providing Frankel with the means of bilking hundreds of millions from US insurance companies with a papal imprimatur, a Vatican bank account, and a new Catholic foundation named after the patron saint of the poor and destitute.

Frankel quickly set about purchasing insurance companies throughout the United States for the St. Francis of Assisi Foundation. The pamphlets for the foundation displayed pictures of John Paul II and Mother Theresa of Calcutta, and Fr. Peter Jacobs, a priest from Manhattan, was appointed by Frankel to serve as the foundation's president.[15]

A CALL TO THE VATICAN

In the midst of Frankel's negotiations to buy Capital Life of Golden, Colorado, attorney Kay Tatum inquired where the St. Francis Foundation had acquired the money for the purchase. She was told that the money came from the Holy See, which had provided $51 million to the foundation through Monitor Ecclesiasticus. With due diligence, Ms. Tatum called Monsignor Colagiovanni at the Vatican and recorded the conversation. Monsignor Colagiovanni assured the lawyer that Monitor Ecclesiasticus was a Vatican organization that had provided the St. Francis Foundation with the money.[16]

Of course, it wasn't true. Holy Mother Church hadn't shelled out a single dime to Frankel or the St. Francis of Assisi Foundation. There was no money. Payments to the companies that Frankel purchased for the scam would come from companies previously purchased by the St. Francis Foundation, that is, from the cash reserves of these companies and from the money that the companies had set aside to settle insurance claims.

VATICAN FRAUD

To further the fraud, Monsignor Colagiovanni signed and sent a declaration that Monitor Ecclesiasticus was "a channel and instrument in fulfilling the will and wish of the Supreme Administrator," that is, the pope.[17] It requires a stretch of the imagination to believe that this declaration would have been issued without John Paul II's approval. Frankel now set about purchasing an insurance company in Spokane, Washington, from Metropolitan Mortgage & Securities (MMS). C. Paul Sandifur, the president of MMS, wrote a letter to the Vatican, inquiring about Monitor Ecclesiasticus and the St. Francis of Assisi Foundation. "The foundation [St. Francis]," Sandifur wrote, "claims to be an agent of the Holy See and desires to engage in a business transaction of $120 million. The foundation also claims that it was established by Monitor Ecclesiasticus . . . which they represent as a Vatican foundation."[18] Two weeks later, Sandifur received a reply from Archbishop Giovanni Battista Re, the third-highest ranking Vatican official. The archbishop made no mention of Monitor Ecclesiasticus and its official status within the Roman Catholic Church. He confined his one-sentence response to the St. Francis of Assisi Foundation and said, "No such foundation has the approval of the Hole See or exists in the Vatican."

BOGUS BILLION-DOLLAR BENEFACTION

An alarmed Sandifur brought Archbishop Re's response to the attention of Kay Tatum, who again contacted Monsignor Colagiovanni, only to receive another false affidavit. In this statement, dated February 3, 1999, the monsignor said that Monitor Ecclesiasticus had endowed the St. Francis of Assisi Foundation with a benefaction of $1 billion and that this money had come from "various Roman Catholic tribunals and charities."[19] The Vatican's lies were compounded with more lies.

After purchasing seven insurance companies in five states, Frankel siphoned the cash reserves of the companies into a group of offshore investment firms. One such firm was the Jupiter Capital Growth Fund that Frankel had set up in the British Virgin Islands. Jupiter Capital possessed no real assets and served no purpose except to perpetuate a shell game.[20] A look at the transactions within this dummy corporation for a six-month period shows how the game was played. In December 1997, $51 million was wired into the Jupiter account at Merrill Lynch; one month later, $40.34 million was wired out to Frankel's bank accounts in Switzerland and Italy. On February 5, 1998, $40.38 million was wired in; 19 days later, $40.38 million was wired out. On April 14, 1998, $90 million was wired in; two days later, $90 million was wired out. On April 28, 1998, $50 million was wired in; ten days later, $50 million was wired out.[21]

HANGED HOUSE GUEST

Frankel used the money to purchase mansions, a fleet of expensive automobiles, diamonds, and gold. In one of his mansions, located in Greenwich, Connecticut, Frankel established his headquarters with a network of eighty computer terminals hooked to satellite dishes, and a virtual harem of more than one hundred female assistants. He had solicited the assistants—most of whom were recent immigrants—from the Internet and personal ads in the *Village Voice*.[22] According to the women who stayed at the Greenwich mansion, Frankel roamed through the estate in pajamas like a Hugh Hefner of high finance. On weekends he visited the Vault, a New York City nightclub that catered to sadomasochists before it went out of business in 1997.[23]

Details of Frankel's personal life came to light on August 8, 1997, when twenty-two-year-old Frances Burge was found dead, hanging by her neck from the deck of the Greenwich mansion. Burge was one of Frankel's "houseguests." She had met him by responding to one of his personal ads. According to Frankel, his relationship with Burge was "rocky" from the start. "Frances did not look as I expected," he told the police. "She was overweight but she was a nice person. During that evening, Frances had taken her clothes off and wanted to have sex. I didn't want to."[24]

While most of the women at the estate were Frankel's sex partners, indulging his taste for sadomasochism, Frances served the financier as an "office assistant." One woman hired to organize the household recalled a pecking order, with fights among the women over who got the right to serve Frankel his glass of orange juice in the morning. When police searched the house, they found leather riding crops, an assortment of ropes, and films and books on sexual bondage.[25]

FINAL FRAUDULENT STATEMENT

Frankel's scheme gathered steam until George Dale, a Mississippi Insurance Commissioner, noticed a massive wire transfer from the reserve accounts of three Mississippi insurance companies that were owned by the St. Francis of Assisi Foundation. Dale noted that the funds were sent to a New York firm called Liberty National Securities. Upon making a series of calls, he discovered that Liberty National was nothing more than a post office box with a telephone answering service. As he probed deeper, Dale came to realize that the St. Francis of Assisi Foundation, the owner of the insurance companies, served no parochial or charitable purpose save to channel funds to Swiss, Italian, and Vatican banking accounts.[26]

When the Mississippi insurance commissioner contacted the Holy See about the matter, he received an official letter from the Curia stating that neither Monitor Ecclesiasticus nor the St. Francis of Assisi Foundation fell under the jurisdiction of the Vatican. This was the final fraudulent statement to be issued from Holy Mother Church about the sordid matter, and, for Frankel, the game was up.[27]

SUITCASES STUFFED WITH DIAMONDS

Before arrest warrants were issued, Frankel consulted his astrological guide in his Greenwich mansion and noticed that his stars were misaligned. He quickly packed his bags—twenty suitcases, including three stuffed with diamonds—leased a jet and headed off to Europe with two of his girlfriends.[28]

In October 1999, a federal grand jury indicted Frankel for looting more than $200 million from seven insurance companies. Two months later, the scam artist was collared at the upscale Hotel Prem in Hamburg, Germany, and charged with carrying false passports and smuggling $10 million in diamonds into the country.[29]

FORT DIX

The FBI seized one of Frankel's estates in Greenwich, valued at $3 million, in May 2000, claiming that it served as headquarters for money laundering and fraud operations. At the same time, the Internal Revenue Service (IRS) took possession of his second Greenwich estate, valued at $2.5 million, saying that the property had been purchased with stolen money from insurance funds.[30]

The next month, Frankel pleaded guilty in Hamburg to charges of evading $1.2 million of custom duties on the diamonds that he had brought into the country. His plea delayed his extradition to the United States. Going into the courtroom, Frankel said that he would rather serve time in Germany than the United States, where prison conditions were "inhumane." "The German constitution," he told reporters, "has laws that let a person rehabilitate himself and I am being tried under German law."[31]

In March 2002, after serving half of his three-year German prison term and realizing that his extradition to the United States was imminent, since he was now eligible for parole, Frankel made a desperate attempt to escape from the prison in Hamburg. Using a piece of wire, he tried to cut through the bars of his cell. Frankel failed to notice that a security camera was monitoring his actions. Two week later, he pleaded guilty to charges of grand theft, racketeering, money laundering, and fraud before a federal judge in New Haven, Connecticut.[32] He was sentenced to two hundred months (sixteen years, eight months) at the Fort Dix Federal Correctional Facility for committing the greatest insurance theft in US history—a crime aided through the complicity of the Roman Catholic Church.[33]

"WE HAVEN'T LOST MONEY, HAVE WE?"

On August 30, 2001, Monsignor Emilio Colagiovanni was arrested in Cleveland, Ohio, and charged with wire fraud and criminal conspiracy.[34] He pled guilty and offered a plea statement in which he named other Vatican officials who were complicit in setting up the scheme with Frankel, including Monsignor Francesco X. Salerno, secretary of the prefecture for the economic affairs of the Holy See, and Archbishop Giovanni Battista Re.[35] On September 9, 2004, Colagiovanni, at the age of eighty-four, was fined $15,000 but spared from a ninety-seven-month prison sentence. Judge Ellen Bree Burns justified the leniency on the grounds of the monsignor's age and his willingness to cooperate with the federal investigators.[36]

In May 2001, insurance commissioners from five states initiated a lawsuit in accordance with the Racketeer Influenced and Corrupt Organizations (RICO) Act against the Roman Catholic Church, claiming that the Vatican had acted as a front for Frankel's criminal activities. "High ranking officials of the Vatican," the lawsuit stated, "authorized and ratified the plan whereby Monitor Ecclesiasticus would be used as a conduit for the flow of Frankel's money to the St. Francis Foundation to purchase U.S. insurance companies."[37] The suit sought more than $600 million in damages. Receiving word of the criminal charges, Pope John Paul II reassured the members of the Roman Curia that the Vatican as a sovereign state was immune from such litigation. "Ignore them," he said. "It will pass." Then the Holy Father added, "We haven't lost any money, have we?"

And so it came to pass twenty years after the Ambrosiano affair that the Roman Catholic Church was presented in US court as a criminal organization in compliance with the RICO statute—the same statute that had been drafted to dismantle the Italian Mafia in America.

Chapter Eighteen

STEALING FROM THE COLLECTION PLATE, LIVING LARGE

If the connection between church embezzlements and possible sexual immorality seems tenuous, consider the case of former San Francisco Msgr. Patrick O'Shea, who was named in a 1996 sexual abuse claim brought against the San Francisco Archdiocese which was settled for $2.5 million. In June 2000 O'Shea was indicted by a San Francisco County grand jury on 224 counts of child molestation, and served two years in jail before the charges were thrown out due to statute of limitations issues. While sparing readers the sordid details of the alleged molestations, it is relevant to note that, several months prior to his indictment, the San Francisco Archdiocese filed a lawsuit accusing O'Shea of embezzling more than $250,000 donated by nuns and parishioners during his 16-year tenure as pastor of two San Francisco-area parishes.

—Michael W. Ryan, "The Second Greatest Scandal in the Church," *New Oxford Review*, June 17, 2005

As financial scandal gave way to more financial scandal within the Vatican, reports of theft and embezzlement by prelates began to mount throughout the United States. In 2007, Robert West and Charles E. Zech released the findings of a national survey which showed that 85 percent of the bishops reported having funds stolen from their dioceses.[1] Drawing on data from the Center for Applied Research at Georgetown University, Michael Ryan, a federal law enforcement official specializing in financial audits and security investigations, calculated that $90 million in funds are embezzled every year from the Sunday collection at US Catholic churches.[2] "Assuming Sunday collection embezzlements are on-going at 10 percent of the approximately 17,900 parishes at any given time," Ryan states, "the average parish loss falls somewhere in the neighborhood of $1,000 per week, or roughly $50,000 per year."[3]

DRINKING URINE

From 2003 to 2015, Fr. Peter Miqueli, fifty-two, pastor of St. Frances de Chantal in the Bronx, reportedly stole more than $1 million in collection plate donations. He used the money to act out unholy fantasies as a sex slave under a homosexual sex master, identified in court papers as Keith Crist. The priest shelled out $1,000 for each encounter with Crist, which often culminated in the priest drinking the sex master's urine.[4] In addition to the sex sessions, Miqueli used the pilfered cash for "illicit and prescription drugs" he used with Crist ($60,000 in 2012 alone), $264,000 for a house in Brick, New Jersey, and $1,075.50 a month for his sex master's apartment in East Harlem. The lawsuit, filed by the parishioners of St. Frances de Chantal, also alleged that Crist had lived for many months in the rectory.[5]

WALKING-AROUND MONEY

In November 2015, Fr. Edward Belczak, seventy, was sentenced to twenty-seven months in prison for stealing $573,000 from St. Thomas More Church in Troy, Michigan, where he had served as a pastor for more than thirty years. He had used the cash to purchase a luxurious condo overlooking the ocean in Palm Beach, Florida, and to play the stock market. In a related case, Janice Verschuren, the office manager at St. Thomas More, also pleaded guilty to dipping into the parish's collection plate and stealing more than $25,000.[6]

Monsignor John Woolsey, sixty-nine, pastor of the Church of St. John the Martyr in Manhattan, was convicted in 2006 of pilfering more than $800,000 from his parish. He used the funds for golf outings, cosmetic dental work, the purchase of sixty expensive watches, and walking-around money.[7] He was sentenced to four years in prison. After serving less than a year at the Oneida Correctional Facility, the monsignor was set free by the parole board. The decision to release him was based on his behavior in prison, messages of support from his parishioners, and a plea from Cardinal Edward Egan of the Archdiocese of New York.[8]

GAMBLING HABITS

Fr. John Regan, forty-seven, pastor of St. Walter's in Roselle, Illinois, was convicted on August 16, 2011, of stealing $300,000 in parish funds to fuel his gambling habit. He was sentenced to 60 days in county prison, 150 days of work release, and four years of probation. He was also order to provide $290,000 to the parish as compensation. In 2015, Regan was released from probation even though he "willfully" neglected to provide the restitution.[9]

In May 2008, Fr. Patrick Dunne, sixty-three, pastor of Our Lady of Sorrows in White Plains, New York, was arrested and charged with stealing hundreds of thousands from church accounts, including a fund set aside for victims of Hurricane Katrina. Dunne took the money because of a "very powerful gambling addiction."[10] On October 20, 2010, Dunne pleaded guilty to second degree larceny and was placed on five years' probation, with the stipulation that he could not be placed in charge of the finances of his parish.[11]

"EPITOME OF PRIESTHOOD"

In 2006, Monsignor John Skehan, seventy-nine, and Fr. Francis Guinan sixty-three, who served at St. Vincent Ferrer, a wealthy parish in West Palm Beach, Florida, were accused of stealing $8.6 million in cash from the collection plate.[12] Skehan, who served St. Vincent's for forty years, used the stolen cash to buy a Palm Beach County condominium overlooking the ocean, a $275,000 coin collection, a cottage on the scenic cliffs of Moher in his native Ireland, and a pub in his hometown of Kilkenny. Described by June Hefti, a parishioner at St. Vincent's, as "the epitome of priesthood," the monsignor also made regular payments to a woman, described in the arrest affidavit, as a "girlfriend."[13] Fr. Guinan, who arrived at St. Vincent's in 2003, bought a luxurious home in Port St. Lucie and an expensive Juno Beach condo. A compulsive gambler, Fr. Guinan made regular trips to the casinos in Las Vegas and the Bahamas, paying for his losses from the collection plate cash. Guinan, too, had a "girlfriend," who received regular payments from the prelate."[14]

In 2009, a jury in West Palm Beach, Florida, convicted Fr. Guinan of grand theft. He was sentenced to four years in prison and fined $100,000. Monsignor Skehan received a sentence of fourteen months after he entered a guilty plea and a pledge to make $780,000 restitution.[15]

DEATHBED CONFESSION

On his deathbed in August, 1998, Fr. Walter Benz, seventy-two, confessed to stealing $1.35 million from the collection plates of two Pittsburgh parishes—Most Blessed Sacrament and St. Mary Assumption—where he had been stationed for twenty-six years. Benz had also developed a close relationship with Mary Anne Albaugh, with whom he "kept house." The two went on elaborate vacations and made regular trips to Atlantic City, where they gambled for high stakes at the Showboat, Tropicana, and the Taj Mahal.[16]

Ms. Albaugh entered a no-contest plea to a theft charge. Under the terms of the plea agreement, she was required to make restitution for only $25,000 of the $1.35 million. Her theft charge was reduced from a felony to a misdemeanor, and the other charges against her, including tampering with church records and criminal conspiracy, were dismissed.[17]

PAY TO PREY

Theft by priests was not limited to pilfering the collection plates but extended to embezzlement from parochial schools, Catholic charities, and various religious orders. In 2007, a grand jury charged Fr. Charles Newman with stealing $1,033,748 from the Archbishop Ryan High School, where he had served as teacher, principal, and president, and from his own Franciscan order. Newman stole the money, in part, to appease a school boy he had sexually molested. The youth later died of a drug overdose. In 2009, the priest entered a guilty plea and received a sentence of three to four years in prison.[18]

In 1999, Archbishop Rembert Weakland, seventy-two, of Milwaukee used $450,000 in church funds to pay off one of his disgruntled gay lovers. The archbishop, at that time, had steered $1.5 million to the Vatican for an endowed chair in social teaching to be established in his name at the Pontifical Gregorian University and a $500,000 chair (again in his name) in liturgy and music.[19]

PRINCES OF THEIR OWN DOMAIN

Within the Roman Catholic fiduciary system, parishes pay an assessment charge to the bishop ranging from 5 percent and 20 percent of the weekly collection. This fee is known as the *cathedraticum*. Within this realm, the bishop is the tax collector and central banker. The bishop can charge interest on late payments and stipulate the amount that each parish must raise for capital campaigns. Bishops, in turn, are required to pay a fee to the Vatican called the *taxa*. The amount of the *taxa* fluctuates according to the size of the diocese. Some diocese are accessed as low as 5 percent, others at 15 percent.[20] Gaining an episcopate is similar to obtaining a business franchise, except that front money (paying for an episcopal position) is no longer required as in the heyday of simony, when all church offices were up for sale.

Each bishop is the prince of his own domain and remains largely unaccountable for his actions and expenditures. This lack of oversight was exemplified by the case of Cardinal Anthony Bevilacqua of the Archdiocese of Philadelphia. During the late 1980s and early 90s, the cardinal spent $5 million renovating his thirty-room Main Line Philadelphia mansion and his seaside villa near Atlantic City, New Jersey. At the same time, Bevilacqua closed fifteen parishes in North Philadelphia, one of the city's poorest neighborhoods, since they ran a combined deficit of $1.2 million a year.[21]

MURPHY'S CHOICE

In 2007, Bishop William Murphy of the Rockville Center diocese on Long Island, New York, shelled out $5 million on renovations to St. Agnes Cathedral and his palatial mansion, which included a new fireplace with an oak mantel and a state-of-the-art kitchen, equipped with a double zero refrigerator and a six-burner Viking professional range. The pantry was updated to include two under-the-counter temperature-controlled wine cabinets. One wine cabinet, set at 50 degrees, contained fifty bottles of vintage red wine. The other cabinet, set at 45 degrees, was for bottles of champagne and white wine. Bishop Murphy spent $120,000 for three Oriental rugs, a dining room table, and six specially upholstered chairs. The bishop's suite was enhanced with a spacious new marble bathroom. A separate suite was set up for Fr. Joseph De Grocco, the bishop's secretary, and another for visiting ecclesiastical dignitaries.

The six Dominican sisters who taught at the St. Agnes School were ousted from their residence on the fourth floor of the mansion so that it could be converted into a "public space" to accommodate influential friends. At the same time the renovations were underway, Bishop Murphy terminated a $1.1 million home health care program that served five hundred area indigent and mentally ill people.[22]

HIGH LIVING

Since bishops have to right to spend the money they receive from parishes at their own discretion, many opt to live large in palatial splendor. Cardinal Timothy Dolan lives in a 15,000-square-foot mansion on Madison Avenue in New York City that has been appraised in excess of $30 million. Cardinal Francis George lives in a ritzy palace in Chicago's Gold Coast neighborhood, with an unobstructed view of Lincoln Park. His residence has been modestly appraised at $14.3 million. Archbishop Thomas Wenski of Miami lives in a six bedroom, six bath house that overlooks Biscayne Bay. His residence, priced at $1.38 million, contains a tiki hut with a wet bar and a backyard swimming pool. Archbishop Jose Gomez of Los Angeles resides in a new rectory that was built for $7 million; Archbishop Samuel Aquila lives in a 13,500-square-foot home in Denver that was constructed with diocesan funds for $6.5 million; Archbishop James Sartain of Seattle dwells in a three-story Victorian worth $3.84 million; and Archbishop Leonard Blain lives in a 9,000-square-foot palace in Hartford, Connecticut, with a cut-rate appraisal of $1.85 million.[23] "There's no reason a bishop has to live like a prince or medieval monarch, even if he inherited the place from his predecessor," said the Rev. Steven Avella, a Catholic priest and professor of religious history at Marquette University. "They should convert the mansions to museums and move into rectories."[24]

THE SAINTS' FACTORY

Lack of financial oversight was not confined to the dioceses but also extended to the Vatican, where the problem became endemic.

During the reign of Pope Paul VI, the Roman Catholic Church came up with a novel way of obtaining new revenue: the creation of a saints' factory. By the time of his death in 1978, Paul VI had canonized more saints, 84, than any of his papal predecessors.[25] In addition, he beatified 39 additional religious figures, a record number. But these figures were soon shattered by John Paul II, who canonized 482 saints and proclaimed 1,338 blessed.[26]

As the saints went marching into the Kingdom of Heaven, the Vatican's coffers swelled to overflowing. To open a cause for beatification and canonization costs the friends of the would-be saint $75,000 to $100,000, an amount that must be supplemented with payments to the theologians, bishops, and physicians who must examine the background and physical remains of the candidate. When the cause is deemed worthy and advanced, the cost skyrockets to $750,000 and more. This price covers the work of the researchers, the postulators (who guide causes through the judicial process), and the drafters of the *positio* (a portfolio of the candidate's deeds and accomplishments). Upon the candidate being pronounced suitable for sainthood, appropriate gifts must be provided for the preparation and performance of liturgical celebration.[27]

A BILLION-DOLLAR BUSINESS

By the time of John Paul II's death, the Congregation for the Causes of the Saints had become a billion-dollar business. But, unlike other businesses, it issued no statements of its income and expenses, kept no books to inspect for possible malfeasance, and maintained no flow charts to show how the money was spent. The funds for the causes (petitions for beatification and canonization) were deposited in the Vatican Bank or the Administration of the Patrimony of the Holy See, only to disappear without a trace. In 2013, the problem of the missing money was brought to the attention of Pope Francis, who attempted to address it by the creation of a new commission of inquiry into the Vatican's finances: the Commission on the Organization of the Economic-Administrative Structure of the Holy See (COSEA).[28] The new commission's attempt to obtain financial records from the Congregation for the Causes of the Saints was answered by this seraphic response: "The Causes of the Saints is not in possession of the requested documentation."[29]

PETER'S PENCE

But the saints' factory became only one of several means for Holy Mother Church to raise "ghost money" (i.e., money that mysteriously vanishes into thin air). Every year, Catholics are encouraged to "give generously" to Peter's Pence (known in the Vatican as the *obolo*), a charity under the direct control of the pope that was set up to serve the needs of the poor and the victims of war and natural disasters. Quotas for the fundraising are set for every diocese. Appeals are issued from the pulpits of every parish. Visits are made by ecclesiastical dignitaries to wealthy Catholic benefactors. The amount collected every year ranges from $70 million to $110 million.[30]

On February 28, 2003, John Paul II addressed the Circle of St. Peter on the vital purpose of the charity, saying, "You are aware of the growing needs of the apostolate, the request for aid that come from peoples, individuals and families in precarious conditions. Many expect the Apostolic See to give them support they often fail to find elsewhere. In this perspective, the Peter's Pence Collection is a true and proper participation in the work of evangelization."[31] In a speech to the same society, Benedict XVI, on February 25, 2006, said, "Peter's Pence is the most typical expression of the participation of all the faithful in the Bishop of Rome's projects of good for the universal Church. The collection is a gesture that not only has practical value but is also highly symbolic as a sign of communion with the Pope and attention to the needs of the brethren, and for this reason your service has a particularly ecclesial value."[32]

THE BLACK HOLE

Yet the expenditures of these funds remain shrouded in mystery. Less than 40 percent go to the impoverished and those most in need. The bulk of the money is sucked into the swirling black hole that remains at the core of the Holy See.[33] The Venerated Financial Report, as issued on January 30, 2015, contained only this information about the charity from the Vatican Secretariat of State: "While on the other hand an analytical report on the revenue relative to the Peter's Pence is published annually, on the other absolute confidentiality has been maintained to date, in compliance with Superior instructions, on how the report is used, since it is excluded from the consolidated financial report of the Holy See."[34] A query about the fund from a COSEA auditor was met by this vague but illuminating response from the Secretariat: "The collection is used for charitable initiatives and / or specific projects indicated by the Holy Father (14.1 million), for the transmission of offerings with specific targets (6.9 million) and for the maintenance of the Roman Curia (28.9 million). Plus the setting aside of 6.3 million from the Peter's Pence fund [money donated directly by the Catholic laity to the Holy See]." An analysis of this statement shows that 58 percent, not counting the money "set aside," did not go to the needy but rather the needs of the Curia, including upkeep on their lavish living quarters[35]

CARDINAL SINS

The cardinals of the Curia, as Gianluigi Nuzzi points out in *Merchants in the Temple*, "reside in princely dwellings . . . [with] rooms for every whim and fancy: waiting rooms, television rooms, bathrooms, reception rooms, tea rooms, libraries, rooms for the personal assistant, the secretary, and the files. . . . And these dwellings are often in stunning buildings, like the Palace of the Holy Office, immediately behind the colonnade of St. Peter's Square: it dates back to the sixteenth century and had been the headquarters of the tribunal of the Inquisition."[36]

Cardinal Tarcisio Bertone, the Vatican secretary of state, occupied a penthouse that was created by combining two Vatican-owned rooftop apartments. The renovations, according to the Italian daily *Il Tempo*, were worth more than one million euros.[37] Herringbone parquet flooring was installed throughout the climate-controlled living quarters. Each of the six bedrooms had its own spacious Carrara marble bath; the kitchen facilities were fitting for an elaborate banquet hall; and eight independent sound systems were installed, including one for a rooftop chapel. How did Bertone come up with the cash for his opulent digs? He took the cash from a fund set aside for the Bambino Gesu Children's Hospital in Rome.[38]

Despite the creation of the saints' factory and the funds diverted from Peter's Pence, the Holy See continued to display a budget deficit that continues to escalate at an alarming rate. In 2011, the deficit stood at $15 million euros. By 2015, the amount in the red ran to $25.6 million euros. Ongoing financial hemorrhages will leave the Holy See severely crippled.[39] Throughout the ages, the church had weathered financial calamities, including the East-West schism, the Reformation, and the loss of the Papal States. But this situation was different because it came with a fifth and final plague—far greater than the pestilences of aggiornamento, religious indifferentism, financial corruption, and unbridled clerical homosexuality—that would strike and still the once sacred heart of the Bride of Christ.

Chapter Nineteen

THE PLAGUE OF PEDOPHILIA

Even the most loyal of Catholics and their faithful priests must concede there is something rotten in our Church. Not only did Cardinal Bernard Law protect Father John Geoghan, who abused 100 Catholic boys over a career of seduction, molestation and rape, the cardinal moved him from parish to parish like a Mafia don providing safe houses for one of his button men. Rather than act as the good shepherd who lays down his life for his sheep, Law covered up the predator tracks of the wolf preying on his lambs.
— Patrick J. Buchanan, "Clean House in the Catholic Church," March 20, 2002

In 1969, Pope Paul VI consulted with Dutch psychiatrist Anna Terruwe, who informed him of her discovery that a high level of immaturity existed among the priesthood and estimated that 25 percent suffered from serious psychiatric disorders.[1] Dr. Terruwe and Dr. Conrad Baars, her American colleague, subsequently issued this finding: "Priests in general—and some to an extreme degree—possess an insufficiently developed or distorted emotional life."[2]

Following the Terruwe/Baars report, the American bishops commissioned their own study, which was concluded in 1972. Entitled *The Catholic Priest in the United States: Psychological Investigations*, the study, which involved a psychological evaluation of 271 priests, found that only 19 (7 percent) were "developed" as mature male adults while 252 (93 percent) were "not developed."[3] It further showed that a high percentage of priests "do not relate deeply or closely to other people" and use the church and their religious status as "cover ups for psychological inadequacy."[4]

Something was psychologically amiss among the priesthood—but no steps were taken by the Holy See or the American bishops to address it.

"EVERY SEXUAL ACT IMAGINABLE"

In 1985, Fr. Gilbert Gauthe of Lafayette, Louisiana, confessed to sexually molesting eleven boys and later admitted to dozens more.[5] He began molesting Scott Gastal when the boy was seven. As one attorney would later say, Gauthe engaged boys in "every sexual act you can image two males doing."[6] At the age of nine, Scott described how the priest befriended him and made him feel appreciated as an altar boy. Like other boys at the parish, Scott stayed overnight at the rectory on several weekends. In the course of these stays, Gauthe engaged him in play and then coerced him into oral and anal sex. The rapes continued, but the boy remained too frightened and confused to tell his parents. "Scott," as Michael D'Antonio writes in *Mortal Sins*, "was most affected by the memory of Gauthe ejaculating in his mouth and forcing his erect penis into his rectum. Once he was injured so severely that he reported the bleeding to his parents, hours after the assault, and had to be treated at a hospital."[7] Fr. Gauthe was sentenced to twenty years in prison and out-of-court settlements, amounting to $5 million, were made with the victims.[8]

PRIVILEGED STATUS

Even though he had sexually molested thirty-seven boys in four parishes during his eleven years of a priest, Gauthe was granted privileged status at the David Wade Correctional Center in Homer, Louisiana. He was provided with his own air-conditioned studio so that he could pursue his dream career of becoming a portrait painter. He was allowed to leave the prison for extended furloughs to visit his mother and to go for lunch at a nearby country club with several of his old friends. Gauthe was released from prison in 1995, eleven years early. He moved to Polk County, Texas, where he was arrested several months later for molesting a three-year-old boy.[9]

The press attention surrounding the Gauthe case opened the flood-gates. Within the same diocese of Louisiana, nineteen additional priests were accused of sexual abuse of children within the next two weeks. Eventually, that number rose to twenty-three.[10]

In 1985, the same year Gauthe was sent to the slammer, Fr. Thomas Doyle, a canon lawyer for the Vatican in Washington, DC, wrote a confidential memo to US bishops citing thirty cases of priests engaged in pedophilia and projected a cost to the American Catholic Church of over $1 billion within the next ten years.[11]

PARADISE FOR PEDERASTS

In 1989, Bishop Joseph Ferrario of the Diocese of Honolulu, Hawaii, became the first member of the Catholic hierarchy in the United States to be accused of pederasty. In 1975, while serving as pastor of St. Anthony of Padua in Kailua, Hawaii, Ferrario began molesting David Figueroa, a fifteen-year-old Portuguese boy who did odd jobs around the rectory. According to Figueroa, sex took place several times a week until he graduated from high school.[12] In 1978, Pope Paul VI appointed Ferrario as an auxiliary bishop of Honolulu, and, in 1982, Pope John Paul II elevated him to Bishop of Honolulu. His rise in ecclesiastical stature occurred despite the fact that Ferrario was engaged in sexual solicitation of seminarians at St. Stephen's and had carried on a homosexual liaison with another island priest.

Word quickly spread that the Diocese of Hawaii was a safe haven for "problem priests." Bishop Leo Maher of San Diego (also the first bishop of Santa Rosa) sent his close friend and wealthy sodomite Msgr. William Spain to Honolulu. Archbishop James Hickey of Washington, DC, hid convicted boy-molester Father Arthur O'Brien on the islands. Career pederast Father Robert N. Burkholder, from the Archdiocese of Detroit, who molested as least twenty-three young boys, took up residence in Ferrario's backyard and said Mass at St. Elizabeth's Parish, which operated a K–8 grade school.[13]

A court dismissed the case, not for lack of evidence, but rather because of a technicality: the plaintiffs had filed too late. Bishop Ferrario, who denied the allegation, retired early in 1993, after excommunicating everyone who raised charges against him.[14] He died on December 12, 2004, at the age of seventy-seven. Ferrario's obituary stated that he had preached "tolerance and community outreach," and that he "openly welcomed gays into the church."[15]

PORTER'S PROTECTION

On May 8, 1992, Fr. James Porter of the Fall River diocese was sentenced to eighteen to twenty years in prison, thanks to a plea agreement his attorney had worked out with a Massachusetts judge. His criminal career showed that he had been protected from prosecution by being moved from parish to parish by Cardinal Bernard Law. Ultimately, Porter was banished by Cardinal Law to a parish in Bemidji, Minnesota, with the hope that the exile would put an end to his criminal escapades. It didn't. Ultimately, the church was forced to settle 131 claims that had been brought about by Fr. Porter's pedophilia, including several in Minnesota.[16]

Prison officials said that the priest continued to exhibit a voracious sexual appetite while incarcerated. Porter was granted an early release in 2004 and died of pancreatic cancer a year later.[17]

By 1992, more than four hundred American priests had been accused of child molestation and more than $400 million had been shelled out to settle the claims of the victims.[18] For the most part, the priests involved in these cases were neither defrocked nor dispatched to psychological treatment facilities. They were simply reassigned to other parishes in other dioceses. In this way the cancer within the church metastasized and spread from one location to another in an unchecked manner.

FIVE HAIL MARYS

In 1992, Fr. Wilputte Alanson Sherwood was sentenced to ten years in prison by Judge Cheryl Hendrix, who had viewed a videotape of the priest performing oral sex on a fourteen-year-old boy. The tape was one of many that the Phoenix police discovered in his rectory. "Father Lan," as he was called, liked to film his encounters so that he could view them again and again. He also chronicled his sexual exploits with young kids in his diaries, which the police also confiscated. By the time of his trial, prosecutors were able to document that he had sexually molested more than twenty-two children. Prior to his conviction, Father Lan had been arrested for masturbating in full view of police officers at the Pleasure World Adult Bookstore in Phoenix.[19]

Father Lan's diaries also revealed a great deal about Bishop Thomas O'Brien of the Archdiocese of Phoenix, who had protected the priest for many years by moving him from parish to parish. On one occasion, when the priest confessed his sins to the bishop, he received a penance of five Hail Marys.[20]

"MY RESPONSE WAS APPROPRIATE"

Questioned by the judge about the arrest of Father Lan in the bookstore, Bishop O'Brien said that it was not unusual for a priest to get busted while performing an act of public lewdness.[21] At a press conference, the bishop defended his decision not to laicize Father Lan for his actions, saying: "I believe my response was appropriate. If you asked me what I would do today faced with a similar situation, in the context of 1993 and considering what we know about this type of behavior, my actions might have been different."[22]

In 2008, Father Lan was arrested by the Northern California Fugitive Task Force as he was leaving the Most Holy Redeemer Church in San Francisco, California. After his release from an Arizona prison in 2003, the priest not only failed to register as a sex offender but also engaged in over 1,800 sexual encounters with individuals he met while roaming the streets of Phoenix. He targeted hitchhikers and young boys who had run away from home.[23]

AN IMPERFECT HUMAN BEING

In 1997, a Dallas jury heard charges from eleven victims of Fr. Rudy Kos. The victims were former altar boys who said that the priest had molested them on hundreds of occasions from 1981 to 1992. Kos was sentenced to life in prison. The Dallas diocese, where Kos had served three parishes, was fined $120 million by the state.[24] The award was later reduced to $31, but the diocese, nevertheless, was forced to take out mortgages and sell property to cover the judgment.[25]

In a 2016 interview with the *Dallas Morning News*, Kos said, "I would like for them [the public] to think of me as a human being, not perfect, tried to be, tried to be all things to all people, and, in the process, things went wrong." He went on to say that he, too, was a victim in the case against him: "I have become a victim simply because my family [the diocese] has deep pockets."[26]

ELUDING JUSTICE

In 1999, Bishop J. Keith Symons of Palm Beach, Florida, became the first US bishop to be forced into retirement after admitting to molesting five altar boys.[27] Symons was replaced by Bishop Anthony O'Connell. Within the year, O'Connell, too, was forced to resign, after the *St. Louis Dispatch* discovered that he had molested a student at a seminary in Missouri. The student had been paid $125,000 in hush money by the Missouri diocese.

After the bishop's resignation, a group of Catholics, including Susan Vance, cofounder of the Survivors Network of Those Abused by Priests,

sought to have the photo of O'Connell removed from the wall of a parochial high school, his name expunged from a Catholic family life center,
and his bust carted away from the chancery. Their efforts were in vain. In
2012, shortly before O'Connell's death, Ms. Vance said, "Ten years after
admitting abuse and moving to a life of security and peace at Mepkin
Abbey, South Carolina, O'Connell eludes civil justice and remains a Catholic priest to his dying day. He was never defrocked despite admission of
crimes that the Catholic Church says it abhors. Victims must settle for the
justice that O'Connell avoided on earth awaiting him before his Creator."[28]

PAPAL CONCEALMENT

The problem continued to escalate until John Paul II, on April 30, 2001,
issued a confidential apostolic letter stating that all cases of sexual abuse
involving the clergy were be handled by the Vatican office under Cardinal
Ratzinger and not by bishops who governed the dioceses in which the
crimes were committed. The pope further declared that all cases were to
be kept secret so that the reputation of Holy Mother Church would not be
sullied.[29] News of the letter created widespread outrage since it provided
proof that the church was engaged in concealing criminal activity from
law enforcement officials.[30]

Despite the papal efforts of concealment, more and more reports of
priests engaged in pedophilia captured international headlines. On January
6, 2002, the *Boston Globe* revealed that Fr. John J. Geoghan of greater Boston,
despite reports that he had molested or raped 130 boys, was simply relocated to new parishes by Cardinal Law as soon as new complaints reached
the chancery. While in protective custody at the maximum security Souza-
Baranowski Correctional Center in Shirley, Massachusetts, Geoghan was
strangled and stomped to death by another inmate.[31]

THE JOHN JAY STUDY

On February 27, 2004, the John Jay College of Criminal Justice, in a study
that had been commissioned by the US Conference of Catholic Bishops,
revealed that between 1950 and 2002, 4,392 US priests had been charged
with sex abuse and that the allegations had been made by more than 10,667
alleged victims. The study contained the following findings:

- 81 percent of the victims were male.

- Female tended to be younger than the males. Data analyzed by the researchers showed that the number and proportion of sexual misconduct directed at girls under eight years old was higher than that directed at boys the same age.

- 22.6 percent were age ten or younger, 51 percent were between the ages of eleven and fourteen, and 27 percent were between the ages of fifteen to seventeen years.

- A substantial number (almost two thousand) of very young children (six and under) were victimized by priests during this time period.

- In 6,696 (72 percent) cases, an investigation of the allegation was carried out. Of these, 4,570 (80 percent) were substantiated, 1,028 (18 percent) were unsubstantiated, and 83 (1.5 percent) were found to be false. In 56 cases, priests denied the allegations.

- More than 10 percent of these allegations were characterized as not substantiated because the diocese could not determine whether the alleged abuse actually took place.

- In 20 percent of the cases, the priest was deceased or inactive at the time of the receipt of the allegation and typically no investigation was conducted.

- In 38.4 percent of allegations, the abuse was alleged to have occurred within a single year, in 21.8 percent the alleged abuse lasted more than a year but less than two years, in 28 percent between two and four years, in 10.2 percent between five and nine years, and in under 1 percent ten or more years.

Concerning the 4,392 priests, the study displayed the following results:

- 56 percent had one reported allegation against them, 27 percent had two or three allegations against them, 14 percent had four to nine allegations against them, and 3 percent (149 priests) had ten or more allegations against them. These 149 priests were responsible for almost three thousand victims, or 27 percent of the allegations.

- The allegations were substantiated for 1,872 priests and unsubstantiated for 824 priests. The researchers thought the charges to be credible for 1,671 priests and not credible for 345 priests. Not included in the study were 298 priests and deacons who had been completely exonerated.

- 50 percent of the priests were thirty-five years of age or younger at the time of the first instance of alleged abuse.

- Almost 70 percent had been ordained before 1970.

- Fewer than 7 percent were reported to have themselves been victims of physical, sexual, or emotional abuse as children. Although 19 percent had alcohol or substance abuse problems, only 9 percent were reported to have been using drugs or alcohol during the instances of abuse.[32]

PROSECUTION UNDER RICO

By the close of the first decade of the twenty-first century, US bishops had received complaints of child sexual abuse by approximately 6,000 priests—5.6 percent of the country's Catholic clerics. Of these, 525 were behind bars, and over three thousand civil and criminal lawsuits were pending.[33] The cost of this scandal exceeded $3 billion, forcing eight dioceses to seek bankruptcy protection.[34] Ten percent of the Roman Catholic priests in America had been accused of pedophilia—a number so alarming that legal activists called upon federal and state attorneys to prosecute such clerics under the guidelines of RICO (the Racketeer Influenced Corrupt Organizations Act), thereby, once again, treating the Roman Catholic Church as a criminal and corrupt organization.[35]

A GLOBAL PROBLEM

This problem of pedophilia, of course, was not confined to America. It extended to Ireland, Canada, the United Kingdom, Latin America, Belgium, France, Germany, and Australia, increasing the cost to $10 billion and creating financial havoc in dioceses and parishes throughout the world. And this mounting problem had been addressed by the continuous rotation of problematic and perverse priests between dioceses and a conspiracy of silence among the Curia. Not only had John Paul II condoned this practice, but he also went on to insist that the abusers were in fact the victims. Cardinal Ratzinger said, "It has to do with the reflection of our highly sexualized society. Priests are also affected by the general situation. They may be especially vulnerable, or susceptible, although the percentage of abuse cases is no higher than in other occupations."[36]

John Paul II's refusal to demand the dismissal of priests from holy office who had been found guilty of child molestation has been likened to the silence of Pope Pius XII during the Nazi Holocaust.[37] One of the pope's greatest shames was giving sanctuary to Cardinal Law, who resigned in disgrace from the archdiocese of Boston in 2002. Another unforgiveable act was the pope's stubborn and self-righteous defense of Marcial Maciel Degollado, a Mexican priest who serially abused adolescent seminarians, some as young as twelve, along with several of his own illegitimate children.[38]

UN CONDEMNATION

On January 16, 2014, the Roman Catholic Church became the first and only religious institution to be condemned by the United Nations. The global organization took the Vatican to task for transferring abusive priests from parish to parish rather than turning them over to the police. Monsignor Charles Scicluna, the Vatican's former sex crime prosecutor, admitted to the Office of the UN High Commissioner for Human Rights that the Holy See had been "slow" to face the crisis and that "certain things need to be done differently."[39]

But neither Monsignor Scicluna nor the other members of the Vatican committee could provide an answer to a question raised by Sara Oviedo, the UN human rights investigator. Ms. Oviedo asked how the Vatican, given its zero-tolerance policy toward clerical sex abuse, could continue, as a religious institution, "to cover up and obscure these kinds of cases?"[40] Nor could the Vatican committee offer a response to Maria Rita Parsi, another UN investigator, who asked, "If these events continue to be hidden and covered up, to what extent will children be affected?"[41]

A CARDIAC INCIDENT

Archbishop Józef Wesolowski, the papal nuncio to the Dominican Republic, was accused in June 27, 2014, of picking up boys on the waterfront, paying them to perform sexual acts, and taking pornographic pictures of them. As soon as the charges were filed by Dominican officials, Wesolowski was whisked away to the Vatican and placed in protective custody. The requests for his extradition were denied on the grounds that the Polish prelate possessed diplomatic immunity.[42] He was the highest ranking Catholic cleric to be labeled a pedophile.

The uproar over the incident caused Pope Francis to set a trial date for Wesolowski, who would become the first person ever to be tried at a criminal court within the Vatican. The trial never occurred. On August 27, 2017, the archbishop was found dead within his Vatican residence at 5:00 a.m. His death was attributed to a "cardiac incident."[43]

A FORTRESS IMPREGNABLE

Largely because of the pedophilia scandal, the Holy See by 2005 began to display deficits in excess of $12 million. However, the Roman Curia remained blithely unconcerned about these mounting shortfalls. They knew that the real worldly riches of the church remained safe and secure within the Apostolic Palace, which houses the Vatican Bank. Dioceses may be sued and fall into bankruptcy; parochial schools, universities, and hospitals may be strapped with multimillion-dollar settlements; but the accounts within the IOR remain out of the reach of altar boys who were sexually molested by their parish priests. As a sovereign state, the Holy See cannot be subjected to any ruling by a foreign court. It remains an institution with over $50 billion in securities, gold reserves that exceed those of some industrialized nations, real estate holdings that equal the total area of many countries, and opulent palaces containing the world's greatest art treasures.[44] Such wealth will remain and grow even though the contributions of the Catholic faithful have been cut back to a trickle.

REFUGEES AS REVENUE

Due to the enormous cost of the pedophilia scandal, Roman Catholic dioceses throughout the United States became more and more reliant on obtaining tax payer dollars to stay afloat. One of the most innovative means of tapping into public funds came with Muslim refugees, who began arriving in the United States at the rate 90,000 a year. They arrived in need of housing, food, medical care, educational services, and employment, if not welfare checks. To address these needs, Catholic Social Services (CSS) became a "resettlement contractor." For every refugee or "client," CSS came to receive $2,025 from the Reception and Placement Program (RPP), which operates under the US State Department.[45] Since the number of Muslim refugees has continued to increase year after year throughout the first years of the twenty-first century, the CCS developed into a multibillion dollar business.

The cost to CCS was purely administrative. The agency does not provide actual food, shelter, or financial subsidy to the refugees. It merely refers them to federal and state agencies where the refugees can get public housing, food stamps, emergency welfare assistance, and other benefits.

STEADY FLOW OF "CLIENTS"

In Milwaukee, Wisconsin, alone, CSS processed more than five hundred refugees, most of whom are devout Rohingya Muslims from Burma. The processing proved to be very profitable. From 2013 to 2016, CSS received more than $7 million from Milwaukee alone.[46]

In addition to RPP, CSS received additional funding from other governmental offices, including the Department of Health and Human Services, the Administration of Children and Families, and Refugee and Entrant Assistant Funds.[47] CCS also received a financial windfall from other "clients," including the legal and illegal immigrants who flowed into the country from the southern border.

THE CHURCH AND STATE

Because federal agencies in many major US cities are now maxed to the limit with refugees and migrants, CSS undertook the task of relocating thousands of them to various places throughout the country, including Reno, Nevada; Ithaca, New York; Eugene, Oregon; and even Ogden, Utah, where the director of CSS for the local diocese is a former Somali refugee.[48] Catholic Social Services (CSS) receives $1,850.00 for every enrolled refugee (including every child), and $2,200.00 for every refugee (including every child) as a matching grant. To receive the match grant, CSS must show that it has spent $200 in administrative or other costs and given more $800 of donated clothes, furniture, or cars. CSS also pockets 25 percent of every transportation loan it collects from the refugees that it sponsors. In addition, the administrative expenses and overhead of the CSS in Washington, DC, where the processing takes place, is paid by the federal government.[49]

Someone has to pay for the plague of pedophilia and it might as well be the US taxpayer.

Chapter Twenty

THE MARK OF THE ANTICHRIST

What increasingly dominates my interest is the effort to establish within myself and to diffuse around me, a new religion—let's call it an improved Christianity if you like—whose personal God is no longer the great Neolithic landowner of times gone by, but the Soul of the world.
—Teilhard de Chardin, "Letter to Leontine Zanta,"
January 26, 1936

Pope John Paul II never censured, let alone excommunicated, any ecclesiastical official who belonged to P-2, despite the canon law mandating immediate excommunication of anyone who joins a Masonic lodge. Cardinal Agostino Casaroli remained the Vatican secretary of state until his death in 1989, Cardinal Ugo Poletti held his positions as president of the Preservation of the Faith and of the Liturgical Academy, and Cardinal Leo Suenens stayed on as protector of the Church of St. Peter in Chains (outside Rome). Other clerics who were members of Gelli's lodge were elevated in rank and dignity:

- Cardinal Sebastiano Baggio rose from his position as president of the Vatican City State to become *camerlengo* (treasurer) of the Holy See.

- Bishop Fiorenzo Angelini left the diocese of Messene in Greece to become a member of the College of Cardinals and the president of the Pontifical Council for the Pastoral Care of Health Workers.

- Bishop Cleto Bellucci climbed in rank from coadjutor bishop of Fermo to archbishop of Fermo.

- Bishop Gaetano Bonicelli relinquished his position as the presiding cleric of Albano to become archbishop of Siena-Colle di Val d'Elsa-Montalcino.

- Archbishop Giuseppe Ferraioli, who was a member of the Second Congregation of Public Affairs, became a leading official of the Vatican Secretariat of State.

- Fr. Pio Laghi, the papal nuncio to Argentina, received his red hat to become a cardinal and the head of the Congregation for Catholic Education.

- Fr. Giovanni Lajolo, a member of the Council of Public Affairs of the Church, became a cardinal and president of the Pontifical Commission for Vatican City State.

- Fr. Virgilio Levi was promoted from assistant director of the official Vatican newspaper to executive director of Vatican Radio.

- Fr. Pasquale Macchi, the private secretary to Paul VI, rose in rank to become the archbishop to the Roman Catholic Territorial Prelature of Loreto.

- Fr. Francesco Marchisano ascended from his post as prelate of honor of the pope to become a cardinal and president of the Permanent Commission for the Care of the Historic and Artistic Monuments of the Holy See.

- Fr. Dino Monduzzi, the regent of the Pontifical House, emerged from the scandal to join the College of Cardinals as prefect of the Papal Household.

- Fr. Virgilio Noe, the undersecretary for the Congregation for Divine Worship, was also elevated to the cardinalate as president of the Fabric of St. Peter.

- Fr. Pio Vito Pinto, an attaché to the Vatican secretary of state, became a monsignor and dean of the Apostolic Tribunal of the Roman Rota (the highest appellate court of the church).

- Msgr. Mario Rizzi, prelate bishop of the Honor of the Holy Father, ascended in dignity to serve as archbishop of Bagnoregio and apostolic nuncio to Bulgaria.

- Fr. Pietro Rossano, rector of the Pontifical Lateran University, became consecrated as the auxiliary bishop of Rome.

- Fr. Roberto Tucci, director-general of Vatican Radio, climbed the ecclesiastical ladder to emerge as cardinal-priest of Sant'Ignazio di Loyola a Campo Marzio.

- Fr. Pietro Vergari, protocol officer of the Vatican Office Segnatura, became rector of the St. Apollinaire Palace, the institution from which Emanuela Orlandi had been kidnapped.

UNIVERSAL SALVATION

Although presented to the faithful as a conservative prelate who sought to safeguard *sacra doctrina*, John Paul II perpetuated the process of *aggiornamento* and the false doctrines of Vatican II, while advancing heresies that were uniquely his own. Traditionally, the church taught that salvation was offered only to those who had been cleansed of original sin by the Sacrament of Baptism, absolved of mortal sins by the Sacrament of Penance, and united to Christ through the Sacrament of Holy Communion. The Council of Trent in 1547 proclaimed, "But although Christ died for all, yet not all receive the benefit of His death, but only those to whom the merit of His Passion is communicated."[1] But John Paul II espoused universal salvation, stating that because of Christ's Passion all of mankind resides in a state of sanctifying grace. On December 27, 1978, he said, "Jesus is the Second Person of the Sacred Trinity who became a man; and, therefore, the whole of mankind is redeemed, saved, enabled to the extent of participating in divine life by means of Grace."[2] Similarly, on January 22, 1980, he proclaimed: "Jesus makes us in Himself once more sons of the Eternal Father. He obtains, once and for all, the salvation of man, of each man, of all."[3]

The implications of such teachings produced earthquakes that cracked the Rock upon which St. Peter had built the church. All of humanity, according to John Paul II, had been saved by Christ's work, thereby eradicating the need of a religious institution; humans no longer were born in a state of original sin, thereby eradicating the need of the Sacrament of Baptism; and mortal sin had become a thing of the past, thereby eradicating the need of the Sacraments of Penance and Holy Communion.

PAN CHRISTIANITY

From the stance of universal salvation, John Paul II espoused a new religion of pan-Christianity that was designed to unite all of mankind in one body of belief. On October 27, 1986, he invited leaders of various religions throughout the world to unite with him in a celebration of prayer and worship at the Basilica of St. Francis in Assisi, Italy. The gathering was attended by rabbis, Islamic muftis and mullahs, Buddhist monks, Jains, ministers from mainstream Protestant denominations, African and Native American Animists, Hindus, and Zoroastrians, who came forward before the altar which housed the remains of St. Francis to offer prayers for peace and religious unity. The Dalai Lama, before offering his prayer, placed a statue of Buddha on the sacred tabernacle and lit candles of incense.[4]

Throughout the ages, the church had condemned such interreligious events as apostasy. On January 6, 1928, Pope Pius XI, in his encyclical *Mortalium animos*, issued the following declaration:

> For which reason conventions, meetings and addresses are frequently arranged by these persons, at which a large number of listeners are present, and at which all without distinction are invited to join in the discussion, both infidels of every kind, and Christians, even those who have unhappily fallen away from Christ or who with obstinacy and pertinacity deny His divine nature and mission. Certainly such attempts can nowise be approved by Catholics, founded as they are on that false opinion which considers all religions to be more or less good and praiseworthy, since they all in different ways manifest and signify that sense which is inborn in us all, and by which we are led to God and to the obedient acknowledgment of His rule. Not only are those who hold this opinion in error and deceived, but also in distorting the idea of true religion they reject it, and little by little. turn aside to naturalism and atheism, as it is called; from which it clearly follows that one who supports those who hold these theories and attempt to realize them, is altogether abandoning the divinely revealed religion.[5]

UNDER THE SPELL OF VOODOO

On January 24, 2002, John Paul II hosted another pan-Christian gathering at the Basilica of St. Francis of Assisi. In preparation of this event all the crucifixes and trappings of tradition Catholicism were covered with drapes. Within the convent within the lower level of the basilica, Muslims were granted a room which faced Mecca; Zoroastrians were allocated a room with windows so that they could burn wooden chips; and the Jews were provided with a room that had not been blessed in the name of Jesus Christ. A highlight of the gathering came when a voodoo priest ascended to the pulpit within the central sanctuary of the basilica to shake a rattle at all those in attendance, including the Holy Father, before placing them under a voodoo spell of tranquility.[6]

Reacting to the gathering, Robert Sungenis, in an article for *Catholic Apologetics International*, wrote, "If the pope believes a world religion can pray for physical and spiritual blessings as a mutual concern with Catholics, then it appears he must also believe that the pagan has an established, not just incidental, relationship with God, to the point where God would hear the prayers of a pagan the same as he would hear the prayers of any faithful Catholic. Moreover, it suggests that God is not the least bit disturbed by the pagan's worship of false gods and sinful lifestyle, nor the least bit disturbed that the Catholic is not discouraging the pagan from his false worship and lifestyle."[7]

KISSING THE KORAN

Of all the world religions, John Paul II displayed a special fondness for Islam. On May 14, 1999, while receiving a delegation from Iraq, he planted a kiss on the Koran, the sacred book of the Muslim faith, which decries the dogma of the Trinity as polytheism and denies the divinity of Jesus Christ. Joseph Sobran, writing in *Catholic Family News*, provided this reaction:

> One of the most amazing symbolic acts in the history of the modern Catholic Church occurred on May 14, 1999, when Pope John Paul II, when receiving a delegation from Iraq, publicly kissed the Koran. It is hard to imagine how "ecumenical dialogue" can go further. This is not your father's Catholic Church.
>
> The papal kiss seemed to me far less likely to bring Muslims into the Church than to drive Catholics out. Surely the Vicar of Christ was aware that the Koran has taught untold millions to deny Christ's Divinity and condemns believers in the Trinity to Hell. Personal charity to Muslims is one thing; honoring their holy book is another. For the Pope himself to do so, in this public manner, was not only without precedent, it was stunningly contrary to all Catholic precedent. As he himself also knew. No Pope before the Second Vatican Council could conceivably have done such a thing.

Since the Council, the Catholic Church has certainly entered a new and extremely troubled phase in its long history. Doctrines, liturgy, discipline, architecture, vocabulary, and demeanor have all changed profoundly. Mass attendance has plunged. So have vocations to the priesthood. Priests, nuns, and theologians [of those who remain within the Church at all, that is] openly defy the Vatican—often appealing to the spirit of the Council itself. The laity routinely ignore Church teaching on contraception, one of the few things that haven't changed. [There is a widespread feeling that if so many other things can be discarded or disregarded, so can this.] Many Catholics no longer believe in the Real Presence of Christ in the Eucharist. Shocking sexual scandals, implicating bishops [and forcing one Cardinal to resign his Archbishopric], now appall even Catholics inured to horrors. The Church has apologized to the world for everything short of damaging the ozone layer. And the Pope himself has publicly kissed the Koran.[8]

Two months after kissing the Koran, John Paul II called upon St. John the Baptist "to protect Islam and all the peoples of Jordan."[9] A prayer for such a blessing was unique in the history of Roman Catholicism. A leading saint had been called upon to protect a religion that was intent upon the forceful submission of all of mankind to the throne of Allah.

EXTREME ISLAMOPHILIA

Such an invocation betrayed the pope's belief that there existed scant difference between Muslim and Christians since both religions worship the same God and venerate the same sacred books. On December 30, 1987, he issued *Sollicitudo rei socialis* in which he held forth the following:

I am certain that the concern expressed in this Encyclical as well as the motives inspiring it will be familiar to them, for these motives are inspired by the Gospel of Jesus Christ. We can find here a new invitation to bear witness together to our common convictions concerning the dignity of man, created by God, redeemed by Christ, made holy by the Spirit and called upon in this world to live a life in conformity with this dignity. I likewise address this appeal . . . to the Muslims who, like us, believe in a just and merciful God.[10]

To reinforce this proclamation, John Paul II stated to a general audience in 1999,

We Christians joyfully recognize the religious values we have in common with Islam. Today I would like to repeat what I said to young Muslims some years ago in Casablanca: "We believe in the same God, the one God, the living God, the God who created the world and brings his creatures to their perfection . . ." The patrimony of revealed texts in the Bible speaks unanimously of the oneness of God . . .

The worship of the one God, Creator of all, encourages us to increase our knowledge of one another in the future.[11]

SAINTS OF ALL SECTS

Naturally, as a proponent of pan-Christianity, John Paul II taught that all non-Christian sects may lead their adherents to the kingdom of heaven. The New Catechism, which he authorized in 1985, declared, "The Spirit of Christ makes use of these Churches and ecclesial communities as means of salvation."[12] What's more, he decided that such sects have saints and martyrs who are worthy of veneration by all Catholics. In *Ut unum sint*, an encyclical issued on May 25, 1995, John Paul II said,

> Albeit in an invisible way, the communion between our Communities, even if still incomplete, is truly and solidly grounded in the full communion of the Saints—those who, at the end of a life faithful to grace, are in communion with Christ in glory. These *Saints* come from all the Churches and Ecclesial Communities which gave them entrance into the communion of salvation.
>
> When we speak of a common heritage, we must acknowledge as part of it not only the institutions, rites, means of salvation and the traditions which all the communities have preserved and by which they have been shaped, but first and foremost this reality of holiness.[13]

Such statements represented a repudiation of the principles that had earmarked Catholicism throughout the ages. In 1441, the Council of Florence under Pope Eugene IV had proclaimed *ex cathedra*, "No one, even if he has shed blood in the name of Christ, can be saved, unless he has remained in the bosom and unity of the Catholic Church."[14] Upholding this dogma, Pope Pius XI in *Rappresentanti in terra*, as promulgated on December 31, 1929, declared,

> The true Christian does not renounce the activities of this life, he does not stunt his natural faculties; but he develops and perfects them, by coor-

dinating them with the supernatural. He thus ennobles what is merely natural in life and secures for it new strength in the material and temporal order, no less then [*sic*] in the spiritual and eternal.

This fact is proved by the whole history of Christianity and its institutions, which is nothing else but the history of true civilization and progress up to the present day. It stands out conspicuously in the lives of the numerous Saints, whom the Church, and she alone, produces, in whom is perfectly realized the purpose of Christian education, and who have in every way ennobled and benefited human society.[15]

NEITHER HEAVEN NOR HELL NOR ANY PLACE IN BETWEEN

During the summer of 1999, John Paul II decided that heaven was not a real place. Before a general audience on July 21, he said, "In the context of Revelation, we know that the "heaven" or "happiness" in which we will find ourselves is neither an abstraction nor a physical place in the clouds, but a living, personal relationship with the Holy Trinity. It is our meeting with the Father which takes place in the risen Christ through the communion of the Holy Spirit."[16]

Seven days later, he came to the conclusion that hell also was not an empirical terrain. Addressing another general audience, he said, "The images of hell that Sacred Scripture presents to us must be correctly interpreted. They show the complete frustration and emptiness of life without God. Rather than a place, hell indicates the state of those who freely and definitively separate themselves from God, the source of all life and joy."[17]

The pope was on a roll. On August 4, he announced that purgatory also was not real. He explained his new stance by saying, "Every trace of attachment to evil must be eliminated, every imperfection of the soul corrected. Purification must be complete, and indeed this is precisely what is meant by the Church's teaching on *purgatory.* The term does not indicate a place, but a condition of existence. Those who after death exist in a state of purification, are already in the love of Christ who removes from them the remnants of imperfection."[18]

THE 1910 *CATHOLIC ENCYCLOPEDIA*

A realization of how far John Paul II had strayed from traditional church doctrine on the subject of eternity can be discovered by turning to the pages of the 1910 *Catholic Encyclopedia*. Regarding heaven, the encyclopedia says, "The heaven of the blessed is a special place with definite limits. Naturally, this place is held to exist, not within the earth, but, in accordance with the expressions of Scripture, without and beyond its limits."[19]

Hell in the encyclopedia is presented as follows:

> The damned are utterly estranged from God; hence their abode is said to be as remote as possible from his dwelling, far from heaven above and its light, and consequently hidden away in the dark abysses of the earth. However, no cogent reason has been advanced for accepting a metaphorical interpretation in preference to the most natural meaning of the words of Scripture. Hence theologians generally accept the opinion that hell is really within the earth.[20]

Purgatory, the 1910 text states, "in accordance with Catholic teaching is a place or condition of temporal punishment for those who, departing this life in God's grace, are, not entirely free from venial faults, or have not fully paid the satisfaction due to their transgressions."[21]

THE DIVINITY OF HUMANS

But the most outrageous heresy of the Polish pope for many believers came with his persistent claim that every man and every woman is Jesus Christ. He set forth this bizarre teaching in his first homily as pope on Sunday, October 23, 1978, as follows:

> "You are the Christ, the Son of the living God" (Matt. 16:16). These words were spoken by Simon, son of Jonah, in the district of Caesarea Philippi. . . . These words mark the beginning of Peter's mission in the history of salvation. . . . Please listen once again, today in this sacred place, to the words uttered by Simon Peter. In those words is the faith of the Church. In those same words is the new truth, indeed, the ultimate and definitive truth about man: the son of the living God—"You are the Christ, the Son of the living God."[22]

John Paul II reiterated this message throughout his pontificate. On December 25, 1978, John Paul II announced, "I'm addressing this message to every human being, to man in his humanity. Christmas is the feast of man."[23] In a sermon delivered on June 11, 1982, John Paul II said, When we look at the cross, we see in it the passion of man: the agony of Christ."[24] On

Good Friday 1998, he proclaimed,

> As we contemplate Christ dead on the Cross, our thoughts turn to the countless injustices and sufferings which prolong his passion in every part of the world. I think of the places where man is insulted and humiliated, downtrodden and exploited. In every person suffering from hatred and violence, or rejected by selfishness and indifference, Christ continues to suffer and die. On the faces of those who have been "defeated by life" there appear the features of the face of Christ dying on the Cross.[25]

Addressing the Missionaries of the Precious Blood in 2001, he said: "And at the moment of Easter this joy came to the fullness as the light of divine glory shone on the face of the Risen Lord, whose wounds shine forever like the sun. This is the truth of who you are, dear brothers."[26]

Humans were also in the pope's mind the first and second persons of the Holy Trinity. In his *Urbi et Orbi* message of 1985, John Paul II announced, "Grace is God as 'Our Father.' It is the Son of God as the Son of the Virgin. It is the Holy Spirit at work in the human heart. . . . Grace is also man."[27] At the close of the second gathering of the world's religious leaders at Assisi on January 24, 2002, the pope proclaimed, "To offend against man is, most certainly, to offend against God."[28] The implication of this teaching was that no one should be castigated or offended for any reason, not even for upholding blasphemous beliefs.

THE MARK OF THE ANTICHRIST

In accordance with his humanistic perspective, John Paul II maintained that the purpose of Catholic churches and communities was not to bear witness to a transcendent God, let alone to serve as centers of Christian proselytism, but rather to serve as places that uphold the exalted status of humanity. In his address to the ambassador of Tunisia on May 27, 2004, the pope said, "For its part, the modest Catholic community that lives in Tunisia has no other ambition than to witness to the dignity of man."[29]

Reflecting John Paul's teachings concerning the divinity of humanity, knowing traditionalists remembered *E supremi*, an encyclical of October 4, 1903, in which Pope Pius X declared, ". . . the distinguishing mark of Antichrist, man has with infinite temerity put himself in the place of God, raising himself above all that is called God; in such wise that although he cannot utterly extinguish in himself all knowledge of God, he has contemned God's majesty and, as it were, made of the universe a temple wherein he himself is to be adored. 'He sitteth in the temple of God, showing himself as if he were God.'"[30]

Whence came John Paul II's apostasy? Digging deeper than the Second Vatican Council, one comes upon the writings of Fr. Pierre Teilhard de Chardin, arguably the most influential Catholic theologian of the twentieth century. The French Jesuit's writings were very much in vogue during Wojtyla's formative years when he was a seminarian in Krakow. According to Teilhard, all of creation is headed toward a Plethora and nothing in nature changes by chance. Evolution is not an endless process but rather a divine plan that culminates in plentitude, a state in which all things—time and space, climate and creation, life and death—come under the control of humans. "Is evolution a theory, a system or a hypothesis?" Teilhard wrote in *The Phenomenon of Man*. "It is a general condition to which all theories, all systems, all hypotheses must bow. . . . Evolution is a light illuminating all facts, a curve that all lines must follow."[31] As envisioned by Teilhard, the end process of evolution would be the unification of world government, culture, language, and religion and the establishment of an earthly utopia in which all humanity would live in peace, harmony, and enlightenment.[32]

Before Teilhard's death in 1955, his works had been condemned by the Holy See and could not be sold in Catholic bookstores. Still and all, his influence in Catholic theology was enormous and had a profound effect not only on John Paul II but also on Benedict XVI, who wrote,

> It must be regarded as an important service of Teilhard de Chardin's that he rethought these ideas from the angle of the modern view of the world and, in spite of a not entirely unobjectionable tendency toward the biological approach, nevertheless on the whole grasped them correctly and in any case made them accessible once again. Let us listen to his own words: The human monad "can only be absolutely itself by ceasing to be alone." In the background is the idea that in the cosmos, alongside the two orders or classes of the infinitely small and the infinitely big, there is a third order, which determines the real drift of evolution, namely, the order of the infinitely complex. It is the real goal of the ascending process of growth or becoming; it reaches a first peak in the genesis of living things and then continues to advance to those highly complex creations that give the cosmos a new center: "Imperceptible and accidental as the position which they hold may be in the history of the heavenly bodies, in the last analysis the planets are nothing less than the vital points of the universe. It is through them that the axis now runs on them is henceforth concentrated the main effort of an evolution aiming principally at

the production of large molecules." The examination of the world by the dynamic criterion of complexity thus signifies a complete inversion of values. A reversal of the perspective.[33]

This inversion of values and reversal of perspective certainly characterized the reigns of John Paul II and Benedict XVI, with disastrous effects on the church whose teachings they had been sworn to safeguard against the "present evil age" (Acts 2:40).

Chapter Twenty-One

RESIGNATION

The missionaries of the 16th century were convinced that the unbaptized person is lost forever. After the [Second Vatican] Council, this conviction was definitely abandoned. . . . Why should you try to convince the people to accept the Christian faith when they can be saved without it?
        —Pope Benedict XVI, interview with *Avvenire*, March
                                                                16, 2016

By the time of John Paul II's death on April 2, 2005, Roman Church membership in the United States was falling at the astonishing rate of 400,000 a year, despite the influx of Catholics from Mexico and Latin America. Thousands of parishes that were once thriving and vibrant had closed, while thousands more lacked a resident priest. Four American-born Catholics were leaving the church for every new convert.[1] In Spain, 81 percent of the people identified themselves as Catholics, but two-thirds never went to Mass. Despite the rulings of the Vatican, 40 percent of the Spaniards believed that abortion was a fundamental right, 24 percent maintained that the practice should be tolerated, and 50 percent of pregnancies occurring in girls between the ages of fifteen and seventeen were terminated.[2]

By 1996, the moral decline in Italy, where Catholics number 95 percent of the populace, became so dire that John Paul II called upon volunteers to go from door to door in an effort to persuade people to "return to church." The effort was a complete failure.[3] By 2000, less than 25 percent of Italian Catholics made an appearance at Sunday Mass.

At the dawn of the twenty-first century, the magnificent churches and cathedrals in France, many dating back to the eleventh century, were visited almost entirely by tourists, since less than 8 percent of the country's Catholics opted to sit through the liturgy once a month.[4] Of the few French people who showed up for Mass, 28 percent were aged seventy-five years or older, and the overwhelming majority consisted of poorly educated, rural women.[5]

Britain, according to Cardinal Cormac Murphy-O'Connor, the head of the Catholic Church in England and Wales, "has become a pagan country."[6] Vandalism, theft, drug dealing, arson, pagan rites, and "inappropriate behavior on the high altar" had become so commonplace throughout the United Kingdom that churches were kept locked outside of the hours for worship and guarded by closed-circuit TV cameras. The number of Catholics showing up to fulfill their Sunday obligation declined from 2.63 million in 1963, when the Vatican Council was in full session, to less than 1 million in 2000.[7] Three years later, the disparity between nominal and practicing Catholics stood at 83.4 to 18.9 percent.[8] During this same time, only 12 percent of the Catholics in Scotland attended Mass with any regularity. Cardinal Keith O'Brien, the country's head prelate, said there was a danger of Scotland declining "into a Bacchanalian state where everyone is just concerned with their own pleasures or to sleep with whoever they want."[9]

Throughout Europe, the church has lost more than 1.5 million members since the close of Vatican II. And every year the situation continued to worsen. When the crowds lined up for the traditional *Novendiales* to view John Paul II's remains, the outlook for the future of Catholics was not even sunny in Mexico, where the number of worshippers in recent years fell from 96 percent to 82 percent.[10]

HOLY HYPERBOLE

The true miracle of John Paul II is that he remained remarkably immune from criticism and condemnation. As scandal gave way to scandal, the world's leading investigative reporters and news commentators refused to take the pope to task, not even to question his judgment in allowing money changers to remain in the holy temple. Nowhere was the lack of critical analysis more apparent than in the biography of the Polish pope by Carl Bernstein and Marco Politi. The very title of the work—*His Holiness*—betrayed the obsequiousness of the authors before their lofty subject. Throughout the lengthy text, Bernstein and Politi never made reference to Sindona, Calvi, or Gelli; never pressed for information about the Ambrosiano affair and the Sicilian connection; never made mention of Archbishop Paul Marcinkus and the Vatican Bank; and never approached the subject of Gladio and the funneling of black funds to Solidarity.

The hyperbole regarding John Paul II rose to near hysteria after his death. "A colossus," some newspapers reported.[11] "The greatest Pole," others said.[12] One Italian newspaper depicted the pope as a solitary Atlas holding the world on his shoulders.[13] During the *Novendiales*, massive crowds gathered in St. Peter's Square to demand, "*Santo Subito!*" ("Sainthood now!")[14] Before the end of January 2006, the Vatican had received over two million letters testifying to the virtuous life of the Polish pope.[15]

JOHN PAUL II'S SUCCESSOR

Since the Vatican Bank remained a magnet for notoriety, Cardinal Ratzinger, who ascended to the papal throne as Benedict XVI, pledged to initiate a new era of compliance with international financial regulations and complete transparency of all transactions. The first step toward this "reform" took place on May 24, 2012, with the dismissal of Ettore Gotti Tedeschi as the bank's president. Tedeschi had become the target of a criminal investigation by Italian officials for his alleged role in the laundering of millions of euros from an unknown source to J. P. Morgan in Frankfort and Banca del Fucino in Italy.[16] But the real cause of the firing, according to informed sources, was neither Tedeschi's ties to organized crime nor his involvement in bank fraud but rather his release of papal documents—all highly damaging to Ratzinger—to the Italian press.[17]

The move backfired. Following his dismissal, Tedeschi informed Italian investigators that he had compiled an exhaustive dossier of compromising information about the Vatican that had never seen the light of day because he feared for his life. The banker had given copies of the documents to his closest companions and told them, "If I am killed, the reason for my death is in here. I've seen things in the Vatican that would frighten anyone."[18] When the investigators seized the dossier, Pope Benedict demanded that the documents be returned to the Holy See since all Italian judicial authorities are obliged to respect the sovereign status of the Vatican.[19]

A LACK OF TRANSPARENCY

In another ill-advised attempt to suppress growing scandal, Pope Benedict agreed to submit the records of the bank's transactions to Moneyval, the Council of Europe's anti–money laundering agency. The records, as expected, were doctored and incomplete. Moneyval announced in July of 2012 that the bank had failed the transparency test in eight of sixteen key categories.[20]

Full disclosure would have raised embarrassing questions. Why had the church obtained controlling interest in companies that sharply conflicted with its dogma, including Raffaele del Monte Tabor in Milan, a biochemical center that specializes in stem cell research,[21] and Fabbrica d'Armi Pietro Beretta, a munitions company that provided ongoing shipments of arms to Gaddafi in Libya?[22] And these questions would lead to more questions. How had the Vatican Bank become the laundry for the Sicilian and Turkish Mafias and the international trade in illegal narcotics? Why is a prominent *capo* (Enrico De Pedis) buried in a cathedral with popes and cardinals? Why had the Vatican Bank sold counterfeit securities and established shell companies to bilk thousands of ill-informed investors? How had it profited from the Nazi ratlines? Why did it engage in black operations with the CIA and subversive political activity on a global scale? At last, Pope Benedict became aware that it was best to allow matters to rest. He retired from the holy office on February 28, 2013.

THE CONDOR'S EGG

By the time Jorge Mario Bergoglio transformed into Pope Francis on March 13, 2013, Islam had replaced Roman Catholicism as the world's leading religion and the spiritual devastation caused by John Paul II had spread to every corner of the globe, save for some regions of Africa. Throughout Europe and the United States, parishes were boarded up, seminaries were shut, convents were closed, and parochial schools were consolidated. In the United States the percentage of Catholics who attended Mass on a regular basis fell from 47 percent in 1974 to 24 percent in 2012, while the number of "strong" Catholics declined from 46 percent to 27 percent.[23] The plague of pedophilia persisted and the Vatican Bank remained one of the world's leading laundries for dirty money.

It would have taken a spiritual Hercules to clean out the Augean stable of Vatican, Inc. But Francis, who exuded considerable charm, refused to shoulder a shovel. The cardinals and archbishops who sheltered the pedophile priests by moving them from diocese to diocese were neither defrocked nor condemned. The Vatican Bank was not closed but rather remained as a separate identity within the sovereign state.

Pope Francis announced his decision on April 7, 2014, to keep the IOR open for business despite the eruption of new scandals regarding money laundering, which involved Monsignor Nunzio Scarano, a senior accountant at the IOR.[24] At the close of 2013, Moneyval uncovered 105 transactions within the Vatican Bank that smacked of money laundering, a significant upturn in apparent criminal activity from 2012, when only a half dozen suspicious cases were reported.[25]

SANTO SUBITO

On April 28, Pope Francis presided over the canonization of John Paul II, thereby perpetuating the decades of hypocrisy that had made the Roman Catholic Church one of the world's most disgraced institutions. In his homily, Francis said, "John Paul II cooperated with the Holy Spirit in renewing and updating the church in keeping with her pristine features, those features which the saints have given her throughout the centuries."[26]

John Paul II had cleared his own way to the community of saints by streamlining the canonization process, reducing to five years the waiting period after a person's death before a pronouncement of sainthood can be made. The Polish pope also abolished the position of a *promotor fidei*—in popular language the "devil's advocate." The purpose of the *promotor* was "to point out any flaws or weaknesses" in the evidence presented to establish a candidate's sainthood and "to raise all kinds of objections."[27] For this reason, no Vatican official was permitted to question John Paul II's accomplishments or to point out his failings.

END OF PONTIFICATION

On July 29, 2013, when asked how he would deal with the problem of homosexual priests, Francis replied, "If someone is gay and he searches for the Lord and has good will, who am I to judge?"[28] His response was problematic. The purpose of a pope is to pontificate, to provide moral certainty, to distinguish between right and wrong. But the statement by Francis was an admission that one could no longer turn to the church for direction and clarity, even though the decisions of the pope on matters of morality were supposedly infallible. What's worse, the question for a Catholic was easy to answer. For centuries, the church had proclaimed that homosexuality was an act against nature, an offense so grievous that it could only be absolved by a bishop. But Francis had abandoned tradition and the teachings of the church fathers. Morality, like matters of faith, was now in flux and no one, not even the bishop of Rome, could provide answers to the most perplexing questions of modern people.

Francis's inability to answer a basic catechetical question concerning sexuality spoke volumes and gave rise to the widespread assumption that the new pope affirmed gay lifestyles. On December 17, 2013, the face of the pope graced the front cover of *The Advocate*, the world's leading LGBT magazine, which named him "the Person of the Year." The article announcing the award said, "Pope Francis's stark change in rhetoric from his two predecessors—both who were at one time or another among *The Advocate*'s annual Phobie Awards—makes what he's done in 2013 all the more daring."[29]

THE DEVIL'S DAUGHTER

The pope took pride in gaining such favor. On January 27, 2015, Francis met and hugged Diego Neria Lejarraga, a forty-eight-year-old transgender person called "the devil's daughter" by his parish priest. Rather than castigating Neria for undergoing gender reassignment, the pope said, "God loves all his children, however they are; you are a son of God, who accepts you exactly as you are. Of course you are a son of the Church."[30] The problem with this statement did not arise from his display of compassion but rather his pronouncement that those who live in relationships deemed sinful by canon law are acceptable to almighty God and the church "exactly" as they are—without need of repentance. It was a deliberate display of rejection by the presiding pontiff of the moral teaching of traditional Catholicism.

NO NORMAL MOMENT

Solidifying his stance on gay issues, Francis informed Cardinal Dolan that Catholics should not dismiss, let alone oppose, same-sex marriages.[31] This statement prompted Virginia governor Tim Kaine, a practicing Roman Catholic, to tell an audience of LGBT activists in his bid for vice-president that he expected the church to bless same-sex marriages in the near future. Bishop Francis X. DiLorenzo, in his reaction to Kaine's statement, declared that the Catholic understanding of marriage would remain "unchanged and resolute."[32] Commenting on this exchange, syndicated columnist Ross

Douthat of the *New York Times* wrote, "In a normal moment, it would be the task of this conservative Catholic scribbler to explain why the governor is wrong and the bishop is right, why Scripture and tradition makes it impossible for Catholicism to simply reinvent its sexual ethics. But this is not a normal moment in the church."[33]

The pope's ambiguity over gay marriage spilled over to his stance on the canon law that prohibits divorced and remarried Catholics from receiving Holy Communion. On February 18, 2016, Francis said that the prohibition now should be lifted since it represented an obstacle to couples who wished "to proceed on the path to integration."[34] After making this pronouncement, he attempted by hook and crook to get the world's bishops to agree that the obstacle should be removed. But he met with considerable resistance from conservatives, who pointed out that such a reform would constitute a repudiation of the two-thousand-year-old teaching that sacramental marriages are indissoluble and second marriages adulterous.[35]

UNDERMINING MARRIAGE

Francis persisted in his argument that divorced and remarried couples should be allowed to partake of the Eucharist. Such a change, he maintained, could be effected by simply ignoring the canon law that prohibits such action. On April 18, 2016, he said, "It is important that the divorced who have entered a new union should be made to feel part of the Church." This should be accomplished, he said, not by "a new set of general rules, canonical in nature and applicable to all cases," but by "a responsible personal and pastoral discernment of particular cases."[36]

Regarding the institution of marriage itself, Francis said, "The great majority of our sacramental marriages are null. . . . Because they say 'yes, for the rest of my life!' but they don't know what they are saying. . . . They say it, they have good will, but they don't know."[37] This view of marriage implied that the marriage vows were not binding and that the sacrament was not efficacious, since it failed to impart an increase of sanctifying grace so that the couple could "love each other faithfully and to bear with each other's faults."[38] Francis, by his remarks, was undermining not only the sacred institution of marriage but the fundamental meaning of a sacrament as "an outward sign instituted to give grace through the merits of Jesus Christ."[39]

ENDORSING COHABITATION

Francis went on to say that cohabitations often display the spiritual fruits of sacramental marriage. "I've seen a lot of fidelity in these cohabitations," he said, "and I am sure that this is a real marriage, they have the grace of a real marriage, because of their fidelity."[40] And so, a pope, at last, had announced that the church in the age of sexual enlightenment was spiritually and morally superfluous. Couples could live together, have children, and receive the full measure of God's blessings.

"It's very odd that on the one hand the people who are married are told ... you're not really married, and the people who are cohabiting, 'I see elements of fidelity there and those are, those are marriages,'" said Robert Royal, editor of *The Catholic Thing*. "It's as if the culture—the sexual revolution of the culture is recalibrating the Church at both ends."[41]

"DON'T BLAME THE REPORTING!"

Phil Lawler of *Catholic Culture* added, "Don't blame the reporting. Don't blame the editing. The Pope's shocking remarks on marriage fall into an unsettling but consistent pattern ... the astonishing statements, the headlines, the confusion, followed by the explanations and clarifications that never clear away the fallout. When will Pope Francis realize—when will other prelates make clear to him—how much damage he does with these impromptu remarks. ... There are two problems, really: that the Pope speaks so often without first considering what he is about to say, and that when he makes these impulsive remarks, his first unguarded thoughts so rarely show the imprint of sound Catholic teaching."[42]

But the pronouncements by Francis were not haphazard remarks. They bore a logic and consistency that displayed a theological perspective of religious indifferentism in which all matters of morals and beliefs were relative; in which all things were in flux; and in which the Roman Catholic Church with its rosaries and rituals, its saints and sacraments, its laws and liturgy had come to represent little more than a historical curiosity.

ENDORSING INDIFFERENTISM

Transforming the heresy of indifferentism into new Catholic orthodoxy, Francis permitted for the first time in history an imam to recite Muslim prayers and to read from the Koran within the confines of the Vatican. The prayer service was conducted on June 6, 2014, in conjunction with a visit to the Holy See by Palestinian president Mahmoud Abbas and Israeli president Shimon Peres. A beaming pope told the press, "It is my hope that this meeting will mark the beginning of a new journey where we seek things that unite, so as to overcome the things that divide."[43] Francis, unfortunately, was unaware that imam's prayer, which was offered in Arabic, called for "victory over all infidels."[44] In another display of indifferentism, Pope Francis released a prayer video in January 2016, which featured Muslim prayer beads, but no rosary; a statue of Buddha but not statue of any Catholic saint, let alone the Virgin Mary; and a Menorah but no cross.[45]

CONFESSION AND COMMUNION FOR PROTESTANTS

Nothing distinctly or exclusively Catholic was to remain. Protestants were now invited to receive Holy Communion. "Explanations and interpretations [of the meaning of the Eucharist]" may differ, Pope Francis maintained, but "life is bigger than explanations and interpretations."[46] On January 15, 2016, after a personal meeting with the pope, a delegation of Lutherans from Finland attended Mass at St. Peter's Basilica. At the time of communion, they placed their right hands on their left shoulders as an indication that they were Protestants who were ineligible to receive the sacrament. But the presiding priest insisted and placed the sacred hosts within the hands of every member of the delegation. "I myself received it," said Lutheran bishop Samuel Salmi.[47] On March 3, 2016, as part of a "confession drive," Pope Francis encouraged non-Catholics to go to confessionals where they could speak in strict confidence with a priest about "problems and issues in their lives" and receive a sacerdotal blessing.[48]

The pope's mission, as he saw it, was to free the church from its own fetters—its dogmas and doctrines, its binding proclamations and claims of spiritual exclusivity, its own canon laws. "I believe in God," Francis said, "not a Catholic God. There is no Catholic God."[49] Regarding the deposit of faith, he declared, "It is not Catholic to say 'or this or nothing.' This is not Catholic; this is heretical. Jesus always knows how to accompany us. . . . He frees us from the chains of the laws' rigidity and tells us: 'But do that up to the point you are capable.' And He understands us very well."[50]

PAS MON PAPE

For Pope Francis, no matter of doctrine or dogma was to be upheld as a spiritual absolute. "We Catholics," he said, "have some, not just some, so many, who believe they have the absolute truth and they move forward with calumnies, with defamation and they hurt (people), they hurt. And, I say this because it's my Church, also us, all of us. It must be combated."[51] Absolution, the pope explained, is a manifestation of "fundamentalism," which he described as "a sickness that exists in all religions."

Since no faith has an exclusive claim to the truth, no religion is to be censored or condemned. Responding to the assassination of Fr. Jacques Hamel, an eighty-five-year-old priest whose throat was slashed by a Muslim extremist while he was saying Mass, Francis said, "There are violent Catholics! If I speak of Islamic violence, I must speak of Catholic violence . . . and no, not all Muslims are violent, not all Catholics are violent. It is like a fruit salad; there's everything. There are violent persons of this religion . . . this is true: I believe that in pretty much every religion there is always a small group of fundamentalists. Fundamentalists. We have them. . . . I do not believe it is right to identify Islam with violence."[52] As a reaction to this statement, #PasMonPape ("Not my Pope") became the number one hashtag in France.[53]

But it didn't matter. In 2016, Francis remained impervious to criticism and retained his position as "the world's most popular leader," even though his popularity failed to produce any increase in church membership or attendance.[54] Within the once hallowed Ark of Salvation, all that remained were the "bare, ruined choirs."[55]

Epilogue

YOU CAN'T GO HOME AGAIN

O waste of loss, in the hot mazes, lost, among bright stars on this weary unbright cinder, lost! Remembering speechlessly we seek the great forgotten language, the lost lane-end into heaven, a stone, a leaf, an unfound door. Where? When? O lost, and by the wind grieved, ghost, come back again.
—Thomas Wolfe, *Look Homeward Angel*

The Mass began on Saturday at 5:00 p.m. The time commemorated neither the Jewish Sabbath nor the Lord's Day. It simply represented convenience. The congregants could sit through the liturgy and still have time for dinner and a movie. What's more, they could sleep late on Sunday morning, even though most of them had retired years ago, or they could go shopping, since the blue laws (brought about in part by Catholic prelates) were a thing of the past.

Those in attendance were casually dressed. Most wore baggy jeans and carelessly pressed shirts or blouses. In its heyday, the sanctuary of this church in suburban Scranton was overflowing with the faithful, who crammed the church for each of the four Masses that were celebrated on Sunday. People lined the walls, the vestibule, and even the front steps leading into the sanctuary. In those days, it was essential for all Catholics to catch at least a glimpse of the Consecration in order to fulfill their Sunday obligation. Now the church was mostly empty and the few who occupied the pews were old and gray and full of sleep. No one was kneeling and saying the rosary, and no one was lighting a candle before the statue of a saint. The saints were gone. So were the candles. And offering prayers as indulgences for the suffering souls in Purgatory was a time of the past.

Before the Mass began, the organist stood and informed the congregation to silence their electronic devices. She then struck the chord to start the processional. The priest entered from the rear of the church behind four ladies in white gowns, known as Eucharistic ministers, two female lectors in attire that seemed to be snatched from the wardrobe of Hillary

Clinton, and the song leader—a mousey, middle-aged woman in a black, knee-length dress. The congregation promptly stood, some on shaky knees, and the rite got underway.

Following the Kyrie Eleison and the Gloria, which had been stripped of their Greek and Latin majesty, the two lectors took to the stage, one reading from the prophet Amos, the other from the apostle Paul, and both displaying a good deal of amateur theatrics. The homily for this twenty-fifth Sunday in Ordinary Time was based on Luke 16:1–13, a parable that the priest said no one really understood. His attempt at a hermeneutic was mercifully short.

At the conclusion of the Credo, the congregation was called upon to sing a hymn—"Come to the Water"—that no one could sing, not even the song leader. All four stanzas were played so that the elderly ushers could take two collections. The service proceeded to the Canon, the most sacred part of the liturgy. At various times during the course of the Canon, including the proclamation of the "mystery of faith," the priest broke out in a mock Gregorian chant, which served as a faint reminder of the old Latin rite.

Following the chanting and the recitation of the Protestant version of the Lord's Prayer, the congregants were called upon to share greetings with a "sign of peace." Most exchanged limp and clammy handshakes in a spirit of resignation. This addition to the liturgy was meant to foment spiritual brotherhood, but it rather served to make the parishioners aware that they were, for the most part, total strangers to the other occupants of their pew.

Everyone in attendance went forward to receive communion, which was handed out by the Eucharistic ministers. The real mystery of the Mass resided not in the act of transubstantiation but rather the necessity of four quasi-prelates and one priest to administer Communion to such a sparse congregation. For their part, the communicants lined up to receive the sacred elements with all the reverence of customers headed to a checkout counter at the local Wal-Mart. And then it was over.

How had it come to this? A time when Saturday night became Sunday morning, when the sacred altar transformed into a common table, when potted plants replaced the statues of the saints, when sacraments, including penance, became superfluous, when sanctifying grace was no longer necessary to dissolve mortal sin, when the majestic Mass that inspired many of the world's greatest thinkers, artists, and composers, transformed into a religious travesty.

The congregants walked from the church into the descending darkness. Many had come in search of some hint of transcendence, a measure of sanctity, a sense of spiritual belonging that they had experienced in the church of their childhood. What was lost could never be recaptured. It could only be remembered.

It was time to leave.

NOTES

CHAPTER ONE: THE GRAND ILLUSION

1. Clement of Rome, *Letter to the Corinthians*, in *The Ante-Nicene Fathers*, vol. 1, *The Apostolic Fathers: Justin Martyr and Irenaeus*, ed. Alexander Roberts and James Donaldson, trans. A. Cleveland Coxe (Grand Rapids, MI: William B. Eerdmans, 1981), pp. 52–52.

2. Irenaeus, *Against Heresies*, in *Ante-Nicene Fathers*, vol. 1, pp. 415–16.

3. Barbara Tuchman, *A Distant Mirror* (New York: Alfred A. Knopf, 1978), p. 335.

4. W. H. C. Frend, *The Early Church* (Philadelphia: J. B. Lippincott Company, 1966), p. 38. See also Henry Chadwick, *The Early Church* (Baltimore: Penguin Books, 1969), p. 18.

5. Cyprian, "Epistle LXXIV," in *The Ante-Nicene Fathers*, vol. 5, *The Fathers of the Third Century*, ed. Alexander Roberts and James Donaldson, trans. Ernest Wallis (Grand Rapids, MI: William B. Eerdmans, 1981), p. 384.

6. Anselm of Canterbury, "Proslogion," in *A Scholastic Miscellany*, ed. John Baillie, John T. McNeill, and Henry Van Dusen (Philadelphia: Westminster, 1956), pp. 69–93.

7. Ellamay Horan, *The Illustrated Revised Edition of Baltimore Catechism*, no. 2 (New York: W. H. Sadlier, 1945), pp. 188–89.

8. Ibid., p. 65.

9. Ibid., p. 109.

10. William J. Bausch, *A New Look at the Sacraments* (Mystic, CT: Twenty-Third Publications, 1984), pp. 174–75.

11. Toby Lester, "Catholic Confession's Steep Price: Former Seminarian John Cornwell Traces How a Sacrament Went Astray—and How It Could Be Revived," *Boston Globe*, February 16, 2014, https://www.bostonglobe.com/ideas/2014/02/16/catholic-confession-steep-price/NbMVFfYljv26Gcphu17yPJ/story.html (accessed March 2, 2017).

12. Thomas Bokenkotter, *Essential Catholicism: Dynamics of Faith and Belief* (Garden City, NY: Image Books, 1985), p. 227.

13. Malachi Martin, *The Decline and Fall of the Roman Church* (New York: G. P. Putnam and Sons, 1981), pp. 33–34.

14. "Host" was derived from the Latin *hostia*, meaning sacrificial victim. "Host," *The Catholic Encyclopedia* (New York: Robert Appleton Company, 1912), available online at: http://www.newadvent.org/cathen/07489d.htm (accessed March 2, 2017).

15. "The Real Presence of Christ in the Eucharist," in *Catholic Encyclopedia*, http://www.newadvent.org/cathen/05573a.htm (accessed March 2, 2017).

16. Garry Wills, *Bare Ruined Choirs: Doubt, Prophecy, and Radical Religion* (Garden City, NY: Doubleday, 1971), p. 65.

17. Thomas Aquinas, *Summa Theologiae*, book 3, question 63, article 4, trans. Fathers of the English Dominican Province (London: Burns, Oates, and Washbourne, 1923), pp. 51–53.

18. Joseph Martos, *Doors to the Sacred* (Garden City, NY: Image Books, 1982), p. 480.

19. Hugo Hoever, ed., *Saint Joseph Daily Missal* (New York: Catholic Publishing Company, 1956), p. 677.

20. Dominic Grassi and Joe Paprocki, *Living the Mass* (Chicago: Loyola Press, 2011), p. 93.

21. Aquinas, *Summa Theologiae*, Book III, question 83, article 1, p. 164.

22. Wills, *Bare Ruined Choirs*, p. 67.

23. Ibid., p. 66.

24. Center for Applied Research in the Apostolate, *Self-Reported Mass Attendance of U.S. Catholics Unchanged during Last Five Years* (Washington, DC: Georgetown University, January 10, 2005), http://cara.georgetown.edu/AttendPR.pdf (accessed March 2, 2017).

25. Augustine, "To the Consecrated Virgins," in *St. Augustine's Letters 240–270*, trans. Fr. Wilfrid Parsons (New York: Fathers of the Church, 1956), p. 44.

26. Lawrence S. Cunningham, *The Catholic Heritage* (New York: Crossroad Publishing, 1983), pp. 38–39.

27. Tertullian, "On the Veiling of Virgins," in *Fathers of the Third Century*, trans. S. Thelwall (Grand Rapids, MI: William B. Eerdmans, 1982), pp. 35–36.

28. Horan, *Baltimore Catechism*, p. 127.

29. Ibid., p. 128.

30. Will Herberg, *Protestant, Catholic, Jew* (New York: Doubleday, 1960), p. 6.

31. Ibid., p. 12.

32. Ibid., p. 40.

33. "American Religious Affiliations," Public Opinion News Service, July 21, 1954.

34. Herberg, *Protestant, Catholic, Jew*, p. 60.

35. Robert Slater, "Religion: Get Ready, the Pope Is Coming," *Time*, September 7, 1987.

36. John Cooney, *The American Pope: The Life and Times of Francis Cardinal Spellman* (New York: Times Books, 1984), p. 109.

37. Seth Meehan, "Catholics and Contraception," *New York Times*, March 15, 2012.

38. J. A. M. Quigley, "The Changing Concept of Servile Work," *Catholic Periodical Index*, 2012, http://ejournals.bc.edu/ojs/index.php/ctsa/article/viewFile/2441/2074 (accessed March 2, 2017).

39. Wills, *Bare Ruined Choirs*, p. 23.

40. Ibid., p. 20.

41. "The Teachings of the Twelve Apostles Commonly Called the Didache," in *Early Christian Fathers*, trans. Cyril C. Richardson (New York: Macmillan, 1970), p. 175; Hippolytus, "The Apostolic Tradition," in *Readings in Church History*, vol. 1, trans. Gregory Dix (New York: Newman Press, 1960), pp. 47–49.

42. Vern L. Bullough, "Chaste Marriage and Clerical Celibacy," in *Sexual Practices and the Medieval Church, ed. Vern L. Bullough and James Brundage* (Amherst, NY: Prometheus Books, 1982), pp. 24–28.

43. Richard McBrien, *The HarperCollins Encyclopedia of Catholicism* (New York: HarperCollins, 1995), p. 1297.

CHAPTER TWO: THE SEISMIC SHIFT

1. Bertrand L. Conway, *The Question Box* (New York: Paulist Press, 1929), p. 429.

2. Ibid.

3. David Wayne Jones, *Reforming the Morality of Usury* (Washington, DC: University Press of America, 2004), p. 31.

4. Thomas Aquinas, *Summa Theologiae*, part II, book 2, question 78, available online at: http://www.newadvent.org/summa/3078.htm (accessed March 2, 2017).

5. Dante Alighieri, *Inferno*, canto XI, trans. Mark Musa (New York: Penguin Books, 2003), pp. 135–37.

6. Third Lateran Council, Canon 25, Papal Encyclicals Online, http://www.papalencyclicals.net/Councils/ecum11.htm (accessed March 2, 2017).

7. Second Council of Lyons, Canon 26, Papal Encyclicals Online, http://www.papalencyclicals.net/Councils/ecum14.htm#26 (accessed March 2, 2017).

8. Council of Vienne, Canon 29, Papal Encyclicals Online, http://www.papalencyclicals.net/Councils/ecum15.htm (accessed March 2, 2017).

9. Benedict XIV, *Vix Pervenit*, November 15, 1745, Papal Encyclicals Online, http://www.papalencyclicals.net/Ben14/b14vixpe.htm (accessed March 2, 2017).

10. Leo XIII, *Rerum Novarum*, May 15, 1891, Papal Encyclicals Online, http://www.papalencyclicals.net/Leo13/l13rerum.htm (accessed March 2, 2017).

11. Ibid.

12. Will Durant, *The Age of Faith* (New York: Simon and Shuster, 1950), p. 378.

13. Hermann Kellenbenz, "Ancient Jewish History: Banking and Bankers," in *Encyclopedia Judaica*, Jewish Virtual Library, 2008, http://www.jewishvirtual library.org/jsource/judaica/ejud_0002_0003_0_01978.html (accessed March 2, 2017).

14. Gerald Posner, *God's Bankers: A History of Money and Power at the Vatican* (New York: Simon and Schuster, 2015), p. 23.

15. Malachi Martin, *Rich Church, Poor Church* (New York: G. P. Putnam's Sons, 1984), pp. 155–56.

16. Ibid., pp. 154–55.

17. Posner, *God's Bankers*, p. 13.

18. Martin, *Rich Church, Poor Church*, p. 155.

19. Clive Gillis, "The Popes at War and the Fall of the Papal States," *The English Churchman*, September 15, 2000, http://www.ianpaisley.org/article.asp?ArtKey=papalstates (accessed March 2, 2017).

20. "The Syllabus of Errors Condemned by Pius IX," December 8, 1864, Papal Encyclicals Online, http://www.papalencyclicals.net/Pius09/p9syll.htm (accessed March 2, 2017).

21. *Decrees of the First Vatican Council*, session 4, ed. Norman Tanner, July 18, 1870, http://www.papalencyclicals.net/Councils/ecum20.htm#Chapter 2 (accessed March 2, 2017).

22. Ibid.

23. Kevin Considine, "Is There a List of Infallible Teachings?" *US Catholic* 76, no. 6 (June 2011): 44–46, http://www.uscatholic.org/church/2011/05/there-list-infallible-teachings (accessed March 2, 2017).

24. David I. Kertzer, *Prisoner of the Vatican: The Popes, the Kings, and Garibaldi's Rebels in the Struggle to Rule Modern Italy* (New York: Houghton Mifflin, 2004), pp. 106–107.

25. Leo XIII, "Concerning New Opinions, Virtue, Nature, and Grace, with Regard to Americanism: *Testem Benevolentiae Nostrae*," January 22, 1899, Papal Encyclicals Online, http://www.papalencyclicals.net/Leo13/l13teste.htm (accessed March 2, 2017).26. Ibid.

27. "Black nobles" were members of aristocratic families that opposed the merger of the Papal States with Italy for the creation of a national government under Giuseppe Garibaldi.

28. Martin, *Rich Church, Poor Church*, p. 28.

29. The complete text of the Lateran Treaty may be found at Vicarus Filii Deli, "666, The Number of the Beast," aloha.net/~mikesch/666.htm (accessed March 2, 2017).

30. Ibid.

31. Ron Chernow, *The House of Morgan* (New York: Simon and Shuster, 1990), p. 285.

32. Ibid.

33. David Yallop, *In God's Name: An Investigation into the Murder of John Paul I* (New York: Bantam Books, 1984), p. 94.

34. Ibid.

35. John T. Noonan, "Development in Moral Doctrine," *Theological Studies* 54 (1993), http://cdn.theologicalstudies.net/54/54.4/54.4.3.pdf (accessed March 2, 2017).

36. Jay W. Richards, "Did the Church Change Its Doctrine on Usury?" *Crisis*, December 8, 2014, http://www.crisismagazine.com/2014/church-change -doctrine-usury (accessed March 2, 2017).

37. Conway, *Question Box*, p. 429.

38. John Cooney, *The American Pope: The Life and Times of Francis Cardinal Spellman* (New York: Times Books, 1984), p. 46.

39. Martin, *Rich Church, Poor Church*, p. 40.

40. Paul I. Murphy and R. Rene Arlington, *La Popessa: The Controversial Biography of Sister Pascalina, the Most Powerful Woman in Vatican History* (New York: Warner Books, 1984), p. 76.

41. Posner, *God's Bankers*, pp. 69–70.

42. Martin, *Rich Church, Poor Church*, p. 41.

43. Ibid.

44. Ibid., p. 45.

45. Ibid.

CHAPTER THREE: THE CATHOLIC MASONS

1. Alexander Lucie-Smith, "Most of Us Would Laugh at the Idea of a Masonic Mafia at Work in the Vatican. I'm Not Sure That We Should," *Catholic Herald*, July 30, 2013, http://www.catholicherald.co.uk/commentand blogs/2013/07/30/most-of-us-would-laugh-at-the-idea-of-a-masonic-mafia-at -work-in-the-vatican-im-not-sure-that-we-should/ (accessed March 2, 2017).

2. Alfred McCoy, *The Politics of Heroin: CIA Complicity in the Global Drug Trade* (Chicago: Lawrence Hill Books, 2003), p. 24.

3. Philip Willan, *Puppetmasters: The Political Use of Terrorism in Italy* (London: Constable, 1991), p. 57.

4. Richard Cottrell, *Gladio: NATO's Dagger at the Heart of Europe* (Palm Desert, CA: Progressive, 2012), p. 114.

5. John Cooney, *The American Pope: The Life and Death of Francis Cardinal Spellman* (New York: Times Books, 1984), p. 46. See also Malachi Martin, *Rich Church, Poor Church* (New York: G. P. Putnam's Sons, 1984), p. 40.

6. Cooney, *American Pope*, p. 159.

7. Gay Talese, *Honor Thy Father* (New York: World Publishing, 1971), p. 271. See also Claire Sterling, *Octopus: How the Long Reach of the Sicilian Mafia Controls the Global Narcotics Trade* (New York: Simon and Schuster, 1990), p. 58.

8. Bradley Earl Ayers, *The War That Never Was: An Insider's Account of CIA Covert Operations against Cuba* (New York: Bobbs Merrill, 1976), p. 82.

9. Peter Dale Scott, "Deep Events and the CIA's Global Drug Connection," *Global Research*, September 8, 2008, http://www.globalresearch.ca/deep-events -and-the-cia-s-global-drug-connection/10095 (accessed March 2, 2017).

10. Alexander Cockburn and Jeffrey St. Clair, *Whiteout: The CIA, Drugs, and the Press* (New York: Verso, 1998), p. 137.

11. Martin A. Lee, "Their Will Be Done," *Mother Jones*, July / August 1983, http://www.motherjones.com/politics/1983/07/their-will-be-done (accessed March 30, 2017).

12. Greg Szymanski, "Vatican in Possession of Top Secret CIA Documents," *The Truth Seeker*, April 28, 2006, http://www.thetruthseeker.co.uk/?p=4537 (accessed March 2, 2017).

13. Natalino Zuanella, *Gli anni bui della Slavia: attività delle organizzazioni segrete nel Friuli orientale* [in Italian] (Cividale del Friuli: Società Cooperativa Editrice Dom, 1996).

14. Ibid.

15. Robert Hutchison, *Their Kingdom Come: Inside the Secret World of Opus Dei* (New York: Dunne Books, 2006), pp. 208–209.

16. Rudolph Bozic, "Venetian Slovenia," Washie.com, 2017, http://www.washie.com/venetian-slovenia/ (accessed March 30, 2017).

17. "The CIA in Western Europe," *Wake Up Magazine* (UK), 2007, http://www.american-buddha.com/cia.westeurope.htm (accessed May 20, 2014) (site discontinued).

18. Victor Marchetti, quoted in David Yallop, *In God's Name: An Investigation into the Murder of Pope John Paul I* (New York: Bantam Books, 1984), p. 108.

19. Luigi DiFonzo, *St. Peter's Banker: Michele Sindona* (New York: Franklin Watts, 1983), p. 68.

20. Alphonse Cerza, *The Truth Is Stranger than Fiction* (Washington, DC: Masonic Service Association, 1967).

21. Congregation for the Doctrine of the Faith, "Declaration on Masonic Associations," Holy See, November 26, 1983, http://www.vatican.va/roman_curia/congregations/cfaith/documents/rc_con_cfaith_doc_19831126_declaration-masonic_en.html (accessed May 20, 2014).

22. "Ten Reasons Catholics Cannot Be Masons," Militia of the Immaculata, 2013, http://freemasonrywatch.org/ten.reasons.catholics.cannot.be.masons.html (accessed May 20, 2014).

23. Pierre Fautrad a Fye, "Vatican et Franc-Maconnerie" [in French], *Bulletin de l'Occident Chretien*, no. 12, July 1979.

24. Ibid.

25. Paul Williams, *Operation Gladio: The Unholy Alliance between the Vatican, the CIA, and the Mafia* (Amherst, NY: Prometheus Books, 2015), pp. 281–82.

26. For a full account of the involvement of Catholic clerics in Operation Gladio, see Willan, *Puppetmasters*; Cottrell, *Gladio*; and Daniele Ganser, *NATO's Secret Armies: Operation Gladio and Terrorism in Western Europe* (London: Frank Cass, 2005).

27. Albert G. Mackey, *Encyclopedia of Freemasonry*, vol. 1 (Chicago: Masonic History Company, 1929), p. 9.

28. Leon Zeldis, "Some Thoughts about Freedom and Freemasonry," *Pietre-Stones: Review of Freemasonry*, 1996, http://www.freemasons-freemasonry.com/zeldis04.html (accessed March 2, 2017).

29. Will Durant and Ariel Durant, *Rousseau and Revolution* (New York: Simon and Schuster, 1967), p. 939.

30. Paul Ginsborg, *Italy and Its Discontents* (London: Palgrave Macmillan, 2003), pp. 144–48.

31. John Kenneth Weiskittel, "Freemasons and the Conciliar Church," *The Athanasian* 14, no. 4 (June 1, 1993).

32. Carlos Vazquez Rangel, quoted in Weiskittel, "Freemasons and the Conciliar Church."

33. Greg Szymanski, "Portugal Newspaper Shows Pope John XXIII Was a Practicing Freemason," *Arctic Beacon*, September 19, 2006, http://www.arcticbeacon.com/articles/19-Sept-2006.html (accessed March 2, 2017).

34. Ibid. See also Giovanni Cubeddu, "John XXIII and Masonry," *30 Days* 2, 1994, p. 25.

35. Piers Compton, *The Broken Cross* (London: N. Spearman, 1983). Although out of print, Compton's book is available in its entirety at http://www.bibliotecapleyades.net/vatican/brokencross/brokencross.htm (accessed March 2, 2017).

36. Fautrad a Fye, "Vatican et Franc-Maconnerie."

37. Weiskittel, "Freemasons and the Conciliar Church."

38. Joseph Fort Newton, *The Builders: A Story and Study of Masonry* (Cedar Rapids, IA: Torch Press, 1914), pp. 250–51.

39. Weiskittel, "Freemasons and the Conciliar Church."

40. Jean-Andre Faucher, "Interview with Baron Yves Marsaudon," *Le Juvenal*, September 25, 1964.

41. Ibid.

42. Supreme Council of the Ancient and Accepted Scottish Rite of Masons, *Masonic Bulletin*, The Masonic District of the United States of Mexico, No. 220, May 1963.

43. John XXIII, *Pacem in Terris*, April 11, 1963, Holy See, http://w2.vatican.va/content/john-xxiii/en/encyclicals/documents/hf_j-xxiii_enc_11041963_pacem.html (accessed March 2, 2017).

44. "Lucius Caecilus Firmanus Lactantius," *The Catholic Encyclopedia* vol. 8 (New York: Robert Appleton Company, 1911).

45. John XXIII, *Pacem in Terris*.

46. Faucher, "Interview with Baron Yves Marsaudon."

47. Jacques Mitterand, quoted in Marcel Lefebvre, *A Bishop Speaks* (St. Marys, KS: Angelus Press, 2007), p. 182.

48. Sanford Holst, "Founding of the Grand Lodge of England in 1717," Masonic Sourcebook, http://www.masonicsourcebook.com/grand_lodge_of_england.htm. See also Albert G. Mackey, *The History of Freemasonry*, part 2, 1898, available online at *Pietre-Stones: Review of Freemasonry*, http://www.freemasons-freemasonry.com/mackeyhi08.html (accessed March 2, 2017).

49. Laurence Gardner, *The Shadow of Solomon: The Lost Secret of the Freemasons Revealed* (London: HarperCollins, 2009), pp. 63–65.

50. Tessa Morrison, "Isaac Newton and Solomon's Temple: A Fifty Year Study," *Avello Publishing Journal* 3, no. 1 (September 2013).

51. Albert G. Mackey, *The Symbolism of Freemasonry*, 1882, reprinted by the Grand Lodge of Colorado, available online at http://www.coloradofreemasons.org/pdfDocuments/library/SymbolismOfFreemasonry.pdf (accessed March 2, 2017).

52. James Anderson and Benjamin Franklin, *The Constitutions of Free Masons*, ed. Paul Royster (Philadelphia: R.W. Grand Lodge of Pennsylvania, 1734; Lincoln: University of Nebraska, 2006), p. 18, http://digitalcommons.unl.edu/cgi/viewcontent.cgi?article=1028&context=libraryscience (accessed March 2, 2017).

53. Ibid.

54. Durant and Durant, *Rousseau and Revolution*, p. 939.

55. Clement XII, *In Eminenti*, April 28, 1738, Papal Encyclicals Online, http://www.papalencyclicals.net/Clem12/c12inemengl.htm (accessed March 2, 2017).

56. Ibid.

57. Benedict XVI, *Providas Romanorum* [in Italian], March 18, 1751, http://digilander.iol.it/magistero/b14provi.htm (accessed March 2, 2017).

58. Robert F. Gould, "Freemasons in the French Revolution," in *The History of Freemasonry: Its Antiquities, Symbols, Constitutions, Customs, etc.*, vol. III (New York: John C. Yorston, 1886), reprinted by the Grand Lodge of Columbia and Yukon, available at http://freemasonry.bcy.ca/texts/revolution.html (accessed March 2, 2017).

59. Will Durant and Ariel Durant, *The Age of Napoleon* (New York: Simon and Schuster, 1975), pp. 51–52.

60. Roger Dachez, *Histoire de la Franc-Maconnerie Française* [in French] (Paris: Presses Universitaires de France, 2003), p. 79.

61. Michael Collins and Matthew A. Price, *The Story of Christianity* (New York: DK, 2003), pp. 174–77.

62. Giuseppe Mazzini ("Piccolo Tigre"), *The Permanent Instruction of the Alta Vendita*, English ed., 1885, http://files.meetup.com/574112/Permanent_Instruction_of_the_Alta_Vendita.pdf (accessed March 2, 2017).

63. Pius IX, *Etsi Multa*, November 21, 1873, Papal Encyclicals Online, http://www.papalencyclicals.net/Pius09/p9etsimu.htm (accessed March 2, 2017).

64. Leo XIII, *Humanum Genus*, April 20, 1884, Papal Encyclicals Online, http://www.papalencyclicals.net/Leo13/l13human.htm (accessed March 2, 2017).

65. Albert Pike, "1st Praelocution," October 19, 1884, Grand Orient of Charleston, South Carolina, http://www.preciousheart.net/fm/Pike_vs_Leo.htm (accessed March 2, 2017).

66. Ernest Jouin, *Papacy and Freemasonry* (Hawthorne, CA: Christian Book Club of America, 1955), https://archive.org/stream/papacyfreemasonr00joui/papacyfreemasonr00joui_djvu.txt (accessed March 2, 2017).

67. Edward N. Peters, ed., *The 1917 Pio-Benedictine Code of Canon Law* (San Francisco: Ignatius Press, 2001), p. 472.

68. Christopher Butler, "Who Was Who at Vatican II: The Voices of Council Fathers," Vatican II—Voice of the Church, http://vatican2voice.org/4basics/fathers.htm (accessed March 2, 2017).

69. "Leon Joseph Suenens—Biography—Second Vatican Council," Liquisearch, http://www.liquisearch.com/leo_joseph_suenens/biography/second_vatican_council (accessed March 2, 2017).

70. John W. O'Malley, *What Happened at Vatican II* (Cambridge, MA: Belknap Press, 2010), pp. 236–38.

71. Annibale Bugnini, cited in Michael Davies, "Annibale Bugnini: The Main Author of the *Novus Ordo*," *Catholic Apologetics*, http://www.catholicapologetics.info/modernproblems/newmass/bugnini.html (accessed March 2, 2017).

CHAPTER FOUR: SPIRITUAL SUICIDE

1. Michael Davies, *Pope John's Council*, vol. 2 of *Liturgical Revolution* (Kansas City, MO: Angelus Press, 1977), p. 21.

2. Will Herberg, *Protestant, Catholic, Jew* (Garden City, NY: Anchor Books, 1960), p. 153.

3. Felician A. Foy, ed., *1959 National Catholic Almanac* (Paterson, NJ: St. Anthony's Guild, 1959), pp. 407–11.

4. Herberg, *Protestant, Catholic, Jew.*

5. Walter J. Ong, "American Catholicism and America," *Thought* 27, no. 4 (Winter 1952–1953).

6. Herberg, *Protestant, Catholic, Jew*, p. 154.

7. "Pope Speaks of Unity and the Council," *The Criterion* (Indianapolis, IN), July 7, 1961.

8. John XXIII, *Humanae Salutis*, Second Vatican Ecumenical Council, December 25, 1961, http://www.diocesecc.org/pictures/Vatican%2520Documents/humanae-salutis.pdf (accessed March 2, 2017).

9. James Hitchcock, *The Decline and Fall of Radical Catholicism* (New York: Herder and Herder, 1971), pp. 22–23.

10. Henry Manning, *The Temporal Mission of the Holy Ghost* (London: Burns and Oates, 1909), p. 24.

11. Thomas Bokenkotter, *A Concise History of the Catholic Church* (Garden City, NY: Image Books, 1979), p. 412.

12. Vincenzo Carbone, quoted in Ralph Wiltgen, *The Rhine Flows into the Tiber: A History of Vatican II* (Bristol, UK: Hawthorn Books, 1979), p. 22.

13. Marcel Lefebvre, *Un Eveque Parle* [in French] (Paris: D. Morin, 1974), p. 190.

14. Ibid.

15. John XXIII, "Opening Speech for the Council of Vatican II," (speech, St. Peter's Basilica, October 11, 1962), http://www.ourladyswarriors.org/teach/v2open.htm (accessed March 2, 2017).

16. Augustine, *The City of God*, trans. Gerald Walsh et al. (Garden City, NY: Image Books, 1958), pp. 272–79.

17. F. R. Tennant, *The Sources of the Doctrines of the Fall and Original Sin* (New York: Schocken Books, 1968), p. 285.

18. John XXIII, "Opening Speech for the Council of Vatican II."

19. Francisco Radecki and Dominic Radecki, *Tumultuous Times: The Twenty General Councils of the Catholic Church and Vatican II and Its Aftermath* (Wayne, MI: St. Joseph's Media, 2002), p. 310.

20. Jürgen Mettepenningen, *Nouvelle Théologie: New Theology—Inheritor of Modernism, Precursor of Vatican II* (London: T&T Clark, 2010), pp. 3–6.

21. Karl Rahner, *Zum Problem Unfehlbarkeit* [in German] (Freiburg im Breisgau: Verlag Herder, 1971), p. 101.

22. Henri de Lubac, quoted in James Larson, "The Philosophy of Henri de Lubac and Hans Urs van Balthasar," *The War Against Being*, 2008, http://www.waragainstbeing.com/partii-byartsentirelynew (accessed March 2, 2017).

23. Brian E. Daley, "Knowing God in History and in the Church: *Dei Verbum* and '*Nouvelle Théologie*,'" ch. 22 in *Ressourcement: A Movement for Renewal in Twentieth-Century Catholic Theology, ed. Gabriel Flynn and Paul D. Murray* (New York: Oxford University Press, 2012), p. 338.

24. Karl Rahner, *Foundations of Christian Faith* (New York: Crossroads Publishing, 1982), p. 266.

25. Ibid., p. 279.

26. Hans Küng, *On Being a Christian* (Garden City, NY: Image Books, 1981), p. 374.

27. Karl Rahner, *Karl Rahner in Dialogue: Conversations and Interviews, 1965–1982* (New York: Crossroads, 1986), p. 135.

28. Ibid.

29. Karl Rahner, *Maria Mediazioni* [in Italian] (Brescia, Italy: Herder-Morcelliana, 1968), p. 50.

30. Pius IX, *Ineffabilis Deus*, apostolic constitution, December 8, 1854, Papal Encyclicals Online, http://www.papalencyclicals.net/Pius09/p9ineff.htm (accessed March 2, 2017).

31. Karl Rahner, "Virginitas in Partu," in *Theological Investigations*, vol. 4, *More Recent Writings* (New York: Seabury Press, 1974), p. 156.

32. Pius XII, *Munificentissimus Deus*, apostolic constitution, November 1, 1950, Holy See, http://w2.vatican.va/content/pius-xii/en/apost_constitutions/documents/hf_p-xii_apc_19501101_munificentissimus-deus.html (accessed March 2, 2017).

33. Karl Rahner, ed., *Encyclopedia of Theology: A Concise Sacramentum Mundi* (New York: Burns and Oates, 2004), p. 1754.

34. Ibid., p. 1755.

35. Brendan J. Cahill, *The Renewal of Revelation Theology (1960–1962): The Development and Responses to the Fourth Chapter of the Preparatory Schema* De deposito Fidei (Rome: Gregorian University Press, 1999), p. 143.

36. Bokenkotter, *Concise History of the Catholic Church*, p. 413.

37. Ibid., p. 414.

38. Pierre Fautrad a Fye, "Vatican et Franc-Maconnerie," *Bulletin de l'Occident Chretien*, no. 12, July 1976.

39. Richard Hutchison, *Their Kingdom Come: Inside the Secret World of Opus Dei* (New York: Dunne Books, 2006), pp. 208–209.

40. Bokenkotter, *Concise History of the Catholic Church*, pp. 414–15.

41. Michael Davies, *Liturgical Time Bombs in Vatican II* (Rockford, IL: Tan Books, 2003), p. 10.

42. Marcel Lefebvre, *A Bishop Speaks* (Kansas City, MO: Angelus Press, 1987), p. 131.

43. Davies, *Liturgical Time Bombs*, pp. 17–19.

44. Edward Schillebeeckx, quoted in Wiltgen, *Rhine Flows into the Tiber*, p. 23.

45. Pius XI, *Auctorem Fidei*, August 28, 1794, Church Militant, http://www.churchmilitant.tv/cia/05rebellion/12.pdf (accessed March 2, 2017).

46. "Constitution on the Sacred Liturgy," as promulgated on December 4, 1963, in Walter Abbott, ed., *The Documents of Vatican II* (New York: Guild Press, 1966), pp. 140–41.

47. Annibale Bugnini, quoted in John Grasmeier, "The Man behind the Novus Ordo Liturgical Curtain," Angel Queen, February 2004, http://www.angelqueen.org/articles/04-02_bugnini.shtml (accessed March 2, 2017).

48. "Constitution on the Sacred Liturgy," pp. 144–45.

49. Ibid., p. 151.

50. Ibid., p. 152.

51. Ibid., pp. 42–43.

52. Andrew Greeley, "Voices from the Underground," *Concilium*, February 1971.

53. "Constitution on the Sacred Liturgy," p. 150.

54. Prosper Gueranger, quoted in Davies, *Liturgical Time Bombs*, p. 60.

55. Paul VI, "Changes in the Mass for a Greater Apostolate," (address to a general audience, November 26, 1969), taken from *L'Osservatore Romano*, December 4, 1969, https://www.ewtn.com/library/PAPALDOC/P6691126.HTM (accessed March 2, 2017).

56. "Constitution on the Sacred Liturgy," p. 138.

57. Ibid., p. 147.

58. Davies, *Liturgical Time Bombs*, p. 20.

59. Thomas Aquinas, *Summa Theologiae*, book 3 (London: Burns, Oates, and Washbourne, 1923), pp. 51–53.

60. Davies, *Liturgical Time Bombs*, pp. 21–22.

61. Keith Kenney, "*Te Igitur*," *Sancta Liturgia* (blog), September 17, 2004, http://sanctaliturgia.blogspot.com/2004/09/te-igitur.html (accessed March 2, 2017).

62. Bokenkotter, *Concise History of the Catholic Church*, p. 425.

63. Edward McNamara, "Why 'For All' in the Words of Consecration?" *Zenit* (Rome), September 7, 2004, https://www.ewtn.com/library/Liturgy/zlitur46.htm (accessed March 2, 2017).

64. Aquinas, *Summa Theologiae*, book 3, pp. 68–69.

65. Susan Benofy, "The Day the Mass Changed," *Adoremus* 15, no. 10 (February 15, 2010), http://www.adoremus.org/0210Benofy.html (accessed March 2, 2017).

66. Bokenkotter, *Concise History of the Catholic Church*, p. 416.

67. Theresa Potenza, "Vatican's Secret, and Deadly, Project to Mummify Saints," *New York Post*, March 22, 2014.

68. Philip Pullella, "Pope John XIII Looks Like He 'Died Yesterday,'" ABC News, March 27, 2001, http://abcnews.go.com/International/story?id=81350&page=1 (accessed March 2, 2017).

69. Philip Pullella, "Pope John XXIII Was Embalmed," Reuters, March 27, 2001, http://www.fisheaters.com/johnxxiiiembalmed.html (accessed March 2, 2017).

70. Keith F. Pecklers, *Dynamic Equivalence: The Living Language of Christian Worship* (Collegeville, MN: Liturgical Press, 2003), pp. 182–84.

71. John Cooney, *The American Pope: The Life and Times of Francis Cardinal Spellman* (New York: Times Books, 1984), pp. 277–78.

72. Ibid.

73. "Change in the Church," CIA report, May 13, 1963, obtained under the Freedom of Information Act.

CHAPTER FIVE: THE THING WITH TWO HEADS

1. Andrea Lazzarini, *Paolo VI* [in Italian] (Rome: Casa Editrice Herder, 1978), pp. 20–21.

2. Gay Talese, *Honor Thy Father* (New York: World Publishing, 1971), p. 271.

3. Frederic Laurent, *L'Orchestre Noir* [in French] (Paris: Editions Stock, 1978), p. 29.

4. Douglas Valentine, *The Strength of the Wolf: The Secret History of America's War on Drugs* (New York: Verso, 2006), p. 167.

5. Luigi DiFonzo, *St. Peter's Banker: Michele Sindona* (New York: Franklin Watts, 1983), p. 35.

6. Ibid., p. 31.

7. Richard P. McBrien, *Lives of the Popes* (San Francisco: HarperCollins, 2000), p. 375.

8. Thomas Bokenkotter, *A Concise History of the Catholic Church* (Garden City, NY: Image Books, 1979), pp. 413–16.

9. Eric Frattini, *The Entity: Five Centuries of Vatican Espionage* (New York: St. Martin's Press, 2008).

10. Ibid.

11. Andres Vazquez de Prada, *The Founder of Opus Dei: The Life of Josemaría Escrivá*, vol. 2, *God and Daring* (New York: Scepter Publishers, 2003), p. 177.

12. John Cooney, *The American Pope: The Life and Times of Francis Cardinal Spellman* (New York: Times Books, 1984), p. 280.

13. McBrien, *Lives of the Popes*, p. 376.

14. Roland Flamini, *Pope, Premier, and President: The Cold War Summit That Never Was* (New York: Macmillan, 1980), pp. 186–89.

15. Patrick Riley, "Pope Paul Sets Agenda as Council's Second Session Opens," *Catholic News Service*, September 29, 1963, https://vaticaniiat50.word press.com/2013/09/29/pope-paul-sets-agenda-as-councils-second-session -opens/ (accessed March 2, 2017).

16. *New Catholic Encyclopedia*, vol. 3, *Can to Col* (New York: McGraw Hill, 1967), p. 104.

17. Will Durant, *The Age of Faith* (New York: Simon and Schuster, 1950), p. 759.

18. Ibid., p. 754.

19. Leo XIII, *Testem Benevolentiae Nostrae*, January 22, 1899, Eternal Word Television Network, https://www.ewtn.com/library/PAPALDOC/L13TESTE .HTM (accessed March 2, 2017).

20. Bokenkotter, *Concise History of the Catholic Church*, p. 200.

21. John Hine Mundy and Kennerly M. Woody, eds., *The Council of Constance*, trans. Louise Ropes Loomis (New York: Columbia University Press, 1961), p. 163.

22. "The Dogmatic Decrees of the Vatican Council Concerning the Catholic Faith and the Church of Christ," *De Ecclesia Christi*, Christian Classics Ethereal Library, April 24, 1870, http://www.ccel.org/ccel/schaff/creeds2.v.ii.i.html (accessed March 2, 2017).

23. Boniface (pseud.), "Collegiality: The Church's Pandora's Box," *Unam Sanctam Catholicam* (blog), http://unamsanctamcatholicam.com/theology/81 -theology/427-what-is-collegiality.html (accessed March 2, 2017).

24. John Timothy Pfeiffer, "Liturgical Movement Review," FSSPX.News, January 1, 1970, http://archives.dici.org/en/news/liturgical-movement-review/ (accessed April 27, 2017).

25. Pius XI, *Mortalium Animos*, January 6, 1928, Papal Encyclicals Online, http://www.papalencyclicals.net/Pius11/P11MORTA.HTM (accessed March 2, 2017).

26. W. H. C. Frend, *The Early Church* (Philadelphia: J. B. Lippincott Company, 1966), p. 38.

27. Boniface, "Collegiality: The Church's Pandora's Box."

28. Basil Wrighton, "Collegiality: Error of Vatican II," *Angelus*, Fall 1984, http://sspx.org/en/collegiality-error-vatican-ii-2 (accessed March 2, 2017).

29. Boniface, "Collegiality: The Church's Pandora's Box."

30. Franz König, quoted in Arthur Wells, "Antioch and the Church of the Third Millennium," Vatican II—the Voice of the Church, June 29, 2009, http://vatican2voice.org/4basics/paulpeter3.htm (accessed March 2, 2017).

31. Boniface, "Collegiality: The Church's Pandora's Box."

32. Xavier Rynne, *Vatican Council II* (New York: Farrar, Straus, and Giroux, 1968), p. 220.

33. Hans Küng, *My Struggle for Freedom: Memoirs* (Grand Rapids, MI: William B. Eerdmans, 2003), p. 364.

34. Leo Joseph Suenens, quoted in Robert de Mattei, *The Second Vatican Council: An Unwritten Story* (Fitzwilliam, NH: Loreto Publications, 2012), p. 319.

35. Ralph Wiltgen, *The Rhine Flows into the Tiber: A History of Vatican II* (Rockford, IL: Tan Books, 1985), p. 232.

36. Ibid.

37. Dino Staffa, quoted in Wiltgen, *Rhine Flows into the Tiber*, p. 230.

38. Wiltgen, *Rhine Flows into the Tiber*, pp. 229–34.

39. Walter Abbot, ed., *The Documents of Vatican II* (New York: Guild Press, 1966), p. 41.

40. George T. Dennis, "1054: The East-West Schism," *Christianity Today*, June 2016, http://www.christianitytoday.com/history/issues/issue-28/1054-east-west-schism.html (accessed March 2, 2017).

41. Abbott, ed., *Documents of Vatican II*, p. 43.

42. "The New Ecclesiology and Collegiality," Society of Saint Pius X, Spring 2016, http://fsspx.org/en/collégialité (accessed March 2, 2017).

43. Abbott, ed., *Documents of Vatican II*, p. 44.

44. Boniface, "Collegiality: The Church's Pandora's Box."

45. Ibid.

46. Wrighton, "Collegiality: Error of Vatican II."

47. Paul VI, *Nota Praevia* to *Lumen Gentium* of the Second Vatican Council, November 16, 1964.

48. Christopher A. Ferrara and Thomas E. Woods, *The Great Façade: The Regime of Novelty in the Catholic Church from Vatican II to the Francis Revolution* (Seattle, WA: Angelico Press, 2015), p. 88.

49. Sacred Congregation for the Doctrine of the Faith, "Declaration in Defense of the Catholic Doctrine on the Church against Certain Errors of the Present Day" (*Mysterium Ecclesiae*), June 24, 1973, Holy See, http://www.vatican.va/roman_curia/congregations/cfaith/documents/rc_con_cfaith_doc_19730705_mysterium-ecclesiae_en.html (accessed March 2, 2017).

CHAPTER SIX: THE KISS OF JUDAS

1. Cyprian, quoted in John A. Hardon, "No Salvation Outside the Church," ch. 10 in *Christ to Catholicism* (Lombard, IL: Real Presence Eucharistic Education and Adoration Association, 1998), http://www.therealpresence.org/archives/Church_Dogma/Church_Dogma_032.htm (accessed March 31, 2017).

2. Eugene IV and the Council of Florence, quoted in "Salvation Outside the Church?" Traditional Catholic, http://traditionalcatholic.net/Tradition/Information/Salvation_Outside.html (accessed March 31, 2017).

3. Pius IX, *Singulari Quidem*, March 17, 1856, Papal Encyclicals Online, http://www.papalencyclicals.net/Pius09/p9singul.htm (accessed March 2, 2017).

4. Pius XII, "Allocution to the Gregorian University," October 17, 1953, quoted in *Extra Ecclesiam Nulla Salus*, Apostolic Apologetics, https://sites.google.com/site/apostolicapologetics/extra-ecclesiam-nulla-salus (accessed March 2, 2017).

5. Avery Dulles, "Who Can Be Saved?" *First Things*, February 2008, http://www.firstthings.com/article/2008/02/001-who-can-be-saved-8 (accessed March 2, 2017).

6. Peter Abelard, *Opera Omnia*, vol. 178 of *Patrologiae Cursus Completus, Series Latina*, ed. J. P. Migne (Paris: J. P. Migne, 1855), col. 161, sec. B–C.

7. Thomas Aquinas, *Summa Theologiae*, part 3, book 1, question 67, vol. 17, trans. Fathers of the English Dominican Province (London: Burns, Oates, and Washbourne, 1923), pp. 143–45.

8. Bertrand Conway, *The Question Box* (Mahwah, NJ: Paulist Press, 1929), p. 3.

9. Ibid., p. 7.

10. Pius IX, quoted in Henry Denzinger, *The Sources of Catholic Dogma* (Fitzwilliam, NH: Loreto Publications, 1955), p. 424.

11. Conway, *Question Box*, p. 103.

12. Ibid., p. 90.

13. Ibid., p. 130.

14. Ellamay Horan, *Baltimore Catechism*, no. 2 (New York: W. H. Sadlier, 1945), p. 65.

15. Conway, *Question Box*, pp. 95–96.

16. Ibid., pp. 93–94.

17. Pius VII, *Post Tam Diuturnas*, letter to Msgr. de Boulogne, Bishop of Troyes, April 29, 1814, http://sedevacantist.com/encyclicals/Pius07/post_tam_diuturnas.html (accessed March 2, 2017).

18. Gregory XVI, *Mirari Vos*, August 15, 1832, Papal Encyclicals Online, http://www.papalencyclicals.net/Greg16/g16mirar.htm (accessed March 2, 2017).

19. Pius IX, *Quanta Cura*, December 8, 1864, Papal Encyclicals Online, http://www.papalencyclicals.net/Pius09/p9quanta.htm (accessed March 2, 2017).

20. Pius IX, "The Syllabus of Errors," December 8, 1864, Papal Encyclicals Online, http://www.papalencyclicals.net/Pius09/p9syll.htm (accessed March 2, 2017).

21. Pius IX, *Graves ac Diuturnae*, March 23, 1875, Papal Encyclicals Online, http://www.papalencyclicals.net/Pius09/p9graves.htm (accessed March 2, 2017).

22. Conway, *Question Box*, p. 219.

23. *Instructio de Motione Oecumenica*, an instruction of the Holy Office, December 20, 1949, Eternal Word Television Network, https://www.ewtn.com/library/CURIA/CDFECUM.HTM (accessed March 2, 2017).

24. Conway, *Question Box*, p. 87.

25. Second Vatican Council, "The Decree on Ecumenism [*Unitatis Redintegratio*]," in *The Documents of Vatican II*, ed. Walter M. Abbott (New York: Guild Press, 1966), p. 342.

26. Leo XIII, *Satis Cognitum*, June 29, 1896, Holy See, http://w2.vatican.va/content/leo-xiii/en/encyclicals/documents/hf_l-xiii_enc_29061896_satis-cognitum.html (accessed March 2, 2017).

27. Second Vatican Council, "Decree on Ecumenism," p. 349.

28. Kenneth Whitehead, "The Four Marks of the Church," from "The Church of the Apostles," *This Rock*, March 1995, https://www.ewtn.com/faith/teachings/churb2.htm (accessed March 2, 2017).

29. John Berchmans, "Catholic Obedience," *Catholicism.org*, June 27, 2005, http://catholicism.org/catholic-obedience.html (accessed March 2, 2017).

30. "The Decree on Ecumenism," quoted in Berchmans, "Catholic Obedience." The decree states: "However, one cannot impute the sin of separation to those at present who were born into these communities and are instilled therein with Christ's faith. The Catholic Church accepts them with respect and affection as brothers. For men who believe in Christ and have been properly baptized are brought into a certain, though imperfect, communion with the Catholic Church." (Vatican II, "Decree on Ecumenism," p. 3, in "The Decrees of Vatican II Compared with Past Church Teachings," The Religious Congregation of Mary Immaculate Queen, 1986, http://www.cmri.org/02-v2_ecumenism.shtml (accessed March 31, 2017).

31. Second Vatican Council, "Decree on Ecumenism," p. 345.

32. Conway, *Question Box*, p. 87.

33. Leo XIII, *Satis Cognitum*.

34. Pius XII, *Mystici Corporis Christi*, June 29, 1943, Holy See, http://w2.vatican.va/content/pius-xii/en/encyclicals/documents/hf_p-xii_enc_29061943_mystici-corporis-christi.html (accessed March 2, 2017).

35. The constitution reads: "We excommunicate and anathematize every

heresy raising itself up against this holy, orthodox and catholic faith which we have expounded above. We condemn all heretics, whatever names they may go under. They have different faces indeed but their tails are tied together inasmuch as they are alike in their pride." Fourth Lateran Council, "Constitution 3: On Heretics," 1215, https://www.ewtn.com/library/COUNCILS/LATERAN4.HTM#2 (accessed March 2, 2017).

36. Bryan Cross, "St. Thomas Aquinas on the Relation of Faith to the Church," *Called to Communion*, February 13, 2010, http://www.calledto communion.com/2010/02/st-thomas-aquinas-on-the-relation-of-faith-to-the -church/ (accessed March 2, 2017).

37. Ibid. See also Colin B. Donovan, "Heresy, Schism and Apostasy," *Catechism of the Catholic Church*, https://www.ewtn.com/expert/answers/heresy _schism_apostasy.htm (accessed March 2, 2017).

38. Pius XII, *Mystici corporis*, quoted in John Du Chalard, "The Errors of Vatican II," part 4, *Si Si No No* 53 (July 2003), http://www.sspxasia.com/ Documents/SiSiNoNo/2003_July/errors_of_vatican_II.htm (accessed March 31, 2017).

39. Ibid.

40. Alec Ryrie, *The Origins of the Scottish Reformation* (Manchester, UK: Manchester University Press, 2006), p. 97.

41. Second Vatican Council, *Unitatis Redintegratio*, 8, Holy See, http://www .vatican.va/archive/hist_councils/ii_vatican_council/documents/vat-ii _decree_19641121_unitatis-redintegratio_en.html (accessed March 31, 2017).

42. Stanislaus Woywod, *The New Canon Law: A Commentary and Summary of the New Code of Canon Law* (New York: Joseph F. Wagner, 1918), p. 258, sec. 1101.

43. John Daly, "The Principal Heresies and Other Errors of Vatican II," *Holy Roman Catholic Church*, http://www.holyromancatholicchurch.org/heresies.html (accessed March 2, 2017).

44. Second Vatican Council, "Decree on Ecumenism," p. 352.

45. Pius XI, *Mortalium Animos*, January 6, 1928, Holy See, http://w2.vatican .va/content/pius-xi/en/encyclicals/documents/hf_p-xi_enc_19280106 _mortalium-animos.html (accessed March 2, 2017).

46. Chalard, "Errors of Vatican II," part 4.

47. Second Vatican Council, "Decree on Ecumenism," p. 348.

48. Eugene IV, Council of Florence, *Cantate Domino*, session 11, February 4, 1442, Eternal Word Television Network, https://www.ewtn.com/library/ COUNCILS/FLORENCE.HTM#5 (accessed March 2, 2017).

49. John Paul II, *Ut Unum Sint*, May 25, 1995, Holy See, http://w2.vatican .va/content/john-paul-ii/en/encyclicals/documents/hf_jp-ii_enc_25051995 _ut-unum-sint.html (accessed March 2, 2017).

50. Paul VI, *Lumen Gentium*, par. 16, November 21, 1964, Eternal Word Television Network, https://www.ewtn.com/library/councils/v2church.htm (accessed March 2, 2017).

51. Thomas Aquinas, "The Five Ways," *Summa Theologica* (1460), available online at University of Notre Dame, https://www3.nd.edu/~jspeaks/courses/2008-9/10100-spring/_LECTURES/3%20-%20Aquinas%202d%20way.pdf (accessed March 2, 2017).

52. Pius IX, "On Revelation," First Vatican Council, session 3, canon 2, Eternal Word Television Network, https://www.ewtn.com/library/COUNCILS/V1.HTM#5 (accessed March 2, 2017).

53. Paul VI, *Lumen Gentium*, par. 16.

54. Eugene IV, *Council of Basel 1431–35 AD*, session 19, September 7, 1434, Papal Encyclicals Online, http://www.papalencyclicals.net/Councils/ecum17.htm (accessed March 2, 2017).

55. Clement V, *Council of Vienne Decrees*, decree 25, 1312, Eternal Word Television Network, https://www.ewtn.com/library/COUNCILS/VIENNE.HTM (accessed March 2, 2017).

56. Benedict XIV, *Quod Provinciale*, August 1, 1754, Papal Encyclicals Online, http://www.papalencyclicals.net/Ben14/b14quod.htm (accessed March 2, 2017).

57. Thomas Chaney, "Koran Kiss," Global Catholic Network, September 19, 2002, http://www.ewtn.com/v/experts/showmessage.asp?number=304721 (accessed March 2, 2017).

58. *Dignitatis Humanae*, "A Declaration on Religious Freedom," sec. 2, in *The Documents of Vatican II*, ed. Abbott, pp. 679–69.

59. Boniface VIII, *Unam Sanctam*, November 18, 1302, Papal Encyclicals Online, http://www.papalencyclicals.net/Bon08/B8unam.htm (accessed March 2, 2017).

60. Boniface VIII, *Unam Sanctam*, in Richard Cavendish, "Boniface VIII's Bull *Unam Sanctam*," *History Today*, November 2002, http://www.historytoday.com/richard-cavendish/boniface-viii%E2%80%99s-bull-unam-sanctam (March 31, 2017).

61. Pius IX, "Syllabus of Errors."

62. *Dignitatis Humanae*, sec. 3.

63. Second Vatican Council, "Decree on Ecumenism," sec. 3, pp. 345–46.

64. Ibid.

65. "Vatican II: The Myths," Eternal Word Television Network, July 1989, https://www.ewtn.com/library/ANSWERS/VAT-2.HTM (accessed March 2, 2017).

CHAPTER SEVEN: HOLY MOTHER CHURCH'S SEX CHANGE

1. Robin Lane Fox, *Pagans and Christians* (New York: Alfred A. Knopf, 1987), pp. 362–63.

2. Justin Martyr, *First Apology*, ch. 29, in *The Ante-Nicene Fathers*, vol. 1, *Apostolic Fathers: Justin Martyr and Irenaeus*, ed. Alexander Roberts and James Donaldson, trans. A. Cleveland Coxe (Grand Rapids, MI: William B. Eerdmans, 1981), p. 172.

3. Cyprian, "Treatise II: On the Dress of Virgins," in *The Ante-Nicene Fathers*, vol. 5, *Fathers of the Third Century*, ed. Alexander Roberts and James Donaldson, trans. Ernest Wallis (Grand Rapids, MI: William B. Eerdmans Publishing, 1981), pp. 435–36.

4. Ibid.

5. "The Protoevangelium of James," in *Women and Religion: A Feminist Sourcebook for Christian Thought*, ed. Elizabeth Clark and Herbert Richardson (New York: Harper and Row, 1977), p. 35.

6. Gregory of Nyssa, *On Virginity*, ch. 3, in *The Nicene and Post-Nicene Fathers*, vol. 5, *Select Writings and Letters of Gregory, Bishop of Nyssa*, trans. William Moore and Henry Austin Wilson (Grand Rapids, MI: William B. Eerdmans, 1955), p. 345.

7. Ambrose, *Concerning Virgins*, ch. 1, in *The Nicene and Post-Nicene Fathers*, vol. 10, *The Principal Works of St. Ambrose*, trans. H. DeRomestin (Grand Rapids, MI: William B. Eerdmans, 1955), pp. 367–68.

8. Jerome, "Letter 22 (To Eustochium, the Virgin's Profession)," in *Women and Religion*, ed. Clark and Richardson, p. 60.

9. *Canons and Decrees of the Council of Trent*, trans. H. J. Schroeder (London: B. Herder, 1955), p. 182.

10. Augustine, "On Marriage and Concupiscence," in *Women and Religion*, ed. Clark and Richardson, p. 72.

11. Ibid.

12. Marina Warner, *Alone of All Her Sex: The Myth and Cult of the Virgin Mary* (New York: Alfred A. Knopf, 1976), p. 77.

13. Thomas Aquinas, *Summa Theologiae*, supplement, question 49, in *Women and Religion*, ed. Clark and Richardson, p. 85.

14. Pius XII, "Allocution to Midwives," Eternal Word Television Network, October 29, 1951, https://www.ewtn.com/library/PAPALDOC/P511029.HTM (accessed March 2, 2017).

15. Ibid.

16. Warner, *Alone of All Her Sex*, pp. 74–75. See also Jerome, "Letter 22," pp. 62–63.

17. Ibid.

18. Vern L. Bullough, "The Christian Inheritance," in *Sexual Practices and the Medieval Church*, ed. Vern L. Bullough and James Brundage (Amherst, NY: Prometheus Books, 1982), p. 15.

19. Justin Martyr, *First Apology*, ch. 29, in *Ante-Nicene Fathers*, vol. 1.

20. Clement of Alexandria, "On Marriage," in *Women and Religion*, ed. Clark and Richardson, p. 47.

21. John Chrysostom, "On Account of Fornication," cited in Bullough, "Formation of Ideals: Christian Theory and Christian Practice," in *Sexual Practices of the Medieval Church*, p. 15.

22. Augustine, "On Marriage and Concupiscence," I, 17, 15, in *Nicene and Post Nicene Fathers*, vol. 5 (Buffalo, NY: Christian Literature Publishing, 1887, http://www.newadvent.org/fathers/15071.htm (accessed March 31, 2017).

23. Thomas Aquinas, *Summa Theologiae*, second part of part 2, question 154, cited in Bullough, "The Sin against Nature and Homosexuality," in *Sexual Practices and the Medieval Church*, p. 85.

24. Anthony Kosnik, William Carroll, Agnes Cunningham, Ronald Modras, and James Schulte, *Human Sexuality: New Directions in American Catholic Thought* (New York: Paulist Press, 1977), pp. 39–40.

25. Reay Tannahill, *Sex in History* (New York: Stein and Day, 1981), pp. 158–59.

26. Pius XI, *Casti Connubii*, December 31, 1930, Papal Encyclicals Online, http://www.papalencyclicals.net/Pius11/P11CASTI.HTM (accessed March 2, 2017).

27. Ibid.

28. George A. Kelly, "Schooling and the Values of People," *Columbia* 29 (June 1986): 22–29.

29. J. D. Conway, *What They Ask About Modesty, Chastity, and Morals* (Notre Dame, IN: Ave Maria Press, 1955), p. 6.

30. Ibid., p. 13.

31. Ibid., p. 17.

32. Ralph Wiltgen, *The Rhine Flows into the Tiber: A History of Vatican II* (Rockford, IL: Tan Books, 1985), p. 268.

33. Alfredo Ottaviani, quoted in Wiltgen, *Rhine Flows into the Tiber*, p. 269.

34. Ibid., p. 270.

35. Ibid., p. 271.

36. The modus read: *Sed ad difficultates superandas omnino requiri ut conjuges castitatem coniugalem sincero animo colant.* See Xavier Rynne, *Vatican Council II* (New York: Farrar, Straus, and Giroux, 1968), p. 561.

37. Ibid., p. 563.

38. Wiltgen, *Rhine Flows into the Tiber*, p. 272.

39. Rynne, *Vatican Council II*, p. 557.

40. Paul VI, *Humanae Vitae*, July 25, 1965, Holy See, http://w2.vatican.va/content/paul-vi/en/encyclicals/documents/hf_p-vi_enc_25071968_humanae-vitae.html (accessed March 2, 2017).

41. Ibid.

42. Thomas Bokenkotter, *Essential Catholicism: Dynamics of Faith and Belief* (Garden City, NY: Image Books, 1986), p. 343.

43. Ibid.

44. Ibid.

45. US Department of Health and Human Welfare, *Trends in Contraceptive Practice: United States, 1965–1976* (National Survey of Family Growth, February 1982).

46. Kosnik et al., *Human Sexuality*, p. xi.

47. Ibid., pp. 82–86.

48. Ibid., p. 86.

49. 1981 Knights of Columbus–sponsored study, cited in Kelly, "Schooling and the Values of People."

50. Gallup poll, cited in Thomas C. Reeves, "Not So Christian America," *First Things*, October 1996, http://www.firstthings.com/article/1996/10/001 -not-so-christian-america (accessed March 2, 2017).

51. Ibid.

52. "Has the Church Lost Its Soul?" *Newsweek*, October 4, 1971, p. 81.

CHAPTER EIGHT: DISSENT, DELUSION, AND DESERTION

1. Leo Rosten, *Religions of America* (New York: Simon and Schuster, 1975), pp. 434–35.

2. Ibid.

3. Ibid., p. 445.

4. *Catholics in America: A Report* (National Opinion Research Center, January 11, 1975).

5. Editorial Staff, "Has the Church Lost Its Soul?" *Newsweek*, October 4, 1971, pp. 81–84.

6. Greeley, McCready, and McCourt survey in Andrew Greeley, *The Catholic Revolution: New Wine, Old Wine Skins, and the Second Vatican Council* (Berkeley: University of California Press, 2004), p. 39.

7. Felician A. Foy, ed., *1970 Catholic Almanac* (New York: Doubleday, 1970), p. 142.

8. "The Great Exodus," *Time*, February 23, 1970.

9. Rosten, *Religions of America*, p. 397.

10. Felician A. Foy, ed., *1973 Catholic Almanac* (Huntington, IN: Our Sunday Visitor, 1973), p. 615.

11. Robert Ostling, "John Paul's Feisty Flock," *Time*, September 7, 1987.

12. Gabriel Garrone, quoted in Ostling, "John Paul's Feisty Flock."

13. "Great Exodus."

14. "The New Nuns," *Time*, March 20, 1972.

15. Lillanna Kopp, quoted in "New Nuns."

16. Margaret Traxler, quoted in Rosten, *Religions in America*, p. 402.

17. Ostling, "John Paul's Feisty Flock."

18. Sara Harris, *The Sisters: The Changing World of the American Nun* (New York: Bobbs Merrill, 1970), pp. 6–7.

19. Ibid.

20. Elizabeth Kuhns, *The Habit: A History of the Clothing of Catholic Nuns* (New York: Doubleday, 2003), p. 156.

21. "New Nuns."

22. Paul VI, *Evangelica Testificatio*, June 29, 1971, Holy See, http://w2.vatican.va/content/paul-vi/en/apost_exhortations/documents/hf_p-vi_exh_19710629_evangelica-testificatio.html (accessed March 2, 2017).

23. Anita Caspary, quoted in "New Nuns."

24. "Frequently Requested Church Statistics," Center for Applied Research in the Apostolate, January 2016, http://cara.georgetown.edu/frequently-requested-church-statistics/ (accessed March 2, 2017).

25. Ostling, "John Paul's Feisty Flock."

26. Steven Greenhouse, "Archbishop Lefebvre, 85, Dies; Traditionalist Defied the Vatican," *New York Times*, March 26, 1991, http://www.nytimes.com/1991/03/26/obituaries/archbishop-lefebvre-85-dies-traditionalist-defied-the-vatican.html (accessed March 2, 2017).

27. John Paul II, *Ecclesia Dei Adflicta*, July 2, 1988, Holy See, http://www.vatican.va/roman_curia/pontifical_commissions/ecclsdei/documents/hf_jp-ii_motu-proprio_02071988_ecclesia-dei_en.html (accessed March 2, 2017).

28. Marcel Lefebvre, "Conference of His Excellency Marcel Lefebvre," Society of Saint Pius X, District of Asia, Angelus Press, November 5, 1983, http://www.sspxasia.com/Documents/Archbishop-Lefebvre/Conference_at_Long_Island.htm (accessed March 2, 2017).

29. Daniel Wojcik, *The End of the World as We Know It: Faith, Fatalism, and the Apocalypse in America* (New York: New York University Press, 1997), p. 87.

30. Joaquin Saenz y Arriaga, *The New Montinian Church* (1971), available online at *Today's Catholic World*, http://www.todayscatholicworld.com/new-mont-church.htm (accessed March 2, 2017).

31. Donald J. Sanborn, "Explanation of the Thesis of Bishop Guerard des Lauriers," Most Holy Trinity Seminary, June 29, 2002, http://mostholytrinityseminary.org/Explanation%20of%20the%20Thesis.pdf (accessed March 2, 2017).

32. Thomas W. Case, "The Society of St. Pius X Gets Sick," *Fidelity Magazine*, October 2002.

33. William J. Collinge, *Historical Dictionary of Catholicism* (Lanham, MD: Scarecrow Press, 2012), p. 399.

34. Natasha Stoynoff, "Inside Mel Gibson's Church," *People*, April 16, 2009, http://people.com/celebrity/inside-mel-gibsons-church (accessed April 26, 2017).

35. PierLuigi Zoccatelli, "The Current Status of Catholic Sedevacantism and Antipopes," *Centro Studi sulle Nuove Religioni*, July 2009, http://www.cesnur.org/2009/plz_sedevacantism.htm (accessed March 2, 2017).

36. Ibid.

37. Paul VI, "Letter to the Bishops of the Netherlands," December 24, 1969, Holy See, http://w2.vatican.va/content/paul-vi/fr/letters/1970/documents/hf_p-vi_let_19700112_episcopato-olanda.html (accessed March 2, 2017).

38. Ibid.

39. Michael Gilchrist, "Growth of a 'New Church': The Dutch Experiment," *AD2000* 1, no. 4 (July 1988), http://www.ad2000.com.au/growth_of_a_new _church_the_dutch_experiment_july_1988 (accessed March 2, 2017).

40. Paul VI, "Remarks to a General Audience," *L'Osservatore Romano*, December 14, 1972.

41. Ellamay Horan, *Baltimore Catechism*, no. 2 (New York: W. H. Sadler, 1945), p. 15.

42. Ibid., p. 11.

43. Ibid.

44. Ibid.

45. Paul VI, "Comments before a General Audience, June 27, 1973," *L'Osservatore Romano*, July 5, 1973.

46. Paul VI, "Address during the Last General Meeting of the Second Vatican Council," December 7, 1965, Eternal Word Television Network, http://www.ewtn.com/library/papaldoc/p6tolast.htm (accessed March 2, 2017).

47. Paul VI, quoted in "Pope Paul Hails Apollo Mission," *Lewiston Daily Sun*, February 8, 1971.

48. Paul VI, *Nostra Aetate*, October 28, 1965, Holy See, http://www.vatican .va/archive/hist_councils/ii_vatican_council/documents/vat-ii_decl_19651028 _nostra-aetate_en.html (accessed March 2, 2017).

49. Paul VI, "To the President of India, for the Centenary Celebrations of the Birth of Mahatma Gandhi," Catholic News Agency, August 22, 1969, http://www .catholicnewsagency.com/document/to-the-president-of-india-for-the-centenary -celebrations-of-the-birth-of-mahatma-gandhi-517/ (accessed March 2, 2017).

50. Paul VI, *Nostra Aetate*.

51. "Pope Greets the Dalai Lama," *L'Osservatore Romano*, October 11, 1973.

52. "Mission Inventory," *US Catholic Mission Handbook* (Washington, DC: US Catholic Mission Association, 2008), p. 21.

53. Piers Compton, *The Broken Cross: The Hidden Hand in the Vatican* (London: N. Spearman, 1983), pp. 118–24.

54. Paul VI, Homily, Ninth Anniversary of the Coronation of His Holiness, June 29, 1972. See Jimmy Atkin, "The Smoke of Satan Homily," Jimmy Atkin.org, November 13, 2006, http://jimmyakin.typepad.com/defensor_fidei/2006/11/the_smoke_of_sa.html (accessed March 2, 2017).

55. Luigi Villa, "Letter to All Cardinals Regarding Pope Paul VI," The Laitytude, November 21, 2012, https://mumbailaity.wordpress.com/2012/11/21/letter-written-by-fr-luigi-villa-to-all-cardinals-regarding-pope-paul-vi-and-who -was-appointed-to-uncover-freemasonry/ (accessed March 2, 2017).

56. Philip Willan, *Puppetmasters: The Political Use of Terrorism in Italy* (London: Constable, 1991), p. 67.

CHAPTER NINE: A CRIMINAL ORGANIZATION

1. Malachi Martin, *Rich Church, Poor Church* (New York: G. P. Putnam's Sons, 1984), pp. 60–62.

2. Douglas Valentine, *The Strength of the Wolf* (New York: Verso, 2004), p. 166.

3. Ibid.

4. "Massimo Spada," Movers and Shakers of the Sovereign Military Order of Malta," August 31, 2008, http://moversandshakersofthesmom.blogspot.com/2008/08/massimo-spada.html (accessed May 20, 2014).

5. Valentine, *Strength of the Wolf*, p. 167.

6. Ibid.

7. Ibid.

8. Dean Henderson, *Big Oil and Their Bankers in the Persian Gulf: Four Horsemen, Eight Families, and Their Global Intelligence, Narcotics, and Terror Network* (New York: Bridger House, 2010), p. 284.

9. R. D. (pseud.), "La Storia sono loro: Michele Sindona e il delitto Ambrosoli" [in Italian], Polis Blog, September 10, 2010, http://www.polisblog.it/post/8528/la-storia-sono-loro-michele-sindona-e-il-delitto-ambrosoli (accessed May 20, 2014); Stefania Limiti, "L'Ultimo Incontro di Michele Sindona" [in Italian] *AltraInformazione*, May 26, 2013, http://alfredodecclesia.blogspot.com/2013/05/di-stefania-limiti-26-maggio-2013.html (accessed March 2, 2017).

10. David Yallop, *In God's Name: An Investigation into the Murder of Pope John Paul I* (New York: Bantam Books, 1984), p. 109. See also David Goldman, "ADL's Sterling Bank Sued in Italian Mafia Case," *Executive Intelligence Review* (*EIR*), February 10, 1982, http://www.larouchepub.com/eiw/public/1982/eirv09n06-19820216/eirv09n06-19820216_030-adls_sterling_bank_sued_in_itali.pdf (accessed April 27, 2017).

11. Luigi DiFonzo, *St. Peter's Banker: Michele Sindona* (New York: Franklin Watts, 1983), p. 37.

12. Ibid., p. 11.

13. Ibid.

14. Martin, *Rich Church: Poor Church*, p. 62.

15. DiFonzo, *St. Peter's Banker*, p. 11.

16. Martin, *Rich Church, Poor Church*, p. 62.

17. DiFonzo, *St. Peter's Banker*, p. 11.

18. Piers Compton, *The Broken Cross: The Hidden Hand in the Vatican* (London: N. Spearman, 1983), p. 212.

19. Yallop, *In God's Name*, p. 125.

20. DiFonzo, *St. Peter's Banker*, p. 124.

21. Ibid., p. 87.

22. Ibid.

23. Martin, *Rich Church, Poor Church*, p. 65.

24. Ibid.

25. G. William Domhoff and Charles L. Schwartz, *Probing the Rockefeller Fortune: A Report Prepared for Members of the United States Congress*, November 1974, http://socrates.berkeley.edu/~schwrtz/Rockefeller.html (accessed April 27, 2017).

26. Martin, *Rich Church, Poor Church*, p. 65.

27. DiFonzo, *St. Peter's Banker*, p. 71.

28. Rupert Cornwell, *God's Banker: An Account of the Life and Death of Roberto Calvi* (London: Victor Gollancz, 1984), p. 28.

29. Ibid.

30. Ibid., pp. 48–49.

31. Andrew Gavin Marshall, "Operation Gladio: CIA Network of 'Stay-Behind' Secret Armies," Global Research, July 17, 2008, http://www.global research.ca/operation-gladio-cia-network-of-stay-behind-secret-armies/9556 (accessed May 20, 2014).

32. Richard Cottrell, *Gladio: NATO's Dagger at the Heart of Europe* (Palm Desert, CA: Progressive Press, 2012), p. 219.

33. Yallop, *In God's Name*, p. 113. See also Philip Willan, "Looking for Licio," interview, 1989, Philip P. Willan, http://www.philipwillan.com/portale/?q=node/13 (accessed March 2, 2017).

34. Penny Lernoux, *In Banks We Trust* (New York: Penguin Books, 1986), p. 175.

35. Alexander Cockburn and Jeffrey St. Clair, *Whiteout: The CIA, Drugs, and the Press* (New York: Verso, 1998), p. 70.

36. John Judge, "Good Americans," in *Selected Writings of John Judge*, Citizens Watch, 1983, http://www.ratical.org/ratville/JFK/JohnJudge/GoodAmericans .html (accessed March 2, 2017).

37. John Cornwell, *Hitler's Pope: The Secret History of Pius XII* (New York: Viking, 1999), p. 265.

38. Yallop, *In God's Name*, pp. 118–19.

39. Ibid., p. 115.

40. Jack Greene and Alessandro Massignani, *The Black Prince and the Sea Devils: The Story of Valerio Borghese and the Elite Units of Decima MAS* (Cambridge, MA: De Capo, Press, 2004), pp. 222–23.

41. DiFonzo, *St. Peter's Banker*, p. 73.

42. Ibid., p. 68.

43. P-2 list, as found among the papers of Licio Gelli, Deep Politics Forum, posted September 2008, https://deeppoliticsforum.com/forums/showthread .php?1222-List-of-P2-Members (accessed March 2, 2017).

44. DiFonzo, *St. Peter's Banker*, p. 8.

45. Cornwell, *God's Banker*, p. 52.

46. Compton, *Broken Cross*, p. 212.

47. Ibid.

48. "Declaration of David Guyatt on IOR," court document, US District Court, Northern District of California, December 5, 2008. See https://deep politicsforum.com/forums/showthread.php?3038-Vatican-Bank#.WLhgvI HyuUk (accessed March 2, 2017).

49. Marshall, "Operation Gladio."

50. Palash Ghosh, "Green, White, and Lots of Red: How Italy Got the West's Biggest Communist Party," *International Business Times*, July 26, 2013, http://www.ibtimes.com/green-white-lots-red-how-italy-got-wests-biggest-communist -party-1360089 (accessed May 20, 2014).

CHAPTER TEN: YEARS OF LEAD

1. Maurizio Cotta and Luca Verzichelli, *Political Institutions of Italy* (New York: Oxford University Press, 2007), p. 38.

2. John Cooney, *The American Pope: The Life and Times of Francis Cardinal Spellman* (New York: Times Books, 1984), pp. 157–59.

3. "The Decline of Political Catholicism in Italy," *Political Theology Today*, March 21, 2014, http://www.politicaltheology.com/blog/the-decline-of-political -catholicism-in-italy/ (accessed March 2, 2017).

4. Dieter Nohlen and Philip Stöver, eds., *Elections in Europe: A Data Handbook* (Baden-Baden, Germany: Nomos Verlagsgesellschaft, 2010), p. 1048.

5. Massimo Introvigne, "The Man Who Changed Italy for the Worse," *Eponymous Flower* (blog), May 20, 2016, http://eponymousflower.blogspot.com/2016/05/marco-pannella-man-who-changed-italy.html (accessed March 2, 2017).

6. Ibid.

7. Philip Willan, *Puppetmasters: The Political Use of Terrorism in Italy* (New York: Authors Choice Press, 2002), Kindle edition.

8. Jack Greene and Alessandro Massignani, *The Black Prince and the Sea Devils: The Story of Valerio Borghese and the Elite Units of Decima MAS* (Cambridge, MA: De Capo Press, 2004), pp. 222–23.

9. Willan, *Puppetmasters*.

10. "1969: Deadly Bomb Blasts in Italy," BBC News, December 12, 2005, http://news.bbc.co.uk/onthisday/hi/dates/stories/december/12/news id_3953000/3953999.stm (accessed May 20, 2014).

11. Willan, *Puppetmasters*.

12. Daniele Ganser, *NATO's Secret Armies: Operation Gladio and Terrorism in Western Europe* (New York: Routledge, 2005), p. 3.

13. Willan, *Puppetmasters*.

14. Ibid.

15. Ibid.

16. Ibid.

17. Alan Cowell, "Italy Re-Examines 1978 Moro Slaying," *New York Times*, November 7, 1993, http://www.nytimes.com/1993/11/07/world/italy-re -examines-1978-moro-slaying.html (accessed March 2, 2017).

18. Arthur E. Rowse, "Gladio: The Secret US War to Subvert Italian Democracy," *Covert Action Quarterly*, December 1994.

19. Ganser, *NATO's Secret Armies*, pp. 3–4.

20. Andrew Gumbel, "The Riddle of Aldo Moro: Was Italy's Establishment Happy to See Him Die?" *Independent* (UK), March 7, 1998, http://www .independent.co.uk/news/the-riddle-of-aldo-moro-was-italys-establishment -happy-to-see-him-die-1149073.html (accessed March 2, 2017).

21. Andrew Gavin Marshall, "Operation Gladio: CIA Network of 'Stay-Behind' Secret Armies," *Geopolitical Research*, July 17, 2008, http://www.global research.ca/operation-gladio-cia-network-of-stay-behind-secret-armies (accessed May 21, 2014).

22. "Inchiesta ProDeo" [in Italian], *La Peste* (Rome), 1995, http://web .mclink.it/MJ4596/pro%20deo.htm (accessed May 21, 2014).

23. Martin A. Lee, "Their Will Be Done," *Mother Jones*, July/August 1983, http://www.motherjones.com/politics/1983/07/their-will-be-done (accessed May 20, 2014).

24. Claudio Celani, "Strategy of Tension: The Case of Italy," 4 parts, *Executive Intelligence Review (EIR)*, March 26, April 2, April 9, April 30, 2004, http://www .larouchepub.com/other/2004/3117tension_italy.html (accessed May 21, 2014).

25. Willan, *Puppetmasters*.

26. Ferdinando Imposimato, *La Repubblica delle Stragi Impunite* [in Italian] (Rome: Newton Compton Editori, 2013), p. 339.

27. Giacomo Galeazzi, "A Londra il Confessore di Moro" [in Italian], *La Stampa*, December 18, 2010, http://www.lastampa.it/2010/12/18/blogs/ oltretevere/a-londra-il-confessore-di-moro-xPVaJTaw95kcpnGoZ0CC4N/pagina .html (accessed May 21, 2014).

28. Gerald Posner, *God's Bankers: A History of Money and Power at the Vatican* (New York: Simon and Schuster, 2015), p. 183.

29. Ibid.

30. Ibid.

31. Robert C. Doty, "Vatican Is Stunned by Plan to Tax It," *New York Times*, July 13, 1968.

32. David Yallop, *In God's Name: An Investigation into the Murder of John Paul I* (New York: Bantam Books, 1984), p. 137.

33. Malachi Martin, *Rich Church, Poor Church* (New York: G. P. Putnam's Sons, 1984), p. 67.

34. Luigi DiFonzo, *St. Peter's Banker: Michele Sindona* (New York: Franklin Watts, 1983), p. 229.

35. Ibid., p. 213.

36. Ibid.

37. Paul VI, quoted in Malachi Martin, *The Decline and Fall of the Roman Church* (New York: G. P. Putnam's Sons, 1981), p. 278.

38. Eric O. Hanson, *The Catholic Church in World Politics* (Princeton, NJ: Princeton University Press, 1987), p. 136.

39. John L. Allen Jr., "Aldo Moro Affair Watershed for the West and for the Church," *National Catholic Reporter*, March 17, 2008, https://www.ncronline.org/news/aldo-moro-affair-watershed-west-and-church (accessed March 2, 2017).

40. Willan, *Puppetmasters*.

41. Editors, "Italy Adopts New Law Providing Free Abortions," *International Family Planning Perspectives and Digest 4, no. 3* (Autumn 1978): 87–89.

42. Harry Hearder, *Italy: A Short History* (Cambridge: Cambridge University Press, 2001), p. 264.

43. Willan, *Puppetmasters*.

44. Maria Rita Latto, "The Massacre of Bologna . . . 30 Years Later," i-Italy, August 3, 2010, http://www.iitaly.org/magazine/focus/facts-stories/article/massacre-bologna-30-years-later (accessed April 27, 2017).

45. Ibid.

46. P-2 List, Report of the Parliamentary Commission, July 12, 1984, in "Elenco Delgi Iscritti alla Loggia P2," Archivo 900, February 2, 2006, http://www.archivio900.it/it/documenti/doc.aspx?id=42 (accessed March 2, 2017).

47. Ganser, *NATO's Secret Armies*, pp. 3–4.

48. Paul VI, *Populorum Progressio*, March 26, 1967, Holy See, http://w2.vatican.va/content/paul-vi/en/encyclicals/documents/hf_p-vi_enc_26031967_populorum.html (accessed March 2, 2017).

CHAPTER ELEVEN: CATHOLIC CONDOR

1. Arthur McGovern, *Liberation Theology and Its Critics* (Maryknoll, NY: Orbis Books, 1989), p. 9.

2. Theresa Keeley, "Nelson Rockefeller's 1969 Mission to Latin America and the Catholic Church," doctoral dissertation, Department of History, Northwestern University, 2011, https://www.yumpu.com/en/document/view/25818280/nelson-rockefellers-1969-mission-to-latin-america-and-the-catholic- (accessed March 2, 2017).

3. Penny Lernoux, *Cry of the People: The Struggle for Human Rights in Latin America—The Catholic Church in Conflict with US Policy* (New York: Penguin Books, 1982), p. 51.

4. Martin A. Lee, "Their Will Be Done," *Mother Jones*, July/August 1983, http://www.motherjones.com/politics/1983/07/their-will-be-done (accessed May 20, 2014).

5. Lernoux, *Cry of the People*, p. 56.

6. Alfonso Lopez Trujillo, quoted in David Yallop, *The Power and the Glory: Inside the Dark Heart of Pope John Paul II's Vatican* (New York: Carroll and Graf, 2007), p. 174.

7. Ibid.

8. Augusto Pinochet, quoted in Yallop, *Power and the Glory*, p. 175.

9. Andrew Orta, *Catechizing Culture: Missionaries, Aymara, and the "New Evangelization"* (New York: Columbia University Press, 2004), p. 95.

10. Robert P. Baird, "The US Paid Money to Support Hugo Banzer's 1971 Coup," *Haiti-Cuba-Venezuela Analysis*, May 30, 2010, http://hcvanalysis .wordpress.com/2010/05/30/us-paid-money-to-support-hugo-banzers -1971-coup-in-bolivia/ (accessed May 21, 2014).

11. Jerry Meldon, "Return of Bolivia's Drug-Stained Dictator," *The Consortium*, Winter 1997, http://www.consortiumnews.com/archive/story40.html (accessed May 21, 2014).

12. Alexander Cockburn and Jeffrey St. Clair, *Whiteout: The CIA, Drugs, and the Press* (New York, Verso, 1998), p. 181.

13. Ibid.

14. Gary Webb, *Dark Alliance: The CIA, the Contras, and the Crack Cocaine Explosion* (New York: Seven Stories Press, 1999), pp. 1–21.

15. David Yallop, *In God's Name: An Investigation into the Murder of Pope John Paul I* (New York: Bantam Books, 1984), p. 311.

16. Yallop, *Power and the Glory*, pp. 174–75.

17. Ibid.

18. Lernoux, *Cry of the People*, p. 332.

19. Brett Wilkins, "'Smoking Gun' Memo Proves Pope Francis Collaborated with Military Junta," Global Research, March 18, 2013, http://www.global research.ca/smoking-gun-memo-proves-pope-francis-collaborated-with-military -junta/5327354 (accessed May 21, 2014).

20. Lernoux, *Cry of the People*, p. 333.

21. Yallop, *Power and the Glory*, pp. 175–76.

22. Robert C. Hill to Henry Kissinger, "Military Take Cognizance of Human Rights Issue," report, February 16, 1976, US Department of State, http://www2 .gwu.edu/~nsarchiv/NSAEBB/NSAEBB185/19760216%20Military%20Take%20 Cognizance%20of%20Human%20Rights%20Issue%2000009FF0.pdf (accessed May 21, 2014).

23. Secretary of State Henry Kissinger, Staff Meeting Transcript, March 26, 1976, http://www2.gwu.edu/~nsarchiv/NSAEBB/NSAEBB185/19760326%20 Secretary%20of%20Stet%20Kissinger%20Chariman%20apgesl%201-39%20-%20 full.pdf (accessed May 21, 2014).

24. Robert C. Hill, "Videla's Moderate Line Prevails," telegram, March 30, 1976, US Department of State, http://www2.gwu.edu/~nsarchiv/NSAEBB/NSAEBB185/19760330%20Videlas%20moderate%20line%20prevails%20%2000009EF2.pdf (accessed May 21, 2014).

25. Luis Granados, "Life Sentence for Gen. Videla," *The Humanist*, January 2011.

26. Ibid.

27. Tom Hennigan, "Former Argentinian Dictator Says He Told Catholic Church of Disappeared," *Irish Times*, July 24, 2012.

28. "Prensa Argentina Vincula a Bergoglio con el Secuestro de Dos Jesuitas Durante la Dictadura de Videla" [in Spanish], *El Periodista*, March 13, 2013, http://elperiodistaonline.cl/globales/2013/03/prensa-argentina-vincula-a-bergoglio-con-el-secuestro-de-dos-jesuitas-en-1976/ (accessed May 21, 2014).

29. Ibid.

30. Iain Guest, *Behind the Disappearances: Argentina's Dirty War against Human Rights and the United Nations* (Philadelphia: University of Pennsylvania Press, 2000), p. 41.

31. John Simpson and Jana Bennett, *The Disappeared: Story of Argentina's Secret War of Oppression* (London: Sphere, 1986), pp. 145–48.

32. "Argentina's 'Death Flights' Trials Begin," SFGate, November 28, 2012, http://www.sfgate.com/world/article/Argentina-s-death-flights-trials-begin-4075675.php (accessed May 21, 2014).

33. Wilkins, "'Smoking Gun' Memo."

34. Ibid.

35. Ibid.

36. Horacio Verbitsky, "Cambio de Piel" [in Spanish], *Pagina 12*, March 17, 2013, http://www.pagina12.com.ar/diario/elpais/1-215961-2013-03-17.html (accessed May 21, 2014).

37. Wilkins, "'Smoking Gun' Memo."

38. Isabel Vincent, "Victims of Argentina's 'Dirty War' of the Late 1970s Blast Pope's 'Deadly' Silence," *New York Post*, March 17, 2013, http://nypost.com/2013/03/17/victims-of-argentinas-dirty-war-of-the-late-1970s-blast-popes-deadly-silence/ (accessed May 21, 2014).

39. Wilkins, "'Smoking Gun' Memo."

40. "New Pope: Austere Jesuit Sometimes at Odds with Liberal Argentina," Globe Span Radio, March 14, 2013, http://www.globespanradio.com/?p=7239 (accessed March 2, 2017).

41. Jonathan Watts and Uki Goni, "New Pope's Role during Argentina's Military Era Disputed," *Guardian* (UK), March 15, 2013, http://www.theguardian.com/world/2013/mar/15/pope-francis-argentina-military-era (accessed May 21, 2014).

42. Ibid.

43. Ibid.

44. Ibid.

45. "Argentine Jorge Bergoglio Elected Pope, Chooses Name Francis," *Inquirer News*, March 14, 2013, http://newsinfo.inquirer.net/373313/argentinian -cardinal-is-new-pope (accessed May 21, 2014).

46. Michel Chossudovsky, "'Washington's Pope?' Who Is Pope Francis? Cardinal Jorge Mario Bergoglio and Argentina's 'Dirty War,'" Global Research, March 14, 2013, http://www.globalresearch.ca/washingtons-pope-who-is -francis-i-cardinal-jorge-mario-bergoglio-and-argentinas-dirty-war/5326675 (accessed May 21, 2014).

47. Ibid.

48. Alana Horowitz, "Pope's Approval Rating Soars: CNN Poll," *Huffington Post*, December 24, 2013, http://www.huffingtonpost.com/2013/12/24/popes -approval-rating-poll_n_4497813.html (accessed May 21, 2014).

49. Chossudovsky, "'Washington's Pope?'"

CHAPTER TWELVE: THE CONTAGION OF CORRUPTION

1. Federal Bureau of Investigation confidential file (58-7146), "Vito Geno- vese," declassified, January 12, 2001.

2. Richard Hammer, *The Vatican Connection* (New York: Charter Books, 1982), p. 216.

3. Ibid., pp. 217–18.

4. Ibid.

5. Ibid., pp. 229–32.

6. David Yallop, *In God's Name*: *An Investigation into the Murder of Pope John Paul I* (New York: Bantam Books, 1984), p. 42.

7. Hammer, *Vatican Connection*.

8. Jack Doherty, *How the Catholic Church Became Naughty . . . and Where the Real Hindrance to Reform Lies* (Parker, CO: Outskirts Press, 2015), p. 83.

9. Yallop, *In God's Name*, p. 45.

10. Paul Marcinkus, interview in Yallop, *In God's Name*, pp. 45–46.

11. Ibid., pp. 46–47.

12. Hammer, *Vatican Connection*, pp. 300–302.

13. Ibid.

14. William Aronwald, quoted in Yallop, *In God's Name*, p. 49.

15. Andrew M. Greeley, *Furthermore! Memories of a Parish Priest* (New York: Tom Doherty Associates, 2000), pp. 88–89.

16. Gerald Posner, *God's Bankers: A History of Money and Power at the Vatican* (New York: Simon and Schuster, 2015), p 251.

17. Yallop, *In God's Name*, p. 191.

18. Ibid., p. 194.

19. Ibid., p. 188.

20. Ibid., p. 189.

21. Posner, *God's Bankers*, pp. 251–52.

22. David Yallop, *The Power and the Glory: Inside the Dark Heart of John Paul II's Vatican* (New York: Carrol and Graf, 2007), p. 36.

23. Posner, *God's Bankers*, p. 281.

24. George Guilfoyle and Paul Boyle, quoted in Posner, *God's Bankers*.

25. Ibid.

26. Joyce Gemperlein, "Probe of Monks Cites Kickbacks," *Pittsburgh Post-Gazette*, September 11, 1979, https://www.newspapers.com/newspage/90055371/ (accessed March 2, 2017).

27. Posner, *God's Bankers*, p. 281.

28. Yallop, *Power and the Glory*, p. 37.

29. Clyde H. Farnsworth, "Orphans of the 1950's, Telling of Abuse, Sue Quebec," *New York Times*, May 21, 1993, http://www.nytimes.com/1993/05/21/world/orphans-of-the-1950-s-telling-of-abuse-sue-quebec.html?pagewanted=all (accessed March 2, 2017).

30. "Duplessis Orphans Want Montreal Burial Site Dug Up," CTV News–Montreal, Canada, June 18, 2004, https://web.archive.org/web/20111022154328/http://www.ctv.ca/CTVNews/Canada/20040619/duplessis_orphans_040618/ (accessed March 2, 2017).

31. Farnsworth, "Orphans of the 1950's."

32. Christine Hahn, "The Worst of Times: How Psychiatry Used Quebec's Orphans as Guinea Pigs," *Freedom*, May 22, 2003, http://www.freedommag.org/english/canada/reports/page01.htm (accessed March 2, 2017).

33. Peter Rakobowchuk, "Duplessis Orphan Can't Forget Sexual Abuse that Occurred Almost 60 Years Ago," *Brooks Bulletin*, December 21, 2006, http://www.bishop-accountability.org/news2006/11_12/2006_12_21_Rakobowchuk_DuplessisOrphan.htm (accessed March 2, 2017).

34. Ibid.

35. Hahn, "Worst of Times."

36. Ibid.

37. Ibid.

38. William Marsden, "Duplessis Orphans Call for Exhumations," *National Post*, June 19, 2004, http://canadiangenocide.nativeweb.org/duplessis_orphans.html (accessed March 2, 2017).

39. Ibid.

40. Ibid.

41. "Duplessis Orphans Accept Quebec's Final Offer," CBC News, July 1, 2001, http://www.cbc.ca/news/canada/duplessis-orphans-accept-quebec-s-final-offer-1.278029 (accessed April 27, 2017).

42. "Canada's Dark Secret: Forgotten Case of the Duplessis Orphans,"

Sputnik News, December 15, 2015, http://sputniknews.com/world/20151215/1031794624/duplessis-orphans-canada-quebec-catholic-church.html (accessed March 2, 2017).

43. "Duplessis Orphans Continue Demand for Church Apology," *Huffington Post*, March 20, 2013, http://www.huffingtonpost.ca/2013/03/30/duplessis-orphans-continu_n_2984767.html (accessed March 2, 2017).

CHAPTER THIRTEEN: THE GAY CHURCH

1. Luigi Marinelli, quoted in Gerald Posner, *God's Bankers: A History of Money and Power at the Vatican* (New York: Simon and Schuster, 2015), p. 463.

2. Leo Lyon Zagami, *Pope Francis: The Last Pope? Money, Masons, and Occultism in the Decline of the Catholic Church* (San Francisco, CA: CCC Publishing, 2015), pp. 16–18.

3. Michael Day, "Vatileaks Scandal: Vatican Properties 'Used as Brothels and Massage Parlours Where Priests Pay for Sex,' Claims Report," *Independent* (UK), November 10, 2015, http://www.independent.co.uk/news/world/europe/vatileaks-scandal-vatican-properties-used-as-brothels-and-massage-parlours-where-priests-pay-for-sex-a6729251.html (accessed March 2, 2017).

4. Franco Bellegrandi, *Nichitaroncalli: Controvita di un Papa* [in Italian] (Rome: Eiles, 1994), pp. 85–86.

5. Paul Hofmann, *O Vatican! A Slightly Wicked View of the Holy See* (New York: Congdon and Weed, 1984), p. 151.

6. Bellegrandi, *Nichitaroncalli*, p. 86.

7. Ibid., pp. 91–92.

8. Paul VI, *Persona Humana*, December 29, 1975, Holy See, http://www.vatican.va/roman_curia/congregations/cfaith/documents/rc_con_cfaith_doc_19751229_persona-humana_en.html (accessed March 2, 2017).

9. Marian T. Horvat, "Paul VI's Homosexuality: Rumor or Reality?" *Tradition in Action*, February 1, 2006, http://www.traditioninaction.org/HotTopics/a02tPaulV_Accusations.html (accessed March 2, 2017).

10. Ibid.

11. Andrew Sullivan, "The Pope Is Not Gay," *Atlantic*, August 15, 2010, http://www.theatlantic.com/daily-dish/archive/2010/08/the-pope-is-not-gay/183564/ (accessed March 2, 2017).

12. A. W. Richard Sipe, "Is Pope Benedict Gay?" Richard Sipe: Priests, Celibacy, and Sexuality, April 4, 2012, http://www.awrsipe.com/Comments/2012-04-04-pope-benedict-gay.htm (accessed March 2, 2017).

13. Angelo Quattrocchi, quoted in Colm Tóibín, "Among the Flutterers," *London Review of Books*, August 19, 2010, http://www.lrb.co.uk/v32/n16/colm-toibin/among-the-flutterers (accessed March 2, 2017).

14. Paul Likoudis, *Amchurch Comes Out: The US Bishops, Pedophile Scandals, and the Homosexual Agenda* (Petersburg, IL: Roman Catholic Faithful, 2002), p. 118.

15. Richard Fragomeni, quoted in Likoudis, *Amchurch Comes Out.*

16. A. W. Richard Sipes, "A Question That Just Won't Go Away: Do Bishops Have a Sexual Orientation?" ch. 4, *Sexual Orientation and American Roman Catholic Bishops,* Richard Sipe: Priests, Celibacy, and Sexuality, August 1, 2006, http://www.awrsipe.com/click_and_learn/2006-08-01-sexual_orientation-4.html (accessed March 2, 2017).

17. Thomas A. Droleskey, "More than a Matter of Legality," Christ or Chaos, April 12, 2010, http://www.christorchaos.com/MoreThanAMatterofLegality.html (accessed March 2, 2017).

18. Likoudis, *Amchurch Comes Out,* p. 137.

19. Eugene Kennedy, quoted in Likoudis, *Amchurch Comes Out,* p. 138.

20. Matt C. Abbott, "Ex-Priest Ellis Harsham 'Returns,'" RenewAmerica, April 19, 2011, http://www.renewamerica.com/columns/abbott/110419 (accessed March 2, 2017).

21. Likoudis, *Amchurch Comes Out,* p. 139.

22. David Gibson, "Pope Francis Breathes New Life into Cardinal Bernardin's Contested Legacy," Religion News Service, October 24, 2013, http://religionnews.com/2013/10/24/pope-francis-breathes-new-life-cardinal-bernardins-contested-legacy/ (accessed March 2, 2017).

23. Margaret Galitzin, "When Cardinals Are Outed for Their Homosexuality," *Tradition in Action,* March 8, 2013, http://www.traditioninaction.org/HotTopics/N002-Cardinals.htm (accessed March 2, 2017).

24. "The Homosexual Colonization of the Catholic Church," *New Oxford Review,* November 2006, http://www.newengelpublishing.com/pages/New-Oxford-Review.html (accessed March 2, 2017).

25. Michelangelo Signorile, "Cardinal Spellman's Dark Legacy," *Strausmedia,* May 7, 2002, http://www.nypress.com/cardinal-spellmans-dark-legacy/ (accessed March 2, 2017).

26. Michael S. Rose, *Goodbye, Good Men: How Liberals Brought Corruption into the Catholic Church* (Washington, DC: Regnery Publishing, 2015), pp. 55–87.

27. Ibid., p. 58.

28. Ibid., pp. 56–57.

29. Michael Shane, quoted in Rose, *Goodbye, Good Men,* pp. 60–61.

30. Ibid., pp. 61–65.

31. Robert Crooks and Karla Baur, *Our Sexuality* (Belmont, CA: Wadsworth, 2008), p. 9. See also Rose, *Goodbye, Good Men,* p. 100.

32. Ibid., p. 11.

33. "Catholic Church Pays $655 Million in Abuse Cases," *Agence France-Presse,* March 8, 2008.

CHAPTER FOURTEEN: YEAR OF THREE POPES

1. Paul VI, quoted in Christopher Lamb, "Shakespeare Tragedy Comes to the Holy See," *Vatican Insider*, April 13, 2016, http://www.lastampa.it/2016/04/13/vaticaninsider/eng/the-vatican/shakespeare-tragedy-comes-to-the-holy-see-LkVQkvKSUhmgIiiWAsIyBN/pagina.html (accessed March 2, 2017).

2. "In Search of a Pope," *Time*, August 21, 1978.

3. Peter Hebblethwaite, *Paul VI: The First Modern Pope* (Mahwah, NJ: Paulist Press, 1993), p. 713.

4. "In Search of a Pope."

5. Daniel Engber, "Why Didn't They Embalm the Pope?" *Slate*, April 7, 2005, http://www.slate.com/articles/news_and_politics/explainer/2005/04/why_didnt_they_embalm_the_pope.html (accessed April 27, 2017).

6. John Cooney, *The American Pope: The Life and Times of Francis Cardinal Spellman* (New York: Times Books, 1984), p. 281. See also the following declassified documents: "Francis Cardinal Spellman," FBI memo, June 6, 1963, declassified February 5, 1980; "Francis Cardinal Spellman," CIA confidential report, November 6, 1964, declassified July 8, 1976; and Department of Defense, "Cardinal Francis Spellman," top secret report, September 6, 1966, declassified September 7, 1978.

7. Giuseppe Siri, quoted in Gloria C. Molinari, "The Conclave: August 25th–26th, 1978," *John Paul I: The Smiling Pope*, September 13, 2012, http://www.papaluciani.com/eng/conclave.htm (accessed May 21, 2014).

8. Ibid.

9. John Cornwell, *A Thief in the Night: The Mysterious Death of John Paul I* (New York: Simon and Schuster, 1989), p. 50.

10. Ibid.

11. Paolo Panerai, "Your Holiness, Is It Right?" *Il Mondo*, August 31, 1978.

12. Ibid.

13. Ibid.

14. David Yallop, *The Power and the Glory: Inside the Dark Heart of John Paul II's Vatican* (New York: Carroll and Graf, 2007), p. 34.

15. Ibid., p. 154. See also Tyler Durden [pseud.], "Vatican Bank to Shut All Embassy Accounts to Halt Money Laundering," *Zero Hedge*, September 20, 2013, http://www.zerohedge.com/news/2013-09-30/vatican-bank-shut-all-embassy-accounts-halt-money-laundering (accessed May 21, 2014).

16. Yallop, *Power and the Glory*, p. 34.

17. David Yallop, *In God's Name: An Investigation into the Murder of Pope John Paul I* (New York: Bantam Books, 1984), pp. 143–45.

18. Concetto Vecchio, "Alessandrini e Quella Carezza del Presidente" [in Italian], *La Repubblica*, April 28, 2011, http://www.repubblica.it/

politica/2011/04/28/news/emilio_alessandrini-15477062/ (accessed May 21, 2014).

19. Yallop, *In God's Name*, pp. 176–77.

20. Canon Law of 1917, which remained in effect at the time of John Paul I, stipulated the following: "Those who join a Masonic sect or other societies of the same sort, which plot against the Church or against legitimate civil authority, incur *ipso facto* an excommunication simply reserved to the Holy See (can. 2335)."

21. Vance Ferrell, *The Murder of John Paul I* (Beersheba Springs, TN: Pilgrim Books, 1999), p. 47.

22. Yallop, *In God's Name*, p. 177.

23. Ibid.

24. Cornwell, *Thief in the Night*, pp. 236–37.

25. Department of State, confidential memo, December 11, 1978, declassified August 17, 1998; CIA official use file, January 7, 1979, declassified February 8, 1988.

26. Avro Manhattan, *Murder in the Vatican* (Springfield, MO: Ozark Books, 1985), p. 155.

27. Ibid.

28. Ibid.

29. Yallop, *In God's Name*, p. 220.

30. Cornwell, *Thief in the Night*, p. 102.

31. Dr. Buzzonetti's pronouncements appeared in the official Vatican press release of John Paul's death. John Julius Norwich, "Was John Paul I Murdered?" *Daily Mail*, May 7. 2011, http://www.dailymail.co.uk/home/moslive/article-1383867/Was-Pope-John-Paul-I-murdered-John-Julius-Norwichs-burning-question-.html (accessed April 2, 2017).

32. Yallop, *In God's Name*, p. 222.

33. Ibid.

34. Cornwell, *Thief in the Night*, p. 272.

35. Yallop, *In God's Name*, p. 222.

36. Ibid.

37. Cornwell, *Thief in the Night*, pp. 274–76.

38. Manhattan, *Murder in the Vatican*, p. 158.

39. Yallop, *In God's Name*, p. 220.

40. Cornwell, *Thief in the Night*, p. 74.

41. News Alert, *Radio Vaticana*, September 29, 1978.

42. Yallop, *In God's Name*, pp. 236–37.

43. Ibid., p. 254. See also Lucien Gregoire, *The Vatican Murders: The Life and Death of John Paul I* (Bloomington, IN: Author House, 2003), p. 24.

44. Carlo Bo, "Perché Dire di No a Un'autopsia?" [in Italian], *Corriere della Sera*, October 1, 1978.

45. Carlo Frizzerio, quoted in Yallop, *In God's Name*, p. 248.

46. Giuseppe Da Ros, quoted in Yallop, *In God's Name*.

47. Yallop, *In God's Name*, p. 244.

48. Manhattan, *Murder in the Vatican*, p. 171.

49. Yallop, *In God's Name*, p. 239.

50. Cornwell, *Thief in the Night*, pp. 312–13.

51. Yallop, *Power and the Glory*, p. 24.

52. Manhattan, *Murder in the Vatican*, p. 222.

53. Carl Bernstein and Marco Politi, *His Holiness: John Paul II and the Hidden History of Our Time* (New York: Penguin Books, 1996), pp. 35–40.

54. Yallop, *Power and the Glory*, p. 28.

55. Manhattan, *Murder in the Vatican*, p. 216.

56. Ibid.

CHAPTER FIFTEEN: THE AMBROSIANO AFFAIR

1. Nick Squires, "God's Banker Linked to Pablo Escobar," *Telegraph* (UK), November 26, 2012, http://www.telegraph.co.uk/news/worldnews/europe/italy/9703479/Gods-banker-linked-to-Pablo-Escobar.html (accessed March 2, 2017).

2. David Yallop, *In God's Name: An Investigation into the Murder of Pope John Paul I* (New York: Bantam Books, 1984), p. 278.

3. Ibid., p. 311.

4. Rupert Cornwell, *God's Banker: An Account of the Life and Death of Roberto Calvi* (London: Victor Gollancz, 1984), pp. 69–72.

5. Philip Willan, *The Vatican at War: From Blackfriar's Bridge to Buenos Aires* (Bloomington, IN: iUniverse, 2013), ch. 3, Kindle edition.

6. Ibid.

7. Malachi Martin, *Rich Church, Poor Church* (New York: G. P. Putnam's Sons, 1984), pp. 68–69.

8. Paul Lewis, "God's Banker: Italy's Mysterious, Deepening Bank Scandal," *New York Times*, July 28, 1982, http://www.bibliotecapleyades.net/vatican/esp_vatican117.htm (accessed May 21, 2014).

9. Penny Lernoux, *In Banks We Trust* (New York: Penguin Books, 1986), p. 206.

10. Cornwell, *God's Banker*, pp. 69–71.

11. Yallop, *In God's Name*, p. 280.

12. Ibid., p. 281.

13. Lernoux, *In Banks We Trust*, p. 196.

14. David Yallop, *The Power and the Glory: Inside the Dark Heart of John Paul II's Vatican* (New York: Carroll and Graf, 2007), p.118.

15. Eric Frattini, *The Entity: Five Centuries of Secret Vatican Espionage*, trans. Dick Cluster (New York: St. Martin's Press, 2004), p. 324.

16. Ibid., p. 326.

17. Yallop, *Power and the Glory*, pp. 169–70.

18. Luigi DiFonzo, *St. Peter's Banker: Michele Sindona* (New York: Franklin Watts, 1983), p. 221.

19. Yallop, *In God's Name*, p. 135.

20. Lewis, "God's Banker."

21. Lernoux, *In Banks We Trust*, pp. 206–208.

22. Cornwell, *God's Banker*, pp. 90–91.

23. Ibid., p. 92.

24. Jesus Lopez Saez, "The IOR-Ambrosian Scandal," ch. 4 in *The Day of Reckoning: John Paul II Examined* (Madrid: Meral Ediciones, 2005), http://www.comayala.es/Libros/ddc2i/ddc2e04.htm (accessed May 21, 2014).

25. Lewis, "God's Banker."

26. Martin, *Rich Church, Poor Church*, p. 68.

27. Yallop, *In God's Name*, p. 287.

28. Cornwell, *God's Banker*, p. 121.

29. Saez, "The IOR-Ambrosian Scandal."

30. Cornwell, *God's Banker*, p. 127.

31. Willan, *Vatican at War*.

32. Cornwell, *God's Banker*, pp. 127–28.

33. Yallop, *In God's Name*, pp. 296–27.

34. Ibid., pp. 294–95.

35. Cornwell, *God's Banker*, p. 250.

36. Ibid.

37. Nick Tosches, *Power on Earth: Michele Sindona's Explosive Story* (New York: Arbor House, 1986), pp. 247–48.

38. Cornwell, *God's Banker*, pp. 179–80.

39. Yallop, *Power and the Glory*, pp. 141–42.

40. Ibid.

41. Richard Cottrell, *Gladio: NATO's Dagger at the Heart of Europe* (Palm Desert, CA: Progressive Press, 2012), p. 228.

42. Willan, *Vatican at War*.

43. Paul Marcinkus, quoted in Cornwell, *God's Banker*, p. 189.

44. Ibid.

45. Roberto Rosone, quoted in Willan, *Vatican at War*.

46. Cornwell, *God's Banker*, p. 190.

47. Jennifer Parmelee, "Deaths of 2 Crooked Bankers Create a Mystery in Italy," *Milwaukee Journal*, May 18, 1986.

48. Avro Manhattan, *Murder in the Vatican* (Springfield, MO: Ozark Books, 1985), p. 259.

49. Willan, *Vatican at War*.

50. Ibid.

51. Ibid.

52. Lernoux, *In Banks We Trust*, p. 192.

53. Cornwell, *God's Banker*, p. 183.

54. Lernoux, *In Banks We Trust*, p. 192.

55. Luigi Cipriani, "Armi e Droga Nell'Inchiesta de Giudice Palermo" [in Italian], *Democrazia Proletaria*, May 1985, http://www.fondazionecipriani.it/Scritti/palermo.html (accessed May 24, 2014).

56. Willan, *Vatican at War*.

57. Roberto Calvi, quoted in Cornwell, *God's Banker*, p. 196.

58. Ibid., p. 198.

59. Ibid., p. 199.

CHAPTER SIXTEEN: THE BOX OF BONES

1. Nick Tosches, *Power on Earth: Michele Sindona's Explosive Story* (New York: Arbor House, 1986), p. 246.

2. Beniamino Andreatta, quoted in Tosches, *Power on Earth*.

3. Malachi Martin, *Rich Church, Poor Church* (New York: G. P. Putnam's Sons, 1984), p. 71.

4. David Yallop, *In God's Name: An Investigation into the Murder of Pope John Paul I* (New York: Bantam Books, 1984), p. 305.

5. Laura Colby, "Vatican Bank Played a Central Role in Fall of Banco Ambrosiano," *Wall Street Journal*, April 27, 1987.

6. David Yallop, *The Power and the Glory: Inside the Dark Heart of John Paul II's Vatican* (New York: Carroll and Graf, 2007), p. 470.

7. Philip Willan, *The Vatican at War: From Blackfriar's Bridge to Buenos Aires* (Bloomington, IN: iUniverse, 2013), Kindle edition.

8. Tobias Jones, "What Happened to the Missing 15-Year-Old Vatican Citizen Emanuela Orlandi?" *Spectator* (UK), June 22, 2013, http://www.spectator.co.uk/2013/06/gone-girl/ (accessed May 24, 2014).

9. Willan, *Vatican at War*.

10. Jesus Lopez Saez, *El Dia de la Cuenta: Juan Pablo II, a Examen* (Madrid: Meral Ediciones, 2005), http://www.comayala.es/index.php/en/libros-es/el-dia-de-la-cuenta-ingles-texto (accessed May 22, 2014).

11. Willan, *Vatican at War*.

12. Vicenzo Parisi, quoted in Saez, *El Dia de la Cuenta*.

13. Ibid.

14. Yallop, *Power and the Glory*, p. 470.

15. Ibid., p. 471.

16. ANSA, quoted in Willan, *Vatican at War*.

17. Giacomo Galeazzi, "L'ex della Magliana: Si Siamostati Noi a Rapire la Orlandi" [in Italian], *La Stampa* (Rome), July 24, 2011, http://www.lastampa

.it/2011/07/24/italia/cronache/l-ex-della-magliana-si-siamostati-noi-a-rapire-la -orlandi-nPsZflW8etENQHZpwgB60I/pagina.html (accessed May 24, 2014).

18. Antonio Mancini, quoted in Galeazzi, "L'ex della Magliana."

19. Ibid.

20. Willan, *Vatican at War*.

21. Gianluca Di Feo, "Sabrina Minardi Ricorda: Le Mie Scopate con Roberto Calvi e Monsignor Marcinkus" [in Italian] *L'Espresso* (Rome), September 24, 2010, http://www.dagospia.com/rubrica-3/politica/sabrina-minardi-ricorda-le-mie -scopate-con-roberto-calvi-e-monsignor-marcinkusla-compagna-del-18855.htm (accessed May 24, 2014).

22. "Caso Orlandi, C'e un Indagato è l'ex Autista di Renato De Pedis" [in Italian], *La Repubblica* (Rome), March 10, 2010, http://www.repubblica.it/ cronaca/2010/03/10/news/indagato_emanuela_orlandi-2586765/ (accessed May 24, 2014).

23. "Caso Orlandi: Inquirenti, in Vaticano Qualcuno sa Verita" [in Italian], *Libero Quotidiano*, April 2, 2012, http://www.liberoquotidiano.it/news/972431/ Caso-Orlandi-inquirenti-in-Vaticano-qualcuno-sa-verita-.html (accessed May 24, 2014).

24. Willan, *Vatican at War*.

25. Antonella Beccaria, "Nicoletti, Banchiere della Banda della Magliana: 'Due Papi Mi Hanno Voluto Bene'" [in Italian], *Domani* (Rome), May 5, 2010, http:// domani.arcoiris.tv/nicoletti-banchiere-della-banda-della-magliana-%E2 %80%9Cdue-papi-mi-hanno-voluto-bene%E2%80%9D/ (accessed May 24, 2014).

26. "The Process of Canonization for Josemaría Escrivá," Opus Dei, March 2, 2006, http://www.opusdei.us/en-us/article/the-process-of-canonization-for -josemaria-escriva (accessed May 24, 2014).

27. Austen Ivereigh, "Secrets of the Tomb," *America*, August 23, 2010, http:// www.americamagazine.org/content/all-things/secrets-tomb (accessed April 27, 2017).

28. Richard Cottrell, *Gladio: NATO's Dagger at the Heart of Europe* (Palm Desert, CA: Progressive Press, 2012), p. 268.

29. Nick Pisa, "Italians Find Mystery Bones in Tomb Linked to Vatican Scandal," *Telegraph* (UK), May 14, 2012, http://www.telegraph.co.uk/news/ worldnews/europe/italy/9263996/Italians-find-mystery-bones-in-tomb-linked -to-Vatican-scandal.html (accessed May 24, 2014).

30. Ibid.

31. Hannah Roberts, "'Lured to Her Death by Vatican Cardinal Paedophile Ring or Kidnapped in Revenge by Italy Mobster?' Enduring Mystery of Girl, 15, Who Vanished on Way Home from Flute Class After Pope Told Family, 'She's in Heaven,'" *Daily Mail* (UK), October 30, 2015, http://www.dailymail.co.uk/ news/article-3295231/Snatched-street-Vatican-cardinal-paedophile-ring -kidnapped-revenge-Italian-mobster-Enduring-mystery-girl-15-vanished-way -home-flute-class-Pope-tells-family-s-heaven.html (accessed March 2, 2017).

32. Martin, *Rich Church, Poor Church*, p. 75.

33. Betty Clermont, *The Neo-Catholics: Implementing Christian Nationalism in America* (Atlanta: Clarity Press, 2009), p. 88.

34. Ibid.

35. Willan, *Vatican at War*.

36. Yallop, *Power and the Glory*, p. 447.

37. James Martin, "Opus Dei in the United States: From February 25, 1995," *America*, December 13, 2012, http://www.americamagazine.org/faith/2012/12/13/opus-dei-united-states-february-25-1995 (accessed April 27, 2017).

38. David Van Biema, "The Ways of Opus Dei," *Time*, April 16, 2006, http://content.time.com/time/magazine/article/0,9171,1184078-3,00.html (accessed May 24, 2014).

39. John Roche, "The Inner World of Opus Dei," Opus Dei Awareness Network (ODAN), September 7, 1982, http://www.odan.org/tw_inner_world_of_opus_dei.htm (accessed May 24, 2014).

40. Martin A. Lee, "Their Will Be Done," *Mother Jones*, July/August 1983, http://www.motherjones.com/politics/1983/07/their-will-be-done (accessed May 20, 2014).

41. Ibid.

42. Ibid.

43. Robert Hutchison, *Their Kingdom Come: Inside the Secret World of Opus Dei* (New York: Macmillan, 2006), pp. 356–57.

44. Henry T. Cason v. Central Intelligence Agency, No. 1:11-cv-00001, US Dist. Court, Southern District of New York, May 30, 2011, http://www.citizen.org/documents/Cason-v-CIA-memorandum-of-law.pdf (accessed May 24, 2014).

45. Luigi DiFonzo, *St. Peter's Banker: Michele Sindona* (New York: Franklin Watts, 1983), p. 258.

46. Ibid., p. 259.

47. Tosches, *Power on Earth*, p. 277.

48. Ibid.

49. Ibid., pp. 277–78.

50. Wilton Wynn, *Keeper of the Keys: John XXIII, Paul VI, and John Paul II—Three Who Changed the Church* (New York: Random House, 1988), p. 172.

51. Ibid.

52. Sherman Skolnick, "The Enron Black Magic—Part Four," Skolnick Reports, January 27, 2002, http://www.rense.com/general19/swind.htm (accessed May 24, 2014).

53. "Report on Calvi Autopsy Returns Spotlight to Vatican Bank Scandal," BBC News World Service, October 16, 1998.

54. "The Fascist's Banker," *Albion Monitor*, November 2, 1998, http://www.hartford-hwp.com/archives/62/269.html (accessed May 24, 2014).

55. "Group Watch: Knights of Malta," Vox News, November 1991, http://www.voxfux.com/features/knights_of_malta_facts.html (accessed May 24, 2014).

56. Adam Lebor, "Revealed: The Secret Report That Shows How the Nazis Planned a Fourth Reich . . . in the EU," *Daily Mail* (UK), May 9, 2009, http://www.dailymail.co.uk/news/article-1179902/Revealed-The-secret-report-shows-Nazis-planned-Fourth-Reich--EU.html (accessed May 24, 2014).

CHAPTER SEVENTEEN: VATICAN, INC.

1. Alan Cowell, "As Pope Visits Sicily, Mafia Sends Gruesome Warning to Priest," *New York Times*, November 6, 1994, http://www.nytimes.com/1994/11/06/world/as-pope-visits-sicily-mafia-sends-gruesome-warning-to-priest.html (accessed April 27, 2017).

2. "Vatican Bank Involved in Mafia's On-Line Washing Money," Xinhua News Agency, October 3, 2000, http://vaticanbankclaims.freeservers.com/xinhua.htm (accessed April 27, 2017).

3. Ibid.

4. "Gangster's Paradise across the Atlantic," *Telegraph* (London), November 19, 2001, http://www.telegraph.co.uk/finance/2742407/Gangsters-paradise-across-the-Atlantic.html (accessed April 27, 2017).

5. Richard Behar, "Washing Money in the Holy See," *Fortune*, August 16, 1999, http://archive.fortune.com/magazines/fortune/fortune_archive/1999/08/16/264285/index.htm (accessed March 2, 2017).

6. Ibid.

7. Alessandra Stanley, "How 2 Priests Got Mixed Up in a Huge Insurance Scandal," *New York Times*, June 26, 1999, http://www.nytimes.com/1999/06/26/business/how-2-priests-got-mixed-up-in-a-huge-insurance-scandal.html (accessed March 2, 2017).

8. Details recorded in a federal lawsuit against the Vatican, filed by the Mississippi Department of Insurance et al., in the US District Court for the Southern District of Mississippi, Jackson Division.

9. Behar, "Washing Money in the Holy See."

10. Ibid.

11. "Frankel's Swiss Banker Pleads Guilty to One Count of Concealing Felony," *Hartford Courant*, November 20, 2004, http://articles.courant.com/2004-11-20/news/0411200155_1_frankel-bear-sterns-vienna-philharmonic (accessed March 2, 2017).

12. Behar, "Washing Money in the Holy See."

13. Stanley, "How 2 Priests Got Mixed Up."

14. Emilio Colagiovanni, quoted in Behar, "Washing Money in the Holy See."

15. Mitchell Pacelle and Ellen Joan Pollock, "Big Firms with Ties to Frankel Could Be Liable for His Losses," *Wall Street Journal*, June 30, 1999, http://www.wsj.com/articles/SB930700423473698252 (accessed March 2, 2017).

16. Behar, "Washing Money in the Holy See."

17. Ibid.

18. Ibid.

19. Ibid.

20. Mitchell Pacelle, Ellen Joan Pollock, and Deborah Lohse, "Some Firms Had Suspicions after Checking into Frankel," *Wall Street Journal*, June 24, 1999, http://www.wsj.com/articles/SB930180863299117464 (accessed March 2, 2017).

21. Behar, "Washing Money in the Holy See."

22. Katherine E. Finkelstein, "Woman's Suicide a Bizarre Note in Fraud Inquiry," *New York Times*, July 7, 1999, http://www.nytimes.com/1999/07/07/nyregion/woman-s-suicide-a-bizarre-note-in-fraud-inquiry.html (accessed March 2, 2017).

23. "Frankel Played Benefactor to a Gaggle of Women," Court TV, July 13, 1999.

24. Ibid.

25. Finkelstein, "Woman's Suicide a Bizarre Note."

26. Rachel Bell, "Martin Frankel: Sex, Greed, and $200 Million Fraud," in *The Crime Library*, http://www.crimelibrary.com/fraud/frankel/ (site discontinued).

27. Ibid.

28. Boris Kachka, "Europe on $10,000 a Day," *New York* (magazine), September 20, 1999, http://nymag.com/nymetro/news/crimelaw/features/1467/ (accessed March 2, 2017).

29. "FBI Says Money Manager Martin Frankel Captured," *Hurriyet Daily News* (Turkey), September 6, 1999, http://www.hurriyetdailynews.com/fbi-says-money-manager-martin-frankel-captured.aspx?pageID=438&n=fbi-says-money-manager-martin-frankel-captured-1999-09-06 (accessed March 2, 2017).

30. Bell, "Martin Frankel."

31. Martin Frankel, quoted in "Rogue US Financier Pleads Guilty to Tax Evasion," Court TV, June 16, 2000.

32. Ellen Joan Pollock, "Financier Frankel Pleads Guilty in a $208-Million Fraud Scheme," *Wall Street Journal*, May 15, 2002, http://www.wsj.com/articles/SB1021498511306772760 (accessed March 2, 2017).

33. John Christoffersen, "Frankel Sentenced to More than 16 Years in Prison," *Boston Globe*, December 10, 2004, http://archive.boston.com/news/local/connecticut/articles/2004/12/10/frankel_sentenced_to_more_than_16_years_in_prison (accessed April 27, 2017).

34. "Vatican Monsignor Arrested in Ohio," *USA Today*, August 31, 2001, http://usatoday30.usatoday.com/news/world/2001/08/31/monsignor.htm (accessed March 2, 2017).

35. Paul Zielbauer, "Ex-Official of Vatican Pleads Guilty in Conspiracy," *New York Times*, September 6, 2002, http://www.nytimes.com/2002/09/06/nyregion/ex-official-of-vatican-pleads-guilty-in-conspiracy.html (accessed April 9, 2017.).

36. "Priest Fined $15K for Fraud Linked to Frankel Plot," *Toledo Blade*, Sep-

tember 10, 2004, http://www.toledoblade.com/local/2004/09/10/Priest-fined
-15K-for-fraud-linked-to-Frankel-plot.html (accessed March 2, 2017).

37. David Yallop, *The Power and the Glory: Inside the Dark Heart of John Paul II's Vatican* (New York: Carroll and Graf, 2007), pp. 438–39.

CHAPTER EIGHTEEN: STEALING FROM THE COLLECTION PLATE, LIVING LARGE

1. Robert West and Charles Zech, "Internal Financial Controls in the US Church," *Journal of Forensic Accounting* 9, no. 1 (2008).

2. Jason Berry, *Render unto Rome: The Secret Life of Money in the Catholic Church* (New York: Crown, 2011), p. 10.

3. Michael W. Ryan, quoted in Berry, *Render unto Rome*.

4. Julia Marsh, "Priest Paid His Male 'Sex Master' from Collection Plate: Lawsuit," *New York Post*, December 10, 2015, http://nypost.com/2015/12/10/priest-paid-his-male-sex-master-from-collection-plate-lawsuit/ (accessed March 2, 2017).

5. Ibid.

6. Candice Williams, "Troy Priest Sentenced to 27 Months in Fraud," *Detroit News*, December 1, 2015, http://www.detroitnews.com/story/news/local/oakland-county/2015/12/01/priest-stole-money-faces-possible-prison-sentence/76600586/ (accessed March 2, 2017).

7. Anemona Hartocollis, "Monsignor Gets 4-Year Sentence for Large Thefts from His East Side Parish," *New York Times*, September 23, 2006, http://www.nytimes.com/2006/09/23/nyregion/23priest.html (accessed March 2, 2017).

8. "Msgr. John G. Woolsey," *Catholic New York*, August 4, 2016, http://cny.org/stories/Msgr-John-G-Woolsey,14319? (accessed March 2, 2017).

9. Clifford Ward, "Priest Who Gambled Away Church's $300,000 May Lose Probation over Repayment," *Chicago Tribune*, February 18, 2016, http://www.chicagotribune.com/suburbs/ct-gambling-priest-court-hearing-0219-20160218-story.html (accessed March 2, 2017).

10. "Priest Is Charged in Church Theft," *New York Times*, May 24, 2008, http://www.nytimes.com/2008/05/24/nyregion/24priest.html (accessed March 2, 2017).

11. "Father Dunne Receives Five Years' Probation for Theft," *Catholic New York*, January 14, 2010, http://cny.org/stories/Father-Dunne-Receives-Five-Years-Probation-for-Theft,117 (accessed March 2, 2017).

12. Jerome Burdi and Mike Clary, "2 Priests Accused of $8.6-Million Theft in Florida," *Los Angeles Times*, September 29, 2006, http://articles.latimes.com/2006/sep/29/nation/na-churchtheft29 (accessed March 2, 2017).

13. Ibid.

14. Ibid.

15. Berry, *Render unto Rome*, p. 9.

16. Mark Fritz, "A Mystery of the Cloth," *Los Angeles Times*, November 16, 1998, http://articles.latimes.com/1998/nov/16/news/mn-43412 (accessed March 2, 2017).

17. Jan Ackerman and Ann Rodgers-Melnick, "DA Won't Prosecute in Death of Priest," *Pittsburgh Post-Gazette*, March 13, 1999, http://old.post-gazette.com/regionstate/19990313benz2.asp (accessed March 2, 2017).

18. Berry, *Render unto Rome*, pp. 11–12.

19. Ibid., pp. 4–5.

20. Ibid., p. 7.

21. Ralph Cipriano, "Lavish Spending in Archdiocese Skips Inner City," *National Catholic Reporter*, June 19, 1998, http://natcath.org/NCR_Online/archives2/1998b/061998/061998a.htm (accessed March 2, 2017).

22. Dick Ryan, "One Bishop's High Cost of Living," *National Catholic Reporter*, October 25, 2002, http://www.natcath.org/NCR_Online/archives/102502/102502d.htm (accessed March 2, 2017).

23. Daniel Burke, "The Lavish Homes of American Archbishops," CNN, August 8, 2014, http://www.cnn.com/interactive/2014/08/us/american-archbishops-lavish-homes/ (accessed March 2, 2017).

24. Steven Avella, quoted in Burke, "Lavish Homes of American Archbishops."

25. Felician A. Foy, ed., *1984 Catholic Almanac* (Huntington, IN: Our Sunday Visitor, 1983), p. 140.

26. Gianluigi Nuzzi, *Merchants in the Temple: Inside Pope Francis's Secret Battle against Corruption in the Vatican* (New York: Henry Holt, 2015), p. 33.

27. Ibid.

28. Ibid., pp. 24–25.

29. Ibid., p. 32.

30. Kevin Roose, "The Vatican's Financial Empire, in Charts," *New York*, March 12, 2013, http://nymag.com/daily/intelligencer/2013/03/vaticans-financial-empire-in-charts.html (accessed March 2, 2017).

31. "Pope Thanks St. Peter's Circle for Unstinting Charity," Vatican Information Service, February 28, 2003, http://visnews-en.blogspot.com/2003/02/pope-thanks-st-peter-circle-for.html (accessed March 2, 2017).

32. Benedict XVI, "To the Members of the Circle of St. Peter," February 26, 2006, Holy See, http://w2.vatican.va/content/benedict-xvi/en/speeches/2006/february/documents/hf_ben-xvi_spe_20060225_circolo-s-pietro.html (accessed March 2, 2017).

33. Edward Pentin, "Peter's Pence Probe?" *National Catholic Register*, November 23, 2015, http://www.ncregister.com/site/article/peters-pence-probe (accessed March 2, 2017).

34. Nuzzi, *Merchants in the Temple*, p. 55.

35. Ibid., p. 56.

36. Ibid.

37. Filippo Caleri, "Le Spese Folli di Casa Bertone Marmi di Carrara e Luci di Design" [in Italian], *Il Tempo*, November 13, 2015, http://www.iltempo.it/cronache/2015/11/13/le-spese-folli-di-casa-bertone-marmi-di-carrara-e-luci-di-design-1.1478683 (accessed March 2, 2017).

38. Matthew Fox, "Cardinal Bertone's Sins against Children," *Huffington Post*, April 18, 2016, http://www.huffingtonpost.com/matthew-fox/cardinal-bertones-sins-ag_b_9708216.html (accessed March 2, 2017).

39. Francis X. Rocca, "Vatican Releases Financial Statements," *Wall Street Journal*, July 16, 2015, http://www.wsj.com/articles/vatican-releases-financial-statements-1437046714 (accessed March 2, 2017).

CHAPTER NINETEEN: THE PLAGUE OF PEDOPHILIA

1. Michael D'Antonio, *Mortal Sins: Sex, Crime, and the Era of Catholic Scandal* (New York: St. Martin's Press, 2013), p. 17.

2. Anna Terruwe and Conrad Baars, quoted in D'Antonio, *Mortal Sins*.

3. Patrick Guinan, "Modern Psychology and Priest Sex Abuse," *Culture Wars*, May 2004, http://www.culturewars.com/2004/ModernPsych.html (accessed March 2, 2017).

4. D'Antonio, *Mortal Sins*, p. 18.

5. Jason Berry, *Lead Us Not into Temptation: Catholic Priests and the Sexual Abuse of Children* (Chicago: University of Illinois Press, 2000), pp. 34–66.

6. D'Antonio, *Mortal Sins*, p. 13.

7. Ibid.

8. "Ex-Pastor Given 20-Year Sentence," *New York Times*, October 15, 1985, http://www.nytimes.com/1985/10/15/us/ex-pastor-given-20-year-sentence.html (accessed March 2, 2017).

9. Evan Moore, "Church Abuse Case Haunts Lawyer Who Defended Priest," *USA Today*, October 5, 2013, http://www.usatoday.com/story/news/nation/2013/10/05/gilbert-gauthe-catholic-priest/2926325/ (accessed March 2, 2017).

10. "Database of Publicly Accused Priests in the United States," Bishop Accountability.org, http://bishop-accountability.org/priestdb/PriestDBbydiocese.html#LA (accessed March 2, 2017).

11. "Priest Sex Abuse Timeline," *Catholic Church in Crisis*, CBS News, April 23, 2002, http://www.cbsnews.com/htdocs/catholic_crisis/framesource_time.html (accessed March 2, 2017).

12. Matt C. Abbott, "'Sodomy' Book Author Exposes Santa Rosa Bishop,

Priest," *Renew America*, June 27, 2006, http://www.renewamerica.com/columns/abbott/060627 (accessed March 2, 2017).

13. Ibid.

14. Mary Vorsino, "Retired Bishop Helped Poor, Gays," *Star Bulletin* (Honolulu), December 14, 2003, http://archives.starbulletin.com/2003/12/14/news/story4.html (accessed March 2, 2017).

15. Ibid.

16. Rick Foster, "Father Porter: Remembering the Evil," *Sun Chronicle*, May 13, 2012, http://www.thesunchronicle.com/news/local_news/father-porter-remembering-the-evil/article_1f621267-2287-5f81-a1fb-4bce1ea0f10d.html (accessed March 2, 2017).

17. Ibid.

18. David Briggs, "Sex Abuse Cases Have Church Reeling: Crisis: Catholic Dioceses across US Prepare to Pay Tens, If Not Hundreds of Millions of Dollars in Legal Fees and Reparations," *Los Angeles Times*, January 29, 1994, http://articles.latimes.com/1994-01-29/local/me-16561_1_sexual-abuse (accessed March 2, 2017).

19. Michael Lacey, "The Sins of the Bishop," *Phoenix New Times*, September 8, 1993, http://www.phoenixnewtimes.com/news/the-sins-of-the-bishop-6425686 (accessed March 2, 2017).

20. Ibid.

21. Paul Likoudis, *Amchurch Comes Out: The US Bishops, Pedophile Scandals, and the Homosexual Agenda* (Petersburg, IL: Roman Catholic Faithful, 2002), pp. 3–4.

22. Michael Lacey, "Sins of the Bishop."

23. US Marshal's Office, Department of Justice, "US Marshals Arrest Former Catholic Priest Turned Fugitive Sex Offender," press release, November 17, 2008, https://www.usmarshals.gov/news/chron/2008/111708.htm (accessed March 2, 2017).

24. "Former Priest Gets Life Term in Sex Abuse Case," *New York Times*, April 2, 1998, http://www.nytimes.com/1998/04/02/us/former-priest-gets-life-term-in-abuse-case.html (accessed March 2, 2017).

25. Rod Dreher, "Showdown in Dallas," Catholic Culture, June 2, 2003, http://www.catholicculture.org/news/features/index.cfm?recnum=23289 (accessed March 2, 2017).

26. Michael Saul, "Kos Says He's Sorry for Crimes and Hopes for Forgiveness," *Dallas Morning News*, February 29, 2016, http://www.dallasnews.com/news/metro/20160229-4-4-98-kos-says-he-s-sorry-for-crimes-hopes-for-forgiveness.ece (accessed March 2, 2017).

27. Scott Gold, "Family of Fallen Bishop in Despair," *Sun Sentinel* (Fort Lauderdale), June 7, 1998, http://www.bishop-accountability.org/news3/1998_06_07_Gold_FamilyOf_Joseph_Keith_Symons_4.htm (accessed March 2, 2017).

28. "Bishop Who Resigned because of Sex Abuse Dies," *National Catholic Reporter*, May 11, 2012, https://www.ncronline.org/news/people/bishop-who-resigned-because-sex-abuse-dies (accessed March 2, 2017).

29. John Paul II, *Sacramentorum Sanctitatis Tutela*, April 30, 2001, Bishop Accountability.org, http://www.bishop-accountability.org/resources/resource-files/churchdocs/SacramentorumAndNormaeEnglish.htm (accessed March 2, 2017).

30. Laurie Goodstein and David M. Halbfinger, "Church Office Failed to Act on Abuse Scandal," *New York Times*, July 1, 2010, http://www.nytimes.com/2010/07/02/world/europe/02pope.html (accessed March 2, 2017).

31. Fox Butterfield, "Long Planning Is Cited in Death of Former Priest," *New York Times*, August 26, 2003, http://www.nytimes.com/2003/08/26/us/long-planning-is-cited-in-death-of-former-priest.html (accessed March 2, 2017).

32. John Jay College of Criminal Justice, City University of New York, *The Nature and Scope of Sexual Abuse of Minors by Catholic Priests and Deacons in the United States, 1950–2002* (Washington, DC: US Conference of Catholic Bishops, February 2004), http://www.usccb.org/issues-and-action/child-and-youth-protection/upload/The-Nature-and-Scope-of-Sexual-Abuse-of-Minors-by-Catholic-Priests-and-Deacons-in-the-United-States-1950-2002.pdf (accessed March 2, 2017).

33. Michael D. Shaffer, "Sex Abuse Crisis Is a Watershed in the Roman Catholic Church's History in America," *Philadelphia Inquirer*, June 25, 2012, http://www.bishop-accountability.org/news2012/05_06/2012_06_24_Schaffer_SexabuseCrisis.htm (accessed April 27, 2017).

34. Annysa Johnson and Paul Gores, "Archdiocese of Milwaukee Files for Bankruptcy Protection," *Milwaukee Journal Sentinel*, January 4, 2011, http://www.jsonline.com/features/religion/112878494.html (accessed May 24, 2014).

35. "Catholic Church Pays $655 Million in Abuse Cases," *Agence France-Presse*, March 8, 2008.

36. Benedict XVI (Joseph Ratzinger), quoted in David Yallop, *The Power and the Glory: Inside the Dark Heart of John Paul II's Vatican* (New York: Carroll and Graf, 2007), p. 352.

37. Berry, *Lead Us Not into Temptation*, pp. vii–xii.

38. Maureen Dowd, "Pope Saint, Victims Asterisks," *Scranton Times-Tribune*, April 24, 2014, p. A13.

39. Charles Scicluna, quoted in "UN Committee Criticizes Vatican for Allegedly Enabling Child Sex Abuse," *New York Daily News*, January 16, 2014, http://www.nydailynews.com/news/world/u-n-committee-criticizes-vatican-allegedly-enabling-child-sex-abuse-article-1.1581758 (accessed March 2, 2017).

40. Sara Oviedo, quoted in "UN Committee Criticizes Vatican."

41. Maria Rita Parsi, quoted in "UN Committee Criticizes Vatican."

42. Elisabetta Povoledo, "Josef Wesolowski, Ex-Archbishop Accused of Sexual Abuse, Dies at 67," *New York Times*, August 28, 2015, http://www.nytimes

.com/2015/08/29/world/europe/jozef-wesolowski-polish-ex-archbishop -accused-of-child-sexual-abuse-is-found-dead.html (accessed March 2, 2017).

43. Cindy Wooden, "Former Nuncio Dies in Vatican Residence while Awaiting Sex-Abuse Trial," *Catholic News Service*, September 1, 2015, http://www.catholicnews.com/services/englishnews/2015/former-nuncio-dies-in -vatican-residence-while-awaiting-sex-abuse-trial.cfm (accessed March 2, 2017).

44. Richard Behar, "Washing Money in the Holy See," *Fortune*, August 16, 1999, http://archive.fortune.com/magazines/fortune/fortune_ archive/1999/08/16/264285/index.htm (accessed March 2, 2017).

45. Melissa Whitworth, "What Does It Take to Come to Ithaca as a Refugee," *Ithaca Voice*, August 20, 2016, http://ithacavoice.com/2016/08/what-does-it -take-to-come-to-ithaca-as-a-refugee/ (accessed March 2, 2017).

46. "USA Spending: Data Research," USASpending.gov, 2016, https://www .usaspending.gov/Pages/AdvancedSearch.aspx?sub=y&ST=C,G&FY=2016,201 5,2014&A=0&SS=USA&k=Archdiocese%20of%20Milwaukee (accessed March 2, 2017).

47. Ibid.; Whitworth, "What Does It Take to Come to Ithaca as a Refugee."

48. Joseph Walker, "Embracing Refugees: 'How Can I Not Give Back?'" *Deseret News*, November 9, 2013, http://www.deseretnews.com/article/ 865590204/Embracing-refugees-How-can-I-not-give-back.html (accessed March 2, 2017).

49. Ann Corcoran, "Refugee Resettlement Fact Sheet," Refugee Resettlement Watch, June 20, 2013, https://refugeeresettlementwatch.wordpress.com/refugee -resettlement-fact-sheets/ (accessed April 12, 2017).

CHAPTER TWENTY: THE MARK OF THE ANTICHRIST

1. "On Justification," Council of Trent, session 6, ch. 3, January 13, 1547, http://www.thecounciloftrent.com/ch6.htm (accessed March 2, 2017).

2. John Paul II, "Address to a General Audience," *L'Osservatore Romano*, January 1, 1979, p. 8.

3. John Paul II, "Address to a General Audience," *L'Osservatore Romano*, January 23, 1980, p. 3.

4. Roberto Suro, "12 Faiths Join Pope to Pray for Peace," *New York Times*, October 28, 1986, http://www.nytimes.com/1986/10/28/world/12-faiths-join -pope-to-pray-for-peace.html (accessed March 2, 2017).

5. Pius XI, *Mortalium Animos*, January 6, 1928, Holy See, http://w2.vatican .va/content/pius-xi/en/encyclicals/documents/hf_p-xi_enc_19280106 _mortalium-animos.html (accessed March 2, 2017).

6. Michael Dimond and Peter Dimond, "John Paul II: Manifest Heretic Who Claimed to Be Pope (1978–2005)," Most Holy Family Monastery, http://www

.mostholyfamilymonastery.com/catholicchurch/anti-pope-john-paul-ii/#.WPADmdQrKUk (accessed April 13, 2017).

7. Robert Sungenis, "A No, No to Assisi—Another Loyal Son Protests," *Catholic Apologetics International*, June 14, 2002, http://www.freerepublic.com/focus/religion/712755/posts (accessed March 2, 2017).

8. Joseph Sobran, "The Papal Kiss," *Catholic Family News*, April 2003, http://www.royaltymonarchy.com/links/sobran_papal_kiss.html (accessed March 2, 2017).

9. John Paul II, "Prayer of the Holy Father," March 21, 2000, Holy See, http://w2.vatican.va/content/john-paul-ii/en/travels/2000/documents/hf_jp-ii_spe_20000321_wadi-al-kharrar.html (accessed March 2, 2017).

10. John Paul II, *Sollicitudo Rei Socialis*, December 30, 1987, Holy See, http://w2.vatican.va/content/john-paul-ii/en/encyclicals/documents/hf_jp-ii_enc_30121987_sollicitudo-rei-socialis.html (accessed March 2, 2017).

11. John Paul II, "Address to a General Audience," May 5, 1999, Holy See, http://w2.vatican.va/content/john-paul-ii/en/audiences/1999/documents/hf_jp-ii_aud_05051999.html (accessed March 2, 2017).

12. Michel Simoulin, "The New Catechism—Is It Catholic?" part 3, *The Angelus*, March 1994, http://archives.sspx.org/New_Catechism/new_catechism__is_it_catholic_part_3.htm (accessed March 2, 2017).

13. John Paul II, *Ut Unum Sint*, May 25, 1995, Holy See, http://w2.vatican.va/content/john-paul-ii/en/encyclicals/documents/hf_jp-ii_enc_25051995_ut-unum-sint.html (accessed March 2, 2017).

14. Eugene IV, quoted in E. Christopher Reyes, *In His Name: Vol. IVC, Who Wrote the Gospels?* (Bloomington, IN: Trafford, 2014), p. 306.

15. Pius XI, *Rappresentanti in Terra*, December 31, 1929, Papal Encyclicals Online, http://www.papalencyclicals.net/Pius11/P11RAPPR.HTM (accessed March 2, 2017).

16. John Paul II, "Address to a General Audience," July 21, 1999, Holy See, http://w2.vatican.va/content/john-paul-ii/en/audiences/1999/documents/hf_jp-ii_aud_21071999.html (accessed March 2, 2017).

17. John Paul II, "Address to a General Audience," July 28, 1999, Holy See, http://w2.vatican.va/content/john-paul-ii/en/audiences/1999/documents/hf_jp-ii_aud_28071999.html (accessed March 2, 2017).

18. John Paul II, "Address to a General Audience," August 4, 1999, Holy See, http://w2.vatican.va/content/john-paul-ii/en/audiences/1999/documents/hf_jp-ii_aud_04081999.html (accessed March 2, 2017).

19. "Heaven," *Catholic Encyclopedia* 7 (New York: Robert Appleton, 1910), http://www.newadvent.org/cathen/07170a.htm (accessed April 6, 2017).

20. "Hell," *Catholic Encyclopedia* 7 (New York: Robert Appleton, 1910), http://www.newadvent.org/cathen/07207a.htm (accessed March 2, 2017).

21. "Purgatory," *Catholic Encyclopedia* 16 (New York: Robert Appleton, 1910), http://www.newadvent.org/cathen/12575a.htm (accessed March 2, 2017).

22. John Paul II, "Homily for the Inauguration of His Pontificate," October 22, 1978, Holy See, http://w2.vatican.va/content/john-paul-ii/en/homilies/1978/documents/hf_jp-ii_hom_19781022_inizio-pontificato.html (accessed March 2, 2017).

23. John Paul II, *Urbi et Orbi*, Christmas message, December 25, 1978, Holy See, http://w2.vatican.va/content/john-paul-ii/en/messages/urbi/documents/hf_jp-ii_mes_19781225_urbi.html (accessed March 2, 2017).

24. John Paul II, "Discovering the Mystery of God's Love," homily, Luján, June 11, 1982, http://www.ssvmusa.org/About/lujan/homilyJPII.shtm (accessed March 2, 2017).

25. John Paul II, "Words at the End of the Via Crucis," April 10, 1998, Holy See, http://w2.vatican.va/content/john-paul-ii/en/speeches/1998/april/documents/hf_jp-ii_spe_10041998_via-crucis.html (accessed March 2, 2017).

26. John Paul II, "Address to Members of the 17th General Assembly of the Congregation of the Missionaries of the Precious Blood," September 14, 2001, Holy See, http://w2.vatican.va/content/john-paul-ii/en/speeches/2001/september/documents/hf_jp-ii_spe_20010914_missionaries-precious-blood.html (accessed March 2, 2017).

27. John Paul II, "*Urbi et Orbi* Message," *L'Osservatore Romano*, January 6, 1986.

28. John Paul II, "Address to the Representatives of the World's Religions," January 24, 2004, Holy See, http://w2.vatican.va/content/john-paul-ii/en/speeches/2002/january/documents/hf_jp-ii_spe_20020124_discorso-assisi.html (accessed March 2, 2017).

29. John Paul II, "To H. E. Mr. Afif Hendaoui, Ambassador of Tunisia," May 27, 2004, Biblia Clerus, http://www.clerus.org/bibliaclerusonline/en/fob.htm (accessed April 13, 2017).

30. Pius X, *E Supremi*, October 4, 1903, Papal Encyclicals Online, http://www.papalencyclicals.net/Pius10/p10supre.htm (accessed March 2, 2017).

31. Pierre Teilhard de Chardin, *The Phenomenon of Man* (New York: Harper and Row, 1965), p. 219.

32. Henry M. Morris, "Evolution and the Pope," Institute for Creation Research, 1996, http://www.icr.org/article/evolution-pope/ (accessed March 2, 2017).

33. Joseph Ratzinger, *Introduction to Christianity*, 2nd ed. (San Francisco, CA: Ignatius Press, 2004), pp. 149–50.

CHAPTER TWENTY-ONE: RESIGNATION

1. "Catholics in Crisis," *The Week*, April 30, 2010, http://theweek.com/article/index/202388/catholics-in-crisis (accessed May 24, 2014).

2. David Yallop, *The Power and the Glory: Inside the Dark Heart of John Paul II's Vatican* (New York: Carroll and Graf, 2007), p. 212. See also Zoë Schlanger, "Spain's Government Pushes Unpopular Abortion Ban," *Newsweek,* February 11, 2014, http://www.newsweek.com/spains-government-pushes-unpopular-abortion-ban-228760 (accessed April 13, 2017).

3. Yallop, *Power and the Glory*, p. 214.

4. "Catholics in Crisis."

5. Yallop, *Power and the Glory*, p. 210.

6. Jonathan Petre and Daniel Johnson, "Britain Is a Pagan Society, Says Cardinal," *Telegraph* (UK), January 20, 2003, http://www.telegraph.co.uk/news/uknews/1419421/Britain-is-a-pagan-society-says-Cardinal.html (accessed May 24, 2014).

7. Yallop, *Power and the Glory*, p. 227.

8. Ibid., p. 228.

9. Peter Moore, "Scots Cardinal Uses Christmas for Gay Attack," *Bondings* 24, no. 3 (Spring 2004), pp. 6–7, http://www.newwaysministry.org/pastissues/Bondings-Vol24N3.pdf (accessed May 24, 2014).

10. Ioan Grillo, "Protestants on the Rise as Pope Visits Mexico," Reuters, March 21, 2012, http://www.reuters.com/article/2012/03/22/us-mexico-pope-idUSBRE82L06E20120322 (accessed May 24, 2014).

11. "Obituary: John Paul II," *The Economist*, April 7, 2005, http://www.economist.com/node/3839698 (accessed April 13, 2017).

12. Timothy Garton Ash, "Christian Europe RIP," *The Guardian*, April 20, 2005, https://www.theguardian.com/world/2005/apr/21/catholicism.religion5 (accessed April 13, 2017).

13. Yallop, *The Power and the Glory*, p. 671.

14. Philip Willan, *The Vatican at War: From Blackfriars Bridge to Buenos Aires* (Bloomington, IN: iUniverse, 2013), Kindle edition.

15. Yallop, *Power and the Glory*, p. xii.

16. "Vatican Bank 'Investigated over Money-Laundering,'" BBC News, September 21, 2010, http://www.bbc.co.uk/news/world-europe-11380628 (accessed May 24, 2014).

17. "The Vatican's Woes: God's Bankers," *Economist*, July 7, 2012, http://www.economist.com/node/21558249 (accessed May 24, 2014).

18. Nick Squires, "Ex-Head of Vatican Bank Has Archive on Senior Italian and Church Figures," *Telegraph* (UK), June 7, 2012, http://www.telegraph.co.uk/news/worldnews/europe/vaticancityandholysee/9316219/Ex-head-of-Vatican-bank-has-archive-on-senior-Italian-and-Church-figures.html (accessed May 24, 2014).

19. Juan Vicente Boo, "Vatican Protests the Seizure of Documents" [in Spanish], ABC News (Spain), June 9, 2012, http://www.abc.es/20120609/sociedad/abci-vaticano-protesta-duramente-incautacion-201206082200.html (accessed May 24, 2014).

20. David Gibson, "Vatican Bank Needs More Transparency, Regulators Say," *Huffington Post*, July 18, 2012, http://www.huffingtonpost.com/2012/07/18/vatican-bank-needs-more-transparency-regulators-say_n_1684198.html (accessed May 24, 2014).

21. Marta Paterlini, "Court Endorses Vatican Bank's Rescue of Italian Research Center," *Science Insider*, October 31, 2011, http://www.sciencemag.org/news/2011/10/court-endorses-vatican-banks-rescue-italian-research-center (accessed May 24, 2014).

22. "Beretta and IOR" [in Italian], *Ecclesia Dei: Cattolic Apostolici Romani*, February 2, 2012, http://musicasacra.forumfree.it/?t=60356939 (accessed May 24, 2014).

23. "Strong Catholic Identity at a Four-Decade Low in US," Pew Research Center, Washington, DC, March 13, 2013, http://www.pewforum.org/2013/03/13/strong-catholic-identity-at-a-four-decade-low-in-us/ (accessed May 24, 2014).

24. Robert W. Wood, "Vatican Money Laundering and Tax Charges Ensnare Flashy Monsignor," *Forbes*, January 23, 2014, https://www.forbes.com/sites/robertwood/2014/01/23/vatican-money-laundering-tax-charges-ensnare-flashy-monsignor/#e5cca285ed7d (accessed April 27, 2017). See also Tom Kington, "Pope Francis Opts to Keep Scandal-Plagued Vatican Bank Alive," *Los Angeles Times*, April 7, 2014, http://www.latimes.com/world/worldnow/la-fg-wn-pope-francis-vatican-bank-20140407-story.html (accessed May 24, 2014).

25. Nicole Winfield, "Vatican Gets Mixed Report Card on Finance Reforms," *US News and World Report*, December 12, 2013, https://www.usnews.com/news/world/articles/2013/12/12/vatican-gets-mixed-report-card-from-evaluators (accessed March 2, 2017).

26. Nicole Winfield and Daniela Petroff, "Pope Francis Presides over John Paul II, John XXIII Historic Canonization," *Journal News* (New York Lower Hudson Valley), April 28, 2014, http://www.lohud.com/story/news/religion/2014/04/28/franis-makes-john-paul-ii-john-xxiii-saints/8386411/ (accessed May 24, 2014).

27. Yallop, *Power and the Glory*, p. xii.

28. Rachel Donadio, "On Gay Priests, Pope Francis Asks, 'Who I Am to Judge?'" *New York Times*, July 29, 2013, http://www.nytimes.com/2013/07/30/world/europe/pope-francis-gay-priests.html (accessed March 2, 2017).

29. Lucas Grindley, "*The Advocate*'s Person of the Year: Pope Francis," *Advocate*, December 16, 2013, http://www.advocate.com/year-review/2013/12/16/advocates-person-year-pope-francis (accessed March 2, 2017).

30. Austen Ivereigh, "'Of Course You Are a Son of the Church,' Francis Tells Transgender Man," *Catholic Voices*, January 28, 2015, https://cvcomment.org/2015/01/28/of-course-you-are-a-son-of-the-church-francis-tells-transgendered-man/ (accessed March 2, 2017).

31. David Gibson, "Cardinal Dolan: Pope Francis Opened Door to Gay Civil

Unions Debate," *National Catholic Reporter*, March 11, 2014, https://www
.ncronline.org/news/politics/cardinal-dolan-pope-francis-opened-door-gay
-civil-unions-debate (accessed March 2, 2017).

32. Ross Douthat, "Pope's Clever Line on Marriage," *Times-Tribune*
(Scranton), September 20, 2016, https://www.pressreader.com/usa/the-times
-tribune/20160920/281921657517646 (accessed April 27, 2017)

33. Ibid.

34. Cindy Wooden, "Fresh Start: Pope Calls for Integration of Divorced into
Church Life," Catholic News Service, February 25, 2016, http://www.catholic
news.com/services/englishnews/2016/fresh-start-pope-calls-for-integration-of
-divorced-into-church-life.cfm (accessed March 2, 2017).

35. Douthat, "Pope's Clever Line on Marriage."

36. James Carroll, "The New Morality of Pope Francis," *New Yorker*, April 8,
2016, http://www.newyorker.com/news/news-desk/new-morality-of-pope
-francis-joy-of-love (accessed March 2, 2017).

37. Michelle Boorstein, "Conservatives Decry Pope Francis's Statement That
'the Great Majority' of Marriages Are Religiously Null," *Washington Post*, June 17,
2016, https://www.washingtonpost.com/news/acts-of-faith/wp/2016/06/16/
pope-francis-the-great-majority-of-marriages-are-null-because-couples-dont
-understand-what-theyre-doing (accessed April 13, 2017).

38. Ellamay Horan, *Baltimore Catechism*, no. 2 (New York: W. H. Sadlier,
1945), p. 172.

39. Ibid., p. 119.

40. Claire Chretien, "EWTN Panel: Pope's Remarks on Marriage, Cohabita-
tion Were 'Reckless,' Depart from Church Tradition," LifeSite News, July 1, 2016,
https://www.lifesitenews.com/news/ewtn-panel-popes-remarks-on-marriage
-cohabitation-were-reckless-depart-from (accessed March 2, 2017).

41. Robert Royal, quoted in Chretien, "EWTN Panel."

42. Phil Lawler, "The Damage Done (Again) by the Pope's Statements on
Marriage," *Catholic Culture*, June 17, 2016, http://www.catholicculture.org/
commentary/otn.cfm?id=1159 (accessed March 2, 2017); Phil Lawler, quoted
in Claire Chretien and John Jalsevac, "Pope's Comments on Marriage Widely
Criticized," LifeSite News, June 20, 2016, https://www.lifesitenews.com/news/
popes-comments-on-marriage-cohabitation-widely-criticized (accessed April 13,
2017).

43. Josephine McKenna, "Pope Francis Calls for 'Courage' toward Peace
between Israel, Palestine," *National Catholic Reporter*, June 9, 2014, https://www
.ncronline.org/news/global/pope-francis-calls-courage-toward-peace-between
-israel-palestine (accessed April 13, 2017).

44. "Islamfachmann: Koran-Rezitation bei Friedensgebeten Ist Legitim"
[in German], Radio Vatikan, June 11, 2014, http://de.radiovaticana.va/
storico/2014/06/11/islamfachmann_koran-rezitation_bei_friedensgebeten_ist
_legitim/ted-806221 (accessed March 2, 2017).

45. Gregory Tomlin, "Pope Again Stresses 'Dialogue' with Other Religions as Video Depicts All as Equal," *Christian Examiner*, January 12, 2016, http://www.christianexaminer.com/article/pope-again-stresses-dialogue-with-other-religions-as-video-depicts-all-as-equal/50031.htm (accessed March 2, 2017).

46. Francis, quoted in John-Henry Westen, "Vatican's Liturgy Chief Contradicts Pope Francis on Communion for Non-Catholics," LifeSite News, November 30, 2015, https://www.lifesitenews.com/news/vaticans-liturgy-chief-contradicts-pope-francis-on-communion-for-non-cathol (accessed April 13, 2017).

47. Matthew Cullinan Hoffman, "Lutherans Receive Communion at Vatican after Meeting with Pope: Report," LifeSite News, January 21, 2016, https://www.lifesitenews.com/news/lutherans-receive-communion-at-vatican-after-meeting-with-pope-report (accessed March 2, 2017).

48. John Bingham, "Non-Catholics Invited to the Confessional," *Telegraph* (UK), March 4, 2016, http://www.telegraph.co.uk/news/religion/12183838/Non-Catholics-invited-to-the-confessional.html (accessed March 2, 2017).

49. Keith Fournier, "How the Church Will Change: Evangelical Catholic Pope Francis Gives Another Interview," *Catholic Online*, October 6, 2013, http://www.catholic.org/news/international/europe/story.php?id=52593 (accessed March 2, 2017).

50. "Pope: Those Who Say 'This or Nothing' Are Heretics Not Catholics," Vatican Radio, September 6, 2016, http://en.radiovaticana.va/news/2016/06/09/pope_those_who_say_"this_or_nothing"_are_heretics_/1235939 (accessed March 2, 2017).

51. Francis I, "Full Text of Pope's In-Flight Interview from Africa to Rome," Catholic News Agency, November 30, 2015, http://www.catholicnewsagency.com/news/full-text-of-popes-in-flight-interview-from-africa-to-rome-48855/ (accessed March 2, 2017).

52. Claire Chretien, "Did Pope Francis Really Say Islam Is Not Violent?" LifeSite News, August 3, 2016, https://www.lifesitenews.com/news/did-francis-really-say-catholics-are-as-violent-as-islamic-terrorists (accessed March 2, 2017).

53. "'Not My Pope' Hashtag Highlights French Divisions," *BBC Trending* (blog), August 2, 2016, http://www.bbc.com/news/blogs-trending-36954425 (accessed March 2, 2017).

54. "Pope Francis 'World's Most Popular Leader,'" BBC News, March 23, 2016, http://www.bbc.com/news/world-europe-35892917 (accessed March 2, 2017).

55. "Bare Ruined Choirs," a quote from Sonnet 73 by Shakespeare and the title of a book by Garry Wills (New York: Doubleday, 1971).

INDEX